A BRIEF HISTORY OF ANCIENT GREECE

A BRIEF HISTORY OF ANCIENT GREECE
Politics, Society, and Culture

Sarah B. Pomeroy
*Hunter College and
the City University of New York
Graduate Center*

Stanley M. Burstein
*California State University,
Los Angeles*

Walter Donlan
*University of
California, Irvine*

Jennifer Tolbert Roberts
*City College and
the City University of New York
Graduate Center*

New York • Oxford
OXFORD UNIVERSITY PRESS
2004

Oxford University Press

Oxford   New York
Auckland   Bangkok   Buenos Aires   Cape Town   Chennai
Dar es Salaam   Delhi   Hong Kong   Istanbul   Karachi   Kolkata
Kuala Lumpur   Madrid   Melbourne   Mexico City   Mumbai   Nairobi
São Paulo   Singapore   Taipei   Tokyo   Toronto

Published by Oxford University Press, Inc.
198 Madison Avenue, New York, New York 10016
www.oup.com

Library of Congress Cataloging-in-Publication Data

A brief history of ancient Greece : politics, society, and culture / by Sarah B. Pomeroy . . .
     [et al.].
        p. cm.
     Includes bibliographical references and index.
     ISBN-13 978-0-19-515680-5; 978-0-19-515681-2 (PBK)
     ISBN 0-19-515680-3 — ISBN 0-19-515681-1 (pbk.)
        1. Greece—History—To 146 B.C.   I. Pomeroy, Sarah B.

DF214.B74 2004
938'.09—dc22   2003060873

Printing (last digit): 9   8   7   6

Printed in the United States of America
on acid-free paper

For Our Children and Grandchildren

CONTENTS

LIST OF MAPS

ACKNOWLEDGMENTS

The authors wish to acknowledge the following publishers for their kind permission to reprint material from their publications:

Cambridge University Press:

The Hellenistic Age from the Battle of Ipsos to the Death of Kleopatra VII, edited and translated by Stanley M. Burstein. Copyright © 1996. Reprinted with the permission of Cambridge University Press.

Hackett Publishing Company, Inc.:

Homer: Iliad, translated by Stanley Lombardo. Copyright © 1997. Reprinted by permission of Hackett Publishing Company, Inc. All rights reserved.

Johns Hopkins University Press:

Hesiod: Theogony, Works and Days, Shield, translated by Apostolos N.Athanassakis, p. 73. Copyright © 1983. Reprinted with permission of The Johns Hopkins University Press.

Pindar's Victory Songs, translated by Frank Nisetich, pp. 256–257. Copyright © 1980. Reprinted with permission of The Johns Hopkins University Press.

Oxford University Press:

The Republic of Plato, translated by Francis MacDonald Cornford. Copyright © 1945.

Xenophon: Oeconomicus: A Social and Historical Commentary, edited and translated by Sarah B. Pomeroy. Copyright © 1994.

Schocken Books:

Sappho and the Greek Lyric Poets, translated by Willis Barnstone. Copyright © 1962, 1967, 1988. Reprinted by permission of Schocken Books, distributed by Pantheon Books, a division of Random House, Inc.

University of California Press:

Sappho's Lyre: Archaic Lyric and Women Poets of Ancient Greece, translated by Diane J. Rayor. Copyright © 1991.

University of Chicago Press:

Aeschylus: The Persians, translated by S. Bernardete, and *Aeschylus: Agamemnon*, translated by R. Lattimore, in *The Complete Greek Tragedies: Aeschylus*, edited by David Grene and Richmond Lattimore. Copyright © 1992.

Sophocles: Antigone, translated by E. Wyckoff, in *The Complete Greek Tragedies: Sophocles*, edited by David Grene and Richmond Lattimore. Copyright © 1992.

W.W. Norton and Company, Inc.:

Herodotus: The Histories, edited by Walter Blanco and Jennifer Tolbert Roberts, translated by Walter Blanco. Copyright © 1992.

Thucydides: The Peloponnesian War, edited by Walter Blanco and Jennifer Tolbert Roberts, translated by Walter Blanco. Copyright © 1998.

PREFACE

The history of the ancient Greeks is one of the most improbable success stories in world history. A small people inhabiting a country poor in resources and divided into hundreds of squabbling mini-states created one of the world's most remarkable cultures. Located on the periphery of the Bronze Age civilizations of Egypt and Mesopotamia, the Greeks absorbed key technical skills such as metallurgy and writing in the process of developing a culture marked by astonishing creativity, versatility, and resilience. Finally, having spread from Spain to the borders of India, Greek culture gradually transformed as it became an integral part of other civilizations: Latin, Iranian, Arabic, and Byzantine. In the process, however, the Greeks left a rich legacy in every area of the arts and sciences that is still alive in Western and Islamic civilizations.

Almost ten years ago the authors of this book set out to write a new history of the country the English poet Byron called "the land of lost gods." We hoped that our work, *Ancient Greece: A Political, Social, and Cultural History*, would flesh out the romantic images of Greece with the new understanding of the realities of Greek history gained from the patient scholarship of a half-century of talented Greek historians. Thanks to their achievements, we were able to give full recognition to the significance of the Dark Age in the formation of Greek civilization and incorporate into the story of Greece the experiences of those who did not belong to the "scribbling class," such as women and slaves.

A Brief History of Ancient Greece is not merely an abridgement of our previous work, but a new book in which greater emphasis is given to social and cultural history. At the same time we have tried to retain all those qualities that made our first book such a success. Every paragraph and sentence has been carefully reviewed. The suggested readings have been updated, and suggestions and corrections sent to us by our readers have been incorporated into the text. The maps have been completely redesigned and new translations selected or prepared wherever necessary. An old saw has it that the purpose of studying Greek history is to understand Greek art and literature. We hope that the result of our efforts is a book that will prove a valuable guide for those people who wish to follow that recommendation and enable them to better appreciate the remarkable legacy of the ancient Greeks.

All works of historical synthesis depend on the contributions of innumerable scholars whose names do not appear in the text. We would like to thank them and our generous readers and students, from whose comments and suggestions we have greatly benefited. We again are indebted to Robert Miller and his talented staff at Oxford University Press, who have been generous with their support and assistance throughout the long gestation of this project. Beth Cohen and H. Alan Shapiro have again given our illustration program their careful attention but are not responsible for any lapses in judgment on the part of the authors. We would also like to express our gratitude to Professor Walter Blanco of the Department of English at Lehman College of the City University of New York for the excellent new translations of Herodotus that he prepared for our book and to Professor Miriam E. Burstein of the Department of English at the State University of New York at Brockport for again taking charge of the difficult tasks of acquiring permissions from various publishers and reminding us that our prose was intended for the elusive "general reader" and not specialists in Greek history.

We would also like to thank the various publishers who have granted us permission to reprint translations. Unattributed translations in the text are by the authors.

Jennifer T. Roberts, New York City   Walter Donlan, Irvine, California
Stanley M. Burstein, Los Alamitos,   Sarah B. Pomeroy, New York City
  California

TIME LINE

Period	Military Events	Political/ Social Events	Cultural Development
6500–3000 **Neolithic**		Permanent farming villages	Domestication of plants and animals; pottery
3000–2100 Early **Bronze Age** (Early Helladic 2800–1900)		Social ranking emerges; villages and districts ruled by hereditary chiefs	
			2500 Widespread use of bronze and other metals in the Aegean
2100–1600 **Middle Bronze Age** (Middle Helladic 1900–1580)	2100–1900 Lerna and other sites destroyed	2100–1900 Incursions of Indo-European speakers into Greece	2100–1900 Indo-European gods introduced into Greece
			2000 First palaces in Crete
			1900 Mainland contacts with Crete and the Near East
			1800 Cretans develop Linear A writing
1600–1150 Late Bronze **Age** (Late Helladic 1580–1150)		1600 Mycenae and other sites become power centers; small kingdoms emerge	1600 Shaft graves

continued

Time Line

Period	Military Events	Political/ Social Events	Cultural Development
	1500–1450 Mycenaeans take over Crete		1500 Tholos tombs
			1450 Linear B writing
	1375 Knossos destroyed	1400–1200 Height of Mycenaean power and prosperity	1400 New palaces in Greece
	1250–1225 "The Trojan War" (?)		
	1200 Invaders loot and burn the palace centers	1200–1100 Palace-system collapses	1200 Cultural decline
1150–900 Early Dark Age (Submycenaean 1125–1050) (Protogeometric 1050–900)		1050 Small chiefdoms established; migrations of mainland Greeks to Ionia	1050 Iron technology
		1000 Dorian Greeks settle in the mainland and the islands	950 Monumental building at Lefkandi
900–750/700 Late Dark Age (Early Geometric 900–850) (Middle Geometric 850–750)		900 Population increases; new settlements established; trade and manufacture expand	
		800 Rapid population growth	800 Greeks develop an alphabet; earliest temples built
			776 Traditional date of first Olympian games
750/700–490 Archaic Period (Late Geometric 750–700	730–700 First Messenian War	750–700 City-states emerge	750–675 *Iliad* and *Odyssey* composed
		750 Overseas colonization to the West begins	720 "Orientalizing period" in art begins
	700–650 Evolution of hoplite armor and tactics		700 Hesiod; period of lyric poetry begins
	669 Battle of Hysiae	670–500 Tyrants rule in many city-states	

continued

Period	Military Events	Political/ Social Events	Cultural Development
	650 Second Messenian War	650 Colonization of Black Sea area begins; earliest known stone inscription of a law; "Lycurgan" Reforms at Sparta; the "Great Rhetra" (?)	650 Temples built of stone and marble; Corinthian black-figure technique
		632 Cylon fails in attempt at tyranny in Athens	
		620 Law code of Draco in Athens	
		600 Lydians begin to mint coins	600 Beginnings of science and philosophy (the "Presocratics")
			582–573 Pythian, Isthmian, Nemean games inaugurated
		560–514 Peisistratus and his sons tyrants of Athens	Peisistratus expands religious festivals at Athens
		550 Sparta dominant in the Peloponnesus	530 Athenian red-figure technique
		507 Cleisthenes institutes political reforms in Athens	
	499 Ionian Greeks rebel from Persian Empire		
			5th-century rationalists and scientists; Hippocrates; advances in medicine; increase in literacy
490–323 Classical Period	490 Battle of Marathon		Classical style in sculpture
		486 Decision to choose Athenian archons by lot	
		482 Ostracism of Aristides	
	480–479 Persian Invasion of Greece		

continued

Period	Military Events	Political/ Social Events	Cultural Development
		477 Foundation of Delian League	
			470–456 Construction of temple of Zeus at Olympia
		Growth of democracy in Athens	
	463 Helot rebellion in Sparta		
		461 Reforms of Ephialtes at Athens	
	460–445 "First" Peloponnesian War		
			458 Aeschylus' *Oresteia*
		454 Athenians move treasury from Delos to Athens	
		Flourishing of Greek trade and manufacture	451 Pericles carries law limiting citizenship at Athens
		445 Thirty Years' Peace	Herodotus at work on his *Histories*
			447–432 Construction of Parthenon at Athens
			Sophists active in Athens
	431–404 Peloponnesian War		Thucydides begins his *History*
		429 Death of Pericles	428 Sophocles' *Oedipus Tyrannus*
			425 Aristophanes' *Acharnians*
		423 Thucydides exiled from Athens	
		421 Peace of Nicias	

continued

Period	Military Events	Political/ Social Events	Cultural Development
	415–413 Sicilian campaign		415 Euripides' *Trojan Women*
		411–410 Oligarchic coup in Athens; establishment of Council of 400; regime of the 5000	411 Aristophanes' *Lysistrata*
	403–377 Sparta the most powerful state in Greece	404–403 Regime of the Thirty Tyrants in Athens	
		399 Trial and execution of Socrates	399–347 Dialogues of Plato; foundation of the Academy
	395–387 Corinthian War	Fourth century: Rise of class of *rhetores* at Athens; economic inequalities and social *stasis* throughout Greece	
	377–371 Athens the most powerful state in Greece		
	371–362 Thebes the most powerful state in Greece		
		Serious population decline in Sparta; impoverished class of "Inferiors" at Sparta; increasing amount of property in hands of Spartan women	
	359 Defeat of Perdiccas III	359 Accession of Philip II	
		357 Marriage of Philip II to Olympias	
		356 Birth of Alexander the Great	356 Philip II's Olympic victory
			355 Demosthenes' first speech
			347 Death of Plato
		356–346 Third Sacred War; Peace of Philocrates	346 Isocrates' *Philippus*

continued

Period	Military Events	Political/ Social Events	Cultural Development
	338 Battle of Chaeronea	338 Assassination of Artaxerxes III; foundation of Corinthian League; marriage of Philip II and Cleopatra	338 Death of Isocrates
	336 Invasion of Asia by Philip II	336 Accession of Darius III; assassination of Philip II; accession of Alexander III	
	335 Revolt of Thebes	335 Destruction of Thebes	335 Aristotle returns to Athens; founding of Lyceum
	334 Battle of Granicus		
	333 Battle of Issus	333 Alexander at Gordium	
	331 Battle of Gaugamela	331 Foundation of Alexandria	331 Visit to Siwah by Alexander
	330–327 War in Bactria and Sogdiana	330 Destruction of Persepolis; death of Philotas	
		329 Assassination of Darius III	
		328 Murder of Clitus	
	327–325 Alexander's invasion of India	327 Marriage of Alexander and Roxane	
	326 Battle of the Hydaspes		
323–30 Hellenistic Period		323 Death of Alexander III; accession of Philip III and Alexander IV	
	323–322 Lamian War	322 Dissolution of the Corinthian League	322 Deaths of Aristotle and Demosthenes
	321 Invasion of Egypt	321 Death of Perdiccas; Antipater becomes regent	321–292 Career of Menander
	318–316 Revolt against Polyperchon		
	315–311 Four-year war against Antigonus	315 Freedom of Greeks proclaimed by Antigonus the One-Eyed	

continued

Period	Military Events	Political/ Social Events	Cultural Development
		311 Peace between Antigonus and his rivals	
	307 Demetrius invades Greece		307–283 Foundation of the Museum
	306 Battle of Salamis	306 Antigonus and Demetrius acclaimed kings	306 Epicurus founds Garden
		305 Ptolemy, Seleucus, Lysimachus, and Cassander declare themselves kings	
	301 Battle of Ipsus	301 Death of Antigonus; division of his empire	301 Zeno founds Stoa
			300–246 Construction of the Pharos
		283 Death of Ptolemy I; accession of Ptolemy II	
	281 Battle of Corupedium	281 Deaths of Lysimachus and Seleucus	
	279 Invasion of Gauls		
		235–222 Reign of Cleomenes III at Sparta	
	222 Battle of Sellasia	222 Exile of Cleomenes III; end of his reforms at Sparta	
	200–197 Second Macedonian War		
		196 Romans proclaim freedom of the Greeks at Isthmian games	
	171–168 Third Macedonian War		
		167 End of the Macedonian monarchy	167 Polybius comes to Rome
	31 Battle of Actium		
		30 Suicide of Cleopatra VII; Rome annexes Egypt	

Greece and the Aegean world.

INTRODUCTION

Historians who study ancient civilizations have the daunting task of following the path of societies and cultures on the basis of scant sources. Actually, as past civilizations go, ancient Greece has left us a comparatively rich record. Even so, we possess only a tiny fraction of what was originally there. Inevitably, then, many aspects of society and culture, even in the most well-documented periods of Greek antiquity, cannot be viewed in bold relief. Yet there is good news, too. Every year new discoveries are made that continue to enlarge our fund of information, while, at the same time, new ways of looking at the old sources have broadened our perspectives.

SOURCES: HOW WE KNOW
ABOUT THE ANCIENT GREEKS

Sources are the raw material of history out of which historians weave their stories. Just about everything preserved from antiquity is a potential source for the history of antiquity. Our sources fall into two broad categories: the physical remains, which include anything material, from bones to buildings, and the written remains, which include the words of the Greeks themselves or of others who wrote about them in antiquity. Of course, the line between the material and the written is often blurred, as in the case of words scratched on a piece of pottery, or an inscription carved on a stone pillar.

Given that our primary sources are at least two thousand years old, and in many cases much older, it is not surprising that most of them require rehabilitation or reconstruction even before they can be of substantial use. But, fortunately, historians do not have to examine them from scratch. They rely on archaeologists to excavate, classify, and interpret most of the material evidence; paleographers to decipher and elucidate the texts written on papyrus and parchment; epigraphists and numismatists to interpret inscriptions on stones and coins. Without the expertise of those specialists who process the raw sources, the work of historians would not be possible.

Archaeologists study past societies primarily through the material remains—buildings, tools, and other artifacts. They create a history of the material culture on the basis of the changing patterns that they discern in the physical record. Historians, on the other hand, primarily use documents, inscriptions, and literary texts to construct a narrative of events and the people who were involved in them: what they did, why they did it, and the changes brought on by their actions. Nevertheless, both disciplines are engaged in a single collaborative project, the reconstruction of the lifeways of the Greek peoples over time.

RETRIEVING THE PAST: THE MATERIAL RECORD

Ancient Greece lies underground. Except for a few stone buildings, mostly temples, which have survived above ground, everything we have has been dug up from beneath, very often from dozens of feet below the present surface. Materials decay, and the soil of Greece is not good for preserving things. Accordingly, artifacts made of wood, cloth, and leather are rarely found. Metals fare better: gold and silver last almost forever; bronze is fairly durable; while iron is more subject to corrosion. Another material, which is virtually indestructible, is terra-cotta, clay baked at very high temperatures. Clay was used in antiquity for many different objects, including figurines and votive plaques, but most of our clay objects are vessels that have been found by the thousands in graves and other sites. It was mainly on the basis of pots that archaeologists were able to construct a chronology for prehistoric and early historic Greece that could be translated into actual dates.

Clay pots were made wide-bellied or slender-bodied, long-necked or wide-mouthed, footed or footless, with one, two, or no handles. Some pots, such as the perfume flasks called *aryballoi*, stood only two or three inches high; others, like the *pithoi* used for storing olive oil and grain, were often as big as a human being. In the ancient world, clay vessels had to be made in all sizes and shapes, because they served virtually every purpose that a container can serve. They were our bags, cartons, and shipping crates, our cooking pots, bottles, and glasses, as well as our fine stemware and "good" china bowls. Because their basic shapes remained much the same, yet they underwent gradual changes in style and decoration, pots could be placed in relative chronological sequences. Earthenware from one site is cross-dated with examples from other sites, thus confirming that site A is older or younger than sites B and C. But the big breakthrough for establishing "absolute" or calendar dates comes about when a datable object from an outside culture is found amidst the Greek material. Such an object might be a scarab inscribed with the name of an Egyptian king. Since the actual dates of his reign are known independently from the Egyptian king-lists, it follows that the Greek objects found with it in that deposit belonged to approximately the same time. Through the repeated process of establishing key cross-dates, a workable chronology emerges that allows us to place an object, or grave, or building in real time: "late fourteenth century BC" or "around 720 BC." Today's archaeologists also have at their disposal more scientific techniques for dating objects and sites, such as measuring the radioactive decay of organic materials (carbon-14 dating).

Yet, notwithstanding the considerable success that modern archaeology has had in bringing the ancient past to light, the fact is that wordless objects can tell us only so much about how people lived, what they experienced, or what they thought.

RETRIEVING THE PAST: THE WRITTEN RECORD

Ancient writings were inscribed upon many different materials including clay, stone, metal, and papyrus (and from the second century BC on, parchment). Most of the written sources that have come down to us were composed in the Greek alphabet, which was introduced in the eighth century BC; but we also have clay tablets from a very brief time in the second millennium BC that were written in a syllabic script called Linear B. (We shall discuss Linear B writing in Chapter One and the Greek alphabet in Chapter Two.)

With the rapid spread of the alphabet came a torrent of written texts that would continue unabated throughout the rest of antiquity. Unfortunately, most of this has been lost; yet that so much has survived is something of a miracle in itself. We may lament that of the more than 120 plays written by Sophocles, one of the most famous of the fifth century BC dramatists, only seven have come down to us whole. We are grateful, however, to have as much as we have. After all, 20,000,000 words are stored in the electronic database of Greek literary texts written down from the late eighth century BC to the second century AD.

The most common medium for writing in the ancient Mediterranean was papyrus (the paper of antiquity), which had been used in Egypt since the third millennium. Papyrus sheets were made by bonding together layered strips sliced from the papyrus reed; these were then glued together to form a long roll, 20 or more feet long. Words were written horizontally to form columns, which the reader isolated by scrolling back and forth along the roll. A papyrus roll could hold, on average, a play of about 1,500 lines or two to three "books" of Homer's *Iliad* or *Odyssey*. Every text had to be copied by hand (usually by slaves), a time-consuming and expensive proposition. The ancient Greeks were fairly assiduous in preserving the authors from their past. A reader visiting the great library at Alexandria during the first century BC would have had access to about 500,000 book-rolls, while the collection at Pergamum is said to have exceeded 200,000 rolls.

But already by this time the process of selection had begun. The Alexandrian scholars themselves appear to have used the term "those included" to denote a list of authors who were deemed most worthy of being studied in schools. Naturally the "included" writers had the best chances for survival. And as literary tastes continued to change during later antiquity, many manuscripts ceased to be copied and crumbled into dust. Fortunately, papyrus endures well in a hot, dry environment, as in the desert sands of Egypt, where many thousands of Greek papyri, dating from the fourth century BC onward, have been found. Most of these are contemporary documents; however, papyri rescued from desert dumps have also preserved major literary works from all periods of Greek antiquity that otherwise would have been lost completely. In addition to texts originally written on papyrus, hundreds of inscriptions on stone and metal, including coins, survive

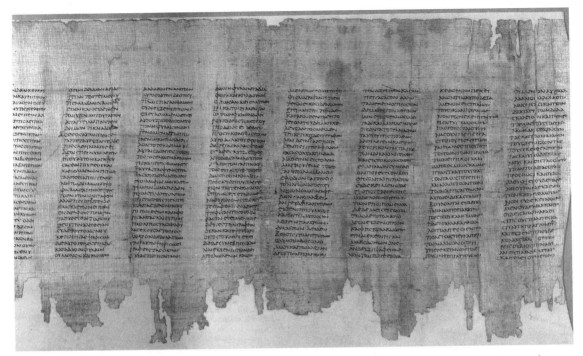

Figure i. Part of a papyrus roll from the second century AD, showing how the text is divided into columns. This and other papyri are our only sources for the speeches of Hyperides, one of the leading Athenian politicians of the fourth century BC.

Figure ii. A school-room scene from Athens (c. 490–480 BC). In the center, a pupil is reciting his lesson before a teacher who is holding a papyrus roll.

that range in subject matter from private funerary epitaphs and dedications to public decrees, treaties, and laws. The latter are especially valuable, because they preserve information about public life that is seldom recorded elsewhere.

Our sources vary in both quantity and quality according to time and place. For the Mycenaean Age (c. 1600–1200 BC), we have a wealth of material evidence (including the Linear B tablets) that permits a fairly detailed picture of the society. For the subsequent period, the Dark Age, down to the eighth century BC, material remains are very sparse and there are no written records. After the seventh century BC, however, when both material and literary remains start to proliferate, we begin to have a dynamic picture of change and continuity. The picture will show how the Greeks responded to environmental pressures with ideas and technological innovations, how they interacted as individuals within communities and as communities within communities, and how they developed a distinctive culture while preserving individual distinction.

Our literary sources are a diverse group, written in many different genres, that is, categories of composition defined by form and content. These include various types of poetry such as epic, lyric, tragedy, and comedy, as well as the prose genres of history, biography, oratory, and philosophy. Naturally, modern historians rely especially on the writings of ancient historians and biographers, but the other genres, both of poetry and of prose, are no less essential as sources.

Of course, there is a big distinction between mythical and historical narratives of the past. We don't expect historical veracity from Homer's account of the Trojan War. At the same time, not even an historian who strives for veracity can give us a truly objective and unbiased account of the past. The ancient historians, no different from us really, aimed to convey only what they deemed historically significant. Because they selected some facts to the exclusion of others, even two roughly contemporary historians—the fifth-century Herodotus and Thucydides, for example— would necessarily produce different accounts of the same past events. Another limitation of our written sources is that, with very few exceptions, they are all produced by a privileged group: urban males, mostly from the upper class. In order to illuminate the lives of women, the very poor, and slaves, who do not generally speak for themselves, historians employ a variety of strategies, often drawing upon feminism, Marxism, cultural studies, and other interdisciplinary approaches.

A SYNOPSIS OF WRITTEN SOURCES BY PERIODS 3000–700 BC

As we have seen, the Greeks of the Bronze Age (c. 3000–1150 BC) left no written records except for the Linear B tablets near the end of the Late Bronze Age. The long silence which followed baffled the efforts of even ancient Greek historians to describe the centuries before the reappearance of writing in the eighth century. Their source material was a body of orally transmitted myths and legends, some of which probably went back to the second millennium. The Greeks of the historical period generally regarded these stories as their ancient history. The central event of their distant past was the Trojan War, which, if it really happened, would have taken place in the thirteenth century BC. The Trojan War and its immediate aftermath are the setting for the earliest texts that we have, Homer's *Iliad* and *Odyssey*, which are believed to be the end product of a tradition of oral poetry going back many centuries. It is currently thought that they were committed to writing in the later eighth century or early in the seventh. The use of these two very long epic poems as historical sources has been debated since the end of antiquity and is still a matter of controversy. Do they reflect a real society? If so, when? Or do they reveal, rather, the values and norms of later ancient Greeks who contrasted their own time with a former "age of heroes"?

700–490 BC

Hesiod (c. 700) stands at the beginning of the Archaic Age. The two texts that have come down under Hesiod's name, the *Theogony* and the *Works and Days*, are, like the *Iliad* and the *Odyssey*, lengthy poems composed in the epic meter. In content, however, they differ not only from Homer but also from each other. While the *Theogony* reaches back in time to tell the origins of the Greek gods and the creation of the universe, the *Works and Days* is set in the poet's own day and is our earliest source that directly addresses contemporary social concerns.

The Archaic Age poets—who composed in the variety of forms we lump together under the rubric of lyric—abuse their enemies, praise the gods, argue politics, and pine over unrequited love in their verses. Even in the fragmentary shape in which we have them, the poems let us glimpse the political, social, and intellectual movements that distinguished the seventh and sixth centuries BC.

Yet, in a sense the Archaic Age is still prehistory, for there are no historical writings from this period. The fifth-century historians, Herodotus (c. 484–425) and Thucydides (c. 460–400), however, provide us with much valuable information about the development of the early city-states, especially Athens and Sparta. Sources for early Athens, though meager, are not quite as sparse as they are for Sparta. By good fortune, a papyrus from Egypt has preserved part of *The Athenian Constitution*, written by the philosopher Aristotle (384–322) or one of his students. This document, as well as Plutarch's *Life of Solon*, quotes fragments of the poetry of the lawgiver Solon (c. 600), who is our earliest source for Athenian society. The bulk of what we know about early Sparta and its institutions, however, comes primarily from later writers, particularly the fourth-century BC historian Xenophon and the biographer Plutarch (46–120 AD). Since the Spartans themselves left almost no written records, and the accounts of later writers tended to idealize or criticize their culture, it is particularly challenging for historians to separate the real Sparta from the fictional Sparta.

490–323 BC

What modern historians call the Classical period of Greece begins in 490 with the victory of the Greeks over the Persians in the Battle of Marathon and ends with the death of Alexander the Great. The sources for this period are fuller than for any other period of ancient Greece and are drawn from all over the eastern Mediterranean world, not from Greece alone. The wars of these two centuries formed the themes of our first extant Greek historians. *The Histories* of Herodotus (c. 485–420 BC) ask the question "why did Greeks and non-Greeks go to war?" and respond with a chain of mutual wrongful acts and cultural misunderstandings reaching far back in time and space. Herodotus is our primary source for the Persian wars from the Greek perspective, and provides much information about relations among Greek city-states in the sixth and early fifth centuries, especially Athens and Sparta.

The principal source for the actions that led to the Peloponnesian War between Athens and Sparta and their allies and for the war itself is the *History* of Thucydides (c. 460–395 BC). Thucydides aimed for accuracy; his account is informed by contemporary documents as well as by interviews with witnesses on both sides. But, as we have noted, no historian is ever truly impartial. As an interpreter of events, he couldn't help making judgments with every selection or arrangement of his "facts." Xenophon (c. 428–354 BC), who began his *Hellenica* almost exactly where Thucydides left off and continued his history down to 362 BC, seems to have made an effort to practice what he understood as "Thucydidean historiography." Several other fourth-century historians who wrote about the Peloponnesian War and its aftermath survive in the biographies of Plutarch and the historical books of Diodorus (first century BC).

During these two centuries of alternating war and uneasy peace, poetry, philosophy, and the visual arts flourished, and the extant works reflect changing ideas, tastes, concerns, and lifestyles, particularly in Athens where most of our evidence comes from. Of the hundreds of dramas that were produced during this period, only the tragedies of Aeschylus, Sophocles, and Euripides and the comedies of Aristophanes and Menander have survived (and even their works are mostly lost). With exception of Menander's comedies, the plays do not attempt to mirror society; nor, like today's "docu-dramas," can they be seen as "history with the boring parts taken out." Yet, social historians can extrapolate from them evidence about many aspects of Athenian life. The tragedians Aeschylus, Sophocles, and Euripides use plots and characters from ancient myths, but their dramas often offer insights into the contemporary concerns of the citizenry. Unlike the characters in the tragedies, those of the comic playwright Aristophanes are represented as contemporary Athenians. Some of them are well-known public figures whom he makes the butt of parody and abusive satire. While it is difficult for us to tell how Aristophanes really felt about the people he attacked in verse, his comedies do show us what made male audiences in a democracy laugh.

Philosophers were among the numerous intellectuals in the fourth century who were voicing their dissatisfaction with traditional democracy and suggesting new models of government. The surviving works of Plato (428–348 BC) and Aristotle (384–322 BC) not only fault the fundamental ideals of democracy, liberty, and equality, but even undertake to redefine them. Yet philosophical writings, no less than drama, defy our attempts to fasten down their viewpoints. Plato, for example, conveniently detaches himself from his arguments by expressing them in the form of dialogues in which he does not appear himself. Nevertheless, their theories about statecraft are evidence for the debate among the intellectual elite over the viability of democracy as they knew it in their day.

Varied aspects of Athenian public and private life in the fourth century are made vivid to us by the dozens of extant speeches. Lysias, Andocides, Isocrates, and Demosthenes were among the influential politician-orators (*rhētores*) who composed speeches for delivery in the law courts and the popular assembly. Because they were constructed to dazzle their audiences and persuade them with clever rhetoric, the "facts" brought forth in their arguments (e.g., the wording of a particular law) must be regarded with some skepticism. Demosthenes (384–322 BC) was most famous for his "Philippics," orations against the ruler of Macedon, Philip II, who was then threatening to become the master of all the Greek states.

323–30 BC

The conquests of Philip's son, Alexander III (the "Great") extended as far as the borders of India. Curiously, the huge number of books written about Alexander after his death in 323, survive only in fragments. We are left with five ancient biographies—Plutarch's *Life of Alexander* is one—written three to five hundred years later and thus subject to the biases of their own times. The sources for Alexander's successors, who ruled over the various parts of the huge empire, are equally scanty. Except for Diodorus' account (first century BC) of the final decades of the fourth century and scraps of other later writings that yield some information about the two generations after Alexander, little else remains to tell their story.

Fortunately, ample sources exist that illuminate everyday life and the administrative, military, and economic apparatus of the various Hellenistic kingdoms. In Egypt, for example, numerous inscriptions and thousands of public and private documents preserved on papyrus record all aspects of urban and village life. Among the papyri we find private letters, marriage contracts, wills, tax assessments and records of legal proceedings.

New philosophies such as Stoicism and Epicureanism (whose precepts are preserved in later sources) offered advice on how to cope with the sense of dislocation produced by this vastly enlarged, culturally diverse universe. Not surprisingly, the surviving works of the Hellenistic poets, Callimachus, Theocritus, and Apollonius Rhodius, expressed a double urge: to recreate the past so that it conformed to the needs of a complex world and at the same time to preserve the past exactly as it was.

THE PHYSICAL CONTEXT: THE LAND OF GREECE

The material and written sources are only part of the story, however. History does not occur in a vacuum but in particular places. Greek historians, therefore, must also consider the character of the land of Greece itself, for the natural environment of a people—the landscape, the climate, and the natural resources—is a major factor in determining the way they live and how they develop socially. *Hellas*, the homeland of the Greeks, ancient and modern, covers the southern portion of the Balkan peninsula and the islands that lie to the west and east of the mainland. The Greek islands to the east, in the Aegean Sea, are numerous; some are closer to the coast of Anatolia (modern Turkey) than to the mainland. The largest Greek island, Crete, lies to the south, about midway between the Greek mainland and North Africa. A place of myth and legend, Crete will have a prominent role in the early part of our narrative.

In terms of square miles, Greece is about the size of England in Great Britain or the state of Alabama in the United States. The landscape is very rugged, with mountains covering almost 75 percent of the land. Only about 30 percent of the land can be cultivated at all, and only about 20 percent is classified as good agricultural land. Except in the northern mainland, where there are extensive plainlands, the mountains and lower hills cut the land into many narrow coastal plains, and upland plains and valleys. Except for Mt. Olympus in Thessaly (nearly 10,000 feet), the mountain ranges are not terribly high (3,000–8,000 feet), but they are quite steep and craggy, which made overland travel in antiquity difficult and somewhat isolated the small valleys and their people from one another.

By far the easiest way to travel was by sea, especially in the islands and the southern mainland, where the coast is never more than 40 miles away. The chains of islands in the Aegean Sea facilitated sea voyages. Although the coastlines of the mainland and the islands are generally quite rugged, sailors could usually find a safe landfall where they could beach their boats for the night or wait out a threatening storm. The few locations that offered a good harbor became ports early on, destinations for the exchange of trade goods. Throughout antiquity, the narrow Aegean tied the Greeks to the Near East and Egypt, commercially, culturally, politically, and militarily. The commercial contacts were vital; for, with the exception of building stone and clay, Greece is not well endowed with raw materials. The necessity to trade overseas for raw materials, especially for bronze, destined the Greeks very early in their history to take to the sea and mingle with people from the other, older civilizations to the east and south.

The Mediterranean climate is semiarid, with long, hot, dry summers and short, cool, moist winters, when most of the rain falls. This general pattern varies from region to region in Greece. Northern Greece has a more continental climate, with much colder and wetter winters than the south. More rain falls on the western side of the Greek mainland than on the eastern side, while the Aegean islands receive even less. The generally mild weather permitted outdoor activity for most of the year. The soil in Greece, though rocky, is fairly rich, the most fertile plowland being in the small plains where, over the ages, earth washed down from the hills has formed deep deposits. The lower hillsides, which are rockier, can be cultivated through terracing, which prevents the soil from washing farther down the slope and captures soil from above. The mountains, with their jagged limestone peaks and steep cliffs, support only wild vegetation, but some enclose mountain valleys suitable for farming and for grazing animals. Wood, essential for fuel and construction, especially shipbuilding, was originally abundant in the highland areas. As time went on, however, forests became depleted and by the fifth century BC the more populous regions were forced to import timber. Water, the most precious natural resource, is scarce in Greece, because there are very few rivers that flow year-round and few lakes, ponds, and springs. Unlike in the huge river valleys of Egypt and Mesopotamia, irrigation on a large scale was not possible; farming depended on the limited annual rainfall.

It should be emphasized that this description of the land and resources of Greece is a generalized one. Though small in area, Greece has a variety of local landscapes and micro-climates in which the rainfall, the quantity and quality of farmland, pastureland, and raw materials are decidedly different. On the whole, however, the land, which the Greeks called Gaia ("Mother Earth"), allowed the majority of the farmers a decent though modest living. But she offered no guarantees. Drought, especially in the more arid regions, was a constant and dreaded threat. A dry winter meant a lean year, and a prolonged drought meant hunger and poverty for entire villages and districts. Torrential rainstorms, on the other hand, could send water rushing down the hillsides and through the dry gullies, suddenly wiping out the terraces, flooding the fields, and destroying the crops. Life on the sea was equally unpredictable. The Aegean, though often calm with favoring winds, could just as suddenly boil up into ferocious storms sending ships, cargo, and sailors to the bottom. (Drowning at sea, unburied, was a hateful death for the Greeks.) It is no wonder, considering the extent to which the Greeks were at the mercy of the land, sky, and sea, that the gods they worshiped included personifications of the elements and forces of nature.

Food and Livestock

In general, the soil and climate amply supported the "Mediterranean triad" of grain, grapes, and olives. Bread, wine, and olive oil were the staples of the Greek diet throughout antiquity and for long afterward. Grains—wheat, barley, and oats—grow well in Greek soil, having been cultivated from native wild grasses. Olive trees and grapevines, also indigenous to Greece, flourished in their cultivated state. Legumes (peas and beans) and several kinds of vegetables, fruits (especially figs), and nuts, rounded out and varied the basic components of bread, porridges, and olive oil. Cheese, meat, and fish, which are rich in proteins and fat, supplemented the diet. Meat, however, provided a very small part of the average family's daily food intake, and was usually consumed at feasts and festivals. The Greeks did not care for butter and drank little milk. Their beverages were water or wine (usually diluted with water). Honey was used for sweetening, and various spices enhanced the flavor of food. Though it might appear monotonous to modern tastes, the Greek diet was healthful and nourishing.

The pasturing of small animals did not interfere with agriculture. Flocks of sheep and goats grazed on hilly land that could not be farmed and on the fallow fields, providing manure in return. As suppliers of wool, cheese, meat, and skins, they had great economic importance. The Greeks also kept pigs, relished for their meat, and fowl. The two largest domesticated animals, horses and cattle, occupied a special niche in the economy and the society. Oxen (castrated bulls) or mules (hybrids of the horse and donkey) were necessary for plowing and for drawing heavy loads. A farmer without ready access to a yoke of oxen or a pair of mules would be classified as poor. Herds of cattle and horses did compete with agriculture, since the stretches of good grazing land they required were also prime farmland. Practically speaking, there could be large-scale ranching of cattle and horses (except in the northern plains) only in times of low population density. Because they require so much in the way of resources, only the wealthy could afford the luxury of keeping cattle and horses in large numbers. As the most prestigious animals for sacrifices and feasts, cattle were a status symbol for the rich. Horses, though, were the prime markers of high rank: beautiful creatures, very expensive to maintain, and useful only for riding and for pulling light chariots.

This agricultural and pastoral way of life remained essentially unchanged throughout antiquity. The fundamental economic fact that ancient Greece was essentially a land of small-scale farmers (most of whom lived in farming villages and small towns) governed every aspect of Greek society, from politics to war to religion. It has been estimated that even in the fifth to third centuries BC, the peak population periods, possibly as many as 80 to 90 percent of the male citizens of a city-state were engaged in agriculture in some degree, while their wives worked inside the house. One of the major unifying forces within the Greek city-states was the citizen-farmers' devotion to their small agricultural plain and its surrounding hillsides, and their willingness to die defending their "ancestral earth," as the poet Homer called it. And the primary disunifying force throughout Greek history was the perpetual tension between those citizens who had much land and those who had little or none.

SUGGESTED READINGS

Easterling, P. E. and E. J. Kenney, eds. 1985. *The Cambridge History of Classical Literature*. Cambridge, UK: Cambridge University Press. Separate chapters on individual authors and genres by distinguished critics cover the entirety of ancient Greek literature, from Homer to the period of the Roman Empire.

Renfrew, Colin and Paul Bahn. 1991. *Archaeology: Theories, Methods, and Practice*. New York: Thames and Hudson. Comprehensive introduction to the discipline of archaeology today: what it is, what it does, and how it is done.

Runnels, Curtis and Priscilla M. Murray. 2001. *Greece Before History: An Archaeological Companion and Guide*. Stanford: Stanford University Press. A brief history of the archaeology of Greece from the Old Stone Age to the end of the Bronze Age, written by experts for the general reader.

van Andel, Tjerd and Curtis Runnels. 1987. *Beyond the Acropolis: A Rural Greek Past*. Stanford: Stanford University Press. A description of the topography, flora, fauna, and subsistence strategies of ancient Greek farming life.

EARLY GREECE AND
THE BRONZE AGE

The most charismatic cultural hero of the ancient Greeks was Odysseus, a man who "saw the towns of many men and learned their minds, and suffered in his heart many griefs upon the sea . . ." (*Odyssey* 1.3–4). Like their legendary hero, the Greeks were irresistibly drawn to distant shores. From early in their history and continually throughout antiquity, they ventured over the seas to foreign lands seeking their fortunes as traders, colonizers, and mercenary soldiers. Their limited natural resources forced the Greeks to look outward, and they were fortunate in being within easy reach of the Mediterranean shores of Asia, Africa, and Europe. By the fifth century BC, they had planted colonies from Spain to the west coast of Asia and from north Africa to the Black Sea. The philosopher Plato (c. 429–347 BC) likened the hundreds of Greek cities and towns that ringed the coasts of the Mediterranean and Black seas to "frogs around a pond" (*Phaedo* 109b). The story of those far-flung Greeks is a long and fascinating one.

GREECE IN THE STONE AGES

Humans entered Greece about 40,000 years ago, during the Middle Paleolithic (Old Stone) Age. These early inhabitants lived mainly by hunting and some gathering of wild plants, using finely crafted tools and weapons of stone, wood, and bone. At the end of the Ice Age, when the glaciers that had covered much of Europe were receding (c. 12,000 BC), the climate of Greece warmed considerably; in the process the landscape and its plants and animals evolved into their present forms. Evidence from a cave at Franchthi in the Peloponnesus shows that the inhabitants at the end of the Ice Age hunted deer and smaller game, caught fish in the coastal waters, and gathered wild cereals, wild peas and beans, and nuts.

Early in the Neolithic (New Stone) Age (c. 6500 BC) the inhabitants began to cultivate the wild cereals and other plants, to domesticate animals, and to weave cloth on a loom. Agriculture forces people to settle down permanently. Small farming villages sprang up, made up of one-room mud-brick houses similar to those of the Near East. Under the favorable conditions of the warm New Stone Age, villages grew larger and new village communities were formed.

The society of the small Stone Age villages was probably egalitarian, with no inequality outside of sex, age, and skill. Families cooperated and shared with their neighbors, most of whom were kinfolk. Leadership was probably temporary, assumed now by this man, now by another, as the need for a decisive voice arose. With the growth of population, however, a more lasting leadership role emerged. Anthropologists call such a leader the "big man" or the "head man," the one who is better at "getting things done." His wisdom, courage, skill in solving disputes, and similar qualities propel him to the front and keep him there. In time, this position becomes a sort of "office" into which a new man, having demonstrated that he is better suited than other would-be leaders, steps when the old head man retires or dies (or is pushed out). Henceforth, the division into two status groups, the very small group of leaders and the large group of the led, would be a permanent feature of Greek political life.

GREECE IN THE EARLY AND MIDDLE BRONZE AGES (c. 3000–1600 BC)

Nearly four thousand years after the adoption of agriculture, another fundamental technological innovation was introduced into the villages of Greece: bronze. Neolithic craftsmen in southeastern Europe and western Asia were already skilled at smelting and casting copper, but because it is a soft metal, its usefulness was limited. The pivotal step of adding 10 percent of tin to copper to produce bronze, a much harder metal, was taken in the Near East during the fourth millennium and arrived in Greece about 3000 BC. This was a momentous technical advance, for tools and weapons of bronze were considerably more efficient than those made of stone, bone, or copper. By 2500, metalworkers in Greece and the Balkans had mastered not only the use of bronze but also other metals such as lead, silver, and gold. The high-ranked families, those with greater surpluses of wealth, would have had the greatest access to scarce metals and metal products. Possession of these and other prestige items further distinguished them from the mass of the population. Their increasing demand for metal goods created a need for more specialists and workshops and accelerated trade for copper, tin, and other metals, throughout the Mediterranean region. And as the economy expanded and the settlements grew larger, so did the wealth, power, and authority of their leaders, now established as hereditary chiefs ruling for life and accorded exceptional honors and privileges.

The Civilizations of the Near East

In contrast to Greece and the Balkans in the Early Bronze Age (c. 3000–2100 BC), the Near East had already progressed to that higher level of organization of the natural and social environment termed "civilization." The Aegean civilizations of

Crete and Greece, as we shall see, owe their rise in the second millennium to their close contact with the palace-kingdoms of the East.

Around 3500 BC in the wide fertile plain the Greeks named Mesopotamia, "the land between the rivers" Tigris and Euphrates (in what is now southern Iraq), there appeared, for the first time in history, the markers of advanced civilization: large-scale irrigation, cities with thousands of inhabitants, bureaucratic government, wide trade networks, written documents, legal systems, and science. Egyptian civilization, which arose around 3200 BC along the long, narrow valley of the Nile, followed the same trajectory as that of Mesopotamia, except that very early on it became a united kingdom under a single ruler, the pharaoh.

In Mesopotamia, however, and in the rest of western Asia, societies evolved in the form of discrete polities, centered around great cities which drew the surrounding towns and villages into a single political unit—the city-state—administered from the capital. During the third millennium the more powerful city-states conquered their weaker neighbors, giving rise to territorial kingdoms which were ascendant for a time only to be conquered in turn by rival kingdoms.

Within individual kingdoms society was highly stratified; the masses were heavily dependent on and completely subject to an elite ruling class, headed by a hereditary monarch. The kings and the high nobles, deploying a huge amount of surplus wealth from agriculture, manufacture, and trade, and millions of hours of human labor, built massive defensive walls and temples, as well as luxurious palaces and elaborate tombs for themselves and their families. Architecture especially served religion, which became the most important means of control, for it identified the will of the ruler with the will of the gods. Vast wealth and increased population allowed the frequent wars of conquest and retribution to be fought on a huge scale by well-organized armies.

These early civilizations would have an enormous influence on the cultural development of the Greeks, and increasingly, as time went on, the histories of the Near Eastern and Aegean peoples became more and more entwined.

The First Greek-Speakers

Though far less advanced politically and technologically than the Near East, Greece attained a fairly high level of social complexity during its Early Bronze Age (c. 3000–2100 BC). The remains of Lerna in Argolis, for example, show that it was a large town with stone fortification walls and monumental buildings, the largest of which may have been the house of the ruling chief. At the end of this period, Lerna and similar sites in southern and central Greece were destroyed. Historians have traditionally associated the destructions and the cultural stagnation that followed during the Middle Bronze Age (c. 2100–1600 BC) with the incursion of a new people, who spoke an early form of Greek. That dating is by no means certain, however, and the questions of when the first Greek-speakers arrived and the route they took remain open today.

More certain is that the newcomers were part of a great and lengthy ancient migration of peoples, known collectively as the Indo-Europeans. In the late eighteenth century AD linguists observed that ancient Greek bears many similarities to other dead languages, such as Latin and Sanskrit (the language of ancient India), as well as to entire families of spoken languages, such as the Germanic and Slavic. Take for example our word "mother": Greek *mētēr*, Latin *mater*, Sanskrit *mātar*, Anglo-Saxon *mōdor*, Old Irish *mathir*, Lithuanian *mote*, Russian *mat'*.

The close likenesses in vocabulary and grammar among these ancient languages and their descendants led scholars to conclude that they had all sprung from a common linguistic ancestor, which they termed "Proto-Indo-European." A current hypothesis is that Greek and the other Indo-European languages evolved during the long waves of emigrations from an original Indo-European homeland, located perhaps in the vast steppes north of the Black and Caspian seas. Over the course of many centuries (beginning perhaps in the fourth millennium BC) the Indo-European languages spread across Europe and Asia, from Ireland to Chinese Turkestan.

The Greeks

Eventually, the Greek language completely submerged the non-Indo-European "Aegean" languages. The relatively few words that survived from the old language were chiefly names of places (e.g., Korinthos, Parnassos) and of native plants and animals, such as *hyakinthos* ("hyacinth") and *melissa* ("bee"). During the nineteenth century of our era, there was considerable conjecture about the social organization and culture of the Indo-Europeans. Many assumed that they were a superior race of horse-riding "Aryan" warriors, who swept into southern Europe and obliterated the cultures of the weak, unwarlike, agrarian natives. Such suppositions were the products of a racially biased Eurocentrism. No scholar today accepts this myth of Aryan superiority which was the pretext for so many crimes against humanity in the nineteenth and twentieth centuries, culminating in the horrors perpetrated by the Nazis and Fascists in the 1930s and 1940s. The imposition of their language does suggest that the Greek-speakers came in as conquerors and initially dominated the indigenous populations. It is likely, however, that by the end of the Middle Bronze Age (c. 2100–1600 BC), the two peoples had merged into a single people and their two cultures had fused into a single Hellenic culture that contained elements of both. Indeed, their cultures were similar in many respects. The newcomers were not wild horse-riding nomads, fresh out of the steppes, as they were once portrayed to be (although they may have introduced horses to Greece). Like the indigenous peoples, they subsisted as herders and farmers and practiced metallurgy and other crafts, such as pottery and clothmaking. Indo-European society was patrilineal (descent is reckoned from the father, *patēr* in Greek) and patriarchal (the father is the supreme authority figure). There is no reason, however, to accept the once prevalent notion that this system was imposed by the newcomers on a matrilineal and matriarchal form of social organization.

The Discovery of the Aegean Civilizations

Around the time when Greek-speakers entered the Aegean (c. 2000 BC), the first palaces appear on the island of Crete, signaling that the Cretans had joined the company of complex state societies. Four hundred years later, the Greeks would also reach that level of development, under the general influence of the Near East, but especially through their relationship with the Cretans (who were not Greek-speakers).

That there had been advanced civilizations in the Bronze Age Aegean became demonstrated only in the late nineteenth century when archaeologists unearthed three cities, which up to that time were known only from the legends about the Trojan War, the central event of the Greeks' mythical "age of heroes." First, in 1870 Heinrich Schliemann discovered the ruins of Troy in northwest Anatolia (modern Turkey). In Schliemann's day most historians regarded the Greeks' re-membrance of an ancient war against Troy as just another fable. Four years later, Schliemann turned to the site of Mycenae in southern Greece, which tradition held to be the city of King Agamemnon, the leader of the Greek invasion of Troy. To everyone's surprise, Schliemann's excavations of the Bronze Age level uncov-ered a large fortified palace-complex, worthy of a mighty warrior king.

Although Schliemann's discoveries are not conclusive evidence of a large-scale war between Trojans and Greeks, the impressive ruins unearthed at both sites, with their immense quantities of gold and other costly things, do confirm the Greeks' remembrance of their heroic age (i.e., the Late Bronze Age) as a time of fabulous wealth and splendor. Because of the importance of Mycenae in fact and myth, the Late Bronze Age in Greece (c. 1600–1150 BC) is commonly referred to as the "Mycenaean period."

Equally spectacular was Sir Arthur Evans' discovery in 1899 of the palace com-plex of Knossos on Crete, whose magnificence gave credence to the legends that in ancient times Knossos had been the center of a powerful naval state. Evans named this first Aegean civilization "Minoan," after the mythical King Minos of Knossos, who lived, according to Homer, three generations before the Trojan War.

The Minoans

First settled around 7000 BC by Neolithic farmers and stock-raisers of unknown origin and language, Crete followed the regional path of slow growth helped along by technological innovation. During the fourth millennium, some of the small farming villages had grown into large towns. Eventually, the chiefs of these early centers emerged as monarchs over other chiefs and people in their districts. Thus Crete became a land of small city-kingdoms.

The earliest large, multiroom complex (which Evans named the "Palace of Mi-nos") was built about 2000 BC at Knossos, by then a town with several thousand inhabitants. Other major palaces, not as grand as Knossos, followed at Phaistos, Mallia, Zakro, and elsewhere, each center controlling an area of a few hundred square miles. The political and cultural flowering in Crete (and on other Aegean islands as well) probably can be attributed to their inclusion in the international trade. The island's location and natural harbors made it an important crossroad in the trade routes across the Mediterranean Sea. The palace-centered economies

a

THEATRE AREA

11

9

10

WEST
COURT

4

3

CENTRAL
COURT

1

6

7

2

8

N

0 25 50   100 ft
0   10   20   30   40   50m

The Palace at Knossos.

1 West Porch
2 Corridor of the Procession
3 Palace Shrine
4 Stepped porch
5 Throne Room
6 Grand Staircase

7 Hall of the Double Axes
8 'Queen's Megaron'
9 Pillar Hall
10 Store-rooms
11 Royal Road, to Little Palace

Figure 1.1a. Plan of the Minoan palace at Knossos, Crete (c. 1400 BC).

b

Figure 1.1b. Plan of the Mycenaean palace at Pylos (c. 1200 BC). Note the distinctive *megaron* in the center of the complex, in contrast to the open central court at Knossos.

Figure 1.1c. (Facing page) View of the ruins of the Minoan palace at Phaistos, Crete.

c

that emerged in Crete were replicas, on a much smaller scale, of the economies of the Near Eastern states. It has not been established, however, whether Knossos ever became the center of a unified island-wide kingdom or was the largest and most powerful among a number of self-ruling states.

The Knossos we see today was begun around 1700 BC, after the first palace was destroyed by an earthquake. Knossos and the other smaller Cretan palaces consisted of a maze of rooms—residential quarters, workshops, and storerooms—clustered around a large central courtyard. This impressive residence of the ruler and a few high-ranking subordinates was the political, economic, and administrative center and indeed the focal point of state ceremony and religious ritual for the entire kingdom.

The palace economies were based on storage and redistribution. Food and other products from the palace's lands and from private farms and herds, paid as taxes, were collected and stored in the palace. The income both sustained the palace and its crafts workers and was redistributed back to the villagers as rations and wages. The palace's reserves of grain and olive oil could also be distributed to the population during famines. The main use of the royal surplus, however, was for trade. Produce and goods manufactured in the palace went out on ships along the wide Mediterranean trade network in exchange for goods from foreign lands, especially metal and luxury items.

To administer their complicated economies the Cretans developed a writing system (in a script Evans named "Linear A") comprised of specific signs that stood for the sounds of spoken syllables. Linear A writing, preserved on small clay tablets found not only on Crete but in other Aegean islands, remains largely untranslated. It is clear, however, that its main purpose was for keeping economic and administrative records.

As in the Near East, there was an enormous gulf between the ruling class and the people. The multitude of ordinary Cretan farmers and crafts workers paid for the opulent lifestyles of the few with their labor and taxes, while they themselves lived very modestly, in small mud-brick houses clustered together in the towns and villages. To be sure, the people received benefits in the form of protection from famine and from outside aggressors, but their compliance with the rigid hierarchy suggests something more—a positive identification with the center, that is, the king. In Crete, as in all ancient kingdoms, the king was a symbol as well as the actual ruler. He was the embodiment of the state: supreme war leader, lawgiver and judge, and, most important, the intermediary between gods and the land and people. Indeed, some Mediterranean scholars describe the Minoan kings as priest-kings like their counterparts in Egypt and Mesopotamia, whose legitimacy derived from the official equation of royal power with the will of the gods.

Minoan Art and Architecture

Minoan art and architecture owe a large debt to the civilizations of the Near East, and especially Egypt. Yet, even as they borrowed extensively from the techniques and styles of the older civilizations, the Cretans developed their own distinctive style and spirit. Visitors to the ruins of Knossos are dazzled by its size and complexity (it covered 3.2 acres with perhaps three hundred rooms) and the elegance of its architecture.

The palace was constructed of stone and mud brick and stood two and three stories high with basements beneath. Numerous porticoes, balconies, and loggias, all brightly painted, gave the exterior a theatrical look. Light wells brought daylight and fresh air into the interior of the palace. A system of conduits and drains provided many of the rooms with running water and waste disposal. On the walls and passageways there were brilliantly colored depictions of plant and animal life and scenes of human activity, often religious processions or rituals. Similar subjects and motifs are found not only at other Cretan palaces, but also in wealthy private homes in the towns and villages.

Minoan art is much admired today for its sophistication, vitality, and exuberance. The frescoes, vase paintings, and small sculptures give us a glimpse into how the inhabitants of the palaces and villas saw themselves. Men and women

Figure 1.2. Fresco of a fisherman from Thera.

both are represented as youthful, slender, and graceful. The men are smooth shaven and wear only a short kilt, similar to the Egyptian male dress. The women are shown wearing elaborate flounced skirts and a tight, sleeved bodice that exposes their breasts. Both men and women have long hair, stylishly curled, and wear gold bracelets and necklaces.

A remarkable example of Minoan cultural influence was discovered in 1967 at Akrotiri on the small island of Thera (modern Santorini), north of Crete. A prosperous city of several thousand inhabitants, Akrotiri was destroyed by a powerful volcanic eruption around 1630 BC, which preserved it, nearly intact, under a deep layer of volcanic ash. Its remains show how extensively the Therans absorbed Cretan art, architecture, religion, dress, and lifestyles into their own island culture. Nevertheless, the distinctly "local" features on Thera and the other Cycladic islands suggest that they were independent societies, trading partners, not colonial outposts of a Cretan empire.

GREECE AND THE AEGEAN IN THE LATE BRONZE AGE (c. 1600–1150 BC)

Cretan influence also extended to southern and central Greece by way of trading contacts, which began as early as 2000 BC. That relationship played a major role in the development of the Mycenaean Greek civilization. The Greeks did not just borrow individual elements from the Minoan cultural repertoire; they even adopted wholesale the model of the Cretan state right down to the writing system. But when they had become powerful in their own right, the Mycenaeans repaid their teachers by invading Crete and taking over the Cretan palace-centers. And then, their civilization, too, came crashing down at the end of the Late Bronze Age.

The Early Mycenaeans (c. 1600–1400 BC)

During the course of the Middle Bronze Age (c. 2100–1600 BC) Greece was gradually transformed. In the Peloponnesus and other areas of mainland Greece, population rose, productivity increased, and trade with the outside expanded, all of which led to a further strengthening of the economic and political power of the leaders. Warrior-chiefs were now evolving into monarchs.

Hundreds of Bronze Age settlements have been found in mainland and island Greece, many of which can be identified by name from the ancient legends. Archaeology has confirmed that the famous mainland cities of epic poetry, such as Mycenae, Tiryns, Pylos, Thebes, and Athens, were in fact the major Bronze Age centers. Their grand palaces, however, were not built until the fourteenth and thirteenth centuries, over the remains of the older, less imposing structures. Accordingly, what we know of the early stage of the Mycenaean civilization (roughly 1600–1400 BC) is revealed chiefly through graves and the offerings interred with the bodies of the deceased men, women, and children.

a

b

d

c

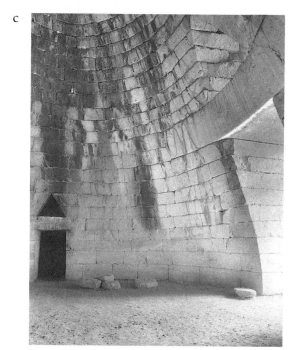

Figure 1.3a. A bronze dagger inlaid with a scene of a lion hunt, from a later shaft grave at Mycenae.

Figure 1.3b. Plan and cross section of a Mycenaean *tholos* tomb.

Figure 1.3c. Interior vault of a *tholos* tomb at Mycenae (the so-called Treasury of Atreus).

Figure 1.3d. Gold mask from an early shaft grave at Mycenae.

In Mycenae, these "shaft" graves—deep rectangular pits into which the bodies were lowered—cover more than a century of burials, from a little before 1600 to a little after 1500. The earlier graves yielded many bronze weapons (swords, daggers, spearheads, and knives) and quantities of local pottery, but little gold or jewelry. By comparison, a single later grave, containing the bodies of three men and two women, held an arsenal of weapons (43 swords, for example), and hundreds of other expensive objects, including gold jewelry adorning the corpses of the women. The increase in luxury imports during this period—from Crete, Cyprus, Egypt, Mesopotamia, Syria, Anatolia, and western Europe—attests both to the growth of Mycenaean trade and to greater control by the ruling class over the economy and the society. Around 1500 BC the noble families began to inter their dead in the more impressive *tholos* tomb, a very large stone chamber, shaped like a beehive. With their high vaulted interiors and long stone entranceways the *tholoi* (plural) were conspicuous signs of the ever increasing power and resources of the leaders.

Shortly after the tholos tombs came into fashion, Greeks from the mainland invaded and defeated the Cretans, destroying a number of palace-centers but leaving Knossos mostly intact. Wealthy Crete was a juicy prize and the Mycenaeans had come to stay. This takeover, however, which occurred around 1450 BC, probably did not bring great changes in Cretan society and culture. Life under the invaders, who were already accustomed to Minoans, went on as before, except that now they paid their taxes to kings who spoke Greek. And the new kings ruled and lived in the manner of Cretan kings, although they did keep to certain mainland ways, as in their burial rites, for example.

Their prosperity, however, was short-lived. Around 1375, Knossos was burned and looted; and although the ruined palace continued to be occupied, Mycenaean Crete sank in importance as Mycenae and the other mainland centers reached the zenith of their prosperity and influence in the Aegean. It is not known who destroyed Knossos and set off the irreversible decline of the Cretan economy and culture. The most likely suspects are other mainland Mycenaeans lured by the riches of the Cretan palaces and perhaps eager to get rid of their biggest rival in the Mediterranean trade.

The Linear B Tablets

We do know that it was Greeks who took over Crete in 1450 BC because of the work of Michael Ventris, an amateur linguist and cryptographer, in the 1950s. As we saw earlier, the Minoans had devised a writing system made up of linear signs incised on clay tablets, which they used to keep palace records. The archaeologist Evans had discovered a few tablets with this script at Knossos, but he also found 3,000 clay tablets inscribed with a more elaborate version of the linear script, which he named "Linear B" to differentiate it from the earlier "Linear A" script. He assumed without question that the language of both was Cretan. The discovery in 1939 of an archive room full of Linear B tablets in the Mycenaean palace of Pylos on the Greek mainland seemed to strengthen Evans' theory that mainland Greece had been controlled by the Minoans throughout the Late Bronze Age.

Ventris, however, demonstrated that the language of the Linear B tablets was not in fact Cretan, but an early form of Greek. Having more than four thousand tablets to work with, he and other linguists were able gradually to obtain the phonetic values of the signs. For example, a combination of three signs— *ti-ri-po*— yields the syllabic equivalent of the Greek word *tripous*, "tripod." Today, the Linear B inscriptions have given up most of their secrets. Despite some successes, however, Linear A, the script of the unknown Cretan language, has not yet been deciphered. The decoding of Linear B has illuminated not only the historical relationship between Greece and Crete, but also the workings of the Mycenaean palace system.

The Later Mycenaeans (c. 1400–1200 BC)

The palace-complexes whose ruins we see today were built in the fourteenth and thirteenth centuries, during the final phase of Mycenaean wealth and power. Their architecture and decoration closely imitated the Minoan style, with some notable differences. They were much smaller and, unlike the largely unfortified Cretan palaces, they were usually located on a commanding hill, encircled by high, thick walls. We may infer that protection from invasion by rival kingdoms was a primary concern of Mycenaean rulers. The walled citadels served also as a refuge for the inhabitants of the unfortified towns below. Later Greeks called them Cyclopean walls, as though they had been built by the mythical race of giant Cyclopes. Indeed, such massive works were probably as much a boast of the king's wealth and power as they were a defense for his palace and people.

The Mycenaeans also utilized space within their palaces differently from the Minoans. In place of the open paved courtyard of the Cretan complexes they made the focus of their palaces the *megaron*, a large rectangular hall. The megaron was the ceremonial center, used for feasts, councils, and receptions of visitors. One entered it through a courtyard, which led into a portico and a small anteroom. In the middle of the great hall stood a large, raised circular hearth, flanked by four columns that supported an open balcony. The megaron room would survive in the form of a chieftain's house during the long Dark Age that followed, and as the essential plan of the Greek temple from the eighth century onward. Although Mycenaean palaces had fewer rooms and lacked some of the architectural embellishments of their Cretan counterparts, they offered such Minoan amenities as indoor plumbing and beautiful wall paintings. The frescoes are completely Minoan in style, though they show a preference for martial themes, such as personal combats, sieges, and hunting scenes.

Despite their cultural similarities, the Mycenaeans were not unified politically, but were divided into separate small kingdoms. Moreover, they were relatively few in number compared to the vast populations of the Hittite empire, which covered Anatolia and Syria, and of Egypt during its brilliant and aggressive "New Kingdom" period (c. 1575–1087 BC). Yet despite their political fragmentation, the Mycenaeans appear to have been a formidable presence in the Mediterranean world and to have had diplomatic relations with these great powers.

ANATOLIA

Troy

Smyrna

Colophon

Ephesus

Miletus

Ialysus

Rhodes

Müskebi

Didyma

Heraion

Cos

Samos

Lesbos

Chios

AEGEAN
SEA

Dêlos

Naxos

Delos

Thera

Melos

Cythera

Crete

Amnisus

Knossos

Karphi

Hagia Triada

Phaistos

Episkopi

Iolcus

Parga

Ithaca

Cephallenia

Pleuron

Dyme

Rhion

Patras

Kallithea

Vrachneika

Olympia

Koukounara

Pylos

Tragana

Rizomylo

Mouriatada

Delphi

Haliartus

Orchomenus Gla

Thebes

Aulis

Dramesi

Eutresis

Menidi

Marathon

Spata Perati

Thoricus

Athens

Eleusis

Salamis

Isthmus

Corinth

Gulf of
Corinth

Zygouries

Mycenae

Prosymna

Argos

Tiryns Lerna

Berbati

Dendra

Asine

Epidaurus

Hagios Kosmas

Iria

Nauplion

Amyclae

Gulf Of
Argos

Hagios Ioannis

Monemvasia

0   20   40   60   80   100 miles

0   40   80   120   160 km

a

b

c

Figure 1.4a. (Facing page) Mycenaean sites in the thirteenth century BC.
Figure 1.4b. View of the ruins of the *megaron* of the Mycenaean palace at Pylos.
Figure 1.4c. The "Lion Gate" entrance to the citadel of Mycenae.

The Hittite archives of the fourteenth and thirteenth centuries record exchanges of letters and of gifts and favors between the Hittite kings and kings of a people they called "Ahhiyawan," who are plausibly identified as Mycenaean "Akhai-woi," that is, "Achaeans," the name given to the Greeks in the *Iliad* and *Odyssey*. Such mentions of Greeks in the Hittite archives (and possibly also in Egyptian records) suggest that the Mycenaeans held a prominent position in the region. Finds of Mycenaean pottery and metalwork show up all across the Mediterranean Sea, from southern Italy and Sicily to the Asian coast, Egypt and the Aegean islands. It is quite possible, too, that a good portion of the immense wealth found in the graves and tombs of these warrior kings and nobles came not only from peaceful trade but also from the Mycenaeans' prowess as seaborne marauders.

The Administration of a Mycenaean Kingdom

A memorable figure for readers of the *Iliad* and the *Odyssey* is the aged warrior Nestor, who, Homer tells us, lived in a magnificent many-roomed house in a town called Pylos, from which he ruled over a large area of Messenia. The discovery of the "palace of Nestor" by the American archaeologist Carl Blegen in 1939 confirmed that the Pylos of the legends had been an actual Bronze Age center. Even more important was Blegen's find of large numbers of Linear B tablets. Clay tablets were not intended to be permanent records; they were preserved only because they were baked hard in the fires that destroyed the palace. What we have, in fact, are just scribes' temporary records from the final year of Pylos' existence. Yet these terse lists (supplemented by the Linear B tablets from Knossos and other centers) tell us much about the economy and society of Mycenaean Greece.

Like other regional centers, Pylos (written Pu-ro in the Linear B script) reached its zenith between 1400 and 1200. Nestor's palace, which lay undisturbed since its destruction around 1200, had been built around 1300 over the ruins of an earlier, smaller complex of buildings. The kingdom of Pylos was large and highly organized. It contained around two hundred villages and towns, spread out over an area of about 1400 square miles, and was divided into two "provinces," each subdivided into several "districts." The clay tablets give us some idea of Mycenaean social structures. At the apex of the pyramid stood the king (*wanax*). Next in rank, apparently, was the *lawagetas*, whose title may be loosely translated as "leader of the army." Below them was a large bureaucracy of military and administrative officers and minor officials who oversaw the functioning of the palace and the outlying areas.

The centralized production and distribution system ensured a luxurious standard of living for the highest officials, and perhaps some portion of the minor ones. But the majority of people, the ones who produced the wealth—the farmers, herders, artisans, and laborers—lived modestly, in small one- or two-room houses, with few luxuries. Many families farmed as tenants on land belonging to the nobles; others held plots of land in their own names. Craftsmen, herders, and priestesses, for example, are listed as "owners" of private land. Just as in later times, most agricultural producers lived in rural villages, while the majority of the crafts specialists were concentrated in the regional centers and the larger settlements.

The palace strictly supervised production. Officials were sent out into the countryside for regular assessments, and the taxes in produce and animals levied on individuals and villages were meticulously recorded. One tablet from Mycenaean Knossos reports: "Men of Lyktos 246.7 units of wheat; men of Tylisos 261 units of wheat; men of Lato 30.5 units of wheat." Yet, the evidence of the tablets does not support the once common view that the free masses were oppressed peasants toiling in misery on the estates of the rich. The men of the village farmed their plots and tended to their trees, vines, and livestock; they paid their taxes, contributed some labor to the palace, and served in the army. The women performed the domestic tasks of spinning and weaving, food preparation, and childcare. A number of the village women were also engaged as textile workers for the palace, for which they received rations of wool and flax.

The truly oppressed were the slaves. References to "captives" and "bought" show that the Mycenaean warrior-aristocrats were active in the slavery business. Tablets from Pylos, for example, record over six hundred slave women, who labored as grinders of grain, bath attendants, flax workers, weavers, and so on. Most of the women listed were attached to the palace; some lived in other towns in the kingdom and received rations of food from the palace. High-ranking individuals also owned slaves, though in far fewer numbers than the wanax. It is also possible that some of the lowest-status workers on the tablets were not true

a

b

Figure 1.5a. A Linear B tablet from Pylos (c. 1200 BC). Note the ideogram for cauldrons on the top line.
Figure 1.5b. A Linear B tablet from Mycenaean-ruled Knossos. On this tablet we can see the numbering system: Circles stand for hundreds, horizontal lines for tens, and vertical lines for units.

slaves, that is, foreigners captured or bought, but native individuals or families who, for whatever reasons, were reduced to a state of permanent dependence on the palace.

The palace-complex was the hub of the kingdom's economy, employing large numbers of workers who turned raw materials into finished products for both domestic consumption and export. Tasks were highly specialized; women were engaged mostly in the textile sector, making cloth goods of wool and linen, while men are listed as carpenters, potters, metal smiths, leather workers, perfume makers, and more. The wanax kept a close eye on the workshops and the storage areas, and his scribes scrupulously wrote down how much raw material the crafts specialists were given, the objects they produced, and the rations of food they received in return. Nothing escaped their attention. Dozens of entries go like this: "one ebony footstool inlaid with figures of men and a lion in ivory." Even chariot wheels are listed individually, and a note is made of their condition: "serviceable," or "unfit for use."

The leading exports were textiles and metalwork, to which we may add olive oil (both plain and perfumed), wine, hides, leather, and leather products. Fine pottery, jewelry, and other costly items also competed well in the international luxury trade. In return, the palaces imported things lacking in Greece, such as copper, tin, gold, ivory, amber, dyes, and spices, as well as foreign varieties of items that they did have, such as wine and jewelry. Needless to say, few luxury goods made their way into the houses and graves of the common people.

Religion

The belief in supernatural forces and beings that control the natural world is probably as old as humankind. Nearly as old are cult and ritual—the acts of devotion to the gods—and religious myths, the suppositions about the gods told in story form as part of ritual activity. Among agrarian peoples, the relationship of mortals to immortals revolves around the continuation of the fertility of the land and animals. To appease the gods, who can bestow or remove the blessings of nature at will, the people make communal displays of respect, including sacrifices of food and animals and even humans at times. The Minoans and Mycenaeans were no exception; they honored their gods with processions, music, and dance, and propitiated them with gifts and sacrifices. The slaughter and butchering of animals on outdoor altars was the most solemn ritual. There may even have been human sacrifice among the early Minoans.

In Minoan art the principal recipient of worship is a goddess, dressed in the Cretan style and placed in outdoor settings that feature trees and other vegetation, and animals. Similar scenes appear on Mycenaean frescoes, vases, and gold and silver rings. The ubiquitous goddess figures depicted in Minoan-Mycenaean art are thought to be representations of an ancient Aegean mother goddess, who presided over nature and fertility. In that case, we must infer that the fertility goddesses brought in by the Indo-European speakers were assimilated into the artistic form of the Aegean nature mother.

a

b

c

Figure 1.6a. Statuette of a goddess or human attendant from Knossos, Crete.
Figure 1.6b. Gold ring from Minoan Knossos showing women worshiping a goddess.
Figure 1.6c. A similar scene on a gold ring from Late Bronze Age Mycenae, indicating Minoan influence on Mycenaean religious rituals.

a

b

Figure 1.7a. (Left) Bronze plate armor and boar's tusk helmet from Dendra in Argolis, c. 1400 BC.

Figure 1.7b. (Above) A vase from thirteenth-century Mycenae, showing a line of ordinary soldiers on the march, armed with helmets, shields, and long spears, and a mourning woman who watches their departure.

There are, however, notable differences between Minoan and Mycenaean religious practices. For example, the Minoans frequently performed their rituals in caves and in sanctuaries built on mountain peaks, while the Mycenaean shrines are mainly confined to the palace-centers. The Linear B tablets also reveal that the Mycenaeans worshipped many of the gods of later Greek religion, including Zeus, Hera, Poseidon, Hermes, Athena, Artemis, and possibly Apollo, Ares, and Dionysus. Zeus, the supreme god of the later Greeks, is plainly the ancient Indo-European "sky-father," and was brought in by the earliest Greek-speakers. *Zeus patēr* "Zeus the father," is the same deity as the Sanskrit *Dyaus pitar* and Roman *Iuppiter*. The names of Hera, Poseidon, and Ares are also formed from Indo-European roots.

The palace was the center of religious activity. The gods, their sanctuaries, and their priests and priestesses received gifts of land, animals, precious objects, as well as human labor, which were requisitioned by the wanax from the people. A ruler with such coercive powers as the wanax could claim that his sovereignty was divinely sanctioned and that he was the special representative of the community to the gods. There is no evidence, however, to suggest that a wanax was considered divine either in his lifetime or after death, or that he functioned as a priest-king over a theocratic state, as in Egypt and Mesopotamia.

Warfare

The wanax was, above all, a warrior-king, who took part in the fighting along with his military commander (lawagetas) and subordinate commanders. In fact, throughout ancient Greek history, most political leaders would also be the commanders-in-chief and many would meet death on the battlefield or on the sea. Mycenaean warriors were heavily armored. Officers wore helmets of bronze or of boars' tusks, corselets of bronze plates, and bronze greaves (knee and shin protectors). The soldiers were equipped with leather and padded linen versions of these. All combatants carried large shields made of ox hide stretched over a wooden frame. Their weapons were bronze swords and daggers, heavy thrusting spears and light throwing spears, and bows and arrows. The Mycenaeans' most impressive weapon was the chariot, adopted from the Near East around 1600 BC. A lightweight platform set atop two high, spoked wheels, and pulled by two horses, the chariot could carry two men at a pace previously unknown in land travel. Throughout the Near East, the chariot corps was the primary military arm, used for massed chariot charges against an enemy's chariots and infantry, one man driving and the other shooting arrows. But because the rough terrain of Greece is unsuited for such tactics, many believe that the Mycenaeans employed chariots only to convey heavily armored elite warriors to and from the fighting. On the other hand, it is conceivable that mini-versions of eastern chariot warfare took place on the plains that lay below the Mycenaean fortresses. In any case, the significance of the chariot was probably not so much its use in battle, but rather its prestige value.

Like other material borrowings, such as the grand palaces and the tholos tombs, chariotry proclaimed the Mycenaean rulers to be the equals of the great kings of Asia and Egypt. Mycenaean art depicts the elite employing chariots also for hunting, racing, and ceremonial processions, as upper-class Greeks would for many centuries after the chariot had ceased to have any military function.

The Fall of the Mycenaean Civilization

At the apparent height of its prosperity, Mycenaean civilization suffered a fatal blow. Beginning around 1200 BC almost all the palace-centers and many of their outlying towns and villages were attacked and destroyed or else abandoned. Order gave way to turbulence and restless wanderings. Many centers, Pylos among them, were never reoccupied after the initial devastation, while others recovered and even enjoyed a brief resurgence, but soon succumbed to further attacks. A few, like Mycenae and Tiryns, lived on as small villages huddled below the ruined fortifications of their once mighty palaces. By 1100, the Mycenaean kingdoms and the complex systems that had supported them no longer existed.

It was not just Mycenaean civilization that suffered: The entire eastern Mediterranean region was overwhelmed by catastrophe at this time. The mighty Hittite empire, which encompassed Anatolia and Syria, fell apart around 1200 BC, crushed by invaders from the north. Egypt was attacked several times by an assortment of warrior bands from all around the Mediterranean. Quite possibly Mycenaeans were among these marauders, who are referred to as the "sea peoples" in Egyptian records. It was also during this period that the fall of Troy occurred (c. 1250–1200). There is no way of knowing whether those who besieged and burned the city were really the Mycenaean Greeks, as the legend of the Trojan War tells.

Until fairly recently it was thought that the Dorians were responsible for destroying and looting the Mycenaean palaces. The modern "Dorian invasion" hypothesis is largely based on the legends of later Doric speakers. Doric was one of the three main dialects of ancient Greek, spoken in the Peloponnesus, Crete and other Aegean islands, and parts of the Anatolian coast. Dorians claimed ancestry from the mythical hero Heracles (Hercules), whose sons, so the story went, were expelled from the Peloponnesus after his death. Several generations after the Trojan War, Heracles' descendants returned south to reclaim by force their rightful ownership of their ancient homeland. The invasion hypothesis was popular because it accounted well for both the initial destructions and the dominant presence of Doric speakers in the Peloponnesus during historical times. Moreover, it was corroborated by the words of the ancient Greeks themselves. Against the theory, however, certain practices, such as cremation of the dead, and objects like the handmade pottery called "Barbarian Ware," supposedly introduced by the invaders, were already present in Mycenaean Greece well before 1200 BC.

Because no single cause could have had such widespread and profound effects, a more plausible explanation for the breakdown of the old order is that the Mycenaeans experienced a massive "systems collapse"; that is to say, the entire "system" (the Mycenaean civilization) suffered a cascading series of negative consequences brought on by disequilibrium between its "subsystems" (its various spheres of activity, such as trade, agricultural production, metallurgy, and the crafting of artifacts). Marauding bands of "sea peoples" could have provided one catalyst, by obstructing sea-trade in the Aegean, which in turn would have cut off the supply of tin and copper for bronze production. If external trade ceased, not only goods but social contacts too would be lost; ideas as well as objects could not be exchanged. At the same time, natural disasters, like prolonged drought, soil exhaustion, and earthquakes, could have put pressure on the food-distribution subsystem, which may have already been undermined by the inefficiency of the top-heavy palace bureaucracies. As food and other crucial resources became scarce, the people might have turned against one another. At this point, when the system had already become weak and vulnerable, internecine warfare, uprisings of the people, or slave revolts might have precipitated the final collapse.

Along with the destruction of the palaces, the centralized, rigidly hierarchical states disappeared forever from Greece. Underneath the veneer of great wealth and stability the Mycenaean economy and government were shallowly rooted, essentially fragile systems. With the end of this stage of Greek history would come the beginning of a new era, so different that when the Greeks looked back upon their own Bronze Age past they could only imagine it as a kind of mythical dreamworld, a time when gods and humans mingled together.

SUGGESTED READINGS

Barber, Elizabeth Wayland. 1994. *Women's Work: The First 20,000 Years. Women, Cloth, and Society in Early Times.* New York and London: Norton. The history of textile manufacture as women's work and art from the Paleolithic through the Iron Age, including weaving techniques and myths about weaving. A major study of women's principal contribution to the ancient economy.

Castleden, Rodney. 1993. *Minoans: Life in Bronze Age Crete.* London: Routledge. Written for the nonspecialist, the book recreates the society and culture of the Cretan civilization.

Chadwick, John. 1967. *The Decipherment of Linear B.* 2nd ed. Cambridge, UK: Cambridge University Press. The story of how the Linear B tablets were deciphered told by one of the principal investigators.

Chadwick, John. 1976. *The Mycenaean World.* Cambridge, UK: Cambridge University Press. A lavishly illustrated description of the workings of the palace societies of Mycenaean Greece, with emphasis on the kingdom of Pylos.

Chadwick, John. 1987. *Linear B and Related Scripts.* Berkeley and Los Angeles: University of California Press. This little monograph describes the relationship between the Linear A script and Linear B, and tells how Linear B was used by the Mycenaeans.

Drews, Robert. 1993. *The End of the Bronze Age: Changes in Warfare and the Catastrophe ca. 1200 B.C.* Princeton, NJ: Princeton University Press. An overview and detailed analysis of the latest theories of the fall of the great civilizations of the Late Bronze Age.

Fitton, J. Lesley. 1996. *The Discovery of the Greek Bronze Age.* Cambridge, MA: Harvard University Press. A sparkling survey of the pioneering excavators, their excavations, and the controversies that swirled around their discoveries of Bronze Age Aegean cultures.

Preziosi, Donald and Louise A. Hitchcock. 1999. *Aegean Art and Architecture* (Oxford History of Art). Oxford: Oxford University Press. A comprehensive introduction to the art and architecture of Greece, Crete, and the Cycladic islands from 3300 to 1000 BC.

THE "DARK AGE" OF GREECE AND THE EIGHTH-CENTURY "RENAISSANCE" (C. 1150–700 BC)

In the middle of the twelfth century BC there were still a few places in Greece where the palaces survived. But these signs of economic and cultural vitality soon fade from the archaeological record. By the early eleventh century, the Greek world had settled into its "Dark Age," a period of steep decline and slow recovery that lasted until the eighth century. During those obscure centuries, new social and political patterns were formed, out of which would emerge, in the eighth century, a new type of political organization, the city-state (*polis*).

DECLINE AND RECOVERY
(C. 1150–900 BC)

There were no more kings, officials, scribes, palace staffs, or state armies; gone was the elaborate redistributive system. Monumental stone buildings were no longer erected, elaborate frescoes and fine furniture were no longer commissioned, and even the art of writing was lost. Bronze, gold, and other luxury imports dwindled to a trickle, as vital trade links were broken. All across the Greek world, towns and village were left abandoned, their inhabitants either dead or gone to other places, some as close as Achaea and Arcadia, some as far away as Palestine and Cyprus. It is true that movements and dislocations of people can exaggerate an impression of overall depopulation; yet it is safe to say that in the two centuries following 1200 Greece emptied out far more than it filled up. By 1000 BC its population was probably the lowest in a thousand years.

For the early twentieth-century historians who coined the phrase "Greek Dark Age," the four centuries that lay hidden between the fall of Mycenae and the birth of the city-state were a period of total obscurity coupled with utter poverty and stagnation. Recent archaeological findings, however, indicate that some regions within Greece recovered much sooner than others and that recovery took different forms. Areas bordering on the Aegean Sea appear to have suffered a briefer period of decline and to have bounced back sooner than regions in western Greece. In fact, at several major centers, including Athens, occupation continued without interruption; many were reoccupied within a generation or two after their destruction.

What survived from the world of the thirteenth century into the world of the eleventh, and what was lost? For those who remained in Greece, life was a lot simpler than it had been during the palace period. But that does not mean that Greece lapsed into a primitive state. Farmers continued to farm, growing the same crops they had always grown; herders tended their flocks as before; women spun and wove their wool and flax. Potters, metalworkers, and carpenters still practiced their crafts (though at a lower level of skill and refinement), and the people kept worshiping their gods and performing religious rituals. In short, the timeless rhythm and activities of the agricultural year and the farming village remained unchanged, and would remain constant over the following centuries.

Even when the material culture appears to have been at its nadir, important technological innovations appeared. Around 1050 the combination of several new techniques and small inventions produced a superior pottery that was well proportioned and finely decorated. A faster potter's wheel improved the shape of the vases. For the first time, potters were using a compass, to which several brushes were attached, to draw perfect arcs, half-circles, and concentric circles. Lines were drawn with a ruler instead of free-hand. New shapes and designs emerged, enhanced by more lustrous glaze achieved by firing at a higher temperature. This new style, called Protogeometric (c. 1050–900), seems to have originated in Attica and spread to other regions.

It was also about this time that Greek metal workers mastered the difficult process of smelting and working iron. Iron weapons and tools were harder than bronze and kept their edge better. Iron technology was long known in the East, but the Mycenaeans had not exploited the sources of iron ore available in Greece. But when the disruption of trade largely cut off access to copper and tin, necessity proved the mother of invention. From 1050 on, small local iron industries sprang up all across the mainland and the islands. By 950, almost every weapon and tool found in graves is made of iron, not bronze.

Beginning around 1050 there was an accelerated movement from the Greek mainland across the Aegean Sea to the Anatolian coast. During this time a number of settlements were established, among them Miletus (the earliest), Ephesus, and Colophon, that would become thriving cities. These population shifts created what the Mycenaeans had not—a large permanent presence in the East—and ensured that the Aegean Sea would one day be known as the "Greek Sea." On the mainland during this time, some major settlements, like Athens and Corinth, might have had populations in the low thousands; however, most sites held no more than a few dozen to a few hundred people.

Figure 2.1a. A Submycenaean vase (c. 1125–1050 BC) from the Kerameikos cemetery in Athens. Note the barely recognizable octopus, which had been a standard motif on Minoan-Mycenaean vases.

Figure 2.1b. A Late Protogeometric amphora (c. 950–900 BC) from the same cemetery, with compass-drawn concentric circles, foreshadowing the Geometric style.

Society in the Early Dark Age

With the dissolution of the intricate ties that had bound the outlying settlements to the palace-complexes and to one another, the former centers and peripheral villages found themselves largely on their own, politically and economically. Some think that the Greeks reverted to government by local "big men"—similar to the leaders who presumably had managed the affairs of villages in the pre-Mycenaean period, before the consolidation of power by a single chief. A local "big man" may have presided over the Dark Age village of Nichoria in south-western Peloponnesus, which was excavated in the 1970s. Originally a large subsidiary town of the kingdom of Pylos, Nichoria was abandoned around 1200, and came back to life about 1075 as a much smaller village-cluster, with a peak population of about two hundred in the early ninth century BC. Dark Age Nichoria was fairly prosperous in a humble way. The forty or fifty families dwelt on a ridge overlooking a plain. There was an abundance of good farmland and plenty of open pasture for animals, notably cattle.

At the center of the ridge top excavators uncovered a large tenth-century building, consisting of a spacious *megaron* and a small porch (room 2), which they identified as the "village chieftain's house." A remodeling in the ninth century added another room at the rear (room 3) and a bigger courtyard in front, enlarging the house to an impressive 52 feet by 23 feet wide. It is suggested that the chieftain's house also functioned as the religious center, and perhaps as a communal storehouse. This was the place where the elders would gather to feast and talk about local affairs. Although much better constructed than the surrounding houses, it had the same shape and was made of the same materials; its floor was packed earth and its walls were of mud brick, supporting a steep thatched roof. Clearly, the family that lived there enjoyed very high status in Nichoria itself and in the surrounding countryside. Yet they lived in a style that was not much different from that of their neighbors.

At the opposite end of Greece from Nichoria—at Lefkandi on the island of Euboea—stood a much wealthier settlement that is still yielding up its secrets today. Like Nichoria, Lefkandi had been a bustling Mycenaean town that revived after the collapse of the palace system and prospered during the Dark Age. In 1981, excavators were examining burial grounds in this area when they uncovered the largest Dark Age building yet found. Dated to about 950 BC, the long narrow structure (150 by 30 feet) covered more than twice the area of that of any contemporary building. But the biggest surprise of all was the discovery of two burial shafts sunk into the building's central room.

In one of the shafts lay two pairs of horses, one on top of the other—reminiscent of the grave offerings given to exceptional warriors during the Late Bronze Age, centuries earlier. The other compartment held the remains of two humans: a cremated man (the warrior) and an inhumed woman, apparently his wife. The man's ashes were well preserved in a large bronze amphora that had been made in Cyprus about a century before the funeral. Next to it lay an iron sword, a spearhead, a razor, and also a whetstone for sharpening the weapons: the toolkit of a fighting man. The horse sacrifices and the costly imports deposited in the couple's grave suggest to some scholars that this man had been a wealthy, hereditary chief with Eastern contacts. Others posit that he belonged to an elite "warrior class."

The woman whose skeleton was found beside the warrior has aroused at least as much curiosity as her spouse. Gold-plated coils flanked her head, broad gold rings decorated her fingers, and her breasts were covered with large disks made of fine gold foil. Around her neck, the excavators found the gold beads and central pendant of an elaborate necklace believed to have been fashioned in the Near East at least 650 years before the time of the burial. This necklace might have been a family heirloom, or it might have been purchased from Near Eastern traders roaming the Aegean Sea. All her adornments reveal that the woman's social status was equal to the man's. But how can we explain the ivory-handled dagger that had been positioned beside her head? Was this woman offered as a sacrifice to the man along with the horses?

Figure 2.2a. Axonometric reconstruction of the "chief's house" at Lefkandi, showing the grave of the basileus of Lefkandi and his consort (c. 950 BC). This is the largest Dark Age building yet discovered.

Figure 2.2b. Plan of the ninth-century "village chieftain's house" at Nichoria.

Figure 2.2c. Artist's rendition of Figure 2.2b.

Figure 2.2d. Artist's conception of an "ordinary" Dark Age house.

Soon after the funeral the whole building was demolished and covered over with a mound of earth and stones so huge that its construction must have required the labor of the entire community. Even the function of the building continues to be a subject of debate: Was it the couple's house or was it erected to be a mausoleum for the chief? In any case, Lefkandi has shown that we cannot presuppose that Protogeometric Greece was uniformly impoverished and isolated.

REVIVAL (c. 900–750 BC)

Around 900 BC, as the conservative Protogeometric style evolves into the Geometric style (c. 900–700), a new artistic and aesthetic spirit becomes evident. There is no dramatic break with tradition, and in some regions the old style continues for some time. Nevertheless, new shapes and new decorative features mark the

Figure 2.3a. Gold jewelry from the cremation grave of a wealthy Athenian woman, c. 850 BC. In addition, she was buried with a number of fine vases, bronze and iron pins, ivory seals, and a faience necklace.

Figure 2.3b. From the same grave, a large terra-cotta chest, surmounted by a lid with five model granaries, as well as a separate granary model, all attesting to the agricultural wealth of her family.

Geometric as a distinctly new period. Circles and semicircles give way to linear angular motifs, such as the famous "meander pattern" (see Figures 2.5a and b).

Eventually painters would fill up the entire surface of a vase with zones of meanders, zigzags, triangles, and crosshatches, alternating them with solid bands and lines. Ninth-century craftsmen were now producing costly luxury items like fine gold jewelry, ivory carvings, and bronze vessels, both for domestic consumption and long-distance trade. This development attests to the renewed availability of raw materials from abroad, including bronze, which now begins to appear in larger quantities.

Homer and Oral Poetry

An oral poet was a skilled storyteller who sang or chanted in verse before an audience, to the accompaniment of a stringed instrument called the *kitharis*. Later Greeks revered Homer, the composer of the *Iliad* and the *Odyssey*, as their greatest poet, although they knew nothing about his life aside from the tradition that he was blind and from Ionia.

The two poems are generally dated to between the later eighth and early seventh century BC, about the time when writing reappeared in Greece. It is possible that Homer, an illiterate bard, dictated his long epics to persons who could write. To us it seems impossible that works of such artistry and length—the *Iliad* is around 16,000 lines and the *Odyssey* 12,000—could have been created without writing. Yet modern comparative studies of traditional oral poetry have shown that bards can in fact compose long, complex narratives as they perform.

Homer and other Greek oral poets would have had at their disposal a store of traditional plots, characters, and themes that they had learned from previous generations of singers, who in turn had learned them from their elders, and so on back in time. In retelling the ancient stories that were familiar to their audiences, poets could also draw on an inherited stock of "formulas" (fixed phrases, lines, and blocks of text), which they had memorized and could vary as the occasion demanded. Over a lifetime of private rehearsals, "writing" and "rewriting" the poetry in his mind, a skilled poet like Homer would have crafted and perfected the poems that bore his personal signature. At the same time, the traditional narrative framework was flexible enough to permit the changing and varied concerns of his audiences to be incorporated into the bard's performances; each performance would be fresh and "updated." When the epics were finally committed to writing—probably within the poet's lifetime—they were fossilized, so to speak, and thus lost this ability to be continuously recreated, yet they gained the advantage of some degree of protection from further modification.

The epics are set in the age of heroes, which encompass a generation or two before, and one generation after, the legendary Trojan War. The tale of the Trojan War is a classically simple folk saga. Paris, the son of King Priam of Troy, seduced and brought back to Troy the beautiful Helen, the wife of Menelaus, ruler of the Spartans. To avenge the insult, Menelaus and his brother, Agamemnon, wanax of Mycenae, gathered a huge army of Achaean warriors. The Achaeans sailed to Troy, destroyed the city after a ten-year siege, and then dispersed, each contingent to its own homeland.

Whether or not a Trojan War actually occurred will probably never be known. For the Greeks, however, it was the pivotal event of their early history. Yet the epics, though set in this distant past, are not really about history nor are they about the Trojan War. History and war are the background for the enactment of social dramas, whose protagonists are caught up in the kinds of dilemmas that every generation experiences and must deal with.

The nagging question for historians is this: Do the epics tell us anything about actual Greek society, whether of Homer's own day (late eighth or perhaps early seventh century) or of some earlier date? Or are they pure fictions, which have only symbolic meaning? The answer, of course, is somewhere in the middle. The Homeric world was a past world that was in every way bigger, better, and more fantastic than the environment of the contemporary audiences. For instance, Hector, the Trojan leader, picks up a stone to use as a weapon, "which two men, the best in the land, could not easily lift from the ground onto a wagon, men such as mortals are today" (*Iliad* 12.445–449). Such a scene serves the purpose of "epic distancing," which gives the aura of a long-ago heroic society. The poet deliberately leaves out innovations that were known to him, such as the reintroduction of writing. Nevertheless, aspects of that imaginary world—its interests, passions, ideologies, and to some degree its social institutions—must have conformed to audience's real-life experiences. The norms and values of Homeric society are internally consistent and coherent enough to be given a place in the not-so-long-ago past, which we may assign roughly to the end of the Greek Dark Age.

HOMERIC SOCIETY

Homer's Greece is divided geographically into independent regions of various sizes, each one constituting a *dēmos*, a word that denotes both the territory itself and the "people" who inhabit it. A typical demos would contain several settlements—towns and villages—along with their adjoining farmlands and pastures. For example, in the catalogue of the contingents that make up the Greek army at Troy there is this entry for the large region of Aetolia.

> Thoas, son of Andraemon led the Aetolians,
> those who dwelled in Pleuron and Olenos and Pylene
> and Chalcis by-the-sea, and rocky Calydon, ...
> and with him followed forty black ships.
> (*Iliad* 2.638–644)

The official title borne by warrior-leaders like Thoas is *basileus*. Interestingly, the word occurs in the Linear B tablets (in the form *qa-si-re-u*) where it denotes a minor official, apparently a sort of mayor or headman of a town or village within a Mycenaean kingdom. In Greek, basileus is usually translated as "king." This is somewhat misleading, however, for clearly *basileis* (plural) in the *Iliad* and the *Odyssey* are not kings in the sense of monarchs who hold absolute sway over their subjects. A Homeric basileus more closely approximates a "chief," the word that anthropologists use to describe a leader with great authority and stature, yet limited in his power to coerce others into obeying him.

A good-sized demos will often contain other chiefs, lower in rank, but called by the same title of basileus. When Odysseus enters the magnificent house of Alcinous, ruler of the island of Scheria, he finds the basileus and his wife Arete, the basileia, entertaining the other basileis. In Alcinous' own words,

> Twelve renowned basileis hold sway as leaders
> in the demos, and I myself am the thirteenth.
> (*Odyssey* 8.390–391)

There is no question that Alcinous is supreme among them—the "paramount chief"—yet he must also take counsel with them, for they are not merely subordinates, but men of power in their own local districts. It is against this background of loosely centralized territorial units that we may envisage social life in the Homeric epics.

Community and Household

Social and economic life at the end of the ninth century was centered in the local communities, most of which were still quite small. The Greeks did not live in isolated farmsteads, but clustered together in small settlements. Farmers would walk out each morning to their plots and return to the village at dusk. Communities were closely knit through generations of intermarrying with other families within the village and in other villages of the same demos. Law was customary law; public disapproval would have sufficed to deter antisocial behavior. Many disputes could be resolved by the local chief and the simple court of the village elders. Homicide, interestingly, was mostly a private matter, to be settled by the families involved, either through material compensation or the exile of the offender. The alternative would be a continuing blood feud, which, if allowed, would disrupt communal solidarity.

The separate settlements were likewise bound together to ensure the survival of the territorial demos. Individual villages within the demos might quarrel with one another but they united against threat from outside. Inside the boundaries of the demos all who shared the demos-name—the "Ithacans," or the "Megarians"—could live and move safely. Once outside the homeland one was "in the demos of others," in an alien country, so to speak, where the protection of tribal ties ended, and one was a stranger, without rights. In Homer, when a stranger appears in an alien demos he is asked to identify himself by naming his "demos and polis." By polis, the questioner means the main town of the demos, the most populous settlement, the place where the paramount basileus lived, and where the assembly of the demos met.

From Homer we may infer that the smallest unit of Dark Age society was the household (*oikos*). The oikos was the center of a person's existence; and every member was preoccupied with its preservation, its economic well-being, and social standing. The word oikos signified not only the house itself but also the family, the land, livestock, and all other property and goods, including slaves. Greek society was patrilineal and patriarchal. The father was supreme in the household by custom and later by law. Descent was through the father, and on his death the property was divided equally among his sons. Although daughters did not inherit directly they received a share of their parents' wealth as a dowry. Because daughters in Homer are prized, suitors customarily give *hedna* (wooing gifts) to the bride's father as part of the marriage contract. The new bride took up residence in the house of her husband; thus their children belonged to the husband's oikos, not to hers.

Among chieftain families—which are the only ones described in Homer—married sons continue to reside in the paternal oikos with their wives and children. Not infrequently, though, the custom is reversed. A powerful chief brings his daughter's new husband into his own household instead. In this way, he gets to keep his daughter and acquires a new man to fight and work for the oikos. Another means of increasing the oikos is for the father to beget additional children by slave women. But that could cause friction in the family. Odysseus' father did not sleep with a newly bought slave woman and so "avoided his wife's anger." Although the male children of slaves are inferior to the legitimate sons in respect to inheritance rights, they are otherwise full members of the family and part of its fighting force and workforce. Illegitimate daughters seem to have the same status as their legitimate half-sisters.

All members of a basileus' oikos do a share of the work. Odysseus, Homer tells us, built a bedroom and bed for him and his wife Penelope all by "himself and no one else." The sons of basileis tend the flocks and herds, the main wealth of the family. Homeric wives work alongside the women slaves in the tasks of spinning and weaving, while young daughters do other tasks, such as fetching water from the communal fountain, or washing clothes by the river. Most of the labor of a wealthy household, however, was provided by female and male slaves (either bought or captured), and by *thētes* (sing. *thēs*), poor free men who worked as hired hands.

The main economic resource for each of the families in a village or town was its ancestral plot of farmland called a *klēros* (literally an "allotment"). Without a kleros a man could not marry. A lotless man (*aklēros*) had two options: He could eke out a precarious existence on a poor patch of unclaimed marginal land, or worse, hire on as a thes. The latter was a galling life, not only because it was hard work for very little pay (essentially his keep), but also because working for another man's family was felt to be an indignity.

The economies of ordinary and elite households in the Dark Age differed primarily in scale. An ordinary farmer would probably have owned a yoke of oxen for plowing, and perhaps a mule. No doubt he pastured enough sheep and goats for the family's consumption of wool, cheese, and meat. The rich man had more of everything, particularly animals, but also more farmland and workers. Even with many more mouths to feed, a wealthy oikos produced a large surplus, while the average family, if it was a good year, would have had just a little extra to spend on its wish list, another ox, for example, or a pair of gold earrings. A wealthy oikos, though, could exchange its surplus production of woolen goods and leather for slaves, metal, and expensive ornaments of the sort that increasingly show up in the ninth-century graves. By this time, we observe such signs of increasing stratification in more and more places. In the ninth century socioeconomic divisions into an elite group and a commoner mass become quite clear.

Chiefs and People

In Homer, the office and title of basileus passes from father to son as in chiefdom societies everywhere. But inheritance alone is not enough to secure the title. In accordance with the aristocratic ethos that permeates the poems, a basileus must be competent to fulfill his role as leader of the people in war and peace. He should be both a good warrior and a persuasive speaker. When Peleus, basileus of the Myrmidons, sends his son Achilles off to the Trojan War, his advice is, "Be both a speaker of words and a doer of deeds." Above all, it is the deeds, "the works of war," that make a leader. In Homer, a chief's status is measured by how many warriors follow him, and few will go fight with a leader who is not a good warrior.

In Homer's world, raiding is a way of life. Any chief may raise his own following of *hetairoi* ("companions") and go on raids against the villages of another demos, either to even the score in some ongoing quarrel, or just to steal or plunder their livestock, valuables, and women.

In recruiting men for a raid, a warlord draws on his large surplus of animals to provide them feasts, thereby showing himself to be a generous leader. Odysseus, for example, describes how he outfitted ships and gathered a following,

> and for six days my trusty companions (hetairoi)
> feasted, and I gave them many animal victims
> both to sacrifice to the gods and to make a feast for themselves,
> and on the seventh we got on board and set sail . . .
>
> (*Odyssey* 14.247–252)

Going on a raid tests manliness and brings honor and glory. Whether on a raid or in a war, the basileus is the one most severely tested, for he is literally the leader, stationing himself "among the front-fighters." Because the leader risks his life fighting in the thick of battle, his people are obligated to repay him with honors and gifts.

Reciprocity—mutual and fair exchange—governs all social relationships in the Homeric world. Accordingly, fairness rules the distribution of the spoils of war. Following a raid, the booty is gathered together. First the chief takes his share, including something extra as his special "prize"; only then is the rest given to the men "to divide up, so that no one may go cheated of an equal share."

A leader who keeps more than his due risks losing the respect of his followers. He cannot afford not to appear generous and openhanded. Similarly, in their relations with one another, chiefs constantly exchange gifts and feasts. In this way basileis show off their wealth, cement alliances, win new friends, and collect obligations that will have to be paid back later.

Despite the authority that comes with his status, a basileus has limited ability to coerce others to do his bidding. He is a chief, not a king. Once, when Odysseus' followers decide to do exactly the opposite of what he has ordered them, he responds that as "one man alone" he must abide by the will of the many.

In a society in which performance is more important than descent, a weak successor will be challenged by rivals eager to replace him as head chief. That is the situation confronting Odysseus' son Telemachus in his father's twenty-year-long absence from Ithaca. Telemachus is barely twenty years old, with no experience of leadership, and he has only a few supporters, since his father's hetairoi have gone to Troy with him. Meanwhile, a group of young chiefs and sons of chiefs have permanently camped out in his courtyard, feasting on his livestock, seducing the slave girls, and wooing his mother, Penelope, now presumed a widow. The suitors assume that the one who succeeds in marrying Penelope will take over as basileus, even though they admit that the office belongs to Telemachus by his "paternal birthright." In the end, Odysseus returns, kills the suitors, and assumes his rightful place as the basileus of Ithaca and the nearby islands. In most instances, however, weakened ruling dynasties would not have fared as well as the house and lineage of Odysseus.

Government and Diplomacy

Governmental institutions in Homeric society were few and simple. A council, the *boulē*, made up of chiefs and other influential men, met in the great hall (megaron) of the ruling chief to feast and to discuss policy for the demos. The leader has the decisive voice, but usually heeds the advice and counsel of the "elders," as the boule-members were called (though many were actually younger men). Their deliberations were presented to an assembly of the people, held outdoors in the *agora* or "place of gathering." The attendees were all the men of fighting age and older. Women did not attend. In the Homeric assembly, only men of high rank bring up a matter for discussion, and although it is permissible for any member of the demos to respond, only rarely does an ordinary man step out of the mass to speak out. Rather, the demos makes its will known collectively, in a chorus of shouting or muttering, or by total silence. The council and the assembly would remain the essential organs of government in the later city-states.

Besides being the military and political leader, the top basileus played a religious role in the life of the community. He was not a priest, nor did he claim to have prophetic powers. But his position was divinely sanctioned; Homer firmly emphasizes that Zeus upholds the ruling authority of the office of basileus. When the basileus prayed to the gods at public sacrifices, he was the spokesman for the people, similar to a father sacrificing on behalf of his family.

Foreign relations among epic heroes are often conducted personally through the institution of *xenia* ("guest-friendship"). Appearing first in Homer, xenia occurs frequently in Greek authors from all periods of antiquity. Xenia was a mutual bond of friendship and trust between individuals who belonged to separate *dēmoi* (plural), often very far apart. *Xenoi* ("guest-friends") would provide each other entertainment, lodging, and valuable parting-gifts whenever they received one another into their demoi and homes. But xenia was more than just hospitality; its duties extended to protection, diplomatic aid, and even intervention to save a guest-friend's life. In some ways, the obligations of xenia are more like those of kinship than friendship. Once the bond was established, it was assumed to be perpetual, and the relationship was passed down from generation to generation through the male line.

In the *Iliad*, Diomedes, a Greek, and Glaucus, a Lycian ally of the Trojans, encounter one another in battle. Hostility, however, turns into amity when Diomedes recalls to Glaucus that his grandfather Oeneus had hosted Glaucus' grandfather Bellerophon for twenty days, and that to cement the xenia-bond Oeneus gave a scarlet belt, and Bellerophon a two-handled golden cup. Now, two generations later, Diomedes proposes that they renew the old ties, saying "Let us exchange armor with each other so that these men [i.e., the Greeks and Trojans] may know that we declare that we are ancestral guest-friends" (*Iliad* 6.231–232).

Social Values and Ethics

The code of behavior followed by Homeric males is typical of warrior societies. A man is called "good" (*agathos*) when he exhibits bravery and skill in fighting and athletic contests. He is "bad" (*kakos*) if he is a coward or useless in battle. A "good man" should honor the gods, keep promises and oaths, and be loyal to friends and fellow warriors. He should exhibit self-control, be hospitable, and respect women and elders. Pity should be shown to suppliant strangers and beggars, who are sacred to Zeus. But these gentler qualities, though they are desirable, are not required; a man may be merciless and cruel and still be agathos.

A warrior society must breed into its future warriors a love of the grim "works of Ares." Thus Hector, the leader of the Trojans, prays to the gods that his infant son may grow up to be a better warrior than his father and "bring back the bloody spoils of a dead enemy and make his mother's heart glad" (*Iliad* 6.479–481). Likewise, when Homer's "good men" capture an enemy village, they are apt to slaughter the male survivors, even including children, and rape and enslave the women and girls.

Being good at slaughtering and pillaging brings honor and glory, as well as wealth, and so warriors compete with one another in the art of killing. The purpose of this excessive striving is to enhance and preserve one's *timē*, one's value and worth, respect and honor. The spirit of competition permeates every facet of life and is not bounded by class or gender. The highest good is to win and be called "best" (*aristos*), whether in spear-throwing, running, playing ball, or chariot-racing; in speaking or in displays of cunning; or in weaving or crafting pots. A poor farmer is roused to work hard when he sees his neighbor getting rich, says Hesiod (c. 700) and "potter resents potter and carpenter resents carpenter, and beggar is jealous of beggar and singer of singer" (*Works and Days* 21–26).

Elite males especially insist that their value be recognized publicly, whether by a seat of honor at a feast, or a choice piece of the booty. Not to be honored when honor is due, or worse, to be dishonored, are unbearable insults. In the *Iliad*, when Agamemnon takes back Achilles' "prize of honor," the captive girl Briseis, Achilles is so keenly stung by the assault against his worth that he refuses to fight.

It is more difficult to access the feelings of Homeric women, because their behavior and motives are revealed to us through a male lens. What the poems do accurately describe is a male-dominated society in which women's roles and the range of behaviors deemed socially acceptable are constructed for them by men. Needless to say, their assigned roles as housewives and mothers dictated a different set of expectations. Like men, women also compete, though only within the few arenas of excellence allowed them; for example, this one or that one, "surpassed her age-mates in beauty and work [e.g., weaving] and intelligence." They are expected to act modestly in public and in the company of men, and above all to be chaste. Although males are permitted to have concubines, adulterous females bring great disgrace and dishonor upon themselves and their families.

Document 2.1. Andromache mourns over the body of her husband Hector, slain by Achilles. Her lament centers on the fate of the helpless women and children.

> White-armed Andromache led the lamentation
> As she cradled the head of her man-slaying Hector:
> "You have died young, husband, and left me
> A widow in the halls. Our son is still an infant,
> Doomed when we bore him. I do not think
> He will ever reach manhood. No, this city
> Will topple and fall first. You were its savior,
> And now you are lost. All the solemn wives
> And children you guarded will go off soon
> In the hollow ships, and I will go with them.
> And you, my son, you will either come with me
> And do menial work for a cruel master,
> Or some Greek will lead you by the hand
> And throw you from the tower, a hideous death,
> Angry because Hector killed his brother,
> Or his father, or son.

Iliad 24.723–737; translated by Stanley Lombardo, Homer *Iliad*. Indianapolis: Hackett Publishing Company, 1997, pp. 489–490.

Despite the severe limitations placed on them by male society, Homeric women are included in the public space. They go freely about the village and countryside, participate in festive and religious events, and serve as priestesses. Nor are they without power. Strong women abound in Homer. Clytemnestra puts a dagger through her husband Agamemnon; Arete, the wife of the Phaeacian basileus, shares some of his authority; and Penelope is as cunning and resourceful as her husband, Odysseus. Nevertheless, in the Dark Age, as in later Greece, women from birth to death were dependent on and under the control of males: fathers and brothers, and then their husbands and grown sons. However much Greek women may have contributed to public opinion, they possessed no political rights of their own.

Gods and Mortals

By the eighth century, the Greek pantheon had attained much the same form it was to have throughout the rest of pagan antiquity. According to the fifth-century historian Herodotus, Homer and Hesiod

> are the ones who created a theogony for the Greeks. They gave names to the gods, decided what their special skills were and what honors they should be given, and described their appearance.
>
> (*The Histories* 3.38; Blanco 1998)

Hesiod's *Theogony* gives a genealogical "history" of the gods. From ancient Mesopotamian narratives Hesiod derives the idea that creation was essentially the separation of an originally undifferentiated mass into its component forces, conceived as deities. This division provoked a series of generational wars among the primordial gods, until the last generation gained control and brought order to the universe.

In the Greek version, Uranus (Sky) is defeated by his son Cronus with the help of his mother Gaia (Earth). Cronus in turn is overthrown by the third generation of gods, after a ten-year war that shook the universe to its foundations. Their leader, Zeus, the youngest child, would rule forever as the unchallenged patriarch of gods and humans, wielding his lightning bolt from cloud-covered Mount Olympus. After their victory, Homer tells us, the brothers divided up the cosmos by lottery, Zeus receiving rule of the sky, Poseidon the sea, and Hades the underworld, where the souls of humans go when they die. Earth is assigned to no particular god, but forever remains the charge of them all, especially of Demeter, the nourisher of the crops.

Unlike in Genesis, the Olympian gods had no hand in creating the physical world, but as descendants of mother Earth and father Sky, were part of it, and they were identified with the particular spheres of nature that they controlled. So, for example, one could say "Zeus rains," or "Demeter smiles." Likewise, Ares, the god of war, is the spirit of blood lust that enters a warrior and makes him eager to kill, and Aphrodite, the goddess of love, is the irresistible force of sexual desire.

As in the Near East, the Greeks anthropomorphized their gods. Greek gods look, think, and act like humans. Zeus and Hera, for example, are notorious for their marital bickering. At one family dinner on Olympus, Zeus accuses Hera of being a suspicious and meddlesome wife, and the other gods become so troubled that the couple's son Hephaestus is forced to intervene, begging his mother to humor his father (*Iliad* 1.536–604).

What sets the gods unbridgeably apart from humans is that they are immortal, ageless, and not subject to disease, and they have the power to manipulate the mortal world. In Homer, humans are the playthings of the gods, who vie with one another to aid their own favorites and to thwart those whom other gods favor.

Did the Greeks believe in their myths? At any given time, many different and often contradictory local versions of the traditional stories would be in circulation around the Greek world. Thus no one version could be taken as literal truth. The myths that exaggerated the gods' "human" flaws were especially entertaining. Yet these same Olympians—as well as countless lesser divinities like nymphs, dryads, and rivers—inspired awe and even dread because of their power to do humans good or harm. Every community had its own protecting god or gods, and the people spared no expense or effort to honor and placate them with elaborate shrines, precious gifts, and animal sacrifices.

In Homer, the gods insist on their proper honors, but not much else. Acts that are condemned as sins by many religions, such as homicide, stealing, or adultery, do not arouse the wrath of the Homeric gods. They do, however, condemn oath-breaking and mistreating strangers, suppliants, and beggars. In both Homer and Hesiod, humans look to Zeus to keep order and justice in the community at large. Thus, Zeus is said to send severe wind and rain storms against those "who make crooked decrees, using force, in the assembly, and drive out justice, heedless of watchfulness of the gods" (*Iliad* 16.384–388).

In many religions, earthly sorrow and suffering are eased by the promise of a paradise after death for those who have lived righteously. Homer's Greeks did not have this consolation: Existence in any meaningful sense ended when the soul (*psychē*) left the body. Most souls carry on a shadowy afterlife in Hades' realm. For a few sorry souls, however—primarily those who had tried to deceive the gods or dared to rival them—Hades was a place of eternal punishment. A handful of fortunate souls were assigned to the Elysian Fields—a place of lush meadows and cool waters in a remote corner of the world—"where life is easiest for men." They were rewarded not because they had led moral lives, or for their achievements, but because they had divine family connections. In the *Odyssey*, the sea-god Proteus prophesizes to Menelaus: "The immortal gods will send you to the Elysian Fields . . . because you have Helen and you are the son-in-law of Zeus" (*Odyssey* 4.563–569).

The prayers, rituals, and sacred objects associated with the cult of a god were in the care of priests and priestesses. While there existed no priestly caste as in the Near East and Egypt, Homeric priests and priestesses were not ordinary members of the community, but were drawn from the noble families. Their official duties generally took up very little time, and required little in the way of preparation and training.

THE END OF THE DARK AGE

For many parts of Greece, the eighth century was a period of population growth, technological innovations, and increasing political centralization. The eighth century was dubbed by modern historians the "Greek Renaissance" because it appeared to be a revival of the glories of the Mycenaean Age. During this period trade links multiplied, communication with the East intensified, writing was reintroduced into Greece, and prosperous new communities were established in the West. As the Mediterranean world became increasingly more interlinked, even the more isolated areas of Greece were drawn into networks of cultural exchange.

People of neighboring areas were meeting together more regularly to celebrate religious rituals, which included competitions among athletes and bards. Communities also vied with one another in the production of luxury items, such as finely decorated pottery and bronze tripods, and in building monumental temples. Still, we should not view the eighth century as a radical break from the past, but rather as an acceleration of trends visible already in the tenth century.

The Rise of a Landowning Aristocracy

Population growth put pressure on the land. Although pasture land was nominally open to all, in reality the elite families had long before appropriated the best for themselves, in particular the lush grassy meadows where they grazed their large herds of cattle and horses. They converted more and more of this fertile soil to growing grain and other crops, a much more productive use of land. In this way, the already land-rich oikoi (households) were able to acquire more arable land until, in the course of a few generations, they came to own a disproportionate amount of the total land. No doubt prior occupancy enabled some oikoi to claim some legal right to plow and plant the traditional pasturelands, but quite possibly chicanery and even use of force were involved in this land grab. In any case, by the early seventh century the elite minority had transformed themselves into an aristocracy of large landowners, while the majority continued to live off small-to-medium farm plots and a few animals.

We should, however, be careful to put scarcity of land into perspective. Nowhere in eighth-century Greece did the population approach the carrying capacity of the land. In fact, the countryside continued to be filled in throughout the seventh and into the sixth century. The problem was not that there was no land, but rather that the most productive land was concentrated in the hands of a minority of the families. Sons whose inherited share of their paternal kleros was insufficient for their growing families would be compelled to seek marginal land in the outskirts of the demos (where they had to work harder for less return). For the ambitious, there was another solution to the problem of land hunger: relocation abroad.

Colonization and the Growth of Trade

In the second half of the eighth century substantial numbers of people left Greece to establish new farming communities in southern Italy and Sicily. These colonizers followed the trail blazed by earlier adventurers, who sailed west, not to farm but to trade. Overseas trade with foreigners, which had been increasing gradually since the tenth century, expanded considerably in the eighth. Shortly before 800, Greeks from Euboea joined the international trading post of Al Mina in northern Syria, and not long after that other Euboeans founded a trading colony at Pithecusae in southern Italy. Once again, Greek ships in significant numbers were plying the trade routes across the Mediterranean, and were even competing with the Phoenicians, who had long been the leading sea merchants in the Mediterranean. The new Greek colonies that sprang up in the West offered the settlers not only a good-sized kleros on good soil but also opportunities to trade their own products and those of old Greece for raw materials, especially metal, with the inhabitants of southern Europe.

Colonization and the expansion of trade and commerce had broad economic effects throughout the towns and villages of the Greek world. There was more work for craftsmen, sailors, shipbuilders and outfitters, and haulers. Even small farmers took advantage of the economic opportunities offered by this expanded world. Hesiod (c. 700 BC) takes it for granted that a farmer will put part of his surplus production in a boat and sail a fair distance for "profit." The big land-holders benefited most, however, because they could produce large surpluses for the market and could subsidize the costs and bear the losses of long sea voyages.

The Alphabet and Writing

The increased contacts with the East led to the most significant cultural achieve-ment of the late Dark Age, the Greek alphabet. Somewhere—most likely in the eastern Mediterranean—Greeks borrowed letters from the Phoenician alphabet, which consisted primarily of signs for consonants. They adapted certain of the Phoenician characters to represent the sounds of the Greek consonants, and changed the value of other consonant signs, making them into vowels. Thus was born an alphabet that was largely phonetic. It is generally believed that this oc-curred around 800 BC. To judge from the evidence, which is very meager, it ap-pears that one of the earliest uses for the alphabet was to write down verses of poetry. Two of the earliest examples of connected Greek words are, in fact, bits of epic-like verse scratched on vases dated to the second half of the eighth cen-tury. While these graffiti do show that the Homeric epics could have been writ-ten down at least by the later eighth century, they do not prove, as some propose, that the alphabet was devised in order to preserve orally composed poems in written form. On the other hand, supporters of this theory point out that the in-vention of signs for vowels was essential to reproduce in writing the metrical rhythms of Greek poetry. Another early function of writing was to record own-ership of personal property and, probably not much later, to keep commercial ac-counts. Whatever the initial motive, once writing was established it was put to many different uses. The earliest specimen of a civic use of writing is a stone in-scription of laws from Dreros in Crete, carved around 650.

Writing spread quickly throughout the Greek-speaking world, though not as one standard alphabet, but rather as numerous local scripts, with variations in

Figure 2.4a. Examples of graffiti on eighth-century vases. The readable portion of inscription (a) says: "He who, of all the dancers, now dances most gracefully" [? will win this pot?]. Inscription (b) identifies the owner: "I am the cup of Qoraqos." Inscription (c) reads: "I am the drinking cup of Nestor, good to drink from. Whoever drinks this cup, immediately the desire will seize him of beautiful-crowned Aphrodite."

Figure 2.4b. Late Geometric jug, c. 740 BC, from Athens, on which graffito (a) was inscribed.

the forms and numbers of characters and in the sounds they represented. The alphabetical script of about twenty-five letters was a huge advance over the cumbersome Linear B syllabic system of eighty-seven signs. Because most of the alphabetical characters stood for a single spoken sound, it was fairly easy to learn to read and even to write Greek. And yet, although the numbers of people who could read and write increased over time, mass literacy was never achieved in ancient Greece. Indeed, through the eighth and most of the seventh century, Greece was almost as completely oral-aural as it had been in the Dark Age. Even in the Classical and Hellenistic periods, when literacy was most widespread, most information passed from mouth to ear.

Art and Architecture

A new direction in artistic representation becomes apparent in the pottery of the Late Geometric period (c. 750–700). Except for an occasional horse or a bird, or, even rarer, a human figure, Greek vases had been essentially without images from the eleventh to the eighth century, when suddenly depictions of animals and humans became frequent. Then, around mid-century artists began to paint action scenes, such as battles, shipwrecks, funerals, and chariot processions. On massive Late Geometric amphorae from Athens that were commissioned as funeral monuments for the wealthy, these pictorial narratives occupy a prominent position among the abstract geometric motifs. Eventually the geometric designs become mere decorative frames for the figure scenes. Vase painters add new pictorial elements, and the figures become increasingly more naturalistic. Other media, such as small bronze sculptures and engraved metalwork, also feature dynamic action. Distinct regional and local styles emerged, as craftsmen experimented with, adapted, and discarded homegrown and imported trends and techniques. Around 720 BC, Greek art begins to feature a variety of ornamental motifs such as rosettes, griffins, and sirens, that are associated with the "orientalizing style." This phase, during which Greeks deliberately used elements of Near Eastern and Egyptian art, sculpture, and architecture, would continue for the next hundred years or so.

The monumental temple, the "signature" Greek architectural form, also emerged in the eighth century. The first temples were small one-room structures that resembled ordinary houses. Early in the century the people of the island of

Facing page

Figure 2.5a. Middle Geometric krater from Athens (c. 800 BC) with meander, zigzag, and other geometric patterns. Note the flanking horses, which enliven the severe geometric decoration, and the jug-shaped knob on the lid.

Figure 2.5b. Large Late Geometric grave amphora (c. 750 BC) from the Dipylon cemetery at Athens.

Figure 2.5c. Detail from the same vase, showing the dead woman lying on her funeral bier surrounded by mourners.

a

b

c

Figure 2.6. A small bronze statuette from the mid-eighth century BC, depicting a hero and a centaur fighting; the preserved part of the man's weapon has pierced the centaur's side.

Samos built a sanctuary for Hera that was a hundred feet long. A little later, architects added a wooden colonnade or peristyle around it, and the Greek temple as we know it was born. By 700, there were dozens of them, built along similar lines, in all parts of the Greek world. Plainly, people wanted and were able to expend their wealth and labor on projects that brought prestige to the whole community. In Athens at this time, votive offerings placed in the temples of the gods—most notably bronze tripods and cauldrons, figurines, and bronze dress pins—greatly exceed the amount of metal objects found in upper-class burials. In this way the elite could give to the community and flaunt their wealth at the same time—a pattern that was to hold throughout the life of the Greek city-state.

Thick brick and stone defensive walls, another architectural feature, first appear in Ionia and the Aegean islands. Smyrna in Anatolia had an impressive circuit wall by around 850, and a number of Cycladic island sites were also fortified in the ninth century. On the mainland, however, the earliest circuit walls date to the later eighth century. The construction of massive defensive walls may mean that actual warfare between communities, as opposed to raiding expeditions, was growing more frequent; they also attest to the growing wealth and communal pride of the communities.

Panhellenism and the Heroic Revival

The eighth century also saw the rise of religious sanctuaries and festivals that were "Panhellenic" (*pan* = "all"), attracting worshippers from all over the Greek world. The most famous of the early shrines were those of Zeus and Hera at Olympia in western Peloponnesus, of Apollo and Artemis at Delos, and the oracles (places of divine prophecy) of Zeus at Dodona and of Apollo at Delphi. Tradition has it that in 776 BC, athletic contests became part of the festival of Zeus at Olympia. Held every four years, the Olympian games at first attracted contestants and visitors only from the vicinity, but by century's end their fame had spread widely, and by the sixth century contestants and spectators would be drawn from all over the Greek world. Panhellenic festivals fostered a sense of Greek identity, reinforcing a feeling that Greeks everywhere shared a common heritage, language, and religion.

The eighth century also saw a new interest in the Bronze Age "ancestors." Quite suddenly, around 750, numerous ancient tombs (mostly Mycenaean) which had been largely ignored throughout the Dark Age began to receive votive offerings, and their anonymous inhabitants were now worshiped as "heroes." Some cult heroes were identified with legendary figures and honored not at graves, but at special shrines set up to them, such as the precincts sacred to Agamemnon at Mycenae and to Menelaus and Helen near Sparta. The reasons for the surge of hero cults at this time are not well understood. Like gods, they were honored with animal sacrifices and other offerings.

We have already seen that in the tenth century at Lefkandi a wealthy man was given a lavish warrior's burial. This practice seems to have been rare throughout the Dark Age until the mid-eighth century, when in some parts of Greece warrior burials become quite common. Like the warrior of Lefkandi, the corpse was cremated and the bones put in an urn; weapons were placed in the grave, and occasionally sacrificed horses. Also around this time vases depicting events from the heroic age begin to turn up in the graves. These practices suggest that the leading families were proclaiming descent from the heroes of old.

The archaeological discoveries of the past thirty years and new interpretive techniques have brought a fresh evaluation of the period called the "Dark Age." We know now that this was not a time of inertia and stagnation as was once thought. Because it was continually fed by new cultural streams, Greece remained vital and vibrant throughout the eleventh, tenth, and ninth centuries. It appears now that the institutions and practices of the city-state society that was to follow were slowly taking shape in the diverse communities of the Dark Age. The rise of the city-states (poleis) and their turbulent early history are the subjects of the next chapter.

TRANSLATION

Blanco, Walter. 1998. *The Histories*, from *Herodotus: The Histories*, Walter Blanco and Jennifer Roberts, eds. New York: W.W. Norton.

SUGGESTED READINGS

Burkert, Walter. 1985. *Greek Religion*. Cambridge, MA: Harvard University Press. A classic history of ancient Greek religion from the Minoan-Mycenaean Age to the Hellenistic period.

Edwards, Mark W. 1987. *Homer, Poet of the Iliad*. Baltimore and London: Johns Hopkins University Press. A reliable, up-to-date general treatment of Homeric poetry and the epic style, with commentaries on selected books of the *Iliad*.

Finley, Moses I. 1978. *The World of Odysseus*. 2nd ed. New York: Viking Press. First published in 1954, this book revolutionized the study of Dark Age society and institutions.

Griffin, Jasper. 1980. *Homer on Life and Death*. New York: Oxford University Press. An insightful literary exploration of the Homeric characterization of the epic hero.

Hurwit, Jeffrey M. 1985. *The Art and Culture of Early Greece, 1100–480 B.C.* Ithaca, NY: Cornell Univerity Press, chaps. 1–3. A keen analysis of Dark Age art in relation to the changing social scene. Chapters 4 to 6 are also recommended reading for art and culture in the Archaic period.

Morris, Ian and Barry Powell, eds. 1997. *A New Companion to Homer*. Leiden: Brill. A valuable collection of thirty new articles, covering all areas of Homeric studies, literary and historical, written by specialists for a nonspecialist audience.

Snodgrass, A. M. 1971 (reprinted in 2000, with new Foreword). *The Dark Age of Greece: An Archaeological Survey of the Eleventh to the Eighth Centuries*. Edinburgh: University of Edinburgh Press. Remains the standard treatment of the archaeological evidence for the whole of the Dark Age.

Thomas, Carol G. and Craig Conant. 1999. *Citadel to City-State: The Transformation of Greece, 1200–700 B.C.E.* Bloomington and Indianapolis: Indiana University Press. Written with the general reader in mind, this book traces the processes of change that led from the destruction of Bronze Age civilization to the emergence of the city-states. Each chapter is devoted to a specific site, among which are Nichoria and Lefkandi.

3

ARCHAIC GREECE
(C. 700–500 BC)

The forces of change that had swept over Greece in the eighth century continued at an accelerated pace in the seventh and sixth. Population continued to rise, and in response Greeks founded more colonies, spreading all across the shores of the Mediterranean and Black Seas. Trade, helped by colonization, dispersed Greek goods far beyond the limits known to the Bronze Age traders. The Panhellenic shrines, festivals, and oracles grew in number and importance, further fostering the sense of a common Greek identity. The Archaic period also saw new forms of literary, artistic, and intellectual expression.

The Archaic period did have its dark side. Wars among Greeks became more frequent, and warfare itself became more lethal. Worse, strife within a demos became commonplace, as the leaders wrangled among themselves over power-sharing and the poorer citizens fought for economic relief and their civic rights. All this movement for good or for bad took place within a new social and political framework, the city-state, which by 700 had replaced the old chieftain system in many parts of the Greek world.

THE FORMATION OF THE CITY-STATE (POLIS)

The term "city-state" is a modern coinage, yet city-states themselves are ancient political formations, going back to the Early Bronze Age in Mesopotamia. Basically, a city-state is a defined geographical area comprising a central city and its adjacent territory, which together make up a single, self-governing political unit. The Greeks called this arrangement a *polis*, which gives us "political," "politics" and "policy."

As we saw in Chapter Two, the essential elements of the Greek city-states were already in place during the later Dark Age. The capital cities of what became city-states existed all through the Dark Age, and most of them had been

61

the major centers of their regions during the Mycenaean period. The territorial community, the *dēmos* in its joint sense as "the land" and "the people" appears fully evolved in the Homeric epics, as are the two primary governmental organs of the Greek city-state, the assembly of men of fighting age and the council of "elders." All that was lacking to make the demos-communities of 800 BC into the polis-states of 700 BC were certain necessary formalities: formal political unification of the demos and the creation of a central government.

Political Unification (Synoecism)

In all city-states, from ancient Mesopotamia to Renaissance Europe, the capital city is the focal point of the state. And it is often the case that those who live outside the city have a lower civic or social status than the city dwellers. Among the Greeks, however, all members of the demos, whether they lived in the capital or the countryside, were called *politai* (members of the polis) as if they all lived together in the polis (city). So, for example, the inhabitants of the several settlements in the plain around the main town of Megara called themselves (and were called by others) "the Megarians."

The process by which a demos became unified is called "synoecism," from *sun-oik-ismos* ("uniting the *oikoi*"). The vast majority of new city-states were quite small (25 to 150 square miles in area) often consisting of a single main town and its adjacent plain, holding a couple of outlying villages. In such cases, political unification was a simple matter. Polis (the state) and polis (the town) were nearly identical entities. Everyone lived within a few miles of everyone else, and many of the few hundred families in the demos would have been interrelated. Drawing them together into a single political unit was merely a matter of making formal the ancient ties of kinship and neighborliness.

Political unification of regional territories that contained several important towns and villages besides the central polis was more complex and is not well understood. It seems likely that synoecism in these regions was a drawn-out process, beginning possibly in the late ninth century BC and crystallizing between about 750 and 700. Regional unification appears for the most part to have been voluntary and peaceful. For some places, however, there is evidence that intimidation and even force were used to integrate reluctant towns and villages into a political union. Such was the case in the region of Laconia, where the four original villages of Sparta absorbed the village of Amyclae, 3 miles south, into the Spartan polis against its will. Synoecism was also incomplete in some regions. Argos, for example, never fully succeeded in unifying the whole of the large region of Argolis. Several small, independent city-states continued to exist outside the plain of Argos, and even in the plain itself some villages retained a good deal of local autonomy.

By the early seventh century, dozens of independent city-states had been established all across the Mediterranean, from Ionia in the east to Sicily and southern Italy in the west, and many more would be added as the Greeks further expanded their geographical horizons. Not all Greeks lived in city-states, however.

In a number of large regions of the Peloponnesus and central and northern Greece the inhabitants opted for a different form of political organization. The *ethnos*, as the city-state Greeks called it, consisted of a people and its territory (a demos) but without a capital polis, or a central government, or formal political union. The separate towns and villages of an ethnos were independent and autonomous, yet they also had a strong sense of common identity: "the Aetolians" as distinct from "the Phocians" to their east, and so on. They were united in religious cult, and they had institutions for reaching common decisions and unified action when necessary, as in the case of attack from outsiders, for example.

GOVERNMENT IN THE EARLY CITY-STATES

Political union could not have occurred unless the local *basileis*, the leaders of the districts, towns, and villages of the demos, wished it. These men, the new landowning aristocracy, were the planners and architects of the new centralized government of the emerging city-states. The key decision was to eliminate the position of the paramount basileus and rule collectively, a relatively easy matter, since the paramount chief had little power over the other chiefs to begin with. The governmental structures of the early poleis differed in specifics, yet all followed a similar pattern: (1) The office of paramount *basileus* was either abolished completely or was greatly reduced in power. (2) The various leadership roles of the basileus were distributed among several officials drawn from the elite. (3) The importance of the council of aristocratic "elders" increased, while that of the assembly of the people decreased. Of course, these decisions were not arrived at in a single year or even a single generation. Yet it is likely that once the process of city-state formation had begun, determining which villages and districts were to be included in the polis and what system of government it would have taken no more than two or three generations.

The new, more complex systems of organization and social control that arose in the city-states were a necessary response to changing conditions: sustained population growth, increasing productivity and trade, and more complicated relationships with neighboring states. Especially pressing was the need for ways to mobilize manpower and resources efficiently for warfare, for as population increased and land became scarcer, poleis fought each other over territory, a more serious business than the raids and counterraids for animals and booty that characterized war in the Dark Age. The new system of governance was thus good for the polis as a whole, but it was especially good for the large landowners who made up the government and, like all dominant groups in human history, were highly motivated to preserve their economic and political power.

The basileus did not disappear completely. In a few poleis, a type of the traditional hereditary chiefdom, with severe limits on the paramount leader's power, appears to have continued on through the Archaic period. The Spartans retained the chieftain system the longest, though in a unique form, with two hereditary, lifelong basileis ruling as equals. In this "dual kingship" the Spartan basileis exercised considerable authority, especially in the military sphere, but their powers were curbed by five annually elected magistrates, called *ephoroi* ("overseers"). Their job was to make sure that the basileis ruled lawfully and to prosecute them if they did not.

In most poleis, however, the title "basileus" became just the name for one of a number of officials who made up the collective leadership of a city-state. The powerful families divided up the spheres of authority—administrative, military, religious, and judicial—among themselves, creating magistracies and boards. Later Greeks called this form of government oligarchy or "rule by the few" (*oligoi* = few). Unlike in the previous system, positions of authority could not be inherited, and their tenure was brief. In most states, by the middle of the seventh century, term of office was limited to a single year and could not be held again until a stipulated number of years had passed. In this way, the power of any single magistrate was checked, and honors were shared among the whole of the aristocratic community. Each city-state developed its own system of magistracies according to its own needs and circumstances. Obviously, small poleis needed fewer officials than the large ones.

In general there was no hierarchy among the major offices, although many states did have a principal official who was regarded as the chief administrator. The most common titles for the chief officer were *archōn* (e.g., at Athens and elsewhere in central Greece) and *prytanis* (e.g., at Corinth and poleis in Ionia). The chief magistrate sometimes retained the old title of basileus. In some poleis, (e.g., at Athens and Megara) an officer called the *polemarchos* ("war leader") was in charge of military operations. Supervision of religious activities fell to another magistrate or, more often, a board of magistrates, which also judged crimes having to do with religion, such as homicides (which polluted the community). The common use of the title basileis to designate these officials speaks to the reverence that is still attached to the name.

The real center of power in the early city-states, however, resided not in the officials and boards but in the council of elders. The *boulē* in the Archaic poleis had even more power than the boule in Homeric society. It met more frequently than in the pre-state period and assumed for itself the task of making policies and drafting laws for the polis. The members were normally recruited from the highest magistrates, who entered the council after their terms of office. Membership in the council was usually for a long term or even for life. The archons and other magistrates, by contrast, had limited terms and would hesitate to oppose the august body of prominent men whose ranks they wished some day to join.

As the authority of the council increased, the limited power of the old assembly of adult male citizens to influence policy was further reduced in the oligarchic city-state. Some states excluded the poorest citizens from membership in the assembly by imposing a property qualification. Some restricted the number of assembly meetings and the business to be brought before it, or they curtailed free discussion of the issues. The sovereignty of the aristocratic council, however, would be relatively short-lived; as time passed, the authority of the assembly to decide policy would increase.

THE COLONIZING MOVEMENT

The widespread emigration of Greeks from their Aegean homelands that had begun in the mid-eighth century continued for more than two centuries. When it ended around 500 BC the Greek world extended from Spain in the west to Colchis in the east. As we saw in Chapter Two, this remarkable expansion was driven by two needs: to satisfy the Greeks' growing appetite for imported goods, especially scarce metals, and to provide citizens of the motherland enough fertile land to live a good life in their new poleis. Founding a colony required careful preparation. The "mother" polis (*mētropolis*) had to choose a site for the colony, obtain divine approval for it, plan out the new settlement, and choose its *oikistēs* (founder), always, of course, a man of high status. As the foundation oath for Cyrene (see Document 3.1) reveals, the decision of the Theraeans to establish the colony involved the whole community and was backed by communal sanctions.

Document 3.1 Foundation Oath of Cyrene, Libya (late seventh century BC). A fourth-century inscription from Cyrene purporting to be a copy of the oath sworn by the Theraeans and the colonists of Cyrene.

Resolved by the Assembly. Since Apollo spontaneously told Battus and the Theraeans to found a colony in Cyrene, the Theraeans decided to dispatch Battus as the founder of the colony and *basileus*. The Theraeans shall sail as his comrades. They shall sail on equal terms; and one son shall be enrolled from each family. Those who sail shall be adults, and any free man from the Theraeans who wishes, may also sail.

If the colonists secure the settlement, any colonist who sails later to Libya shall have a share in the citizenship and honors. He also shall receive a lot from the unassigned land. But if they do not make the settlement secure, and the Theraeans cannot come to their aid and they suffer troubles for five years, the colonists may return without fear to Thera. They may return to their own property and become citizens of Thera.

If anyone is unwilling to sail when sent by the city, let him be subject to the death penalty and let his property be confiscated. Whoever receives or protects such a person—whether a father his son or a brother his brother—shall suffer the same punishment as the person who refused to sail. On these terms oaths were sworn by those remaining at Thera and those sailing to found the colony. They also cursed those who transgressed these conditions and did not abide by them, both those settling in Libya and those staying here.

Supplementum Epigraphicum Graecum 9.3;
translated by Stanley M. Burstein.

It was the oikist who was responsible for leading out the colonists, laying out the city's defenses, establishing the sanctuaries of the gods, and assigning the kleroi to the settlers. If his leadership proved successful, the oikist would become the guardian hero of the new polis after his death. The colony itself would remain linked to its metropolis by bonds of kinship and cult, symbolized by the fire the oikist brought from the metropolis' hearth to kindle the hearth of the new polis. The Greek word for colony was *apoikia*, literally a "home away [from our old home]." Otherwise, however, the colony was a new and completely independent polis, since those who joined a colony gave up their citizenship in the mother-polis.

The colonizing movement had two phases, each lasting a little over a century. The first, beginning in the mid-eighth century, was directed to Italy and the western Mediterranean; the second began about a century later and was concentrated on the north Aegean and the Black Sea. The pioneers in the colonization of Italy were Euboeans, who in the early eighth century established a trading colony on the island of Pithecusae (modern Ischia) in the Bay of Naples. It was a huge success, attracting not only other Greeks but also Phoenicians, who made up 15 percent of the more than 10,000 inhabitants that eventually occupied this tiny island. With its good harbor, Pithecusae was well situated to exploit the iron deposits on the nearby island of Elba and to trade with the Italic populations of the mainland.

The Euboeans followed up their success at Pithecusae with additional poleis: Cumae (757) on the Italian mainland near modern Naples, and four in Sicily between 734 and 712. Poleis in the Peloponnesus, plagued by problems caused by unequal distribution of land at home, also sent out colonists to the fertile areas of Italy and Sicily. The Corinthians, for example, settled the Adriatic island of Corcyra (modern Corfu; c. 734) and a year later founded Syracuse, which would become the major city-state in Sicily and a famous center of culture in the Greek world. Towards the very end of the century, the Spartans established their one and only overseas colony, Taras in southern Italy, settled by exiled dissidents.

Colonization of the West continued into the seventh century as the early colonies spun off daughter settlements and newcomers from other parts of old Greece came looking for farmland and trading opportunities. For example, about 600 BC, colonists from Phocaea on the coast of Anatolia founded Massilia (modern Marseilles) on the coast of southern France. Its location at the mouth of the Rhone River afforded the Massilians easy access to the lucrative trade with the Celtic inhabitants of the upper Rhone Valley. By then, however, opportunities for further Greek expansion in the West were disappearing. Besides, the western Greeks had rivals; Phoenicians from their colony of Carthage (in modern Tunisia) were establishing their own colonial empire in western Sicily, southern Spain, and the islands of Corsica and Sardinia.

There were other places to go, however. For example, the people of the tiny island of Thera, feeling the pinch of land shortage, founded Cyrene in Libya (c. 630). But it was the areas around the Hellespont and the Black Sea, with their good fishing grounds, rich soil, mineral wealth, and trading possibilities that lured the Greeks the most. And they went at it with gusto: Miletus alone is credited in the

Figure 3.1. Greek colonization: 750–500 BC.

ancient sources with having founded ninety colonies. Having no rivals in this area (unlike in the Mediterranean basin), the Greeks were able to establish new colonies throughout the Archaic and Classical periods until the Black Sea was almost entirely ringed by Greek poleis. Many colonies became rich and powerful, among them Byzantium, which a thousand years later, under its new name, Constantinople, would become the capital of the Roman Empire. The transplanted city-states proudly proclaimed their Greekness, building monumental temples, patronizing Panhellenic institutions such as the Delphic oracle and the Olympic games, and eagerly staying abreast of cultural developments in the Aegean. (The earliest examples of the Greek alphabet and hexameter verse in fact come from Pithecusae.)

Relations with the people into whose lands the colonists came were complex. On the one hand, the colonies were gateways through which various peoples of southern Europe and the Black Sea areas obtained access to the products and culture of the Greeks and other Mediterranean societies. The Etruscans in Italy, for example, adapted the Greek alphabet and avidly embraced Greek art and even religious cult. On the other hand, the Greeks were intruders, and conflict with the native inhabitants occurred frequently. For the most part, however, the minority colonists made accommodations with their non-Greek neighbors, trading and intermarrying with them, and sometimes even sharing their territory. Nor indeed was the cultural exchange all in one direction. For instance, cults such as those of the Thracian goddess Bendis and the divine musician Orpheus spread throughout the Aegean and beyond.

ECONOMIC AND SOCIAL DIVISIONS IN THE ARCHAIC POLEIS

The colonizing movement was only a partial remedy for the disparity in land ownership. Not every family could emigrate, and as population at home continued to grow, each new generation of oikoi found it increasingly difficult to gain access to land. The result was a widening of the existing economic and social gulf between the small group at the top—comprising perhaps no more than 20 percent of the families—and all the rest.

The economic power of the aristocratic houses rested on their inherited landholdings. As a group they controlled a disproportionate share of the total agricultural land in the demos and an even greater share of the good land, including lush meadows for grazing their horses and cattle. They became even richer by concentrating on cash crops, such as wine and olive oil. Most significant for their profits was their ability to exploit the plight of the poorest farmers, who made up possibly a third or more of the demos. Some of them mortgaged their kleroi to the rich, paying off the debt with a portion of their crops; others became sharecroppers on rich men's lands. Many were reduced to the status of *thetes*, hired hands who worked for mere subsistence. The majority of citizens in a polis, however—perhaps 40 or even 50 percent of households—though far from wealthy, were economically self-sufficient and therefore not economically dependant on the rich. The fourth-century philosopher Aristotle in his *Politics* called this group, "the middle," the portion of the polis between "the very rich and the very poor."

These three divisions of rich, middling, and poor were not monolithic, of course; within each there were gradations of wealth and social rank. The small upper class was dominated by a smaller number of families that were preeminent because of their nobler bloodlines and greater wealth: an aristocracy within an aristocracy. Moreover, the hierarchy was subject to shifts; one family might rise into the ranks of the upper nobility while another might drop down into the lesser nobilty. Nevertheless, the propertied class as a whole remained clearly marked off from the groups below them. They protected their economic and social exclusiveness by marrying only among themselves. Moreover, they cultivated an image of group superiority, calling themselves "the good" (*hoi agathoi*) on the basis of their wealth and ancestry, while lumping together those outside the landed nobility as "the bad" (*hoi kakoi*) and "the many" (*hoi polloi*).

Within the middle group there was greater economic and social gradation. Some nonnoble oikoi shared in the increasing prosperity of the Archaic Age and were fairly well off; at the other end of the scale were those barely keeping out of debt. The differences in economic status—and therefore in social status—among the independent farmers and craftsmen prevented them from perceiving themselves as a class with their own interests, like the rich landowners. Upward mobility, even for the top of this group, was not easy. Yet, if a commoner family became wealthy enough, it could marry into the nobility. The sixth-century aristocratic poet Theognis complains that although men take pains to make their animals "well-born" by careful breeding, a "good man" (agathos) will not hesitate to marry the daughter of a "bad man" (kakos) if she brings with her a good dowry. "Wealth," he laments, "corrupts a lineage" (*Theognidea* 183–192). Downward mobility, on the other hand, was more common; a couple of bad years could easily push a precarious farmer into insoluble debt, and even into the condition of a thete.

The gradations of the bottom group would have been only in the degree of abjectness, since the chances for economic betterment for the very poor were slight. It was not just poverty that made the lives of thetes miserable; they also had to endure the stigma of working for others, which for the Greeks meant loss of freedom. From a number of poleis come various slang terms denoting persons of inferior status: "the naked ones" (Argos), "dusty-feet" (Epidaurus), "wearers of sheepskins" (Sicyon), "wearers of dog-skin helmets" (Corinth). In addition to the thetes, there existed in some areas of Greece another category of laborers, characterized as "between free persons and slaves." Among those who endured this sort of semi-slavery are the Spartan "helots." These were the original inhabitants of parts of Laconia and most of Messenia who were conquered by the Spartans in war and made to work for the Spartan citizens as serfs on what had been their own land. The helots were given some human rights—they could marry and raise a family and keep a portion of their production—but in all other respects they were chattel, as we shall see in the next chapter.

The only persons of lower status than these were, of course, the actual slaves, males and females acquired from the outside by capture or purchase who had no freedom whatever and no human rights and were legally classed as property. It was not until the sixth century that slaves began to pour into the poleis in large numbers. Some have argued that the increased use of slaves was the result of political reforms abolishing debt bondage within the polis, which forced the rich, who had found it more profitable to exploit the labor of impoverished citizens, to turn to slave labor.

Citizenship

While all free-born members of the polis were citizens (*politai*), they were far from equal in their citizen rights. Aside from their roles in the religious worship of the community, women citizens were denied any participation in public affairs. This was the exclusive domain of adult (over age 18) male citizens. But their share of civic responsibilities and rights—to vote and speak in the assembly, hold office, serve as judges, fight in the army—was divided unequally along economic and social lines. In the early city-states, as we have seen, only the rich and wellborn possessed the full range of citizen privileges. Nonnoble citizens of moderate means were barred from holding office, and in many cases the poorest citizens had no vote in the assembly. The struggle for full participation by all citizens in the governance of their poleis would be achieved only at the end of the Archaic period and then only in the democratic states; in oligarchic states the poorest members would continue to be second-class citizens. Even in the most democratic poleis, citizenship would be denied to ex-slaves and resident aliens.

Resentment from Below and the Beginnings of Social Change

There was strong popular resentment against the wealth, power, and arrogance of the self-styled agathoi in the seventh century. Among the exploited have-nots in many Archaic poleis the rallying cry was "redistribution of the land." The middling oikoi—those that produced enough to live on or enough and some extra—also had cause for resentment. Because the aristocratic households were successful in holding on to most of the fertile soil, these independent farmers had few opportunities to acquire good land. They could choose to emigrate abroad, which many did, or else acquire marginal land far from their villages, which yielded poorer return for extra labor and increased their travel time. The middle group also chafed at the oligarchy's hold on the magistracies, boards, and particularly the council, where the political decisions were formulated. The well-off farmers were just as liable as the poorer ones to be cheated in the law courts and just as helpless against "crooked decisions." In the assembly, the one organ of government to which they were admitted, the people's voice carried little weight against the concentrated power of the rich.

Yet, despite the strength of the ruling oligarchs and the apparent impotence of the rest of the demos, total domination by the former was destined to be short-lived. By the early sixth century, the oligarchical hold was weakening and more inclusive forms of government were emerging that would eventually give political power to the mass of people, including the poor. The spearhead of the protest against aristocratic excess was the middle group of independent farmers, over whom the oligarchs had the least control. We are fortunate to have a very early voice for this group: Hesiod.

HESIOD: A VIEW FROM BELOW

Unlike the *Iliad* and the *Odyssey*, which are about the glories and the sufferings of the mighty Trojan War heroes, Hesiod's *Works and Days* (c. 700 BC) is down-to-earth. Hesiod's world is a rural village in Boeotia, Ascra, which was part of the polis of Thespiae, three miles away. The poem is ostensibly a long lecture (828 lines) to Hesiod's errant brother, Perses. But the advice to Perses to mend his ways and be a good farmer and neighbor is also a way for Hesiod to preach to his audiences the virtues and values that all people should honor.

Perses had apparently defrauded Hesiod of a portion of their inheritance by bribing the judges (basileis) who heard the case. Hesiod addresses the basileis very sternly, not at all deferentially, calling them "gift-swallowing basileis." He accuses them of habitually rendering their verdicts "with crooked judgments," and warns that Zeus himself protects his daughter, Dike, "Justice," and avenges unjust acts against her committed by those in power.

[卐卐卐卐卐卐卐卐卐卐卐卐卐卐卐卐卐卐卐卐卐卐卐卐卐卐卐卐卐卐卐卐卐卐]

Document 3.2 Hesiod Lectures the Aristocrats.

> *Basileis*, give this verdict no little thought,
> for the immortals are ever present among men,
> and they see those who with crooked verdicts
> spurn divine retribution and grind down one another's lives.
>
> . . . .
>
> Justice is a maiden and a daughter of Zeus;
> the gods of Olympos respect her noble title,
> and whenever men mistreat her through false charges
> she rushes to sit at the feet of Zeus Kronion
> and she denounces the designs of men who are not just,
> so that the people pay for the reckless deeds and evil plans
> of *basileis* whose slanted words twist her straight path.
> Keep her commands, O gift-devouring *basileis*, and let
> verdicts be straight; yes, lay your crooked ways aside!

Works and Days 248–264; translated by
Apostolos N. Athanassakis, *Hesiod*. Baltimore and London:
Johns Hopkins University Press, 1983, p. 73, adapted.

[卐卐卐卐卐卐卐卐卐卐卐卐卐卐卐卐卐卐卐卐卐卐卐卐卐卐卐卐卐卐卐卐卐卐]

The tone of the entire poem is moralistic. Hesiod has a litany of proverbial dos and don'ts that we might find in any peasant society. For example, he counsels a strict reciprocity in all dealings. When you borrow from a neighbor, he says, "pay back fairly, the same amount, or more if you can, so that when you need something later you can count on him" (349–351).

At the core of Hesiod's moral program is the virtue of arduous manual labor:

> Through work men grow wealthy and rich in flocks,
> and by working they become much dearer to the gods.
> Work is no disgrace; idleness is the disgrace.
> And if you work, the idle man will soon envy you
> as you grow rich, because fame and renown follow wealth.
>
> (*Works and Days* 308–313)

Only through "work upon work," Hesiod says, can the ordinary farmer win the three prizes of wealth, divine favor, and glory, which in the Homeric epics only heroes could attain. The prizes of work, of course, are just the humble rewards that rural villagers might hope for. For Hesiod and his neighbors wealth meant not golden goblets, but "having their granaries full of the sustenance of life" at harvest time and not having to borrow; renown was being admired and respected by all the folk in the village.

As a social document, the *Works and Days* also provides evidence of class differences in outlook toward institutions such as marriage. Among the upper class, marriage was primarily a means of establishing political alliances and enhancing family prestige; the elite often sought advantageous marriages outside the polis. Hesiod's vantage point, rather, is that of a village farmer. It is not a wife who will bring him political connections that he seeks, but a local girl who will not sully his reputation if she should turn out to be a glutton or lazy or unfaithful.

> Marry a virgin so that you can teach her proper habits,
> and especially marry one who lives near you;
> and check all around so that your marriage will not be a joke
> to your neighbors, for nothing is better for a man than a good wife
> and nothing more horrible than a bad one. . . .
>
> (*Works and Days* 699–703)

That women are weak but dangerous is a common theme in Greek literature. In Hesiod this male attitude is validated in the myth of the first woman, Pandora, told both in the *Theogony* (571–612) and the *Works and Days* (60–105). Pandora, the "beautiful evil," was created as a punishment for the crime of Prometheus of stealing fire from the gods and giving it to humans. It was she who opened the lid of a jar containing all the plagues and diseases of the world and let them out. Thenceforth, all womankind inherited Pandora's "shameless mind and deceitful nature," her "lies and coaxing words." Women live off men like the drones among the bees. "Do not let a woman wiggling her behind deceive you with her wheedling words. She is after your granary. The man who trusts a woman trusts thieves" (*Works and Days* 373–375).

Hesiod's class of middling farmers resembled the wealthy class in one important respect: They exploited the labor of others. Hesiod takes for granted that the farmers he addresses can afford to own at least one slave woman or man, or take on a regular hired hand (thes). The good farmer keeps his eye on the bottom line; the day's food for a hired plowman is to be carefully measured out. He advises hiring a thes who has no oikos (he will work for less) and a childless female ("a worker with a child at her breast is a bother").

However much he railed against the wealthy and powerful, Hesiod, then, was not a "champion of the oppressed," as some have dubbed him. Rather his was the indignant voice of the middle: Zeus will look favorably on those who are pious, hard working, and just and in the end will punish those who are not.

THE HOPLITE ARMY

Battles between poleis were fought by men like Hesiod and his neighbors, average farmers and craftsmen. Developments in military equipment and organization altered the nature of warfare in the early city-states. It is in this new type of military organization that we most clearly observe the polis ideology that the citizen is the slave of the common good. By 650 BC polis armies were made up of heavily armored foot soldiers called hoplites, arranged in a tightly packed formation—the phalanx—which apparently evolved from the looser type of mass

Figure 3.2. A rare depiction of hoplite battle; from a Corinthian vase, c. 640 BC.

formation depicted in the *Iliad*. In the developed phalanx the soldiers lined up almost shoulder to shoulder with each rank almost treading on the heels of the one in front of it.

Battle tactics were quite simple: Opposing phalanxes formed up (normally eight rows deep), charged at one another, and collided. The hoplite's weapons were a long heavy spear, used for thrusting and jabbing, and a short slashing sword for close in fighting. For protection he wore a helmet, breastplate, and greaves (shin-and-knee protectors), all made of bronze and covering as much of the body as possible. The most important piece of equipment was a new type of shield called the *hoplon*, which was quite different from the shields carried by the Homeric warriors. It was round, made of wood covered with a thin sheet of bronze, and was held by inserting the left arm through a central band and gripping a strap at the rim, which gave it maneuverability. Its large size (about 3 feet in diameter) gave cover to the man on the left, allowing hoplites to fight close together with half of their bodies protected by the adjacent man's shield. Seen from the front, a phalanx presented nearly a solid wall of shields, helmeted heads, and spears.

A hoplite battle was a ferocious affair. When the opposing front lines collided, the ranks behind shoved against those in front—the maneuver was called "the pushing"—using their weight to break the enemy's ranks. It took enormous courage to keep place in the ranks when all around you was the sight, sound, and smell of iron piercing into flesh and bone. Most did stand fast, "biting their lip with their teeth," as the Spartan poet Tyrtaeus (c. 650 BC) says, out of personal pride and sense of duty as a citizen.

> This is the common good, for the *polis* and the whole *dēmos*,
> when a man stands firm in the front ranks
> without flinching and puts disgraceful flight completely from his mind.
> (Tyrtaeus fr. 9.15–17 Diehl)

Although the fighting was savage, hoplite battles were usually brief, seldom lasting more than an hour, and casualties were relatively light for both losers and victors, seldom over 15 percent. Once the enemy broke ranks and fled, there was not much pursuit, so that massacres were rare. Campaigns, too, were brief; usually, a single set battle ended the fighting for the summer. Farmer-warriors could not stay long away from their fields and animals.

Not all citizens fought in the phalanx, however. Because hoplites had to furnish their own arms and armor, which were fairly expensive, the poorest men were excluded and served instead as light-armed troops. The proportion of the non-hoplite oikoi in the Archaic period would have varied from polis to polis: perhaps 20 or 30 percent of all citizen families. Although disparities in wealth and social status separated phalanx fighters from light-armed skirmishers, there were no such distinctions within the phalanx itself. In the ranks, where highborn nobles and men from the middle fought side by side, strict equality prevailed. Under these conditions it would become increasingly difficult for the former to claim that they alone were competent to wield political power and formulate policy for their poleis.

THE ARCHAIC AGE TYRANTS

The first serious challenge to oligarchic rule came not from below, but from within the elite group itself, in the form of a new political phenomenon the Greeks called tyranny (*tyrannis*). The "age of tyrants" lasted from about 670–500 BC, affecting a great many of the Greek states. The Archaic Age tyrant (*tyrannos*) was what we call today a dictator or strongman, a single ruler who, however, lacked the legitimacy of the old paramount basileus. Indeed, the Greeks had no name for such a figure; the title tyrannos was likely borrowed from the Lydians, an Anatolian people. Tyrants were only later regarded as evil despots. Their subsequent ill-repute stemmed partly from propaganda spread by the aristocrats themselves, who naturally resented the domination of a single man, and partly from the popular sentiment that dictatorial rule posed a threat to the freedom of all. Yet the early tyrants were probably viewed more favorably by their nonaristocratic contemporaries.

Very few of the dozens of tyrants who grabbed power in their poleis are known in any detail, but we can discern a general pattern. Firstly, most tyrants arose from the elite group, though not necessarily from the top-ranked families. Cypselus of Corinth (c. 657–627), for instance, was marginalized within the prominent "clan" of the Bacchiads, because his mother, a Bacchiad, had married outside the clan. In addition to noble birth, would-be tyrants were distinguished in their poleis for their personal achievements. Cypselus, prior to seizing control, had held the post of polemarch (military commander) in Corinth, as had another famous tyrant, Orthagoras of Sicyon (mid-seventh century). Cylon of Athens, whose attempted coup in 632 failed, had won fame as a victor in the Olympic games. Finally, despite attempts to form dynasties by passing on their rule to their sons, few tyrannies lasted more than three generations and most collapsed after one or two.

Continual feuding among the major aristocratic factions certainly contributed to the emergence of the tyrants. Each faction was associated with a preeminent lineage (*genos*) that extended an umbrella of fictive kinship over less prestigious families, who supported the leader-family in its political ambitions. The frequent bouts of violence and bloodshed among what were basically rival gangs of hotheaded young aristocrats were politically disruptive. The intervention of a strongman who could keep them in check would be welcome to the people, if not to the aristocrats.

The would-be tyrant also needed armed followers. These might be disaffected aristocrats within the polis who were frozen out of the ruling circle, or a mercenary force from outside the polis. Such aid was sometimes supplied by a friendly tyrant (for his abortive coup, the Athenian Cylon received troops from his father-in-law Theagenes, tyrant of Megara). Peisistratus of Athens had a variety of resources in his three attempts to seize power, including local bodyguards, mercenaries, and troops donated by powerful outsiders. His story will be told in Chapter Five.

Yet, no tyrant, however great his resources, could have overthrown the oligarchs without the tacit support of the citizens themselves, particularly the heavily armed farmer-hoplites. These need not have actively helped him; they could just stand aside and refuse to defend the nobles. Those at the bottom of the social pyramid would naturally have supported a coup against the group that was exploiting them. Indeed, the tyrants seem to have presented themselves as champions of the demos against the oligarchs. Aristotle in the fourth century put it concisely:

> A tyrant is set up from among the *dēmos* and the multitude to oppose the notables so that the people may suffer no injustice from them. This is clear from the facts of history. For almost all the tyrants have arisen from being leaders of the people [*dēmagōgoi*; hence "demagogue"], so to speak, having gained their confidence by slandering the notables.
>
> (*Politics* 1310b 12–17; Rackham 1977, adapted)

By and large, the tyrants did favor the poor over the rich, sometimes confiscating the land of the wealthy and redistributing it to the poor, and making laws that limited aristocratic privilege. They initiated the construction of temples, harbors, and fortifications, as well as improvements in the water supply, drainage systems, and the like, all of which provided work for poor citizens. Moreover, they encouraged trade and commerce. For example, Periander, the son of Cypselus, built a stone trackway across the Isthmus of Corinth (where a canal runs today), allowing ships and cargoes to be hauled between the Saronic and Corinthian gulfs. Under tyranny, cultural activities also thrived: New religious cults and festivals were established, and tyrants made special effort to attract the best artists, architects, poets, and thinkers in Greece to their poleis.

The founding tyrants had won popular support because of their charisma and achievements. Their sons, however, as heirs to a nonexistent office, were quite vulnerable to opposition. Although some succeeded on their own merits, most resorted to increasingly "tyrannical" measures, which only exacerbated resentment against them. So, the second or third generation tyrants were overthrown, and their exiled opponents returned, usually to reestablish oligarchic rule. Rarely, however, were the poleis the same after a tyranny. The farmer-hoplites were no longer willing to vote for leaders whom they could not hold accountable, nor could the nobles easily take back from the poor the benefits that the tyrants had bestowed on them.

THE ARTS AND SCIENCES

The poleis of the Archaic Age and later competed with one another for eminence in art and architecture, poetry, philosophy, and science. These were arenas in which even small poleis could gain glory. With contributions from all parts of the Greek world, the arts and sciences reached new heights of excellence in the seventh and sixth centuries.

Art and Architecture

In the Archaic period the various poleis developed their own distinct artistic styles, especially in pottery. During Cypselus' reign as tyrant Corinth emerged as the leading commercial center of Greece. Corinthian potters dominated the trade in finely painted pottery, exporting huge quantities of their specialty item, tiny perfume flasks—exquisitely decorated in the fashionable "orientalizing" style—filled with scented olive oil. The enterprising Corinthians also invented a widely imitated technique called "black figure," which permitted the rendition of minute details. The artist first painted a silhouette (that turned black during firing) on

a

b

Figure 3.3a. Two views of a special Athenian amphora (c. 525–520 BC) decorated in the red-figure technique on one side and black figure on the other. The warriors are playing a board game.

Figure 3.3b. A *symposion* ("drinking party") scene on an Athenian red-figure calyx krater (mixing bowl for wine and water), showing a man and a youth reclining on a couch, as a girl plays the pipes for them.

the clay ground; then with a sharp point he incised the anatomical and decorative details, sometimes filling these in with red or white paint. Corinthian black figure was enormously popular, but as often happens, success led to mass production and a consequent decline in quality.

By 550, Athenian black-figure pottery, featuring differently shaped and larger vessels, had driven Corinthian vases from the export market. Around 530 the Athenians, in turn, invented a new style called "red figure," which reversed the black-figure technique. The artist drew outlines first and then painted the background with a gloss (clay slip) that fired black, leaving the outlined figures in the orange color of the clay itself. Afterwards he painted on the details with a fine brush. This allowed a more subtle and refined rendering of detail than the incised black-figure technique. Portraits of contemporary daily life were added to the standard mythological and heroic scenes; athletics, horsemanship, and rowdy drinking parties are favorite themes. On some vases erotic acts, both heterosexual and homosexual, are represented graphically. In such scenes, the men are citizens, but the women are all prostitutes (slaves or foreigners). Citizen women appear in domestic settings, often accompanied by their female slaves.

Unfortunately, little is left of the large-scale paintings of mythological and patriotic subjects that adorned temples and other public buildings. Some of these must have been "tourist attractions," since the artists who painted them were mentioned centuries later. On the other hand, some monumental (life-size or larger) stone and bronze statues have survived. It was from the Egyptians that the Archaic Greeks learned the techniques of making large freestanding sculptures. Most Greek Archaic statues are in the form of either a naked "young male"(*kouros*) or a clothed "young maiden" (*korē*). Gradually, sculptors departed from the rigidly stylized, static Egyptian model towards a more naturalistic representation of the human body.

The architecture of the Archaic period still centered on religious buildings, the monumental temple and (beginning in the sixth century) smaller edifices, such as the "treasuries," which housed dedications to the gods. A big advance in temple architecture occurred around the middle of the seventh century, when limestone and marble replaced mud brick and wood. Here again, the Greeks were indebted to the Egyptians from whom they learned the engineering skills necessary for handling huge stone blocks. By the early sixth century Greek temples were beginning to look much as they would for the next five hundred years. As other stone buildings were added in the sixth century, all the capital poleis (except Sparta) began to resemble true urban centers. Most construction was in and around the *agora*, "the gathering place," a large open space at or near the center of the city. The agora became the marketplace and public space of the city and therefore of the whole polis. It was the place where male citizens congregated to do business, gossip, and make political deals. Market stalls were sheltered in shaded colonnades called stoas. Official buildings, such as the council house, distinguished the agora as the state center; sanctuaries, fountain houses, and public monuments gave it grace and dignity.

Figure 3.4. Statue of an Egyptian nobleman (early seventh century BC).

Figure 3.5. Marble kouros from Attica (c. 600 BC). The statue imitates the stylized stance of Egyptian sculpture.

Figure 3.6. This marble kouros (c. 510–500 BC), was set atop the grave of Aristodikos in Attica; it shows the growth of naturalism in sculpture.

Figure 3.7. Late Archaic kore from the acropolis of Athens (c. 490 BC), dedicated by Euthydikos.

Figure 3.8. Relief sculpture from the Siphnian Treasury at Delphi (c. 530–525 BC) depicting the Battle of the Gods and the Giants. Apollo and Artemis equipped as archers are striding into battle (left) against the Giants (equipped as contemporary hoplites).

Lyric Poetry

Although heroic epics continued to be produced during the Archaic period, most talented poets preferred to express themselves in other genres, which we lump together under the rubric of "lyric poetry." Indeed the seventh and sixth centuries BC are often referred to as the "lyric age" of Greece. Only a tiny fraction of all the verses composed then are extant today, much of them in fragmentary form, yet what we have provides an ample enough doorway into the thought and concerns of the Archaic Greeks.

The roots of lyric poetry extend far back in time to folk songs created orally for special occasions, such as harvests, weddings, funerals, and religious celebrations. With the advent of writing, songs could now be preserved and circulated. Some kinds of poems were performed to the accompaniment of a lyre (*lyra*; hence the name "lyric"), others to a flutelike instrument (*aulos*). The main division within the genre of lyric, however, was between poems performed by an individual (solo song) and choral poetry, performed by a chorus of young men or women, who sang as they danced to the music of the aulos or a stringed instrument. Solo poetry could be presented before large public audiences or small private gatherings of upper-class males at a drinking party (*symposion*). Choral odes might run to several hundred lines, solo poems were usually much shorter, sometimes just a few lines.

Choral poetry was civic and integrative; the chorus retold the old myths of the polis, paid homage to its gods, and expressed patriotic pride. Most solo poetry, on the other hand, was very personal in both attitude and tone. Solo poets sang about friendship and betrayal, sexual love, old age and death, politics, war, and morality. The tone could be serious or lighthearted, bitter or contemplative; the language elevated or obscene. Much solo lyric was what we would call social commentary. Almost all the lyric poets were of the upper class; their stance, however, was often critical of the aristocrats' elitist ideology. Although we have fragments from about two dozen lyric poets of this period, we can sample only a few of them here. Other Archaic poets such as the Spartan Alcman, the Athenian Solon, and Simonides of Ceos we shall meet in later chapters.

Some Lyric Poets

Archilochus of Paros (early seventh century), represents himself as both a soldier of fortune and an inspired poet. He writes of drinking bouts, his sex life, his comrades and enemies, battles and shipwrecks. He delights in skewering pretentiousness.

> I don't like a general who is big and walks with a swagger,
> or who glories in his curly hair and shaves off his moustache.
> Give me a man who's little, bandy-legged,
> feet firm on the ground, full of heart.
>
> (fr. 114 West)

The Spartans found these next couplets—which mock the ideal of heroic self-sacrifice—so outrageous that they forbade the recitation of Archilochus' poetry at Sparta.

> Well, some Thracian is enjoying the shield which I left—I
>   didn't want to, and it was a perfectly good one—beside a bush.
> But I saved myself. What do I care about that shield?
>   To hell with it; I'll get another one just as good.
>
> (fr. 5 West)

Some lyric poets also derided aristocratic display of luxury. For example, the philosopher-poet Xenophanes (c. 550 BC) censured the elite of his native Colophon who went to the assembly in their all-purple cloaks, "glorying in their well-dressed long hair, drenched with the perfume of elaborate scents" (fr. 3 West). Hipponax of Ephesus (late sixth century) took a more cynical approach toward wealth. He adopted the persona of an urban hustler, always broke and engaging in drunken brawls and escapades. He revels in the low life of the city and even makes fun of his poverty. "Ploutos (the god of wealth)," he says, "never came to my house—for he's quite blind—and said to me, 'Hipponax, I'm giving you thirty minas of silver, and lots else besides.' No, he's too feeble-witted" (fr. 36 West). There are also voices that sound Hesiodic, promoting the commonsense values held by ordinary citizens of moderate means. A collection of homespun maxims, attributed to Phocylides of Miletus, is made up of sayings such as, "Many things are best in the middle; I want to be middle (*mesos*) in the *polis*"; and "What good is noble birth for those who lack grace in words and counsel?"

Most of the surviving poetry, however, appeals more openly to an audience that has wealth and leisure. Much of it was composed specifically for recitation at drinking parties. Partisan politics was naturally a favorite topic. But just as often symposiastic poetry celebrates the pleasures of wine and love (both heterosexual and homosexual) and laments the sad necessity that these joys must fade with old age. This poem by the seventh-century Ionian poet Mimnermus is typical:

> What life is there apart from Golden Aphrodite?
> > What joy can there be? May I die when I
> No longer care for secret love and tender gifts
> > and bed, the alluring blossoms of youth for men
> and women too. And when miserable old age
> > comes on that makes a man both ugly and useless,
> then troublesome worries forever wear and tear at his wits,
> > nor can he enjoy the sight of the sun's rays.
> Boys find him hateful, women contemptible.
> > So sorrowful a thing has the god made old age.
> > > (fr. 1 West; Fowler 1992, adapted)

Similar in style and tone is Ibycus (mid-sixth century) from Rhegium in Italy, who spent some years in Samos under the patronage of the tyrant Polycrates. Ibycus wrote long choral narratives on traditional epic and mythological themes, but he was most famous in antiquity for his homoerotic poetry, full of sensuous imagery. In one poem, Eros ("Love") comes like the north wind from Thrace, and with "parching madness, dark and fearless, shakes me to the bottom of my heart with his might" (fr. 286 Page). In another poem, on falling in love late in life, he compares himself to an old champion racehorse that unwillingly drags his chariot to the contest (fr. 386 Page).

Sappho (late seventh century) is the only known woman poet from the Archaic period, in fact, one of the few in all of ancient Greek literature (women were not encouraged to write). Born into a prominent aristocratic family from Mytilene on the island of Lesbos, Sappho was greatly admired throughout antiquity; later critics listed her among the top nine lyric poets, and hailed her as the "tenth Muse." Sappho appears to have been the leader of a close-knit circle of young upper-class women in Lesbos (hence the modern term "lesbian"), who shared their lives for a brief period before marriage. The little that has survived of her poetry is mostly solo song, highly personal in tone, whose main theme is erotic love between women. In addition to solo poetry, Sappho wrote weddings songs (*epithalamia*) to be performed by choruses of young girls.

Document 3.3. Nine "books" (i.e., papyrus rolls) of Sappho's poetry were collected in the Alexandrian period, of which only one complete poem survives, along with portions of poems. Here is a selection of shorter fragments.

"I simply wish to die."
Weeping she left me
and said this too:
"We've suffered terribly,
Sappho, I leave you against my will."
I answered, go happily
and remember me,
you know how we cared for you,
if not, let me remind you
. . . the lovely times we shared . . . (fr. 94 L-P)

I have a beautiful child, her form
like a golden flower, beloved Kleis,
whom I would not trade for all of Lydia
or lovely. . . . (fr. 132 L-P)

Evening Star who gathers everything
shining dawn scattered—
you bring the sheep and the goats,
you bring the child back to its mother. (fr. 104 L-P)

Translated by Diane J. Rayor, *Sappho's Lyre.*
Berkeley: University of California Press, 1991, pp. 60, 72, 74.

One of Sappho's fellow aristocrats, Alcaeus, also achieved lasting fame as a poet. Like the other symposiastic poets, he wrote of love and wine and the myths of old, but he was most famous for his political poems. Alcaeus puts us in the center of the complicated power relations among the aristocratic factions in Mytilene: the political deals and betrayals, the partisan hatreds and violence, which were wracking the polis.

The largest chunk of symposiastic poetry that we have is a compilation of fourteen hundred lines of poetry all attributed to Theognis of Megara (mid-sixth century), but actually containing poems written by a number of different authors, from the late seventh to the early fifth century. In a stridently elitist tone Theognis vilifies the base-born kakoi while singing the praises of the high-born agathoi. The poet's contempt for nonnoble citizens—whom he deems innately incapable of achieving excellence—reflects the frustration of the minority elite as they watched their power and privilege being eroded while the non-elite were making political and economic gains. Aristocratic resentment over their reversal of fortune comes through in verses such as these (addressed to the young lover of Theognis):

> Cyrnus, those who were *agathoi* once are now *kakoi*, and those who were *kakoi* before are now *agathoi*. Who could bear seeing this, the *agathoi* dishonored and the *kakoi* getting honor?
>
> (*Theognidea* 1109–1112)

Although aristocrats would continue to proclaim their natural right to rule the state, in the end they would find themselves helpless to halt the movement toward political equality.

Philosophy and Science

The sixth century saw the beginning of philosophy (literally "the love of wisdom"). The early Greek philosophers—who may have been the first to write in prose—are called the Presocratics, that is, the thinkers who lived before Socrates (c. 469–399 BC) and his disciple, Plato. Plato (c. 429–347) set the course that Western philosophical thought would follow up to today; the Presocratics were primarily concerned with the structure and development of the physical universe, the cosmos (*kosmos*).

The study of astronomy and mathematics had flourished in Mesopotamia since the early second millennium, and the earliest Presocratics, who were from Miletus in Ionia, built upon the achievements of their eastern neighbors. Greeks had always studied the night sky, of course. They named the planets, stars, and star groups after their gods and characters in their myths, like Orion the hunter and the girls he pursued and never caught, the Pleiades. Basic knowledge of the celestial motions had always been essential in daily life: In Hesiod's *Works and Days*, the rising and setting of the constellations tell the farmer the proper time to begin his various seasonal chores. Sailors, too, navigated by the stars and planets. What the Presocratics introduced to the Greeks was "scientific" astronomy. Thales of Miletus, for example, was said to have predicted the solar eclipse of 585 BC, and his fellow Milesian, Anaximander, was credited with drawing a plan of the heavens (as well as the first geographical map).

The Milesians were also the first to abandon mythical-religious explanations for the origins of the universe and instead to seek purely physical causes. Thales theorized that the origin of all matter was water (for it could be transformed into both gas and solid forms), and that the earth was flat and floated on water. In contrast, Anaximander called the original principle "The Boundless," or "The Indefinite," a limitless entity that governs the material world, harmonizing such opposites as wet and dry and cold and hot. He postulated that the earliest creatures arose out of the sea from slime warmed by the sun's heat. Another Milesian, Anaximenes, thought that everything had evolved from air: It became fire when it was rarefied, could change to wind and cloud, and when condensed was transformed into solid substances. Like Thales, Anaximenes believed that the earth was flat, but he thought that it floated on air.

Pythagoras, one of the most influential cosmologists, is familiar to us from the geometric theorem that still bears his name. Around 531 BC he left his birthplace Samos because of the tyranny of Polycrates and settled in southern Italy with a group of disciples, both male and female. The doctrines of the Pythagoreans combined mysticism (they believed in the transmigration of the soul), political theory, cosmology, and mathematics. Pythagoras taught that arithmetic was the key to understanding the universe. He postulated that the earth was a sphere in the center of a series of hollow spheres. The stars were fixed on the outer spherical shell, and the planets on smaller shells within. The movements of the celestial spheres, dictated by strict arithmetical ratios, gave the universe a musical harmony (which, it was said, he alone could hear).

The ideas of Xenophanes of Colophon (c. 550 BC) about the development of the cosmos were based more on personal observation. For example, when he noticed fossil imprints of marine life and seaweed in three different locations inland, he theorized that they were produced when the earth was covered with the mud created by the primal mixture of seawater and earth. We have fragments of his poems in which he attacks conventional religious and ethical beliefs.

Document 3.4.

Mortals made their gods, and furnished them
with their own body, voice, and garments.
If a horse or lion or a slow ox
had agile hands for paint and sculpture,
the horse would make his god a horse,
the ox would sculpt an ox.

Our gods have flat noses and black skins
say the Ethiopians. The Thracians say
our gods have red hair and hazel eyes.

Xenophanes fr. 12–14 Diehl; translated by Willis Barnstone,
Greek Lyric Poetry. New York: Schocken, 1972, p. 131, adapted.

The writings of the early Greek scientists were circulated all around the Greek world and they freely criticized each other's theories. Heraclitus of Ephesus (late sixth century), for example, rejected Pythagoras' notion of an orderly and regulated cosmos, maintaining instead that everything was constantly changing like a river: You can not step into the same river twice. To reach understanding of this process of change, we must learn the hidden principle, which he calls "logos." For the world is not what it appears to be. The same idea was at the core of Parmenides' (early fifth century) attempt to analyze what it means to say that something is or exists. According to Parmenides, all you can say and think is that "being" exists but that "nonbeing" does not exist. Change is logically impossible because if something changes it is no longer the same and does not exist. Such questions as these, first posed by the Presocratics, would preoccupy philosophers for the rest of antiquity: What do we mean when we say that something exists, and what is the relationship between the world as we perceive it through our senses and what it "really" is?

PANHELLENIC INSTITUTIONS

The ease with which poets, thinkers, artists, and ideas moved from city to city shows how culturally unified the Greek world was even as it remained politically divided. The gatherings at Panhellenic sanctuaries played a prominent part in forging a common Hellenic identity, as ever greater numbers came to worship, consult oracles, and attend musical and athletic competitions.

The oracle of Apollo at Delphi drew Greeks and non-Greeks alike from all over the Mediterranean. For a fairly hefty fee individuals could consult Apollo for prophetic advice on marriage, careers, voyages, etc. Poleis too sought the god's guidance and sanction on serious matters of state, such as colonizing, religion, and laws. Apollo responded through a priestess, called the Pythia, who, in a self-induced trance, divulged his messages. The Pythia's incoherent utterances were turned into verses (often ambiguous in meaning) by "interpreters" (*prophētai*). Because so many tyrants, foreign kings, and aristocratic leaders consulted the oracle, the sanctuary at Delphi became a storehouse of information about political conditions across the Mediterranean world.

The greatest attraction, however, was the sanctuary of Zeus at Olympia. By the end of the seventh century the quadrennial games in Zeus' honor—inaugurated, according to tradition, in 776 BC—were drawing spectators and contestants from the entire Greek world. The success of the Olympics (the games held at Olympia) soon spawned three new Panhellenic athletic festivals: in honor of Apollo at Delphi (582 BC), for Poseidon at Isthmia near Corinth (581), and for Zeus at Nemea in Argolis (573). These festivals were integrated into the four-year Olympiad to form an athletic "circuit," staggered so that there would be one major game each year, two in alternate years, with the Olympics remaining the premier event. Other Panhellenic festivals modeled on the Olympic games were inaugurated at Athens, Thebes, and elsewhere during the sixth century.

The Panhellenic contests and rituals brought Greeks together in peaceful celebration. For the month in which the Olympic games were held, poleis observed a sacred truce banning warfare and channeled their rivalries instead into the athletic contests, much as states do today. The sacred precincts themselves became places for poleis to flaunt their wealth and achievements with costly dedications of statuary and marble "treasuries," commemorating both athletic and military victories. Yet the games featured no team events, just matches among individuals. The contestants showed off their speed, strength, dexterity, and endurance, the very same qualities required of Homer's heroes, whether on the battlefield or in athletic contests.

The main events at the Olympic games were the foot races, the most prestigious of which was the short sprint, called the stade (*stadion*, hence stadium) a distance of about 210 yards. In this contest alone—at a separate festival honoring Hera—maidens participated; their course was one-sixth shorter than the men's stade. The young women did not race completely nude, as the males did, but their tunics barely reached the knees and covered only one side of the chest.

Male athletes vied in a variety of events, including wrestling, boxing, and the *pankration*, a vicious combination of boxing and wrestling with no holds barred except biting and eye gouging. In the *pentathlon* opponents competed in five events: the stade, javelin and discus throws, the long jump, and wrestling. In these events the contestants competed in the nude. Most spectacular of all was the four-horse chariot race, a contest dating back to the Late Bronze Age. (The wealthy owner of the horses and chariot, not the charioteer, was declared the winner.) A number of festivals also featured competitions in choral and solo poetry and in instrumental performances.

At the four principal games the prizes were just honorific tokens, wreaths of foliage: at Olympia olive leaves, at Delphi laurel, at Nemea wild celery, and at Isthmia pine. (The rewards at the less notable festivals were more substantial.) On their return home from a major festival, however, victors could expect triumphal processions, statues in the agora, and even prizes of money.

RELATIONS AMONG STATES

With the emergence of the city-states, the external problem of coexistence became much more complicated. What had been raids among neighboring communities turned into serous warfare. There were several reasons for the heightened tensions. As states began to run out of land, they attempted to extend their boundaries, and disputes often erupted over borderlands that had not required strict definition when populations were still small. Moreover, quarrels of mother-poleis were often taken up by their colonies, with new enmities arising among poleis hundreds of miles away. On the mainland territorial wars between poleis began as early as the late eighth century, when Chalcis and Eretria in Euboea fought over possession of the rich Lelantos River plain that lay between them. In this conflict (known as the Lelantine War), both sides were said to have had distant allies from much farther away—possibly indicating the involvement of rival colonial networks.

Interstate tensions were especially high in the Peloponnesus, which contained three of the major Greek city-states—Sparta, Argos, and Corinth. After their conquest of Messenia in the late eighth century, the Spartans warred against their rivals, the Argives, with some success, though they were badly beaten by them in 669 BC in a battle at Hysiae in Argolis. The Argives in the meantime were trying to expand their own land holdings and influence within the Peloponnesus, particularly around Corinth; the Corinthians themselves were fighting over territory with their smaller neighbors, Megara and Sicyon. Such costly and deadly squabbles over land continued in the Peloponnesus until the middle of the sixth century, when the Spartans began using diplomacy and forming alliances to maintain their supremacy in southern Greece.

In the sixth century the Greek states began in earnest to establish formal mechanisms for avoiding war. Most of these cooperative institutions had their genesis in the prestate period, but it was not until the later Archaic Age that they were refined and regularized. At the same time that formal means were being instituted, diplomatic relations were still being conducted much as they had been in the Dark Age. The tyrants especially conducted foreign policy this way, making pacts of friendship or marriage alliances with other tyrants or with the top aristocrats. For example, Periander (c. 627–587), who succeeded his father Cypselus as tyrant of Corinth, developed a political friendship with Thrasybulus, tyrant of Miletus, ending an old enmity between the two poleis going back to the Lelantine War. The pact aided both Corinthian traders in Egypt and the Black Sea and Milesian traders in the West. Periander also arbitrated a dispute between Athens and Mytilene over control of Sigeum, an important way station on the route to the Black Sea.

Temporary military alliances are as old as war. In the Archaic period they became more formal and longer lasting. States began to make written treaties, pledging friendship and cessation of aggression for a stipulated time. The earliest formal pact we know of comes from the polis of Sybaris in southern Italy (c. 550 BC). An inscription reads: "The Sybarites and their allies and the Serdaioi made an agreement for friendship, faithful and without guile, for ever. Guarantors: Zeus, Apollo, and the other gods, and the *polis* of Poseidonia" (Meiggs and Lewis, 1989, p. 10). There were also multistate alliances or leagues. One such was the amphictyony or "association of neighbors," whereby several poleis were bound together by a common religious cult. Although an amphictyony could not prevent its members from going to war, the cooperating states might pledge not to destroy each other's cities or cut off their water supply.

In the Archaic period, the *ethnē* too began to form loose unions among their separate towns and villages. The vast ethnos of Thessaly, a region rich in land and people, formed one of the most successful federations. Its unity made Thessaly the major power of northern Greece for a period of time in the sixth century, until the confederacy was weakened by quarrels among the local chiefs. Under pressure from the Thessalian confederacy, the ethnos of the Phocians developed a federal union of their own, complete with their own federation coinage and army. And under the pressure from both the Thessalians and the Athenians, the rival poleis of Boeotia formed a league under the leadership of Thebes, which too proved fractious and unstable, because of opposition to Theban hegemony.

It would be an overstatement to say that the polis-system was responsible for the many advances and achievements of the Archaic Age, but it certainly spurred them along. Greeks, no matter where they lived in the wide Mediterranean world, shared in a common culture, what the historian Herodotus called *to hellēnikon,* "the Greek thing." Still, they would never be a single nation, but rather hundreds of independent city-states, unfettered by an overarching government. By the end of the Archaic Age the two most powerful states were Sparta and Athens. It is to Sparta that we now turn.

TRANSLATIONS

Fowler, Barbara Hughes. 1992. *Archaic Greek Poetry*. Madison: University of Wisconsin Press.

Rackham, H. 1977. *Aristotle: Politics*. Loeb Classical Library. Cambridge, MA and London: Harvard University Press.

SUGGESTED READINGS

Andrewes, A. 1956. *The Greek Tyrants*. New York: Harper & Row. Although written almost a half century ago, it remains a standard introduction to the *tyrannoi*.

Boardman, John. 1973. *The Greeks Overseas: Their Early Colonies and Trade*. Baltimore: Penguin. An excellent introduction, with many illustrations, to Greek colonization and the economic and cultural interactions between the Greeks and their neighbors in other lands.

Hanson, Victor Davis. 1995. *The Other Greeks: The Family Farm and the Agrarian Roots of Western Civilization*. New York: The Free Press. A wide-ranging, meticulously detailed study of the "yeoman" farmer-hoplite and his role in the formation of the city-state.

Murray, Oswyn. 1993. *Early Greece*. 2nd ed. Cambridge, MA: Harvard University Press. An important contribution to the understanding of Greek society and culture in the early polis from the end of the Dark Age to the Persian Wars.

Osborne, Robin. 1996. *Greece in the Making 1200–479 BC*. London and New York: Routledge. This book, well illustrated, is a valuable compendium of new information and the latest scholarly research covering the periods from the early Dark Age to the Classical.

Osborne, Robin. 1998. *Archaic and Classical Greek Art*. (Oxford History of Art). New York: Oxford University Press. Splendidly illustrated and engagingly written, this volume places Archaic and Classical art in their social and cultural contexts.

Snodgrass, Anthony. 1980. *Archaic Greece. The Age of Experiment*. Berkeley and Los Angeles: University of California Press. The first major book on Archaic Greece written by an archaeologist, and an important reappraisal of the importance of the Archaic period to Greek history.

Starr, Chester G. 1986. *Individual and Community: The Rise of the Polis 800–500 B.C.* A brief, but thorough, analysis of the emergence of the city-state form of polity.

Tandy, David W. and Walter C. Neale (eds.). 1996. *Hesiod's* Works and Days. *A Translation and Commentary for the Social Sciences*. Berkeley and Los Angeles: University of California Press. A very useful commentary that looks at Hesiod's world through the perspectives of sociologists, anthropologists, and social economists.

4

SPARTA

Admired in peace and dreaded in war, for much of the Archaic and Classical periods Sparta was the most powerful city in the Greek world. It was also different from other *poleis*. To be sure, the Spartans shared many basic institutions with other Greeks: their society was patriarchal and polytheistic, servile labor played a key role, agriculture formed the basis of the economy, law was revered and martial valor prized. Nonetheless, Sparta was unique in many important ways. No other Greek state ever defined its goals as clearly as Sparta or expended so much effort in trying to attain them. While the intrusion of the state into the lives of individuals was substantial in all Greek states, no state surpassed Sparta in the invasive role it played in daily life. Spartans took enormous pride in their *polis,* and other Greeks were impressed by the patriotism and selflessness the Spartan system entailed. The Spartans' denial of individuality fostered a powerful sense of belonging that other Greeks envied, and Sparta continues to cast a spell over historians, philosophers, feminists, and political scientists.

Despite the interest the Spartans sparked in Greek intellectuals, it is difficult to write about Sparta and its surrounding territory, Laconia. The problem is not lack of sources; the volume of ancient writing on Sparta is large. The difficulty lies in the fact that many of our sources are tainted by their acceptance of an idealized image of Sparta that historians call the "Spartan mirage." This idea of Sparta was a vision of an egalitarian and orderly society characterized by patriotism, courage in battle, and tolerance for deprivation.

THE DARK AGE AND THE ARCHAIC PERIOD

Laconia was an important center in the Bronze Age. Like much of the rest of Greece, Laconia experienced a sharp drop in population at the end of the Mycenaean period. Sometime in the tenth century BC Dorian newcomers entered the territory. By the eighth century BC trends similar to those documented elsewhere in Greece had begun to appear in Laconia as well. New villages were founded as population gradually increased, and four of those villages near the Eurotas

Figure 4.1. Peloponnesus.

River in the center of the Laconian plain united to form the city of Sparta. Early in the eighth century the town of Amyclae, 3 miles from the original four villages, was added to the city. Thus the Spartan polis was the city center plus the territory of the plain. Increased contacts with the rest of Greece were reflected in the emergence of a distinctive Spartan version of geometric art.

Like other early Greek poleis, Sparta (or Lacedaemon, as it was often called in antiquity) began to experience difficulties in satisfying its needs from its own territory. Sparta was located inland, with the nearest port, Gythium, 27 miles to the south. This atypical location encouraged the city to seek a novel solution to the need for land to feed a growing population, a solution that would determine the course of Spartan development. Unlike other Greek cities, which repeatedly founded colonies overseas in an effort to alleviate the pressure on resources caused by population expansion, the Spartans founded only one colony, Taras in southern Italy. Instead of looking abroad for a solution to their difficulties, the Spartans sought a military answer to their problem through conquest of their neighbors, and by the end of the eighth century, they had gained control of the plain of Laconia.

Helots and the Social Hierarchy

To ensure control of the Laconian plain, its inhabitants were reduced to the status of helots, hereditary subjects of the Spartan state. The rest of the inhabitants of Laconia, who occupied the area surrounding the city of Sparta, became *perioikoi* ("those who dwell around [Sparta]," or "neighbors"). Unlike the helots, who were in essence slaves, the perioikoi remained free. Although they were obligated to serve in the army, they were not permitted to participate in the government. They did enjoy some local autonomy, however, and in many ways lived like the majority of Greeks who were not Spartans, working as homemakers, farmers, craftsmen, and merchants. Thus they constituted an essential part of the Spartan economic system.

The Spartans also coveted the fertile Messenian lowlands, and at some time in the third quarter of the eighth century they invaded Messenia, beginning what modern historians call the First Messenian War. According to tradition the war lasted twenty years and ended about 720 BC. Messenia became subject to Sparta, and like the Laconians, some of the Messenians became perioikoi, but most became helots, bound to their land and obliged to work it for their Spartan masters with no consolation but the promise that they would not be sold out of Messenia. The Spartan poet Tyrtaeus gloatingly described them as "burdened like asses, bringing to their masters under harsh compulsion one half . . . of the fruits of the land" (fr. 6 West).

The conquest of Laconia and Messenia made Sparta one of the largest of Greek states, controlling a territory of over 3000 square miles (about three times the size of the Athenian state). Sparta was also one of the richest states. Spartan pottery and metalwork were among the finest in Greece. The beauty of Spartan women was widely celebrated, and Sparta's female choruses were famous. A vivid impression of the wealth and elegance of Spartan life is provided by a few surviving fragments of the works of the seventh-century BC poet Alcman, whose hymns, written for choruses of unmarried Spartan girls to sing on ceremonial occasions, mention luxury items including racehorses, purple textiles, and gold jewelry in the shape of serpents.

> There is no abundance of purple sufficient to protect us, nor our
> speckled serpent bracelet of solid gold, nor our Lydian cap, adornment for tender-eyed girls, nor Nanno's hair, (70) nor Areta who
> looks like a goddess, nor Thylacis and Cleesithera. Nor will you go
> to Ainesimbrota's and say "I wish Astaphis were mine," and (75) "I
> wish Philylla would look at me, and Demareta, and lovely
> Vianthemis"—no, it is Hagesichora who exhausts me with love.
>
> (fr. 1.65–78 Alcman; Pomeroy 2002)

Spartan prosperity, however, rested on insecure foundations. Civil unrest in the late eighth and early seventh centuries was avoided by exiling dissidents, who founded Sparta's only colony, Taras. The growing desperation of the Messenians was a more serious threat. Greek political theorists considered it a mistake to enslave people in their own home territory, especially when the enslaved significantly outnumbered their masters, as the Messenians did the Spartans. Not surprisingly, the Messenians rebelled in the wake of a major Spartan military defeat by the Argives at the Battle of Hysiae in 669 BC.

As is true of the First Messenian War, little is known of the details of the Second Messenian War. The poems Tyrtaeus wrote celebrating Spartan courage in the war became Sparta's classics. The following excerpt is from the same poem that is quoted in Chapter Three:

> Here is a man who proves himself to be valiant in war.
> With a sudden rush he turns to fight the rugged battalions
> of the enemy, and sustains the beating waves of assault.
> And he who so falls among the champions and loses his sweet life,
> so blessing with honor his city, his father, and all his people,
> with wounds in his chest, where the spear that he was facing has
>   transfixed
> that massive guard of his shield, and gone through his breastplate
>   as well,
> why, such a man is lamented alike by the young and the elders,
> and all his city goes into mourning and grieves for his loss.
>
> (Tyrtaeus fr. 9 Diehl; Lattimore 1960)

In the end Sparta prevailed and the Messenians had no choice but to resign themselves to the rigors of their former helot status.

The Second Messenian War had been a terrifying revelation of the potential risks of the helot system. As a result of the conquest of neighboring regions the helots outnumbered Spartan citizens by a ratio that may have been seven to one or even higher. The Spartans were forced to find a way to preserve their domination over their helots. The solution they found was drastic, and its implementation gradually transformed Sparta and eventually created the unique regimented society known to us from the Classical sources. Simply stated, the Spartans realized that if all potential hoplites could be trained to the highest degree of skill possible, Sparta would enjoy an overwhelming military advantage over its helots and other enemies. Therefore the Spartans reformed their institutions with a view toward achieving two goals: freeing male citizens from all but military obligations, and socializing them to accept the regimentation and discipline required of a Spartan soldier. Until the fourth century and the Hellenistic period, the Spartans were the only real professional soldiers. In effect they waged a perpetual war against the helots and were consequently always prepared to deploy their military force when necessary.

THE SPARTAN SYSTEM

Little is known about the actual development of the Spartan system. Greek historians followed Spartan tradition and ascribed its creation to Lycurgus, a shadowy figure who may or may not really have lived. Scholars today are agreed that many of the institutions whose creation Greeks ascribed to Lycurgus, such as men's dining groups, organization of the population by age cohorts, and the use of iron money, had, in fact, once existed in other Greek communities. These practices survived at Sparta because their place in Spartan life had been redefined to aid in the production of the ideal Spartan hoplite.

However this evolution occurred, the evidence indicates that the main features of the Spartan system were in place by the end of the seventh or the early sixth century BC. The Spartan regime may be called totalitarian, for it touched on almost every aspect of life, including those we in modern Western society consider private: how to wear our hair, the choice of whether and when to marry, the conditions of conjugal intercourse, and the decision whether to rear a child.

The Education and Upbringing of Boys

As the poetry of Tyrtaeus made plain, the Spartan ideal for a man was to be skilled and courageous in battle, neither to run away nor surrender but to stand his ground and give up his life for his city. Training was designed to produce men who conformed to this pattern alone. The Spartan was liable for military service to the age of sixty and needed to stay fit; hence he never was trained for any other profession or way of life. The educational system, like much else that was unique to Sparta, received legitimacy from the insistence that it was created by Lycurgus.

The process of creating invincible warriors began at birth, for the state took upon itself the right to determine a new baby's viability. Whereas other Greek poleis left the choice to the father, at Sparta officials appointed by the government examined the newborns. The vitality of male infants and their potential as soldiers determined whether they would be raised, or abandoned. (Female babies, apparently, were not subjected to official scrutiny, for their physical prowess did not directly affect the outcome of battles.) Fathers did not decide how to raise their children. Rather, all children received the same education under state supervision. Education in Sparta, as elsewhere, was organized by age groups: children, boys, youths (ephebes), young men, and adults. From the age of seven, boys left home to be trained in groups called "herds" according to principles designed to encourage conformity, obedience, group solidarity, and military skills.

The emphasis in the boys' education was not on reading and writing, but rather on practicing to endure hardships and to fend for themselves as would be necessary when they became hoplite soldiers. To toughen their feet, they went barefoot, and they often went naked as well. When they were twelve, their hair was cut short. They never wore a tunic and were each allocated only one cloak yearly to wear in all kinds of weather. Unlike the rest of the Greeks, who made war only in the summer, the Spartans were perpetually at war with the helots and therefore needed to be prepared to fight year round. Magistrates called ephors ("overseers") inspected the boys daily and examined them in the nude every ten days. The boys slept in groups on rough mats that they had made themselves. To develop cunning and self-reliance, they were encouraged to supplement their food rations by stealing. Whipping awaited anyone who revealed his lack of skill by getting caught.

From the ages of fourteen to twenty the ephebes performed their preliminary military service. At twenty they grew their hair long (unlike men in other parts of the Greek world) and shaved themselves in the distinctive Spartan style—a long beard and no mustache. Between ages twenty and thirty they were permitted to marry but had to continue to live with their army groups until the age of thirty.

Acceptance into a *syssition* ("dining group," "mess") was an essential stage in reaching adulthood. The Spartan man ate his meals with about fifteen members of his army group, an experience that fostered the loyalty and cooperativeness essential to successful hoplite warfare. Each member of the syssition was obliged to contribute a fixed quantity of food and drink. The *syssitia* (plural) were in some ways analogous to the *symposia* ("drinking parties") enjoyed by Greeks elsewhere, but the fact that the Spartan was purposely schooled to drink in moderation points to an important difference. Greeks usually mixed their wine with water. Helots, however, were forced to consume undiluted wine and to perform vulgar and ridiculous songs and dances to exemplify the consequences of lack of control. Young Spartans, who were invited to the syssitia as part of their education, were encouraged to laugh at the spectacle of the drunken helots. The lesson was a double one: From this experience youths were expected to learn both to be wary of drinking to excess—for inebriation could lead to death in conditions of perpetual warfare—and to view the helots as pathetic creatures, patently inferior to the Spartan soldiery.

Inevitably, the success rate in forging soldiers according to the prescribed mold was less than 100 percent. Though the harsh treatment of those perceived as cowards discouraged failure, some boys failed to develop as expected. Since martial valor offered the sole path to the honor and respect of one's peers, life was wretched for boys who were unable to cope with the rigors of military life. When cowards were identified, they were stigmatized and called "tremblers." Their ridiculous appearance announced their disgrace: They were obliged to wear cloaks with colored patches and to only partially shave their beards. Humiliated in public, they were despised even by their own kinsmen, whom they were believed to have dishonored. They could not hold public office, nor was it likely that anyone would marry them or their sisters, with the consequence that their family would die out and the eugenic goals of the state be well served.

Becoming a Spartan Woman

Sparta's military ethos had implications for females as well as males. Just as boys were brought up to become brave fighters, girls were raised to bear stalwart soldiers-to-be. Spartans were the only Greek women whose upbringing was prescribed by the state and who were educated at state expense. For example, unlike other Greek women, who spent most of their time indoors and were regularly given less food than men and no wine, Spartan females exercised outside, were well nourished, and drank wine as part of their daily diet. Childbearing was their only social obligation. Though, like all Greek women, they did know how to weave, they were free from the obligation to engage in any other form of domestic labor.

Specific lines of development were prescribed for Spartan girls much as they were for boys. The educational system for girls was also organized according to

Figure 4.2. Bronze statuette of a Spartan girl running, wearing a racing dress that exposes her right breast.

age classes. Girls were divided into the categories of children, young girls, maidens who had reached puberty, and married women. Hairstyles announced a woman's passage through the life cycle. As a maiden, she wore her hair long and loose; as a bride, her hair was cropped; as a married woman, her hair was covered. As with so much else in their way of life, Spartans ascribed the customary upbringing of Spartan girls to Lycurgus.

As is the case in many warlike societies, the perpetual absence of men on military duty created a division of labor in which women managed domestic affairs. Aristotle, writing in the fourth century BC and considering some four hundred years of Spartan history, complained that for this reason Spartan women enjoyed altogether too much freedom, power, and prestige. The constitution of Lycurgus, he believed, was flawed from the start because only men conformed to it, while women escaped its regulations. He was convinced that Spartan women indulged in "every kind of luxury and intemperance," promoting greed and an attendant degeneration of the Spartan ideal of equality among male citizens. He also maintained that the Spartans' freedom to bequeath their land as they wished and the size of dowries led to two-fifths of the land in his own time having fallen into the hands of women. Spartan daughters received as dowries one-half the amount of their parents' property that their brothers received as inheritance. (In contrast, at Athens daughters received approximately one-sixth the amount that their brothers inherited.) Yet Aristotle no doubt exaggerates when he complains that Sparta was ruled by women, for they had no share in the government. Clearly, however, their ownership and control of property gave Spartan women far more authority than their counterparts in the rest of Greece.

Sex and Marriage

As elsewhere in Greece, marriages in Sparta might or might not entail a close emotional attachment between husband and wife. The Spartan requirement that married men continue to live in barracks until the age of thirty meant that young couples did not live together even in peacetime.

According to Plutarch, Spartan marriages often took on a strikingly clandestine character that struck the ancients as worthy of comment.

> They used to marry by capture, not when the women were small or immature, but when they were in their prime and fully ripe for it. The so-called "bridesmaid" took the captured girl. She shaved her head to the scalp, then dressed her in a man's cloak and sandals, and laid her down alone on a mattress in the dark. The bridegroom, who was not drunk and thus not impotent, but was sober as always, having dined with his mess group, then would slip in, untie her belt, lift her, and carry her to the bed. After spending only a short time with her, he would depart discreetly so as to sleep wherever he usually did with the other young men. And he continued to do this thereafter. While spending the days with his contemporaries, and going to sleep with them, he would cautiously visit his bride in secret, embarrassed and fearful in case someone in the house might notice him. His bride at the same time was scheming and helping to plan how they might

meet each other unobserved at a suitable time. They did this not just for a short period, but for long enough that some might even have children before they saw their
own wives in the day. Such intercourse was not only an exercise in self-control and
moderation, but also meant that partners were fertile physically, always fresh for
love, and ready for intercourse rather than being satiated and impotent from un-
limited sexual activity. Moreover some lingering spark of desire and affection always remained in both.

(Plutarch, *Life of Lycurgus* 15.3–5; trans. Pomeroy 2002)

In addition to the secret marriage, other reported customs include the random
selection of spouses by cohorts of potential brides and bridegrooms groping in a
dark room. In a system of aristocratic endogamy (i.e., marriage within the group),
the haphazard selection of spouses is a symptom of equality, for one spouse is as
good as the next. Since the sole purpose of marriage is reproduction, the secret,
or trial, marriage permits the couple to find other spouses if their union proves
to be infertile. If these customs were ever practiced, they apparently had died out
by the Classical period. The absence of adultery at Sparta, however, continued to
evoke comment among non-Spartans. Xenophon also mentions a combination of
practices that satisfied both the private desires of individual women and men as
well as the state's eugenic goals and insatiable need for citizens:

If, however, it happened that an old man had a young wife—seeing that men of
that age guard their wives—he [Lycurgus] thought the opposite. He required the
elderly husband to bring in some man whose body and spirit he admired, in order to beget children. On the other hand, in case a man did not want to have intercourse with his wife but wanted children of whom he could be proud, he made
it legal for him to choose a woman who was the mother of a fine family and well-
born, and if he persuaded her husband, he produced children with her. Many
such arrangements developed. For the wives want to get possession of two oikoi,
and the husbands want to get brothers for their sons who will share their lineage
and power, but claim no part of the property.

(Xenophon, *Spartan Constitution* 1.7–10; Pomeroy 2002)

Homosexuality and Pederasty

Like other ancient Greeks, Spartans lacked the binary division modern society
tends to impose between people who are considered homosexual and those who
are viewed as heterosexual, and same-sex erotic relationships did not preclude
their participants entering into heterosexual marriages, with which the homosexual relationship might exist simultaneously. Ancient homosexuality differs from
the modern version in several respects. The origins of many same-sex relationships
lay in the educational system. Erotic relationships between members of the same
sex were considered potentially educational for both women and men as long as
the element of physical attraction was not primary. Single-sex education was the
norm in the Greek world, and older men and women often functioned as "teachers" or informal guides to younger members of society. The disapproval that attaches today to romantic connections between teachers and students or between

old and young would have puzzled the ancient Greeks, who viewed the erotic element in the teacher-pupil relationship as a constructive building block in the education of the young. The attraction of teachers to their youthful pupils was considered to have social utility, encouraging the enamored teacher to work hard at educating the student, who in turn was offered an inspiring role model in an older, wiser, more accomplished suitor. The pupils in question were generally in early adolescence. This pattern of same-sex relationships was evident not only in the context of education but in life as a whole. How much physical sexual activity actually was involved is unclear, since many Greek intellectuals who left written records of social customs tended to be embarrassed about sex and were eager to stress the cerebral element in same-sex romantic connections. We know less about the homoerotic bonds between women, but Plutarch in his *Life of Lycurgus* reported that "sexual relationships of this type were so highly valued that respectable women would in fact have love affairs with unmarried girls," and the erotic element in the songs of female choruses (like the poem of Alcman quoted previously) is not hidden.

For males and females alike, liaisons with members of the same sex provided much of the companionship, sexual pleasure, and sense of spiritual well-being that many people in modern Western society nowadays associate with marriage. Homosexuality was integrated into the system. The idealized model of the same-sex relationship involved an older person and an adolescent and consequently was time-limited. With boys it was considered inappropriate to continue the relationship after the teenager's beard began to grow. Nevertheless, some relationships did develop between companions of the same age and endured throughout life.

DEMOGRAPHY AND THE SPARTAN ECONOMY

By their conquests of Laconia and Messenia, the Spartans created a situation where they never constituted more than a small fraction—perhaps a twentieth—of the total population of their territory. Hence, as is often the case with ruling aristocracies, their numbers were never deemed to be sufficient. Furthermore, unlike other Greek states, at the very start the lack of trade and colonization limited the growth of Sparta's population, for it had no colonies to which it might sometime in the future export a population that could no longer be supported at home. Xenophobia also restricted Sparta's numbers. Unlike the Athenians, for example, at no time did Spartans marry foreigners, nor did they recruit large numbers of new citizens of non-Spartan origin, though the desperation occasioned by the long war with Athens during the fifth century known as the Peloponnesian War did move them to take some exceptional measures. In this emergency, they allowed some non-Spartiate boys living in Sparta to be trained for service in the Spartan army, freed some helots for military service, and appointed perioikoi to some positions of command. Some of these practices continued after the end of the war and into the Hellenistic period when the population problem was even more acute.

Sparta's Shrinking Population

The Spartan lifestyle exacerbated the population decline. Sparta was the only Greek state in which male infanticide was institutionalized. Moreover, many deaths can be explained by the Spartan soldier's obligation to stand his ground and give his life for his country, rather than surrender. This ideal was reinforced by peer pressure, epitomized by statements attributed to Spartan women such as that of the mother who told her son as she handed him his shield to come home "either with this or on this." (Spartan soldiers who were not buried on the battlefield were carried home on their shields.)

The reduction in the number of Spartans was gradual. In addition to the high rate of infant and juvenile mortality found throughout the ancient world, the Spartan problem was aggravated by their unusual marriage practices. Women married only several years after they became fertile; opportunities for conjugal intercourse were limited; husbands were continuously absent at war or sleeping with their army groups when wives were in their peak childbearing years; and both sexes engaged in a certain amount of homosexual, nonprocreative sex. As if these obstacles to maintaining the population were not sufficient, some women also declined to bear children. The risks of maternity were considered equal to those soldiers faced on the battlefield: The only Spartans who earned the distinction of having their names inscribed on tombstones were those who had died in childbirth or in battle. Spartans, like other Greek women, probably had access to contraceptives including the use of herbs, douches of vinegar or water, and mechanical barriers made of wads of wool soaked in honey or olive oil. Control over fertility is often indicative of high status for women, and Aristotle may have been correct in contending that Spartan women controlled domestic matters, managing households that constituted a significant portion of the family's fortune.

Sparta's population problem was also accelerated at times by natural disaster, economic problems, and the emigration of men. There were nine thousand male Spartans in the Archaic period. In 479 there were eight thousand male citizens, five thousand of whom served at the battle of Plataea. There, according to Herodotus, each Spartan hoplite was accompanied by seven helots who served as light armed forces and performed the menial jobs. Though these figures are probably not exact, they do give an idea of the proportion of Spartans to helots in the army. In 330 Aristotle reckoned the number of Spartans at one thousand. By 244 there were no more than seven hundred. By Roman times very few Spartans were left to perform their hoary rituals and tests of endurance for tourists. We have no exact information either on the absolute number of female Spartans or on their numbers relative to the number of males.

Helots and the Spartan System

The Spartan economic system was designed to enable citizens to devote all their time and energy to the defense and welfare of the polis. The state saw to it that they had everything they needed as measured by a standard of austerity, not luxury.

Though the perioikoi, who conducted business with the rest of the Greek world, used silver and gold coins, Spartans themselves were permitted to use only iron money: These flat bars or cakes made of iron had originally been used throughout Greece before the invention of coinage. The Spartans used iron until the end of the fifth century, when there was a vast influx of gold and silver after their victory in the Peloponnesian War, though they did not mint their own coins until the Hellenistic period.

The goal for men was economic equality, which was, in reality, a minimum income for all that would allow them to follow the Spartan way of life. The Spartans referred to themselves as *homoioi* ("peers," or "men of equal status"). As we shall see below, however, economic equality was an illusory ideal. When Messenia was conquered, the territory was divided up into nine thousand equal *klēroi*. At birth, each boy was allocated a share of this land by the state, and a family of helots came with the land. The institution of helotry was inextricably tied up with the Spartan system, essential as it was to releasing Spartan men and women from the need to produce or purchase their food.

The owner of each *klēros* was entitled to receive a specified amount of produce annually from the helots who worked it. The helots' burden seems to have varied over the centuries. Tyrtaeus describes them as sharecroppers, forced to give their masters half their yield, but Plutarch mentions a fixed rent of 70 bushels of barley for each Spartan man and 12 for his wife, in addition to oil and wine. Though they were not free, helots were not the same as slaves elsewhere in Greece. They belonged to the state, not to individuals. They lived in stable family groups on a farm assigned to them, and could not be sold abroad. Aside from the obligation to provide sustenance for the owner of the plot of land, to serve as auxiliaries in the army, and to mourn at the death of kings and magistrates, the helots had no specific obligations to their masters. They were permitted to sell excess crops in the market and to accumulate some money in that way.

So that they should never forget that they were enslaved, the helots were subjected to an annual beating. They were also obliged to wear a primitive and humiliating costume that identified them immediately, including animal skins and a leather cap. Submitting to the rule of others but living in their own territory, the helots did not lose their desire for freedom. The service they performed in the Spartan army, moreover, provided them with useful knowledge in their ongoing struggle against their masters. In 464 some of them took advantage of the earthquake that had devastated Sparta and staged a rebellion at Ithome that lasted ten years. In 455 the Spartans agreed to let the rebels depart on condition that they should never return to the Peloponnesus. The Athenians settled many of them at Naupactus, on the northern side of the Corinthian Gulf. Finally, in 369, Messenia regained its independence with the aid of Thebes and other Boeotian enemies of Sparta.

The system of helotry distinguished Sparta sharply from other Greek states, making it the only polis with an economic system totally dependent upon geographical and social distance between landowners and workers on the land. Despite the prevalence of slavery in the Greek world, nowhere else was the labor of the lowest class so essential to survival. Furthermore, though agriculture remained the basis of the domestic economy throughout the Greek world, other sources of gaining a livelihood were customarily developed; at Sparta alone among major states, agriculture remained the sole basis of the citizens' economy.

The Spartan system was a remarkably successful experiment in what is now called social engineering. To be sure, despite the ideology of equality among citizens that was associated with their polis, disparities of wealth did not disappear. Except for the members of the royal family and the tiny group elected to the Council of Elders, however, the role played by differential wealth in determining status and power was far smaller in Sparta than in other Greek poleis. The Spartans called themselves the "Men of Equal Status" for good reason. Rich or poor, they all had survived the same judgment at birth, they had endured the same training, and they wore the same uniform and fought side by side with the same weapons in the phalanx.

SPARTAN GOVERNMENT

Like Sparta's social and educational system, its government was much admired by contemporaries. It consisted of monarchical, oligarchical, and democratic elements: These constituted the kind of system political theorists like Aristotle called a mixed constitution. Spartan conservatism made for a reluctance to abandon traditional institutions like monarchy and the council of elders when other Greek poleis had either abolished or redefined the functions of these institutions and had decreased the importance of hereditary power in government. The various organs of government and shared offices were designed to serve as checks and balances to one another, minimizing the danger that the government would take too rapid, radical action.

Dual Kingship

The executive office was divided between two men. Two kings (*basileis*) served as the head of government. The succession was hereditary. The two kings, who were both cooperative and competitive with one another, and who were equal in authority, served as a mutual check on the power of the monarchy. Sparta, moreover, was never without a leader, and thus avoided what the Greeks called "anarchy" (absence of leadership or of government).

The kings exercised military, religious, and judicial powers. One king served as commander-in-chief of the armed forces, while the other supervised domestic matters at home and took charge if his co-king was killed in action. The kings functioned as the chief priests and conducted all the public sacrifices. They were also expected to serve as moral exemplars. Thus, the courage and self-sacrifice of King Leonidas and his troops, who obeyed the command of the Spartans to fight at Thermopylae in 480 BC against all odds in the war against the Persians, became legendary, although many other Greeks fought bravely at the same battle.

Gerousia

The kings shared their judicial functions with the other members of the *gerousia*, the Council of Gerontes ("Elders"). In addition to the two kings, the gerousia was composed of twenty-eight men over the age of sixty who served for the rest of their lives. Election to the gerousia was the highest honor to which a Spartan could aspire. Candidates appeared in an order determined by lot. The winners were chosen by acclamation in the assembly. Those who received the loudest shouts were considered elected, a procedure Aristotle later criticized as "childish." No bill could be brought before the assembly until it had first been discussed by the gerousia, and the gerousia could decline to accept a decision of the assembly by summarily declaring an adjournment. It also served as a criminal court for cases of homicide, treason, and other serious offenses that carried the penalty of disenfranchisement, exile, or death.

Ephors

Every year the Spartans elected five ephors by acclamation from candidates over the age of thirty. The ephors ("overseers") supervised the kings and represented the principle of law, precious to the Spartans as it was to many Greeks. The ephors took a monthly oath to uphold the office of the kings as long as they behaved in accordance with the laws, and they shared some of the kings' executive powers; but they were also empowered to depose them. Ephors monitored the kings in Sparta, and two of them always accompanied a king who was on campaign. The ephors presided over the gerousia and assembly, and dealt with foreign embassies. They also exercised judicial powers in civic matters and in cases involving perioikoi.

One ephor was always "eponymous," that is, his name was used at Sparta to signify the year. For example, Thucydides dates a treaty of 421 as follows: "The treaty is effective from the 27th day of the month of Artemisium at Sparta, when Pleistolas is an ephor; and at Athens from the 25th day of the month of Elaphebolium, when Alcaeus is an archon" (5.19). As a check on the ephors' power, they served for only one year, could not be reelected, and were subject to an audit by their successors. Thus, they were both a democratic and an oligarchic constituent of government.

The ephors exercised total control over the education of the young and enforced the iron discipline of Sparta. They were in charge of the krypteia ("secret police"), a force designed to control the helots. This feature of government was unique to Sparta among Greek cities. Young men were sent out for a year to spy on the helots and were encouraged to kill any helots they caught, especially the best of them who might be most prone to rebel. The ephors declared war against the helots annually, thus making it possible for the Spartans to kill them without incurring the religious pollution that usually accompanied acts of homicide.

Assembly

In terms of its membership, the assembly was the most democratic organ of Spartan government, for it included all adult male citizens. It met once a month at full moon, outdoors. Unlike the Athenian assembly, however, the Spartan assembly did not debate; citizens listened to a proposal made by the gerousia and simply voted to accept or reject it, without discussion. The Spartan was trained to obey and to conform, not to take sides in public debate. Lycurgus was said to have outlawed rhetoric teachers. This ethos gave rise to the English word "laconic" (derived from Laconia), which is used to describe a spare style of speech or someone who talks very little.

The Mixed Constitution of Ancient Sparta

Since antiquity, many political theorists have admired Sparta's government, believing it to confirm the basic principle that the best guarantee of stability lies in a blend of monarchic, oligarchic, and democratic elements. Certainly Sparta had kings, and the ideology of economic equality among male citizens fostered an egalitarian spirit. In reality, however, the oligarchic element considerably outweighed the other two. Power lay predominantly with the gerousia. As time went by, moreover, the five ephors also gained increasing power over the kings and frequently took the lead in framing foreign policy. Even if we discount the 95 percent or so of disenfranchised residents of Laconia—perioikoi, helots, and Spartan women—the truth is that even within the subgroup of male citizens, participation in government was limited to a very small group of men, most of them rich.

THE PELOPONNESIAN LEAGUE

Until the Roman conquest of Greece, Sparta itself was never subject to the ongoing rule of non-Spartans. After the defeat of Argos in 546 BC, Sparta had become the most powerful state not only in the Peloponnesus, but in all Greece. With Peloponnesian states other than Messenia, Sparta adopted a policy of alliance, rather than conquest, and gradually assumed a position of leadership. Eventually, around 510–500, "Sparta and its allies," or "the Peloponnesian League" as historians today call the Spartan alliance, was organized. The League included all the states in the Peloponnesus except Argos and Achaea, as well as key poleis that lay outside the Peloponnesus, such as Thebes. The purpose of the League was mutual protection. Each state pledged to contribute forces in case of war and swore an oath "to have the same friends and enemies, and to follow the Spartans wherever they lead." The League was not an empire, but an alliance; no tribute was paid except in wartime, and Sparta did not dictate the policy of the League.

The government of the League was bicameral, consisting of the assembly of Spartans and the congress of allies in which each state had one vote. Only Sparta could convene a meeting of the League and only Spartans served as commanders of its armed forces. Sparta's own reputation for distinction in military matters along with the existence of the League made Sparta the natural leader of the Greeks in their war against the Persians. The League remained in existence until the 360s, when Corinth and other member states were obliged to quit it after Sparta's defeat by Thebes.

HISTORICAL CHANGE IN SPARTA

Since there are no witnesses to the full operation of the Spartan community as described by Plutarch, and Xenophon states that the laws of Lycurgus were no longer enforced in his own time, we must admit the possibility that some features of the Lycurgan legislation were observed only briefly, or partially, or not at all. There are twentieth-century parallels for the failure of similar totalitarian dystopias or utopias. Modern historians follow the general model traced by Aristotle of drastic change over time in Spartan society, dating the "normalization," or loss of distinctiveness, to the later fifth century. Such a change may be observed in the public behavior of male Spartiates, but it is not at all clear that women's lives had been fundamentally altered, for, as Aristotle pointed out, women had never completely submitted to the Lycurgan system.

Some change, however, is plainly discernible. One area in which development is apparent is that of land tenure. Land was the most valuable commodity in the ancient world. Two systems of land tenure, a public one and a private one, existed in Sparta. When a man died, his kleros reverted to the state and then was allocated to another Spartan baby, who was not necessarily related to the previous owner. At the end of the fifth century or early in the fourth, the Lycurgan system regulating public property was abandoned. Thenceforth a man could give his kleros and his house to anyone he wished, or bequeath them by testament. This change undermined the ideal of economic equality and eventually led to the concentration of great wealth in the hands of a minority. This shift created an impoverished underclass who failed to meet the economic requirements for full citizenship, for they could not make the necessary contribution to a syssition. They were no longer "Men of Equal Status" but known as "Inferiors."

By the Classical period (if not earlier), in addition to the land designated for distribution as kleroi, some land was held as private property. Though women had probably been excluded from the distribution of kleroi, they owned a larger portion of the private land than women in any other Greek city. Land came into women's possession as dowry and inheritance. It seems likely that before the free bequest of land was introduced, daughters automatically inherited half as much as sons. Some families, of course, had daughters but no sons. Sparta was always plagued by a lack of men, for men were continually lost in battle, left Sparta for mercenary service, or failed to meet the census requirements for full citizenship. Moreover, though male infanticide was systematically practiced, it seems unlikely that female babies were eliminated in this way. Plutarch, who supplies details about the official elimination of male infants, says nothing about girls, though his interest in the rearing of girls is noteworthy. If this inference is correct, then these factors probably created a substantial imbalance in the sex ratio. A woman could inherit all her father's land, and many women became extremely wealthy by this means. Thus Aristotle's statement that in his day women owned two-fifths of the land of Sparta is credible.

THE SPARTAN MIRAGE

The admiration writers like Xenophon and Plutarch felt for Spartan society led them to exaggerate its monolithic nature, minimizing departures from ideals of equality and obscuring patterns of historical change. This perspective in turn made Sparta very attractive to subsequent thinkers, for whom a static society seemed to offer the stability lacking in a more dynamic state (such as democratic Athens).

Figure 4.3. Hilaire Germain Edgar Degas, "Young Spartans Exercising," 1860. London, National Gallery. In Degas' painting of "Young Spartans Exercising," Lycurgus stands among the mothers in the group of adults in back. Degas stated that the source for his inspiration was Plutarch. Thus the painting reveals the power of the utopian, naturalistic view of Sparta that was perpetuated in the modern era. Compare the costume of the girls in this painting to the dress on the Greek bronze statuette in Figure 4.2.

The idealization of Sparta in modern political thought also owes much to Plato. Already in antiquity Sparta served as "the other" vis-à-vis Athens and its democracy, as intellectuals unsympathetic to Athens exaggerated the differences between the two societies. In their writings Sparta became a virtual utopia, a paradise of *eunomia*—a word meaning "governed by good laws." The most dramatic instance of this concept is probably found in the blueprint for the utopian state in Plato's *Republic*, where many features of this idealized Sparta appear. They are evident, for example, in Plato's description of the life of his philosopher-rulers, the "guardians." Central to both social systems are commonality and totalitarian control. Women and men of the top class are given the same education, including physical training. The private family, with its emphasis on women's monogamy and the transmission of property to legitimate male heirs, is eliminated among Plato's guardians. Sexual intercourse is guided by eugenic considerations. Female guardians do not have to perform domestic labor, for members of the lower classes perform the work usually accomplished by Greek women. Their only gender-related task is that of giving birth to children. Marriage is dispensed with, since the state educates all children. Private property and money are likewise outlawed to minimize the envy and class conflict that perpetually threatened to dissolve the fabric of Greek society.

The controversy about Sparta and its critics, both ancient and modern, continues to the present day. For the past 2400 years, historians and philosophers have put forward views that vary radically, though they are based on readings of precisely the same texts. Readers have widely differing reactions to the veritable fountain of anecdotes that has survived from antiquity embodying the underpinnings of the Spartan ethos. Many of these are collected in Plutarch's *Sayings of Spartan Women*. Plutarch reports that a Spartan mother burying her son received condolences from an old woman who commented on her bad luck. "No, by the heavens," the mother replied, "but rather good luck, for I bore him so that he could die for Sparta, and this is precisely what has happened." Another woman, seeing her son coming toward her after a battle and hearing from him that everyone else had died, picked up a tile and, hurling it at him, struck him dead, saying "And so they sent you to tell us the bad news?"

The notion of a people whose response to stimuli is the very opposite of what human nature would seem to dictate has exercised a hold on the human imagination. As late as the twentieth century, critics of Western capitalist society have idealized the Spartans as highly virtuous, patriotic people produced by a stable noncapitalistic society. In recent years, however, those who cherish individual freedom and social mobility have come to see in Sparta a forerunner of totalitarian regimes such as Nazi Germany. Furthermore, the blueprint for twentieth-century Communism had many affinities with the Spartan utopia. Even today, however, the old idealization of Sparta has reappeared in the works of some feminist theorists, who have noted that the lives of women in aristocratic Sparta appear to have been more enjoyable and in many ways preferable to those of women in democratic Athens.

Although Athens was no more a typical Greek polis than was Sparta, examining Athens and Sparta together is a useful way of understanding the ancient Greek view of life. It is to Athens that we now turn.

TRANSLATIONS

Lattimore, Richmond. 1960. *Greek Lyrics.* 2nd ed. Chicago: University of Chicago Press.

Pomeroy, Sarah B. 2002. *Spartan Women.* New York: Oxford University Press.

SUGGESTED READINGS

Cartledge, P. A. and Antony Spawforth. 1989. *Hellenistic and Roman Sparta. A Tale of Two Cities.* London and New York: Routledge. Detailed description of the social, political, and economic conditions of postclassical Sparta.

Fitzhardinge, L. F. 1980. *The Spartans.* London and New York: Thames and Hudson. Extensively illustrated cultural and social history of Sparta.

Forrest, W. G. 1968. *A History of Sparta: 950–192 B.C.* New York: Norton. Brief, but informative history of Sparta.

Pomeroy, Sarah B. 2002. *Spartan Women.* New York: Oxford University Press. Clearly written comprehensive account of the life of Spartan women.

Powell, A., ed. 1989. *Classical Sparta. Techniques Behind Her Success.* London and Norman, OK: University of Oklahoma Press. A collection of essays including Ephraim David, "Laughter in Spartan Society," and Stephen Hodkinson, "Inheritance, Marriage and Demography: Perspectives upon the Success and Decline of Classical Sparta."

Rawson, Elizabeth. 1969. *The Spartan Tradition in European Thought.* Oxford: Oxford University Press. Reprint 1991 with a new introduction by Keith Thomas. The history of the idea of Sparta from Classical Greece through the Renaissance, Whig England, and Nazi Germany, with a short note on the United States.

5

THE GROWTH OF ATHENS
AND THE PERSIAN WARS

During the Archaic period, numerous Greek city-states struggled with a variety of problems—factional quarrels between aristocratic families, tension between aristocrats and the people, and tyranny. Sparta found a unique solution to the Archaic crisis and so did Athens. By 500 BC Athens' problems had been largely resolved. The last tyrant had been expelled, Athens had a democratic government, and aristocratic stasis was largely confined to competing for office and persuading the assembly. Because of their relative harmony, wealth, and great numbers, the Athenians had become the second most powerful Greek polis, they were poised to play a major role in the great war that was about to begin. For while the Greek city-states were evolving, the Persian Empire was growing into an ambitious power that would threaten to engulf the Hellenic world. A strong Athens would be vital to the defense of Greece against invasions by the Persian kings Darius I and Xerxes.

ATHENS FROM THE BRONZE AGE
TO THE EARLY ARCHAIC AGE

Literary evidence and physical remains show that during the Late Bronze Age Athens was the largest and most important settlement on the Attic peninsula and a major Mycenaean palace-center that exercised a loose control over the other fortified palace-centers in the region. These remained, however, independent of the Athenian *wanax*. Archaeology also confirms the tradition that the invasions of the late thirteenth century BC bypassed Athens. Still, if the story about the Achaeans taking refuge at Athens is true, they would have found in Attica the same collapse of the centralized ruling structure, drastic depopulation, and dispersal into small village communities as in the regions from which they had fled.

The first sign of Athenian recovery from the post-invasion slump is the appearance of Protogeometric pottery around 1050 BC. Although reduced to a cluster of villages around the Acropolis, Athens continued without interruption as the central place of Attica. It is likely that by 900 BC, if not earlier, the basileus of Athens was preeminent within Attica. A series of rich ninth-century graves reveals significant growth in wealth and overseas trade during the later Dark Age. The population around Athens rose sharply during the eighth century, and new settlements appeared throughout Attica, perhaps through "internal colonization" from the plain of Athens.

Significantly, Athens did not colonize overseas during the late eighth century. The synoecism or "joining together" of the towns and villages of Attica into a political unity under the leadership of Athens was probably gradual, only being completed around the middle of the eighth century. The Athenians ascribed the unification to Theseus, whom myth linked with his companion, the Dorian hero Heracles. Theseus' exploits, such as defeating the Minotaur in Crete and the Amazons in Athens, were enshrined in Athenian art and literature. In making Theseus the founder of Athens and its democracy, the Athenians followed the common Greek practice of attributing important events of the preliterate period to some great figure from the legendary past.

More important than the details of the process of unification is the fact that after the Dark Ages every settlement in Attica considered itself "Athenian," and none attempted to declare its independence as happened elsewhere, nor were there subordinate populations such as the Spartan helots or perioikoi. The unification of Attica, however, created unique problems. Although all Athenian citizens could participate in the government of Athens, in reality people who lived in or near Athens would find it easier to vote than those who lived farther away. Thus, for example, a visit to Athens by a farmer who lived 15 or 20 miles away would probably require three days. The importance of this fact for understanding Athenian history cannot be underestimated since until the outbreak of the Peloponnesian War in 431 BC most people still lived in the countryside.

The early government of Athens was aristocratic. Probably during the later eighth century the chiefs of Attica replaced the paramount basileus with three civic officials called collectively archons—that is, "the leaders"—who divided the leadership roles among themselves. One of the archons, called the *basileus*, administered the city's cults of the polis and judged lawsuits pertaining to cult property and other religious matters. The *polemarch* (war archon) commanded the army and judged disputes involving noncitizens. The most prestigious office was that of the *archōn*, who had overall supervision of public affairs, including presiding over the council and the assembly and judging nonreligious cases. He was known as the eponymous archon, because he gave his name to the year. Six judicial officials called *thesmothetai* ("layers down of the rules") were added later, making up the governing body of the "nine archons." The nine archons were elected annually from candidates drawn from the small circle of aristocratic families known as the Eupatrids ("people with good fathers").

The archons governed Athens in concert with the council that met on the hill (*pagos*) sacred to the war god Ares and was called for that reason the Council of the Areopagus. Because archons joined the council after the end of their term, sitting archons would probably think twice before flouting its wishes. Citizen males also participated in the assembly, but its precise role in the government and the part that the ordinary citizens played in it are unknown, although Aristotle claimed that it elected the archons (*Politics* 2.1274a 1–2 and 15–17).

Alongside these official state institutions were other forms of social organization that directed the lives of the citizens. In Attica, as in the rest of Greece, the basic social units—the individual households (*oikoi*)—were grouped into larger but poorly understood kin-like associations: tribes, phratries, and clans. Every citizen family belonged to one of four *phylai* ("tribes") and to another smaller group within their tribe, called a *phratry* ("brotherhood"). Since all the Ionian peoples had the same four tribes, these probably originated early in the Dark Age. They probably served as political and military divisions—each tribe furnishing a contingent to the army. The phratry may originally have designated a "brotherhood of warriors," like the warrior bands led by Dark Age chieftains that we see in Homer. By the seventh century, however, the phratries were concerned with matters of family and of descent. Proof of citizenship, for example, was provided by membership in a phratry, and in cases of unintentional homicide, the members of the victim's phratry were obligated to support his family, or, if the victim had no family, to pursue the case on his behalf. The "clans" (*genē*) were associations of aristocratic households dominated by a top *oikos* and claiming descent from a common ancestor. It was within this framework that the events of seventh and sixth century Athens unfolded.

The Conspiracy of Cylon

Only two events of Athenian history are known from the seventh century, both plainly connected with unrest of some kind. About 632 BC, an Olympic victor named Cylon took advantage of his marriage connection with Theagenes, the tyrant of nearby Megara, to seize the Acropolis and attempt to become tyrant of Athens, only to find himself and his supporters besieged by the Athenians. Cylon and his brother escaped, but his supporters, who had taken refuge at the altar of Athena, surrendered to the nine archons on condition that their lives would be spared. The conspirators even tied a thread to the statue of Athena, and descended while holding onto it, hoping the goddess would protect them. When the thread snapped, however, the archon Megacles and his supporters killed them. People believed that Megacles had committed sacrilege, and soon his family was exiled, including dead relatives whose bodies were exhumed and cast beyond the Attic frontier.

Although Cylon's coup failed, it played an interesting role in future Athenian history because of the prominent family to which Megacles belonged. The Alcmaeonid genos would contribute important politicians to Athens, including Cleisthenes and Pericles, two of the most prominent Athenian statesmen of the sixth and fifth centuries. Politically motivated demands for the expulsion of the "accursed" repeatedly sent shock waves through the body politic because people believed that the family's shared responsibility for its members' impious actions might call the wrath of the gods down on the state.

Draco and Early Athenian Law

More is known about the codification of Athenian law by a mysterious man named Draco around 620 BC. Because *drakoñ* is Greek for "snake" and the Athenians worshiped a sacred snake on the Acropolis, some scholars have suggested that priests published the laws of "Draco" on the supposed authority of the sacred snake. It is more likely, however, that Draco was a real person.

The best known of Draco's laws is that concerning homicide, which replaced the family and kin with the state as the arbiter of justice in cases of both intentional and unintentional killings. Before Draco's homicide law, bereaved family members were entitled and obliged to avenge the deaths of their slain relatives, unless the kin could be persuaded to accept compensation. Draco transformed such disputes into trials in which the next of kin, backed by his phratry, prosecuted the accused killer before magistrates who determined the appropriate penalty: death for murder or exile for unintentional homicide.

Little is known about Draco's other laws except that they were severe, naming death as the penalty even for minor offenses. The fourth-century Athenian orator Demades quipped that Draco's laws were written not in ink but in blood. What was significant about Draco's laws was their role in the process of developing the authority of the state at the expense of that of the family, and, it should be noted, of the magistrates also. The establishment of fixed principles of justice limited the magistrates' ability to shape their decisions in accord with their social and professional ties to particular litigants. The problems that were causing unrest in Athens, however, were both economic and political; purely legal reforms could not soothe the tensions that seemed to be inviting tyranny, such as enslavement for debt, which was becoming a principal grievance of the poor.

THE REFORMS OF SOLON

Solon's legislation in the 590s provides the best evidence for the nature of these problems. Solon tried to strengthen the fragile agricultural base of the Athenian economy by grafting onto it a thriving commerce. Because of the poor soil of Attica, the Athenians could not raise enough grain to feed their increasing population. Consequently, they bartered crops suited to their land—olives, vines, figs, and barley—abroad for wheat. High quality olive oil packaged in vases made from the excellent clay of Attica was their most significant export, much of it going to the Black Sea, which came to supply a great deal of the wheat consumed in Attica. Athens fought fiercely to defend the routes that led to the Black Sea, even seizing the strategic city of Sigeum near the entrance to the Hellespont about 600 BC. Besides oil, wine, and pottery the Athenians had at their disposal silver produced in the mines at Laurium in southeast Attica.

Although the Athens of 600 had great potential for economic development, many poor sharecroppers were losing the struggle to survive. For a second time the Athenians turned to a respected individual to resolve the crisis. Probably in

594 they empowered Solon, an aristocratic war hero and moralizing poet, to draw up a new law code that would ease the sufferings of the poor and avoid a tyranny. The poor wanted the abolition of their debts and redistribution of land; what they got was the abolition of debt slavery. Over time, Solon's reforms mitigated the risk of Attica's being divided into haves and have-nots by creating a sliding scale of privilege that contained something for everyone.

Solon defended his work in poetry, fragments of which still survive. Decrying both the selfishness of the rich and the revolutionary demands of the poor, he identified wealth as an unstable and problematic force in human affairs: "There are many bad rich men," he wrote, "while many good men are poor"; but, he went on, he would not exchange his virtue (*aretē*) for the riches of the wealthy, "for virtue endures, while wealth belongs now to one man, now to another" (cited in Plutarch, *Solon* 3). Although Solon urged justice for the people, he was also committed to defending the rights of the elite both to their land and to a pre-eminent role in government:

> I gave the *demos* such privilege as is sufficient to them, neither adding nor taking away; and as for those who had power and were admired for their wealth, I also provided that they should not suffer undue wrong. I stood with a stout shield thrown over both parties, not allowing either one to prevail unjustly over the other.
> (Cited in Plutarch, *Solon* 18.4; Scott-Kilvert 1960,
> and in *The Athenian Constitution*, 12)

"In large things," Solon wrote about his endeavors, "it is hard to please everybody." His rueful lament that in trying to please everyone he pleased no one is ironic in view of the cult that developed after his death, when he would become the beloved "founding father" of Classical Athens. Democrats and antidemocrats alike claimed him as their ideological ancestor and invoked his support for their programs. Although the earliest surviving sources for Solon's reforms—aside from his own poems—were written centuries after his death, the outlines of his thoughtful and original programs can be reconstructed.

Solon's first act was to address the sufferings of the poor. These included share-croppers who were called *hektēmoroi* ("sixth-parters"), presumably because they paid a rent equal to a sixth of their produce to a wealthy landowner, and also failed debtors, who had become the slaves of their creditors. Solon not only made it illegal for loans to be secured by anyone's property or person; he also freed those who had been enslaved for debt and canceled the obligations of the hekte-moroi. This bold measure was known as the *seisachtheia*, the "shaking off of bur-dens," and for many generations was commemorated by a festival of the same name. Solon also redeemed and brought home Athenians who had been sold as slaves outside Attica. None of this should be construed as an attack on slavery per se. Solon had no problem with Athenians enslaving non-Athenians.

Solon's other economic measures were less dramatic but equally important. He revised Athenian weights and measures to facilitate trade with other states. He also encouraged live cultivation and prohibited the export of grain, because it was needed at home. Solon encouraged the immigration of artisans to Athens, moreover, by offering them citizenship if they would settle there permanently with their families. Solon was also credited with a law that sons who had not been taught a trade were not required to support their mothers and fathers in old age. He was even said to have empowered the Council of the Areopagus to inquire into every man's means of supporting himself and to punish those who could show none, a dramatic contrast to the Spartan ethos that soldiering was the only appropriate work for a citizen.

By establishing a constitution in which political privilege was allotted in accord with income Solon also tried to deal with the grievances of the hoplite middle class, which resented the Eupatrid monopoly on privilege. He revised the traditional system of property classes by adding a fourth class at the top. In the new system citizens were ranked according to agricultural wealth. The new class, the *pentakosiomedimnoi*, or "500-measure men," consisted of those whose estates produced at least 500 *medimnoi* ("bushels") of produce; any combination of oil, wine, or grain would do. Below them came the *hippeis* ("horsemen," since they were the men who could afford to keep a horse for the cavalry). Their income was between 300 and 499 medimnoi. The *zeugitai*, men who could afford to own a team of oxen, with 200 to 299 medimnoi, were next, and finally the *thētes*, poor farmers and landless workers, who produced fewer than 200 medimnoi. Although the chief magistracies were limited to members of the first two classes, zeugitai could hold lower state offices; while the thetes could attend the assembly (the *ekklēsia*), which was to meet regularly. Slaves and resident aliens called metics were excluded from the system, as were women, who formed about a third of the citizenbody, since their life expectancy was about ten years shorter than men's. Citizen men from all classes could serve in the *heliaia*, a body of prospective jurors. These people would serve in courts set up to receive appeals from the judicial decisions of the archons and try the cases of magistrates whom someone wished to accuse of misconduct in office. Solon's most revolutionary contribution to the Athenian political system probably was his insistence that any male citizen whatever his rank—not just the victim or the victim's relatives—could bring an indictment if he believed a crime had been committed and serve as a juror in a trial. Once the concern of families, justice was now the business of the community of male citizens as a whole.

Solon did not alter Draco's homicide laws, but he reduced the penalties for other crimes and decreed an amnesty for persons exiled for crimes other than homicide or attempted tyranny. It was probably this amnesty that allowed the Alcmaeonid family to return to Athens. Like Draco, Solon feared the concentration of power in the hands of a few great families. It was probably for this reason that he allowed childless men (like himself) to adopt an heir by means of a will, thereby abrogating the traditional rule that such property passed automatically to the nearest male kin.

Solon's laws regarding sex and marriage reflect the traditional Greek view that a state was a conglomeration of oikoi. Although some of these laws seem intended to extend governmental power to cover women's private life, Solon's concerns about the excessive power of aristocratic families suggest that his more intrusive provisions, such as restrictions on women's dress, reflect his apprehension about conspicuous consumption by rich families rather than a desire to control women's activities. Several of Solon's policies, however, had a significant impact on women's lives. For example, the nearest male relative of a man who died without a son was required to marry the dead man's daughter in order to produce a male heir and thus keep the property in the family. A similar concern for maintaining the purity of family lines probably accounts for the fact that, although Solon had abolished debt slavery and had forbidden fathers as a rule to sell their children into slavery, he made an exception for a man who discovered his unmarried daughter was not a virgin.

Solon's legislation is remarkable for its creativity and scope. Solon had been given an unusual opportunity to think long and hard about the nature of a community. His laws established the principle that the Athenian citizen body as a whole would guide the Athenian state. Indeed, he virtually established the notion of citizenship itself. His law that neutrality was unacceptable in a time of civil strife demonstrates his determination that all male citizens take part in civic affairs, essentially defining a citizen as a person involved in public concerns. His laws also made clear that, while the regulation of women's behavior was essential to a well ordered society, their role was limited to the private sphere; thus he excluded them effectively from the body politic.

Solon's laws were inscribed on wooden tablets called *axones* that were set up in the agora, where everyone could see them even though most could not read them. After the Athenians swore to keep his laws in effect for a hundred years and each archon had been compelled to swear that he would dedicate a gold statue at Delphi if ever he violated any of them, Solon left Attica, partly to see the world and partly to escape pressure to alter his legislation. Solon was neither a democrat nor a revolutionary. There is, nevertheless, some justice in the claim that he was the father of the democracy, for by abolishing the hectemorage (sixth-part) system and debt slavery, Solon not only helped create the free peasantry that formed the basis of the democracy; he also established the distinction between freedom and slavery that was to be central to the Athenian concept of citizenship.

PEISISTRATUS AND HIS SONS

Solon's reforms eased social tensions in Attica. By intensifying the competition for political office, however, they probably indirectly fostered the civil strife that led to the tyranny of Peisistratus. The inhabitants of sixth-century Attica were loosely divided into three factions known as the Men of the Plain, the Men of the Coast, and the Men of the Hill. Historians still debate the composition of each group. The men of the plain were probably large landowners while the men of the coast were fishermen and craftsmen and the poorer inhabitants of the Attic highlands made up the men of the hill; perhaps the city-dwellers were in this last group as well.

Peisistratus' Seizure of Power

Around 560, a distant relative of Solon from northern Attica named Peisistratus successfully carried out a coup. Peisistratus' backers included not only the Men of the Hill but also some of the city dwellers. According to Herodotus, Peisistratus wounded himself and his mules and then appeared in the agora demanding a bodyguard to protect himself from his alleged enemies. Although Solon supposedly warned the Athenians against his kinsman's duplicity, the assembly voted Peisistratus a bodyguard, whereupon Peisistratus seized the Acropolis and with it the reins of government.

After about five years, the parties of the plain and the coast united against Peisistratus and drove him out, but when Megacles, the leader of the coastal party, quarreled not only with the party of the plain but also with his own faction, he decided to ally with Peisistratus and agreed to reestablish him in Athens provided he married his daughter. A century later Herodotus marveled at the story that Peisistratus effected his return to Athens by dressing a beautiful tall woman in armor and putting out the rumor that Athena was escorting him to Athens, although "from the very earliest times the Greeks have been distinguished from the barbarians by their intelligence and freedom from simpleminded foolishness . . ." and "the Athenians . . . are said to be the foremost of the Greeks when it comes to brains" (*The Histories* 1.61: Blanco 1992).

Whatever the truth of the tale, Peisistratus' alliance with his father-in-law Megacles did not endure. Peisistratus already had two grown sons whose position he did not wish to undermine by fathering any children with Megacles' daughter, so, according to Herodotus, he had intercourse with his wife *ou kata nomon*—"not according to the accepted norm." (Herodotus adds that Megacles found out from the bride's mother, who had asked her some pointed questions.) Outraged, Megacles joined with Peisistratus' enemies, and they drove him out a second time.

During his exile, which lasted from about 555 to 546 BC, Peisistratus gathered a force of mercenary soldiers with wealth drawn from the gold and silver mines of Mount Pangaeus in northern Greece. Supported by Lygdamis of Naxos and the cavalry of Eretria, he landed at Marathon and defeated the opposition in a battle at Pallene. He then governed Athens for over ten years until he died of natural causes in 527. Peisistratus gave his tyranny legitimacy by maintaining Solon's system in force but manipulating the laws so that his friends and relatives were elected archons, while mercenaries held in check potential opponents, whose children he used as hostages. When the last of Peisistratus' sons was expelled in 510, the way lay open for the development of the democratic institutions that are still associated with the city of Athens. Although it might seem that a tyranny would roll back Draco's and Solon's efforts to undermine the influence of powerful families, the reality was that after the fall of the Peisistratids the development of democracy profited from the tyranny's equalizing effect: Under the rule of the tyrants, all Athenians—rich and poor—found themselves surprisingly in similar circumstances.

Peisistratus' Policies

Strengthening the economy was a major focus of Peisistratus' program. Like Solon, he was concerned about both agriculture and commerce. He offered land and loans to the needy. He encouraged the cultivation of the olive, and Athenian trade expanded greatly under his regime. During the first half of the sixth century,

Athenian exports had begun appearing throughout the Mediterranean and Aegean, and it is difficult to believe that this explosion was not due at least in part to Solon. Under Peisistratus fine Attic pottery traveled still farther—to Ionia, Cyprus, and Syria in the east and as far west as Spain. Black-figure painting reached its apogee shortly after the middle of the century, and around 530 potters began to experiment with the more versatile red-figure style. Peisistratus or his sons also issued the first "owls"—silver coins stamped with the image of Athena's sacred god—that quickly became the soundest currency in the Aegean.

The growth of commerce was accompanied by an ambitious foreign policy. Peisistratus installed his friend Lygdamis as tyrant at Naxos, conveniently making

Figure 5.1. Water jar (c. 520 BC) from Athens showing women getting water at a fountain house.

Figure 5.2. This silver coin worth four drachmas, and thus known as the tetradrachm, was minted at Athens shortly after Peisistratus' death. The letters alpha, theta, and epsilon indicate that the coin was minted by the Athenians.

Naxos available as a residence for Peisistratus' hostages. Peisistratus also placed Sigeum under the control of one of his sons and established a foothold across the Hellespont in the Thracian Chersonese (the Gallipoli peninsula), by sending Miltiades, a member of the Philaid clan and a potential rival, to rule the Dolonci, a Thracian tribe that lived there.

In Athens, Peisistratus' building projects provided jobs to the poor while focusing attention on Athens as the cultural center of Attica. Replacing the private wells guarded by aristocrats with public fountain houses not only meant construction jobs but also a shift from private to public patronage. With expanded opportunities for jobs and housing in the city, Athens' population grew; and the people who lived in the urban area found it easier to vote. Peisistratus also rebuilt the temple of Athena on the Acropolis and began a temple to Olympian Zeus so large that it was completed only seven centuries later by the Roman emperor Hadrian.

Peisistratus' support of the gods and the arts enhanced both his own reputation and that of the city of Athens. He established two new festivals, the greater and lesser Dionysia, and instituted around 534 BC competition in tragic drama as part of the Dionysia. The worship of Dionysus flourished in Peisistratid Athens, and Dionysiac scenes of drinking and unrestrained merrymaking were popular subjects of vase painting. At the Dionysia, choirs of "satyrs" wearing goat skins honored Dionysus by conversing with their leader in a "goat song" or *trag-ōdia* that evolved into the Attic "tragedies" of the fifth century. Peisistratus also commissioned the first editions of Homer's *Iliad* and *Odyssey* and made Homeric recitations a regular part of the great Panathenaic festival, which was celebrated at Athens every four years. The Panathenaea culminated in a great procession carrying to Athena's temple the robe woven for her by young Athenian women. Ironically the procession up the Acropolis at the Panathenaea would serve as the occasion for the murder of Peisistratus' son Hipparchus in 514.

Figure 5.3. Attic red-figure *psyktēr* ("wine cooler") attributed to Oltos, Armed Warriors Riding on Dolphins, c. 520–510 BC. This vessel probably represents the chorus of an early theatrical production. It was made for use at the drinking party known as a *symposion* (see Fig. 3.3b) and, therefore, also depicts other wine vases as devices on the warriors' shields.

The Collapse of the Tyranny

Patronage of the arts became still more conspicuous after Peisistratus' death in 527. Thucydides believed that Peisistratus' son Hippias ruled alone, although others including Aristotle claimed that Hippias' brother Hipparchus was co-tyrant. In any event, Hippias and Hipparchus adorned their court with celebrated writers—Simonides of Ceos, whose choral odes were famous; the love poet Anacreon of Teos; and Lasus of Hermione, known for composing novel "hissless hymns," that is, poems in which the sound "*s*" was never heard. Cultural prestige, however, could not keep the hereditary tyrants secure. In 514, Hipparchus, spurned by a young man named Harmodius, insulted Harmodius' sister by forbidding her to carry a basket in the Panathenaic procession. Outraged at the suggestion that his sister was not a virgin, Harmodius and his lover Aristogiton plotted to assassinate the tyrants at the procession. When one of the conspirators was observed chatting with Hippias, the others panicked and immediately killed Hipparchus. The results were devastating for Athens: the paranoid autocracy of Hippias replaced the benign government of two aristocrats.

Hippias' tyranny lasted another four years until 510, when he was driven into exile thanks to the efforts of the exiled Alcmaeonids. The key to their success was good relations with Delphi. Taking advantage of the Delphians' failure to rebuild the temple of Apollo, which had burned down, the Alcmaeonids subsidized its reconstruction, even providing a frontage of first-class Parian marble instead of ordinary stone. In return, the priests made sure that whenever the Spartans went to Delphi for advice about future projects they always received the response:

"First free Athens." Inasmuch as the Spartans enjoyed their reputation as the enemy of tyranny, they were receptive to this suggestion, and in 510 King Cleomenes blockaded Hippias on the Acropolis. When Hippias' children were captured, the tyrant capitulated and departed with his family to Sigeum.

The Athenians understandably, however, chose to remember the heroism of Harmodius and Aristogiton rather than the Spartan intervention, as illustrated, for example, by drinking songs like the following:

> I will carry my sword in a bough of myrtle
> The way Harmodius and Aristogiton did
> When they killed the tyrants
> And restored equal laws to Athens.

Figure 5.4. The tyrannicides Harmodius and Aristogiton were commemorated in a lost bronze statue group of c. 477–476 BC that replaced an earlier group, which was taken during the Persian Wars. This Roman marble copy reflects the replacement group.

THE REFORMS OF CLEISTHENES

Predictably, renewed factional strife followed the exile of Hippias. An aristocrat named Isagoras was elected archon in 508 BC on a platform of disenfranchising persons given citizenship by the tyrants. His rival Cleisthenes, the leader of the Alcmaeonid family, opposed the plan and won popular support. Isagoras responded by using the old curse to force Cleisthenes into exile, but despite the support of the Spartan king Cleomenes he failed in his plan to set up an oligarchy. Instead of capitulating, the indignant Athenians blockaded the Spartans on the Acropolis, forced the surrender of Cleomenes and Isagoras, and invited Cleisthenes and his followers back to Athens.

Recognizing the danger to the state posed by family rivalries, Cleisthenes carried in the assembly a package of far-reaching reforms intended to break the power of rich families (other than his own). His methods were ingenious. He transferred the civic functions of the four ancient Ionian tribes to ten new tribes established on a new basis. First he divided Attica into three broad geographical areas: the city, the coast, and the plain. Each area was subdivided into ten *trittyes*, or "thirds" composed of residential units called demes (villages or townships). As the demes (which had been in existence for a long time) varied in size, the number in each *trittys* also varied, but each tribe in the new system contained one trittys from each geographical area. The requirement that citizens identify themselves by their demotic, that is, the name of their deme, instead of their father's name, undermined family loyalty. Tradition was not so easily cast aside, however, so we still think of Pericles as the son of Xanthippus and the historian Thucydides as the son of Olorus.

The ten new tribes also formed the basis for the creation of a new council, the Council (*boulē*) of Five Hundred, with each tribe annually providing fifty members chosen by lot. The use of the lot in determining the composition of each year's boule was a key democratic feature of the Cleisthenic system. The boule's chief functions were to prepare business for the ekklesia (the assembly) and to manage financial and foreign affairs. Because five hundred was an unwieldy number, each tribe represented the whole boule for a tenth of the year. During a tribe's period of service its members were called *prytaneis*, and the term prytany was used to designate a period of time, rather like a "month." The chair and secretary each changed every day by lot. The army also was reorganized on the basis of the ten tribes, with each tribe electing its officers including a *stratēgos*, or chief general. Unlike archons, *stratēgoi* could be reelected repeatedly, so that in time the board of ten strategoi became the most prestigious executive body in Athens.

THE RISE OF PERSIA

The political transformation of Greek poleis occurred at the same time as the emergence of the Persian Empire, the largest of all Ancient Near Eastern empires. The sources for Persian history are, unfortunately, limited. Although the Persians

Figure 5.5. Attica.

developed a cuneiform-based alphabetic script to write their language, no Old Persian literature survives except for inscriptions primarily devoted to recording the building activities of the Persian kings. Persian history necessarily depends, therefore, on non-Persian sources, Babylonian, Aramaic, Hebrew, and especially Greek historians for whom, however, the Persians, despite their achievements, were merely barbarians, that is, people who spoke "barbar, barbar," gibberish. Despite these limitations, historians working with archaeologists have succeeded in reconstructing the story of the rise of the Persian Empire.

Persia Before Darius

The Persians were one of several Indo-European peoples, who had settled in Iran by the early first millennium BC. It was not the Persians, however, but the Medes, who built the first Iranian empire by joining with the Babylonians to overthrow the mighty Assyrian empire in 612 BC. In the mid-sixth century BC, Cyrus II, who governed Persia (ruled 559–530 BC), revolted and made Media the first of the satrapies (provinces) of the Persian Empire. During his long reign Cyrus extended Persia to include all Western Asia, but it was his conquest in 546 of the Lydian king Croesus that brought the Greeks of Asia Minor into the empire and led ultimately to the confrontation between the Persians and the European Greeks that would redefine the course of Greek history. Events within the Persian Empire, however, delayed the confrontation for over half a century. First, Cyrus' son Cambyses (530–522 BC) conquered Egypt; and then, Darius I (522–486 BC), the founder of the dynasty that ruled the empire until its conquest by Alexander the Great, seized power and reorganized the empire.

The Achievements of Darius

Cyrus was praised by Greek and Asian sources alike as a benevolent and talented ruler, who avoided the Assyrian and Babylonian practice of deporting rebellious populations and supported local religions and cultures. Because Cyrus allowed the Jews to return from exile in Mesopotamia, Jewish enthusiasm for him was so great that the prophet Isaiah proclaimed him as one of God's messiahs:

> Thus says Yahweh to his anointed, to Cyrus whom he grasps by his right hand,
> That he might subdue nations before him, and ungird the loins of kings,
> To open doors before him, that gates shall not be closed:
> "I will go before you, and I will level the roads;
> I will shatter gates of bronze, and I will hew bars of iron to pieces.
> I will deliver buried treasures to you, and hidden riches. . . ."
> (Isaiah II, 45:1–3)

Nevertheless, it was Darius I's reorganization of the empire that ensured its survival for almost two hundred years. He centralized the government and moved the

Figure 5.6. Delegations bringing tribute to Persepolis. The Persian king received a wide variety of goods from throughout the Near East in the form of tribute.

Figure 5.7. The Persian Empire in the reign of Darius.

capital to Persepolis. Building inscriptions record that Greeks were among the workforce of men and women drawn from all corners of the empire who built the royal buildings. Darius facilitated travel for commercial purposes in many ways, even building a canal linking the Nile and the Red Sea. This canal made the newly conquered territory of Egypt more prosperous than it had been under native Egyptian rule. Darius was also the first Persian king to mint his own coins of silver and gold. The gold coins, Daric staters or "darics," demonstrated the king's talent at archery, a skill highly prized by the Persians, who, Herodotus reported, learned three skills—to ride, to shoot straight, and to tell the truth. Finally, Darius divided the empire into twenty provinces or satrapies governed by royal appointees and paying an annual tribute to the king. Spies known as the "Eyes and Ears of the King" discouraged rebellions. Supreme political power was unified only in the person of the king, who ruled as the designee of the Zoroastrian god of light and truth Ahuramazda and defended his subjects against the supporters of Ahriman, god of darkness and falsehood. In accordance with his exalted status the king exercised absolute authority over his subjects, who prostrated themselves in obeisance before him and performed at his command forced labor and military service. But unlike the Jews, who were grateful for their liberation, the Greeks pitied the subjects of the Persian king, considering them his slaves.

THE WARS BETWEEN GREECE AND PERSIA

Darius campaigned against the European Scyths and thus became the first Persian king to enter Europe. Although he failed to conquer Scythia, he subdued Thrace and reduced it to a satrapy. Darius' westward expeditions piqued his curiosity about the mainland Greeks, and a rebellion in his empire brought him into direct contact with them.

The Ionian Rebellion

In 499 BC the Ionian Greeks revolted. Discontent in Ionia was considerable. Taxes had risen under Persian rule, and the Greeks resented the puppet tyrants the Persians had imposed. Violence might not have erupted, however, except for the ambitions of Aristagoras, the tyrant of Miletus. Hoping to add Naxos to his domain, Aristagoras had persuaded the Persians to join him in an unsuccessful effort to subdue the Cyclades islands and perhaps to invade mainland Greece. When the plan failed, Aristagoras, noticing the restlessness of the Ionians, decided to recoup his failing fortunes by uniting them in revolt.

Aristagoras resigned his tyranny and then set about overthrowing tyrants in the other Ionian cities. Most fell without bloodshed, but the tyrant of Mytilene was so unpopular that he was stoned to death. The Ionians showed their unity by issuing coinage on a common standard. Herodotus' account of Aristagoras' attempts to gain support from King Cleomenes sought to illustrate the Spartan character as most Greeks imagined it—cautious, conservative, and leery of foreign adventures; it also highlighted the assertiveness of Spartan women and the respect due them. Aristagoras, Herodotus maintains, carried with him a bronze map of the world to show Cleomenes the wealthy peoples the Greeks would conquer if they chose to liberate the Ionians. Capitalizing on the Spartans' dislike of foreign customs, he suggested that they could easily defeat men who fought in trousers and wore peaked caps on their heads. But when Aristagoras told Cleomenes that the Great King lived three months' march from the sea, "Cleomenes cut short the rest of the account Aristagoras planned to give about the journey by saying, 'Get out of Sparta before sundown, Milesian stranger, for you have no speech eloquent enough to induce the Lacedemonians to march for three months inland from the sea'" (*The Histories* 5.50; Blanco).

Not yet willing to abandon his quest, Aristagoras followed Cleomenes to his house, carrying with him the customary sign of supplication—an olive branch, covered with wool—and as he sat in Cleomenes' home as a suppliant he noticed young Gorgo, who was eight or nine years old, standing by her father. He asked that Cleomenes send his daughter away, but Cleomenes told him to say whatever he liked and not to hold back on account of the child; whereupon Aristagoras began by promising ten talents if Cleomenes would do what he wanted. When Cleomenes rejected this, Aristagoras kept upping the amount until he was offering fifty talents. At this point, the child cried out, "Father, if you don't get up and leave, this stranger will corrupt you with a bribe!" Cleomenes, delighted with the child's advice, withdrew into another room and Aristagoras abandoned Sparta without being able to give any more details about the journey inland to the Great King (*The Histories* 5.51; Blanco).

The Athenians were more receptive. More daring than the Spartans, they were not constrained by fear of a slave rebellion in their absence. They also feared that the Persians might try to restore Hippias to power in Athens. As a result, they agreed to send twenty ships to aid the Ionians; the Eretrians to the north were willing to send five.

Six years after it began the Ionian Revolt ended in a major naval defeat off the island of Lade near Miletus in 494 BC. Greek morale had fallen; the tyrants whom Aristagoras had expelled were spreading pro-Persian propaganda; and before the battle was over the Samians and Lesbians had deserted. Miletus was defeated, its women and children enslaved, and the men relocated to the mouth of the Tigris. In addition, Sardis, the capital of the satrapy of Lydia, was burned, whether accidentally or on purpose.

Darius would not forget the destruction of Sardis, nor would the Greeks forget the annihilation of Miletus. Home of the philosophers Thales, Anaximander, and Anaximenes, and the geographer Hecataeus (who had warned Aristagoras of Persia's overwhelming superiority), Miletus had been one of the most cultured cities in the Greek world. When the poet Phrynichus produced a tragedy on its

Figure 5.8. Herm of Themistocles. This Roman marble copy was probably modeled after the head of a bronze statue of Themistocles erected about 460 BC. With its thick neck and coarse features, the head may reflect the earliest known example of individual portraiture in Greek art. We should perhaps associate the unusual physiognomy with the tradition that Themistocles' mother was not Greek.

fall entitled *The Capture of Miletus*, the Athenians fined him one thousand drachmas for reminding them of their misfortune. Although the Athenians had withdrawn from the rebellion after the burning of Sardis, their outrage reveals their sympathy with Miletus in its final hour and a growing sense of identity among the Ionians.

Not surprisingly, they also feared that the mainland Greeks might suffer the fate of Miletus. In this situation, a rising politician named Themistocles, who had just been elected archon, persuaded the Athenians to convert the three rocky harbors of Piraeus into a fortified naval and commercial base. Since Themistocles, unlike most Athenian politicians, lacked strong family connections and the support of the leisured landowning class, he sought the backing of those who made their living by trade. Acutely sensitive to the Persian threat—Thucydides praised him for his ability to foresee what the future held (1.138)—Themistocles served Greece well at this critical time.

Darius' Invasion of Greece

The desire to avenge the burning of Sardis strengthened Darius's interest in Greece. In 492 BC an expedition led by his son-in-law Mardonius failed when the fleet was wrecked rounding the Chalcidic peninsula, although it did restore Persian prestige in northern Greece, conquering Thrace, Thasos, and Macedonia. Two years later Darius sent another expedition straight across the Aegean. Mindful of the fate of Miletus, many Greek cities offered earth and water, the proverbial tokens of submission that signaled recognition of the king's supremacy. On the mainland Argos and Thebes went over to the Persians. Sparta and Athens, however, remained steadfast in their opposition.

Darius' primary goal was to punish Athens and Eretria for their role in the Ionian rebellion. In the summer of 490 his fleet arrived in Greece, commanded by his nephew Artaphernes and Datis, a Mede, who brought with them the aging former Athenian tyrant Hippias. Eretria quickly fell, its temples being burned in revenge for the sack of Sardis and its people exiled to central Asia, where the peripatetic prophet of the Roman Empire, Apollonius of Tyana, reported finding their descendants still speaking their native Greek several centuries later. From Eretria, the Persians sailed to the old Peisistratid stronghold of Marathon in northern Attica.

The Athenian assembly immediately voted to dispatch their forces to Marathon, and a runner, Philippides, was sent to Sparta, supposedly covering fully 140 miles by the next day. The Spartans, however, claimed that they could not march before the new moon because they were celebrating a festival of Apollo, the Carnea. As the Spartans were deeply religious and no cowards in war, their explanation may have been sincere.

The Battle of Marathon

The Athenians were outnumbered, perhaps by a factor of two to one. Although the Persian force included cavalry, archers, and skirmishing troops, the Athenian hoplites were more heavily armed. The most serious problem faced by the Athenians was disunity among the ten strategoi; some wanted to wait for the Spartan reinforcements and others thought delay risky. When the Athenians learned however, that the Persian cavalry was missing and suspected that the Persian forces were heading for Phaleron, the general Miltiades (nephew of the Miltiades whom Peisistratus had dispatched to protect Athenian interests in the Chersonese) persuaded his colleagues to attack immediately. His stirring words appear in Herodotus' *Histories:*

> Callimachus, it is up to you, *right now,* to enslave Athens or to make it free, and to leave for all future generations of humanity a memorial to yourself such as not even Harmodius and Aristogiton have left. *Right now,* Athens is in the most perilous moment of its history. Hippias has already shown what we will suffer if we bow down to the Medes, but if this city survives, it can become the foremost city in all Greece. Now, I'll tell you just how this is possible, and how it is up to you— and only you—to determine the course of events. We ten generals are split right in two, with half saying fight and the other half not. If we don't fight now, I am afraid that a storm of civil strife will so shake the timber of the Athenian people that they will go over to the Medes. But if we fight now, before the cracks can show in some of the Athenians, and provided that the gods take no sides, why then we can survive this battle. All this depends on *you.* It hangs on your decision—*now.* If you vote with me, your country will be free and your city will be first in all of Hellas, but if you choose the side of those who urge us not to fight, then the opposite of all the good I've spoken of will fall to you.
>
> (*The Histories* 6.109; Blanco 1992)

And so, early one morning in late September of 490, the Athenians and their Plataean allies attacked, shouting, covering the mile or so dividing them from the Persians at double speed despite their heavy hoplite armor. Knowing they were outnumbered, they concentrated their forces, even though it meant leaving the center thin. The Persians, who were caught by surprise, broke under the attack of the determined hoplites fighting in defense of their freedom and fled in confusion to their ships.

Arriving too late to participate in the fighting, the Spartans visited the battlefield and surveyed the Persian corpses. Herodotus maintained that the Athenians lost 192 men, the Persians 6400. The number of Greek dead is probably correct, for the names were inscribed on the battlefield; they included Callimachus. The dead were cremated where they had fallen, and a monument was subsequently erected on the site. Some Plataeans and some Athenian slaves also died, but their numbers are unknown. The playwright Aeschylus, who fought at Marathon, later mentioned only his service at Marathon in his epitaph, writing that: "The glorious grove of Marathon can tell of his valor—as can the long-haired Persian, who well remembers it." For the next two generations, the *Marathonomachoi*—the veterans of Marathon—enjoyed singular prestige in Athens as exemplars of traditional Athenian values in an increasingly luxurious and complex society. Not all Athenians, however, rejoiced in their victory. Herodotus reports that a shield signal was flashed from Athens after the battle urging the Persians to hurry to Athens. (Gossip ascribed this act of treachery to the Alcmaeonids, but Herodotus denied indignantly that the Alcmaeonids had been to blame.) For years accusations of Persian sympathies would dog aspiring Athenian politicians as a convenient device to damage a rival's reputation.

Athens After Marathon

Political leadership in Athens changed after the Battle of Marathon in a very specific manner. The need for capable military commanders resulted in a new method of selecting archons, who, as primarily judicial officials, now seemed less important than the strategoi. Beginning in 487, therefore, archons were chosen by lot from candidates drawn from the demes as was the Council of Five Hundred. As a result, ambitious men shifted their interest from the archonship to the *stratēgia* (generalship), leading ultimately to the decline in influence of the venerable Council of the Areopagus, which was composed of former archons.

Themistocles, who was hostile to the aristocratic ethos that granted special power and prestige to the Areopagites, may have inspired this reform, but he cannot have foreseen its long-term effects on Athenian politics. Selection by lot was a procedure associated with democracy in Greece that tended to discourage the machinations of special interest groups. It also ensured that a significant proportion of the men eligible for each office would participate in politics, and gave legitimacy to the process by enlisting the gods in the choice of officials. The Athenians were no fools, however. All would-be officeholders underwent an interrogation known as *dokimasia*, and the lot was not used to select strategoi, leading to the ten strategoi becoming the most prestigious of all Athenian officials.

At the same time, the Athenians first successfully employed one of Cleisthenes' most remarkable innovations, ostracism, a procedure thought to have been intended to prevent the emergence of a new tyrant. Every spring the Athenians had the option of voting to send one of their fellow citizens into exile for ten years. The process took its name from the ostraka—broken pieces of pottery—on which voters scratched the name of the man they wanted to banish. Ostracized Athenians

Figure 5.9. Numerous *ostraka* have been discovered in the Athenian agora. These bear the names of Aristides, son of Lysimachus, and Themistocles, son of Neocles, of the deme Phrearrhioi.

stood accused of no crime and remained citizens, but they had to live in exile for ten years simply because they had received a plurality of six thousand votes cast by their fellow citizens.

Inevitably historians have wondered if Cleisthenes really created this procedure, since the first man so exiled—a Peisistratid named Hipparchus—was not ostracized until 487. The answer may lie in the requirement for six thousand votes to be cast for an ostracism to be valid, so that Hipparchus' ostracism may not have been the first attempted ostracism but merely the first successful one. In any event, it is probably no coincidence that the first man ostracized was related to former tyrant Hippias, and that all but one of the other men ostracized in the 480s—Themistocles' great rival Aristides—were members of the Alcmaeonid family that had been accused of trying to betray Athens to the Persians in 490.

Themistocles' role in the first three ostracisms is unclear, but his dispute with Aristides over how best to face a renewed Persian threat was the central issue in the ostracism of 482. Darius, in fact, began preparations for a new invasion of Greece soon after the Persian defeat at Marathon, but revolts in Babylon and Egypt and Darius' death in the fall of 486 delayed it for almost six years. Meanwhile, the Athenians had made a spectacular silver strike at Laurium in southeastern Attica that yielded over two tons in the first year. In the bitter debate over its use Aristides advocated sharing it among the citizens, while Themistocles argued for building two hundred triremes (light, fast, maneuverable warships with three banks of oars). They were allegedly to be used against Athens' old enemy, Aegina, but were really for defense against the Persians. The ostracism of 482 decided the issue; Aristides left Athens, and the fleet that would save Greece was built. It is difficult to imagine how history might have turned out had the vote in that ostracism been different.

The Invasion of Xerxes

Darius' son and successor, Xerxes (Cyrus' grandson on his mother's side) was at first ambivalent about carrying out the invasion, but by 484 BC he had made his decision, and the Greeks learned that ships were being built in large numbers throughout the ports of the extensive Persian Empire from Egypt to the Black Sea. Engineers and laborers were dispatched to the Hellespont, where they bridged the crossing with boats, and to northern Greece where they cut a canal across Athos so that the shipwreck Mardonius had suffered in 492 could be avoided.

While the Athenians were still constructing warships, Xerxes' heralds arrived in Greece seeking earth and water, and many states including Thessaly and Thebes, complied. At a congress held at Corinth in 481 BC thirty-one states limited mainly to Athens and the Peloponnesian League formed an alliance that historians call the Hellenic League. Even Aegina and Athens reconciled in the crisis, and Aristides and the other exiles were recalled. Sparta received supreme command on land and sea. After an unsuccessful attempt to find a defensible position in northern Greece, the Hellenic League decided to make a stand in central Greece, placing a land force at the pass of Thermopylae on the Malian Gulf while the fleet settled in at nearby Artemisium off northern Euboea. At the instigation of Themistocles, the Athenians probably voted to evacuate Attica and wait out the war on the island of Salamis and in nearby Troezen in the Peloponnesus. A third-century copy of the decree discovered on Troezen in 1959 probably preserves the substance of Themistocles' motion:

> The Gods
> Resolved by the Council and People
> Themistocles, son of Neocles, of Phrearrhioi, made the motion
>
> To entrust the city to Athena the Mistress of Athens and to all the other Gods to guard and to defend against the Barbarian on behalf of the land. The Athenians themselves and the foreigners who live in Athens are to send their children and women to safety in Troezen, their protector being Pittheus, the founding hero of the land. They are to send the old men and their movable possessions to safety on Salamis. The treasurers and priestesses are to remain on the Acropolis guarding the property of the gods.
>
> All the other Athenians and foreigners of military age are to embark on the 200 ships that are ready and defend against the Barbarian for the sake of their own freedom and that of the rest of the Greeks along with the Lacedaemonians, the Corinthians, the Aeginetans, and all others who wish to share the danger.
>
> (Jameson 1970, p. 98 adapted)

The odds facing the Hellenic League were great, so great that the Delphic oracle issued a stream of oracles discouraging resistance to the Persians. The Spartans were told that their only hope lay in the death of a king and the Athenians

Figure 5.10. Photograph of a trireme at sea. Working in England and Greece, twentieth-century scholars and naval architects reconstructed an Athenian trireme of the Classical period.

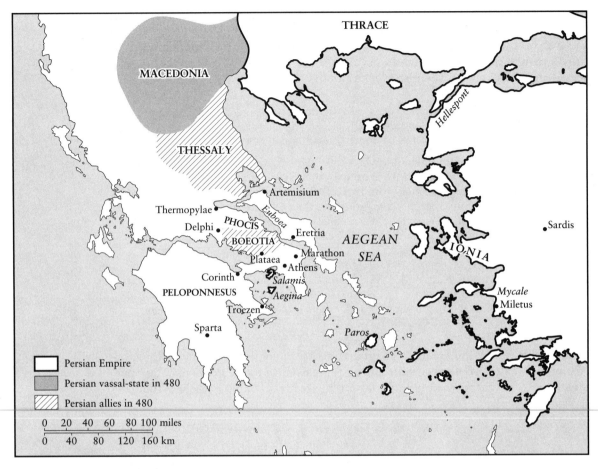

Figure 5.11. The Persian Wars.

that salvation was to be found in the "wooden walls," which Themistocles argued was the new navy. While the oracle may partly explain King Leonidas' tenacity in holding Thermopylae, hard calculation also called for a land operation, however unpromising, to buy time for Greece while the fleet off Artemisium could cripple the Persian navy. As luck would have it, a storm fortuitously intervened so that even before the indecisive fighting at Artemisium the Persians had lost many ships.

The Battle of Thermopylae

Leonidas marched into Thermopylae with about seven thousand men, a fairly small force. But for their dependence on the Athenian fleet, the Peloponnesians would have preferred to focus their defense on the Peloponnesus. Local Phocian forces were assigned to defend a secret path over the mountains leading to the rear of the Greek forces. Unfortunately, a Greek traitor betrayed the secret and guided Xerxes' personal guard, the so-called Immortals, over it. On learning the Persians were in his rear, Leonidas dismissed the bulk of his forces, and with only the Thebans, Thespians, and three hundred Spartans, fiercely defended the pass, killing many "Immortals" including two brothers of Xerxes before being killed themselves. On Xerxes' orders the body of Leonidas was decapitated and impaled. Throughout antiquity Greeks took inspiration from the epitaph composed for the Thermopylae dead attributed to Simonides:

> Go tell the Spartans, stranger passing by,
> That here, obeying their commands, we lie.

The Battle of Salamis

Their victory at Thermopylae opened the road to Athens and central Greece to the Persians. From their refuge on Salamis the Athenians soon saw the smoke of the burning Acropolis. While the Peloponnesians urged withdrawal of the fleet to the Peloponnesus, Themistocles, fearing that the Greeks might indeed pull back from the Isthmus, sent a messenger to Xerxes urging him to occupy the narrows and block the escape of the Greeks. Herodotus, who came from Halicarnassus in Ionia, took delight in telling how Xerxes' prudent adviser Artemisia, queen of Halicarnassus, in vain advised him against fighting a needless battle. Xerxes quickly learned the wisdom of Artemisia's advice as he watched from his throne the Persian fleet, unable to maneuver in the straits of Salamis, suffer a massive defeat, losing over two hundred ships. Rather than confronting the foolishness of his decision to fight, Xerxes reacted to the defeat by furiously executing his Phoenician captains for alleged cowardice in the battle and retreated to Asia with the remainder of his fleet. Less than a year later, in the spring of 479, Xerxes' forces were led by Mardonius was totally destroyed at Plataea by the largest Greek army ever mobilized. Almost at the same time the Greek fleet that had pursued the Persians eastward defeated their navy at the Battle of Mycale near Miletus, finally liberating the Ionians and ending the Persian threat to Greece forever.

The War Through Greek Eyes

Victors celebrate the history of their triumphs; the vanquished try to forget or trivialize them. Until recently, Greek historical sources and scholars who caricatured the Persian Empire as merely an "Oriental despotism" largely shaped our views of the Persian Empire. Modern historians have been overwhelmingly "Hellenocentric," following the lead of fifth-century Greek authors such as the playwright Aeschylus, who believed that Xerxes had incurred the wrath of the gods and was responsible for his own defeat and the death of many noble Persians because of his folly. In 472 BC he produced a tragedy, *The Persians*, celebrating the Athenian role in the Persian defeat and the values for which they had fought—liberty as opposed to slavery, responsible democratic government as opposed to capricious autocracy and monarchy. It was the historian Herodotus, however, who gave definitive form to the Hellenocentric view of the Persian Wars. He highlighted in his *Histories* the unexpectedness of the Greek victory and sought its causes in the fundamental institutions of Greek and Persian society and government. Herodotus depicted Xerxes, in contrast to Cyrus, as an impious madman who was responsible for initiating the decline of Persia. Xerxes' chief character flaw, in Herodotus' view, was *hybris* ("arrogance"). Imagining himself to be on the same level as the gods, he dared to bridge the Hellespont, thereby setting in motion a process that led to his own defeat.

Document 5.1. The chorus from Aeschylus's *Persians* (472 BC).

Aeschylus took the occasion of his drama about Salamis to stress the differences between eastern despotism and what he conceived as Greek freedom. Here the chorus of Persian elders laments Persia's defeat by Greece:

> They throughout the Asian land
> No longer Persian laws obey,
> No longer lordly tribute yield,
> Exacted by necessity;
> Nor suffer rule as suppliants,
> To earth obeisance never make:
> Lost is the kingly power.—
> Nay, no longer is the tongue
> Imprisoned kept, but loose are men,
> When loose the yoke of power's bound,
> To bawl their liberty.
> But Ajax' isle, spilled with blood
> Its earth, and washed round by sea,
> Holds the remains of Persia.

The Persians 584–596; translated by Seth Benardete, in
David Grene and Richmond Lattimore, eds.,
The Complete Greek Tragedies, vol. 1, *Aeschylus*.
Chicago: University of Chicago Press, 1959.

Although Greek historical sources tend to depict Persian history as the gradual degeneration of the mighty empire established by Cyrus the Great, the Persians were not decisively defeated until their conquest by Alexander the Great (from 334–323 BC). They continued to play an influential role in Greek politics, both in civic disputes and in rivalries between Greek states, favoring now one side, now another. They were instrumental in the Spartan victory in the Peloponnesian War, and fourth-century Greek history cannot be understood without constant concern for Persian involvement in Greek affairs.

The unanticipated success of the little city-states over the monolithic empire had little impact in Persia, but in Greece it would give birth to a civilization of extraordinary brilliance and originality. The unity the Persian Empire had sparked, however, would prove short-lived, and its fragility would place limits on how long Greek civilization could endure.

TRANSLATIONS

Blanco, Walter. 1992. *The Histories,* from *Herodotus: The Histories,* Walter Blanco and Jennifer Roberts, eds. New York: W. W. Norton.

Jameson M., "A Decree of Themistocles from Troizen," *Hesperia* 29 (1960) 200–201, modified by P. Green. 1996. *The Greco-Persian Wars.* Berkeley and Los Angeles: University of California Press.

Scott-Kilvert, Ian. 1960. *The Rise and Fall of Athens: Nine Greek Lives by Plutarch.* Harmondsworth, UK: Penguin.

SUGGESTED READINGS

Cook, J. M. 1983. *The Persian Empire.* London: J.M. Dent. A history that provides vital background in understanding fifth-century Persia.

Forrest, W. G. 1966. *The Emergence of Greek Democracy.* New York and Toronto: McGraw-Hill. A lively and readable analysis of the governments of the Greek city-states.

Green, Peter. 1996. *The Greco-Persian Wars.* Berkeley and Los Angeles: University of California Press (revised edition of *Xerxes at Salamis*). A dramatic account of Xerxes' invasion of Greece.

Lenardon, Robert. 1978. *The Saga of Themistocles.* London: Thames and Hudson. The life of the innovative and irreverent politician.

Romm, James. 1998. *Herodotus.* New Haven: Yale University Press. A lucid introduction to Herodotus and his place in Greek literature.

Stanton, G. R. 1990. *Athenian Politics c. 800–500 BC: A Sourcebook.* London and New York: Routledge. A very useful collection of sources that traces the evolution of the Athenian state.

6

THE RIVALRIES OF THE GREEK CITY-STATES AND THE GROWTH OF ATHENIAN DEMOCRACY

In the struggle to prevent a Persian takeover of Greece, a powerful sense of Hellenic identity was forged. Eager to prevent a third invasion, a number of Greek states entered into an alliance led by the Athenians, whose naval strength had been instrumental in winning the war. Tribute from this league enabled Athens to offer state pay for public service such as jury duty, thus expanding the number of men who could afford to participate in government. The fact that the lower-class citizens who rowed the triremes were becoming increasingly pivotal to the city's well-being also made it difficult for the rich and wellborn to maintain their traditional monopoly on political power. Democratic reforms consequently undermined the edge wealthy aristocrats enjoyed in politics, though nothing whatever was done to remove the civic disabilities of women or to abolish slavery. Indeed, Athens' imperial ventures probably increased the number of slaves in Attica, and the status of women seems to have declined with the growth of equality among citizen males.

During the decades that followed Xerxes' defeat, moreover, Athens became a major cultural center. Tourists came from all over Greece to watch the tragedies performed in honor of the god Dionysus, and some of the money Athens received to police the seas was diverted to the celebration of religious festivals and to the erection of magnificent public buildings such as the temple to Athena called the Parthenon; for the Greeks' deliverance from Persian autocracy the gods received ample thanks. The tragedians Aeschylus, Euripides, and Sophocles were all born in Athens, as were the comic dramatist Aristophanes, the sculptor Phidias, and the historian Thucydides. Many Greek thinkers like the historian Herodotus and the philosopher Anaxagoras came from elsewhere to enjoy—and enhance—what Athens had to offer.

Although it exerted a magnetic force on many of the artists and intellectuals of Greece, Athens was far from the only site that could boast major attractions.

At Delphi, for example, donors grateful for deliverance from Persia set up splendid monuments and commissioned superb works of art. Olympia remained a vital religious center as well; the games were extended to five days, and after its completion in 456 BC visitors could admire the imposing temple of Zeus. Democracies similar to that evolving at Athens developed in a number of places, most prominently Syracuse in Sicily, and throughout the Greek world intellectuals could be found bringing new ideas to birth. While Socrates was asking questions about justice and the human community in the streets of Athens, on the island of Cos, Hippocrates was discussing medicine and the human body.

THE AFTERMATH OF THE PERSIAN WARS AND THE FOUNDATION OF A NEW LEAGUE

The Delian League—so called by modern historians because its treasury came to be located on the island of Delos—had not always been under Athenian leadership. While the League's fleet was at Byzantium in 478 seeking to consolidate Greek power in the east, the Greeks began to complain bitterly about their commander Pausanias, regent for Leonidas' underage son Pleistarchus. He conducted himself, they alleged, like an eastern potentate, dressing like a Persian and fortifying his position with a bodyguard of Medes and Egyptians. Sparta's attempts to hold onto its position of primacy by sending out another commander were not successful. It was only then that Athens was offered the chance to lead the League, an opportunity the Athenians were all too happy to seize. In 477 BC representatives from Athens and dozens of other states met at Delos and took oaths binding themselves into an organization designed to fight the Persians. Some members of the old Hellenic League joined; others did not. In exchange for annual contributions in ships or money Athens agreed to lead the League in military operations against Persia while simultaneously respecting the internal autonomy of each polis in the alliance. Though policy was to be established by a League assembly, it would be executed by an Athenian high command that would also control the treasury. Thus from the beginning power in the League was concentrated in Athenian hands. The small size of Greek states is reflected in the number of poleis who enrolled in the alliance—probably about 150. Whereas the goals of the Peloponnesian League had never been defined, those of the Delian League were fairly clear—containment of Persia, the gathering of booty as compensation for damages done to Greece during the war, and simple revenge.

In view of the personality problems that had brought down Pausanias (and with him Spartan naval leadership), it was particularly fortunate for the Athenians that they had at their disposal a man as famous for his probity and affability as Aristides. It was he who was charged with assessing each state's appropriate contribution to the League treasury. Some of the larger states such as Lesbos, Samos, Chios, Naxos, and Thasos chose to make their contributions in ships; most preferred to pay cash. Although records of the tribute paid in the League's first years are lacking, it is possible to track the history of payments beginning in 454

Figure 6.1. Section of Athenian Tribute List inscription showing payments for 433–432 BC. The citizens of Mykonos, Andros, Siphnos, Syros, Styra, Eretria, Grynches, and Rheneia are listed here.

BC through the compendium that survives today called the *Athenian Tribute Lists*, actually lists of the one-sixtieth of each contribution that was dedicated to the goddess Athena Polias; these figures multiplied by sixty give the size of each state's contribution in a given year.

From Delian League to Athenian Empire

For over a quarter century the League fought against Persia and, led by Miltiades' son Cimon, the Athenians and their allies expelled the Persians from Europe and made it impossible for them to establish naval bases in Ionia. In 476, Cimon set out with the League's navy for the northeast. The fortress of Eion on the Strymon River in Chalcidice was taken with little difficulty. The Athenians then moved against Scyros, a rocky island east of Euboea inhabited by pirates. Enslaving the pirates and their families, they established on the island the kind of colony that was known as a cleruchy. Unlike most Greek colonies, which were fully autonomous and independent of the mother city, cleruchies were in effect part of Athenian territory, and all their inhabitants (called cleruchs) retained their Athenian citizenship. Generally chosen by the government from among poor Athenians, each cleruch was granted a parcel of land (a *klēros*, hence the word "cleruch"). Cleruchies filled a double function: They provided an outlet for the disaffected and potentially contentious poor, and they operated as garrisons in the empire to discourage rebellion from Athens.

Shortly afterward, the Athenians and their allies sailed against Carystus in southwestern Euboea, compelling the city to join the Delian League, and when the island of Naxos decided to leave the League, the Athenians forcibly prevented its withdrawal and in fact confiscated its fleet, ordering the Naxians thenceforth to pay their tribute in money rather than ships. These two developments highlight the problematic nature of the Delian League. A strong case could be made—and was made—that since all Greek states benefited from the existence of the League, all should pay tribute and support its fleet. Against this argument, however, resentful *poleis* adduced their right to make their own determinations about the extent of the Persian peril. Because the League's existence was justified only by the need for continued protection of Greece from the Persians, moreover, a problem would be created for the Athenians if Cimon and his navy did too good a job of squelching any designs Persia might have on Greece. This is precisely what happened around 467 when the Persian forces were badly beaten by those of Cimon at the mouth of the Eurymedon River in southern Asia Minor. Cimon's success probably played a role in the revolt in 465 of the important island of Thasos, located just off Thrace. When the Thasians were finally overcome by Athenian might, they were compelled, like the Naxians, to yield their ships and switch to cash payments into the League treasury, an obligation that would be all the more onerous since the Athenians also confiscated the Thracian mines that had previously been in Thasian hands.

The Athenians' refusal to permit states to remain aloof from the League, combined with the gradual conversion of tribute payments from ships (which had been commanded by admirals from their native poleis) to money, sent an increasingly clear

Figure 6.2. The Athenian Empire at its height.

message that Athens ruled the sea and was converting the naval alliance into an empire. Although Athenian leaders seem to have been largely of one mind about the merits of naval imperialism, however, they were divided about Athens' proper relationship to Sparta. These conflicts, moreover, were tied to disagreements about the further democratization of Athenian political life. Although sources for Athenian politics during these decades are sparse, some underlying fault lines are discernible: Themistocles encouraged competition with Sparta and the development of democracy, whereas Cimon favored Sparta and opposed any further democratization.

The forces in Athens favoring warm relations with Sparta and opposing the increasingly democratic trend in the government were strong. So was Themistocles' personality: His sharp tongue and quickness to claim credit for his achievements played into the hands of his enemies, and it seems that he was ostracized around 471 BC. In the 460s the Athenians and the Spartans united against him, claiming that he and Pausanias were engaged in treasonable correspondence with the Persian king. Themistocles fled to Persia, and Pausanias was starved to death by the Spartans in a temple where he had sought asylum.

NEW DEVELOPMENTS IN ATHENS AND SPARTA

Having rid themselves of a keen and colorful politician in Themistocles, the Athenians were left with the genial and gentlemanly Cimon. Themistocles and Cimon were opposites in every way. Slow where Themistocles had been quick, and courteous where Themistocles had been insolent, Cimon was no intellectual, but he had a flair for generalship. Because of his military reputation, he continued to command a good deal of respect in the Athenian assembly even after the development of a calculating and determined coalition led by Ephialtes, whose purpose was to break with Sparta and further the growth of democracy.

For some years Ephialtes and his associates had been making attacks on individual members of the venerable and aristocratic Council of the Areopagus. Matters came to a head in 462, not long after Cimon's return from Thasos. Two years earlier, when an earthquake in Sparta killed thousands of people and destroyed most houses, the helots had seized the moment and revolted. Unable to dislodge the rebels from their stronghold on Mount Ithome, the Spartans appealed for aid to the cities with which they were still technically allied by the terms of the Hellenic League formed in 481 for the defense of Greece during the Persian wars.

The Fall of Cimon and the Reforms of Ephialtes

Sparta's request touched off a vigorous debate in the Athenian assembly. Cimon, it seems, defended the time-honored alliance between Athens and Sparta, imploring the Athenians "not to allow Greece to go lame, or their own city be deprived of its yoke-fellow," while Ephialtes exhorted his fellow citizens to "let Sparta's pride be trampled underfoot" (Plutarch's *Cimon* 16.8; Scott-Kilvert 1960). Cimon carried the day, and he marched off to Sparta backed by four thousand hoplites. But something about the way the Athenian soldiers conducted themselves in Sparta sparked panic in the conservative and fundamentally xenophobic people they had come to help. Alone among the allies, the Athenians were sent home. Their abrupt dismissal imperiled what harmony had been achieved among the Greek states. Athens now made an alliance with Sparta's enemy Argos; Cimon, moreover, was ostracized for his miscalculation, leaving an open highway for Ephialtes and his associates. If the Spartans were alarmed by the Athenians' innovative and forward-looking ways of construing the world, they did a bad job of squelching these. Cimon's ostracism marked the beginning in Athens of full-blown democracy, taking democracy in the Greek sense of diffusing political power throughout the male citizen body, with no votes for women, no citizenship for immigrants, and slaves in abundance. Ironically, moreover, the naval ascendancy that Cimon had done so much to create played a large role in fostering the democratic reforms he opposed. Cimon seems to have supported a moderate hoplite democracy, that is, government by those who could afford to provide their own weapons and armor. The success of his naval operations, however, underlined the increasing importance to the state of the men who rowed the triremes (some moderately poor, some indigent), a development that served to undermine the old-fashioned system associating power with property and contributed to its replacement by a more broadly based form of government.

Ephialtes was able to seize on the discrediting of Cimon's policies by passing some significant democratic reforms. Though the details remain obscure, we know in a general sense that he substantially diminished the power and prestige of the ancient Council of the Areopagus. (Time had already done some of Ephialtes' work for him: Since the Areopagus consisted of ex-archons, it had been growing less and less aristocratic with each year that had passed since 486, when the Athenians had begun selecting archons by lot.) At the instigation of Ephialtes, the assembly passed measures constricting the jurisdiction of this body, transferring many of its functions to the *boulē*, the *ekklēsia*, and the body of prospective jurors known as the *hēliaia*. Ephialtes was careful, however, to show respect for its venerable history and long traditions by leaving it with jurisdiction over homicide and some religious matters.

Shortly after these reforms were enacted, men who presumably disliked the turn the government was taking arranged for Ephialtes' assassination. Upon Ephialtes' death the leadership of the loosely organized political group to which we give the somewhat misleading term "party" devolved upon his dynamic associate Pericles, who remained the most prominent politician in Athens from roughly 461 to his death in 429.

THE "FIRST" (UNDECLARED) PELOPONNESIAN WAR (460–445 BC)

Pericles took the lead in shaping Athenian policy throughout the decade during which Athens chose to wage war with both the Persian Empire and the Peloponnesian League. Hostilities with Persia survived Cimon's ostracism, while tensions with Sparta and its allies escalated. The period from 460 to 445 BC is sometimes called the first Peloponnesian War, an undeclared war between the Athenian and

Spartan leagues that really consisted of a series of battles often punctuated by considerable intervals of peace. (The famous Peloponnesian War, which was fought fairly steadily for twenty-seven years from 431 to 404, was really the second Peloponnesian War.)

Athens' Conflicts with Its Neighbors

Sitting between Corinth and Attica, the commercial state of Megara played an important role in the outbreak of both Peloponnesian wars. Around the time of Ephialtes' death it decided to bolt from the Peloponnesian League and ally itself with Athens to obtain protection from the designs of Corinth. Not surprisingly, the Corinthians were alarmed by the Athenians' possession of the Megarian port of Pegae on the Corinthian Gulf, from which it was easy to sail to the west. They became more agitated still at the upshot of the helot rebellion that had followed the earthquake in the Peloponnesus, for when the helots on Mount Ithome finally surrendered on condition that they be permitted to leave the Peloponnesus, the Athenians settled them at Naupactus near the mouth of the Gulf, on the northern shore. This bold action drove an additional wedge into the Corinthians' sphere of influence. With the two states locked in trade rivalry, moves that promised to expand the territory easily accessible to Athenian shipping were bound to spark hostility in Corinth, and it was predictable that the tension between Athens and Corinth would play a large role in determining the diplomatic relations of the Greek states.

In 459, Corinth and Aegina combined against Athens. The Athenians not only repelled a Corinthian invasion of Megara but also built formidable walls, the so-called Long Walls, linking Athens to the port of Piraeus. This prudent strategy had the effect of making the whole town complex impossible to besiege by land, since supplies could always be brought in by boat. Around the same time they engaged Hippodamus, a native of Miletus who wrote a treatise on town planning, to design the port area, which he laid out on a grid pattern similar to that of his home state in Ionia.

The Spartans' decision to enter the war against Athens in 457 did more harm to them than to their designated enemy. Fighting the Athenians in Boeotia, what the Spartans chiefly accomplished was to draw Athens into Boeotian affairs. By 456, the Athenians had come to control the whole region with the exception of Thebes, and Athenian influence (or pressure) had made democratic governments the norm in the Boeotian poleis. West of Boeotia, Phocis and Locris joined the Delian League, as did the vanquished island of Aegina, and Athens also gained two states in the Peloponnesus itself, Troezen on the east coast and Achaea on the Corinthian Gulf.

Disaster in Egypt and the Transfer of the League Treasury to Athens

Athens' land empire now stood at its maximum extent. Determined to continue operations against Persia, Pericles persuaded the Athenians to send ships both to

Cyprus, where they hoped to inflict damage on the Phoenician fleet, and to Egypt, which had rebelled from King Artaxerxes. The Egyptian campaign, however, ended in disaster; Thucydides reports losses of some two hundred Athenian and allied ships with their crews, a total of 40,000 men. It was at this juncture that the Athenians decided to proclaim their ongoing supremacy by transferring the League treasury from Delos, vulnerable to pirates and Persians alike, to Athens itself. Historians consequently have taken 454 as a convenient date to stop referring to the Delian League and begin speaking of the Athenian Empire, though in reality of course the transformation had been going on for some time.

A Brief Hiatus: Athens at Peace with Persia and Sparta

Returning from his ten years' exile in 451, Cimon negotiated a truce of five years between Athens and Sparta and abandoned Athens' alliance with Argos. Argos in turn signed a thirty-year treaty with Sparta; the expiration of this treaty in 420, eleven years after the beginning of the (second) Peloponnesian War, would create a volatile situation in mainland Greece. When Cimon died campaigning in Cyprus in 450, the Athenians apparently made peace with Persia.

Peace with Sparta followed in 445 when the Athenian land empire collapsed virtually overnight as a revolt in Euboea was followed by the defection of Megara. After sixteen years of imperialism within mainland Greece, the Athenians had lost thousands of lives and had no more territory than they had possessed in 461 when fighting had begun. King Pleistoanax of Sparta invaded. Through delicate diplomacy and probably outright bribery as well, Pericles persuaded Pleistoanax to return home, but terror had been struck in the Athenians' hearts. Though in time Pericles himself subdued Euboea, Megara reverted to the Peloponnesian League, and Athenian influence in Boeotia crashed to a close as Thebes assumed leadership of an antidemocratic Boeotian League.

The peace of 445 was optimistically named the Thirty Years' Peace, though it would not last even half that long. The key provisions of the peace were five: Neither state was to interfere with the allies of the other; neutrals were free to join either side; disagreements were to be settled by arbitration; no allies were permitted to switch sides; and each hegemon was free to use force to resolve conflicts within its own alliance.

PERICLES AND THE GROWTH OF ATHENIAN DEMOCRACY

The guiding spirit of Athenian imperialism was Pericles, who owed his position at Athens in part to his repeated election to the post of strategos and in part to the high regard in which the Athenians held him. Though he always served concurrently with nine other strategoi, none of the other generals exercised a parallel influence in the ekklesia.

The Athenian Assembly

The ekklesia met in the open air on the hill known as the Pnyx. In the early decades of the fifth century it convened only about a dozen times a year, but the number of meetings soon expanded, and in Pericles' time ten days rarely went by without at least one meeting. Rain or shine, assemblies that promised discussion of serious problems were likely to be attended by about six thousand—the quorum for certain important actions such as ostracism. This number was probably an eighth or so of all adult citizen males in Attica during Pericles' career, when the city's population was at its height. During the first half of the fifth century, boys with at least one Athenian parent would be enrolled in their demes as citizens at the age of eighteen, but in 451, for reasons that are uncertain, Pericles persuaded the Athenians to limit citizenship to those whose parents were both Athenians. Citizenship was important for girls as well as boys: Though Athenian women could not vote or hold offices, they were now the only women who could bear Athenian children.

The consequences of this legislation were both wide and deep. Throughout Greece, the discouragement of marriage between citizens and aliens increased the jingoistic tendencies of the polis. The insistence that people marry citizens of their own state eliminated a powerful source of connectedness among poleis and fostered a sense of separateness that frequently led to war. Social problems were also created within the polis. Limited in their choice of marriage partners to Athenian women, married Athenian men frequently opened the door to domestic tensions by maintaining sexual relationships with the exotic "foreign" women whom they could not marry if they wanted their descendants to be citizens.

Those who attended the assembly might be lifelong advocates of certain policies and could well be followers of a popular politician, but they were not members of political parties as we know them today, for there was no such thing in Athens. Classical Greek even lacks a word for a political party; writers used expressions like "those around So-and-So" to identify political groups. Even among men who elected to attend meetings of the assembly, the degree to which citizens chose to participate varied widely. As at gatherings of academic faculties today (or town meetings in New England), some never spoke, some spoke occasionally, a hard core of engaged citizens spoke frequently—and no doubt there were a few who seemed to speak incessantly. Some people spoke extemporaneously; others brought notes or even a text. Speakers had to be prepared for their remarks to be interrupted periodically by laughter, applause, or heckling of various sorts. Once the debate was concluded—assembly meetings rarely went past early afternoon, for some time had to be reserved before supper for the daily meeting of the boule—voting was conducted by show of hands.

Who attended the meetings of the assembly? Common sense would suggest that those who lived in the city were more likely to turn up than those who lived far away, and no doubt the walk in from distant villages discouraged some citizens, especially on rainy days. Nonetheless it seems that people did take the trouble to make the trip when vital matters (like whether or not to go to war) were slated for discussion.

Athenian Officials

Athens had no president or prime minister; the generals exercised power in politics only by virtue of the esteem in which they were held. Until Pericles' death, men who lacked military reputations did not generally become distinguished politicians. The converse tended to be true as well—military heroes expected to be rewarded with political careers. All this changed after Pericles' death, when politics and the military began to diverge as careers and it became less unusual for a man to be just a general or just a politician; concomitantly the government ceased to be dominated entirely by the scions of famous clans. Throughout Athenian history, however, wealth and lineage remained important factors, and generals continued to involve themselves in politics more than they do in many countries today.

The board of ten generals on which Pericles served was only one of many bodies the Athenians established. Including jobs entailed by the administration of the empire, there may have been as many as seven hundred official positions in Classical Athens, and most offices were held, like the strategia, by boards of several men, all serving one-year terms. Many, like the archons, were selected by lot. Most citizen males by the time they died had held some public office at one time or another, and a good number had held several. By diluting power in this way, Athenian voters believed they could inhibit the growth of an identifiable class of permanent officials (what we might call bureaucrats) with interests different from those of the populace at large.

The Judicial System and State Pay for State Service

By the time of Pericles, the Athenians had come to call their form of government *dēmokratia*, a government in which the *kratos* ("power") was in the hands of the *dēmos* ("the people"), by which they meant the male citizens in their capacity as voters in the assembly—and as jurors in the courts. The large size of Athenian juries—several hundred, occasionally as many as 1501—facilitated the legal fiction that a decision of a jury was a decision of the demos, and consequently there could be no appeal from a verdict in an Athenian courtroom. The Athenians were a notoriously litigious people. In Aristophanes' *Clouds*, a lively comedy whose depiction of Socrates contributed substantially to the hostility against the philosopher, one of Socrates' pupils points out Athens on a map to the crotchety Strepsiades, but Strepsiades is not persuaded. "What's that you're saying?" he asks; "I'm not convinced, since I don't see any courts in session" (208).

To ensure that the privilege of serving on juries would be spread as widely throughout the citizen body as possible, not long after Ephialtes' death Pericles introduced a measure providing pay for jury service. It was a small amount, less than a day's wages for an average laborer, but not trivial, and no doubt this legislation bolstered Pericles' popularity at the polls. In time, Athenians came to be paid for serving on the boule and even for attending the assembly; for many years during the fifth century magistrates were also paid for their time. Today it seems natural to compensate people for the time spent serving the community, and state pay for state service is now the norm. But many Athenians—mostly affluent men who could afford to serve without remuneration—viewed this system as a discreditable attempt on the part of democratic politicians to buy popularity and votes. In the aristocratic value system, it was acceptable for Cimon to court popularity by inviting passersby to pick fruit from his orchards and by holding banquets for the hungry at his home, but it was manipulative and underhanded of Pericles to introduce measures in the assembly providing for compensation to those who served the state.

Despite a variety of constitutional reforms and creative innovations designed to maximize popular participation in civic life, rich Athenians continued to enjoy substantial prestige. Democratic politicians, moreover, cleverly harnessed the wealth of the elite into the service of the state by establishing a network of public services known as liturgies. These included major outlays such as maintaining a trireme and training its crew (the liturgy known as the trierarchy), leading and financing a delegation to a religious festival in another Greek state, paying and training a team of runners for the intertribal torch races at festivals within Athens, or offering a banquet to all members of one's tribe on the occasion of a religious festival. Some of the most elaborate (though not as expensive as the trierarchy, which remained the costliest liturgy) involved training choruses for performances at Attic festivals in honor of Athena or Dionysus. About a hundred civilian liturgies were performed each year. Everyone profited from this system. Those who lacked the means to offer such services benefited from the generosity of those who provided them, and the rich could reaffirm their status while simultaneously performing vital military, cultural, religious, and civic functions for the community. A competitive element also fostered excellence, for prizes at contests went to the victorious choregist as well as to the successful poet.

LITERATURE AND ART

A word commonly attached to the art and literature of the earlier fifth century is "grandeur." During this vigorous era of transition, talented poets, painters, architects, and sculptors carried the traditions of the sixth century throughout the wider Greek world, while in Athens the defeat of Persia was marked by innovations in tragic drama (see Chapter Seven) so striking as to constitute a new art form.

Lyric Poetry

Lyric was a necessary precursor of tragedy, and its practitioners were among the most distinguished writers of the fifth century. Simonides (c. 556–468 BC) is remembered chiefly as the unofficial poet laureate of the Persian wars. He was probably in Athens when the Persians invaded Greece, and his epitaphs for the war dead (such as the one cited in Chapter Five) became to Greek literature what the Declaration of Independence and the Gettysburg Address are to Americans (only easier to remember, since they were in verse).

Sicilian tyrants were well known for their interest in culture, and both Simonides and his nephew Bacchylides benefited from their patronage. Though both were famed for their success in the genre known as the epinician ode, that is, poems written *epi-nikē* ("upon [an athletic] victory"), the verdict of posterity went rather to Pindar. At the courts of Sicilian tyrants as well as elsewhere in Greece, Pindar enjoyed the favor of the rich and powerful. His world view was diametrically opposed to that of democrats in Athens and elsewhere. Like Theognis, Pindar took it as axiomatic that merit was inherited. His many odes, rich in allusion and soaring in language, share a deeply held belief in an old-fashioned heroism—an excellence that takes as its starting point the assumption that men of worth spring from illustrious families that can trace their origins ultimately to divine ancestors. Writing numerous epinician odes, he was also disposed to associate physical prowess with all-around virtue. By connecting recent achievements with divine blood and tracing the ancestry of his subjects, he was able to elaborate his poems with powerful myths about gods and ancient heroes. His concern with the notion of excellence lent a lofty and inspirational quality to his verse.

Document 6.1 Excerpt from Pindar's sixth Nemean ode. The occasion of this poem was the victory of Alcimidas of Aegina in the boys' wrestling contest at Nemea, perhaps in 465 BC. The poet recalls the Olympic victory of Alcidamas' grandfather and sings of the immortality conferred by poetry.

There is one race of men,
   one race of gods.
      Yet from one mother
         we both take our breath.
      The difference
   is in the allotment
of all power,
      for the one is nothing
while the bronze sky exists forever,
a sure abode.
      And yet, somehow,
   we resemble the immortals,
      whether in greatness of mind
         or nature, though we know not
      to what measure
day by day and in the watches of the night
      fate has written that we should run.
And now Alkimidas
   gives clear proof
      that the power
         born in the blood
      is like

the fruit-bearing fields
that now, in alternation,
        yield mankind
yearly sustenance from the ground
and now, again, resting
        withhold their strength
. . .

treading in the footprints of his father's father,
Praxidamas—
        for he, victorious at Olympia,
first brought the Aiakidai garlands from Alpheos;
. . .

        come, Muse, direct
    upon this clan
the glorious breath of song—
        for when men have passed out of our midst
poems and legends
        convey their noble deeds. . . .

1–25; translated by Frank Nisetich, *Pindar's Victory Songs*.
Baltimore and London: Johns Hopkins University Press, 1980.

The Visual Arts

Greek painters and sculptors shared a fascination with both the human and the divine. Throughout the decades of change and growth that mark the fifth century, the plastic arts reveal a powerful drive to organize the world in accord with harmony, balance, and proportion. During the fourth century, Plato, in the blueprint for the ideal society he described in his dialogue *The Republic*, would identify justice as the condition that is obtained when all parts of the soul and state are in balance. The connections Plato posited between beauty and truth underlay much of the Greek view of the world throughout the Classical period.

Greek painting and sculpture achieved what they did within the constraints posed by a variety of conventions. Bronze and marble, the customary materials for sculpture, were difficult to work with and did not lend themselves to naturalism. The two generations or so that followed the Persian wars mark a period of transition during which Greek artists begin to emancipate themselves from the canons of the Archaic period, as a spare austerity comes to distinguish Classical styles from those that had gone before. Some of the changes may have had to do with a rejection of eastern influences in the wake of the bitter conflict with Persia; the ties with the Near East that were so conspicuous in Archaic styles now seem more tenuous. The visual arts also become less static during these decades, and action becomes important. Conveying a strong sense of movement in a still medium is no small achievement. Some of the most outstanding artists of these decades managed despite the constraints of their craft to build a sense of anticipation and excitement.

To be sure, the tranquility of Archaic sculpture persists in some of the work of this period. It is evident, for example, in the bronze charioteer dedicated at Delphi in the 470s by Hiero's brother Polyzalus after his victory in the chariot races at the Pythian games. The eerie stillness of the body and the garment that falls from it in perfect folds show precisely the discipline and self-control that Pindar celebrated in the aristocrats who carried off prizes in these events.

Figure 6.3. This bronze charioteer from the Sanctuary of Apollo at Delphi (c. 475 BC) originally stood in the car of a four-horse chariot; it has survived because an earthquake cast it into an ancient drain.

Figure 6.4. Roman copy of the *diskobolos* or "discus thrower" by Myron. Scholars recognized Myron's statue as the model for the Roman copies because of a passage by the second-century AD author Lucian that describes the original work in detail.

Probably the free-standing sculpture that conveys the most dramatic sense of movement to come was the so-called *diskobolos* ("discus thrower") of the Athenian sculptor Myron, who was known for his striking realism: Admirers commented that a bronze cow of his on the Acropolis could easily be mistaken for the real thing. Though the bronze diskobolos Myron made around 460 does not survive, a variety of Roman copies enable us to appreciate the pent-up energy the athlete is about to unleash as he hurls his arm forward leaning into the throw.

The relief sculpture with which Greeks adorned their temples offered still greater opportunities for storytelling. One key example is the temple of Zeus at Olympia, completed between 470 and 456 BC just when the dramas of Aeschylus were defining the Attic stage. Excavations have brought to light remarkable sculptural groups on the portions of the temple known as the pediments—the elongated triangular spaces under the roof that sat atop the columns and cried out for decoration. In the temple of Zeus, each pediment extended for over 80 feet from left to right and rose in the center to a height of 10 feet. The west pediment celebrated the triumph of order and civilization over the animal-like barbarism represented by the Centaurs, who in their characteristic drunkenness had sought to disrupt the wedding of the hero Peirithoos to Deidameia only to find themselves worsted in the melee by Peirithoos and his friend Theseus. In the center of the relief stands a figure whom most scholars identify as Apollo upholding the principles of civility.

The east pediment portrayed a more complicated story—an episode in the life of Agamemnon's ancestor Pelops, who won his bride Hippodameia in a chariot race arranged by her father Oenomaus, an event associated with the beginning of the Olympic games. Numerous figures in the scene depicted on the temple have survived, including one of the most remarkable individuals depicted in relief sculpture, a pensive seer who even before the race has begun knows what is going to happen (Figure 6.5b). (Although the race was fixed, Pelops managed to defeat the duplicitous Oenomaus, who was killed, and marry Hippodameia.)

Grave stelai also provided an important venue for relief sculpture. Although most commemorated the deaths of men, women and girls were depicted on their tombstones as well. One of the best preserved funerary reliefs of the fifth century offers a tender portrayal of a little girl holding her pet doves. This poignant reflection of the dead child makes clear that for all their preoccupation with war and civic engagement the Greeks could also feel private losses deeply.

Thousands of vases survive from the Classical period. Neither vases nor works of sculpture are easy to ascribe to any particular artist; by convention, painters are often known simply by the subject matter of their most memorable works or the places where they were or can be found (e. g., the Berlin painter, the Pan painter). Like sculpture, vase painting of the earlier fifth century was focused on the human figure, to which the curving surfaces of the vessels lent a sense of movement and grace. Even more than in drama, in which actors' faces were covered by masks, the possibilities of facial expression are limited by the medium, and character portrayal is weak; we are often given a clear sense of what the dramatis personae of the vase are experiencing at the moment in time the artist

a

b

Figure 6.5a. The pediments of the temple of Zeus at Olympia (c. 460 BC) show scenes from Greek mythology. The east pediment (a) tells the story of the chariot race between Pelops and Oenomaus, king of Pisa. The west pediment (b) depicts the melee that ensued when Peirothoos made the mistake of inviting the barbarous centaurs to his wedding.

Figure 6.5b. This marble statue of an elderly seer is the third figure from the right in the recontruction of the east pediment. It represents a dramatic blend of naturalistic and stylized elements.

Figure 6.6. This marble grave relief, from Paros, dates from about 450 BC and stands today in the Metropolitan Museum of Art.

has chosen to capture, but little understanding of who they have been over their lifetimes, what their driving anxieties or concerns were. The figures on Greek vases are portrayed in action, not contemplation—they almost never appear to be posing for the artist—and we ask ourselves not only, "What are they thinking? What are they feeling?," but also frequently, "What has just happened, and what will happen next?" As in the Archaic period, classical vases frequently took their subject matter from mythology, as in the fine vase in the Museum of Fine Arts in Boston depicting on one side the murder of Agamemnon and on the other that of his murderer Aegisthus.

Unlike sculpture, however, painting was as likely to treat mundane scenes of daily activities as it was to portray deeds of epic proportion. Vases have provided social historians with a wealth of information about how people spent their time at work and at play, showing women and men in a variety of activities; shoemakers, blacksmiths, agricultural workers, and other laborers are portrayed going about their tasks. We are indebted to vases for images of domestic space and

Figure 6.7. This Attic vase was probably painted around 470 BC, shortly before the production of Aeschylus' *Oresteia*.

Figure 6.8. Some vases depicted crafts-people at work, such as this Attic black-figure neck amphora showing shoes being made and a blacksmith forging.

the depictions of women from all social groups. Vases that were used at drinking parties for mixing and drinking wine frequently show prostitutes entertaining men. Some women are shown playing pipes, others are engaged in various stages of flirtation, and some scenes are frankly pornographic. Common prostitutes were often slaves. A woman of higher status who nevertheless mingled with men and received pay for her services was known as a *hetaira*. Such women were likely to be metics (see pp. 163–164) , either ex-slaves or freeborn, who—like male metics—gravitated to Athens because it was a commercial center. A few of these women, like Aspasia, the common-law wife of Pericles and the most famous hetaira of all, participated actively in the intellectual life of their male associates. In contrast, many paintings on vases used by respectable women depict wedding scenes, or women visiting tombs or sitting at home spinning wool or adorning themselves, often in the company of other women.

OIKOS AND POLIS

The Greek polis comprised *oikoi* ("families," "estates," or "households," each with a male head). The oikos was the primary unit of production, consumption, and reproduction. Citizens became members of the polis not directly as individuals, as they do in most modern states; rather, they first had to be accepted as members of an oikos.

Family Membership

When a baby was born in Attica the father decided whether to raise or expose it. He doubtless evaluated the newborn's health as well as the financial impact of raising another child. Most sons were raised, because male heirs were the normal means of perpetuating the lineage, and it was of great importance that families not die out. The offspring of a daughter was considered to belong to her husband's family, not her father's. As boys grew up, their labor was considered valuable. Moreover, they were expected to support their aged parents, bury them, and look after their tombs. Parents placed less value on girls, who lacked earning power and whose children would belong to a different family. Though the eldest child was normally raised regardless of its sex, some historians have conjectured that as many as 20 percent of newborn Athenian girls were abandoned in places like the local garbage dump. Slave dealers collected a few of the exposed infants and turned them over to wet nurses to be raised and sold as slaves. Most exposed infants, however, died, and exposure quickly became infanticide.

In Athens, after a baby boy was accepted as a member of his father's family, he needed to be approved by his father's quasi- or pseudofamily: A boy inherited membership in his phratry ("brotherhood") and deme ("city ward or country village") from his father. The father introduced and enrolled his baby in his phratry and vouched for him as being his own and born of an Athenian mother.

Demography and the Life Cycle

The average age at death in Classical Athens for adult females was about 36 years and for adult males 45 years. The average woman probably bore about 4.3 children, perhaps 2.7 of whom survived infancy. The death ratio for infants was 500 per 1000 adults. Athenian men married at approximately the age of thirty and women around the age of fifteen. Women were often widowed as a consequence of war, and the age difference heightened the likelihood of widowhood overtaking a woman before old age; men lost young wives in childbirth. Marriages could also be ended by divorce, which was not stigmatized unless some scandal was involved. Widowed and divorced people often remarried, and children of divorced parents generally lived with their fathers, to whose oikos they belonged.

Marriage

Greeks could be married only to one spouse at a time, although there was a double standard for sexual conduct and husbands might have additional sexual partners of either gender. Marriage was the social institution that sustained the oikos,

Figure 6.9. Detail of Attic red-figure *lebēs gamikos* ("wedding bowl") by the Washing Painter, last quarter of the fifth century. A bride displays a baby boy, the hoped for result of her marriage. A standing woman toward the right is holding a *loutrophoros*, a wedding vase used for transporting water for the prenuptial bath. The flying Nike (winged Victory) on the far right holds a vase for perfumed oil.

and its principal purpose was reproduction. At the time of betrothal the bride's father or other guardian declared in the presence of witnesses, "I give you my daughter to sow for the purpose of producing legitimate children." After the bridegroom agreed, "I take her," he and his fiancée's father agreed to the size of her dowry. For respectable girls there was no alternative to marriage, and the obligation to dower each daughter doubtless was a prime motivator in female infanticide.

The wife's dowry plus the husband's contribution constituted the economic foundation of the oikos at the start of a marriage. The ideal, at least for those who farmed their own land, was to furnish most of the basic necessities of life without needing to depend on purchasing supplies at the market. The division of labor was by gender: Women's work was indoors and men's outdoors. The husband brought into the house agricultural products such as fruit, vegetables, grain, and raw wool, and the wife and domestic slaves transformed these products into textiles and edible food. Wives were also responsible for storing the household contents safely, so that there would always be enough to eat and wear, and even to sell if the family fell on hard times.

Document 6.2. The customary division of labor in the oikos is spelled out in Xenophon's Socratic dialogue the *Oeconomicus*, in which Socrates' friend Ischomachus explains to him how he taught his fourteen-year-old bride to manage the household.

He told me he said to her: "Wife, the gods seem to have shown much discernment in yoking together female and male, as we call them, so that the couple might constitute a partnership that is most beneficial to each of them. . . ."

"Those who intend to obtain produce to bring into the shelter need someone to work at the outdoor jobs. For plowing, sowing, planting, and herding is all work that is performed outdoors, and it is from these that our essential provisions are obtained. As soon as these are brought into the shelter, then someone else is needed to look after them and to perform the work that requires shelters. The nursing of newborn children requires shelters, and so does the preparation of bread from grain, and likewise, making clothing out of wool. Because both the indoor and the outdoor tasks require work and concern," he said, "I think the god, from the very beginning, designed the nature of women for the indoor work and concerns and the nature of man for the outdoor work. . . .

For the woman it is more honorable to remain indoors than to be outside; for the man it is more disgraceful to remain indoors than to attend to business outside.

. . .

"And how did you arrange things for her, Ischomachus?"

"Well, I thought it was best to show her the possibilities of our house first. It is not elaborately decorated, Socrates, but the rooms are constructed in such a way that they will serve as the most convenient places to contain the things that will be kept in them. So the rooms themselves invited what was suitable for each of them. Thus the bedroom, because it was in the safest possible place, invited the most valuable bedding and furniture. The dry store rooms called for grain, the cool ones for wine, and the bright ones for those products and utensils which need light. I continued by showing her living rooms for the occupants, decorated so as to be cool in summer and warm in winter. I pointed out to her that the entire house has its facade facing south, so that it was obviously sunny in winter and shady in summer. I also showed her the women's quarters, separated from the men's quarters by a bolted door, so that nothing might be removed from them that should not be, and so that the slaves would not breed without our permission. For, generally, honest slaves become more loyal when they have produced children, but when bad ones mate, they become more troublesome."

Xenophon, *Oeconomicus* 7.18, 20–22, 30, 9.2–5; translated by Sarah B. Pomeroy, *Xenophon Oeconomicus, a Social and Historical Commentary*. Oxford: Clarendon Press, 1994, pp. 141, 143, 155.

Figure 6.10. Attic black-figure *lekythos*, sixth century, attributed to the Amasis Painter, showing textile production. Left: Woman spinning. Center: Woman weaving at a vertical loom. Right: The winged goddess Nike weighing wool.

The fundamental division of domestic space was between men and women. Even in a small house with only two rooms, one upstairs and one on the ground floor, the upper room was normally the women's quarters and the lower room the men's. Entertainment took place in the men's quarters, and so a visitor to the Greek home would meet only male members of the family; when strangers were in the house women and girls would withdraw to the secluded parts of the home and not even be mentioned by name. The females in the household, both free and slave, slept in the women's quarters. They also produced textiles there, though in warm weather they might move their looms into an interior courtyard and work outdoors, protected by the surrounding walls.

Citizen women whom poverty did not compel to work outside rarely ventured far from the house except for festivals and funerals. In this way they avoided encounters with men who were not their relatives and who might compromise their respectability either by actual sexual contact or by the rumor of it. Wherever possible, slaves and husbands did the marketing and other errands that required leaving the immediate environs of the home. The availability of slaves even for families of fairly modest means was vital in perpetuating the social ideal of the virtuous woman who never left the house. Women in straitened circumstances, however, would shop for groceries or household items themselves.

THE GREEK ECONOMY

Like women, slaves were a "muted group." Though they are ubiquitous in literature and the visual arts, their names and thoughts were not recorded, and few have left their mark on the historical record. We do know that the work of slaves did not always take place in the oikos. Large numbers of slaves were employed in the craft industries, some working for their owners and others rented out by them. Their jobs tended to be gender specific. Men worked in factories making swords, shields, furniture, pottery, and other items, while women often worked in textile-related industries. Inscriptions recording expenses incurred in construction on the Athenian Acropolis show that slaves were paid the same as free workers. Of course, the wages of slaves who were rented out were paid to their masters.

By no means were all craftspeople slaves; Aristotle in fact contended that most craftsmen were rich. Greeks whose social and economic status allowed them some choice, however, shunned work that made them subject to the commands of another person, and this included most craft fields. Such a life, they believed, was demeaning to a free male citizen. Unlike farming, to which a certain nobility was always attached, manual work performed indoors was despised by many wealthier Greeks and known by the name "banausic" labor, which means literally work performed over a hot furnace, and distinctions between skilled and unskilled labor were often ignored. It may be that the leisured classes disdained indoor work because of its connection with slaves and women. Litigants in Athenian courtrooms enjoyed making snide remarks about their opponents (or their opponents' relatives) ever having held any kind of job or even having run a business, and political theorists—who always came from the upper classes—contended often that strenuous indoor work ought to disqualify people from voting on the grounds that it damaged the mind as surely as it compromised the body. Most Greeks, however, had limited choices about how to support themselves and their families, and there is no reason to believe that those who worked for others or performed indoor manual labor were embarrassed about their professions. Tombstones frequently boasted of craft skills; surviving examples include epitaphs of a woodcutter and a miner. As elsewhere, the ideology of literate elites was at odds with the daily practice of ordinary people.

The disdain with which some Greeks regarded paid labor did not prevent a great deal of work from getting done or a good bit of money from being made. Sometimes, however, revenue was the product of imperialism and other forms of exploitation. Without the tribute from subject allies it would have been difficult for the Athenians to initiate the system of state pay for state service and thus significantly expand the proportion of citizens able to participate in the business of government. Democracy was not entirely dependent on empire; the Athenians lost their empire in 404 BC but continued to have democratic government for several generations until their conquest by Philip of Macedon in 338 (and in many respects democracy persisted even after that). But it certainly seems to have received its impetus from the surplus funds generated by imperial tribute. The splendid buildings with which the Athenians began adorning the Acropolis shortly after relocating the treasury in Athens certainly owed their existence to imperial revenues; no empire, no Parthenon. In addition, the empire's maritime nature meant that it served as the organizing principle of Greek trade. The centrality of the Athenian Empire to commercial life became abundantly plain in the late 430s when the Athenians banned Megarian merchants from trading in imperial ports, claiming they were simply making rules for their own sphere of influence as stipulated by the Thirty Years' Peace. The consequences of this move were fatal to Megarian trade, and outrage over this prohibition was one cause of the long Peloponnesian War of 431–404.

Agriculture and Trade

Before the nineteenth century AD most people in the world made their living by agriculture, and fifth-century Greeks were no exception. It was trade, however, that united the far-flung states that ringed the seas, and the routes over which material goods traveled also served as vital conduits for the exchange of ideas. Most trade went by boat, land traffic being a slow and expensive business over rocky roads; the cost of carting heavy goods by land might well exceed the price of the goods themselves.

The diversity of natural resources in the ancient world made trade a necessity; no polis had everything, and some poleis had very little indeed. Athenian commerce especially was driven largely by the need for grain to feed a large population. Athens was by far the most populous of the Greek cities, with a population that normally varied between 200,000 and 300,000. Grain might come from north or south. One crucial source was the Black Sea region, which also provided hides, cattle, fish, hemp, wax, chestnuts, iron, and slaves. For this the Athenians exchanged wine and oil, sometimes in decorated vases. These exports were themselves often resold elsewhere; the Phoenicians often sent Attic vases to Egypt, and a good deal of secondhand pottery from Athens has been discovered in Etruria in Italy. Italians also bought a good deal of Attic pottery firsthand. Another key granary lay in Egypt, where Attic olive oil was also traded for papyrus, ivory, glasswork, slaves, and exotic animals. Carthage provided textiles; Etruria fine bronzework and boots; Sicily pigs, cheese, and grain; Phoenicia purple dye and dates. Corinth exported its own wares as well as serving as an intermediary between east and west, sending out tiles and metalwork. Already in the fifth century it seems that some silks from China made their way to Greece via Scythian intermediaries. Arabia exported perfumes, and Persia carpets. Important sources of metals were identified early: Cyprus for copper, Spain for tin, Laconia as well as the Black Sea for iron, Thasos and Mount Pangaeus in northern Greece for gold. All these goods flowed throughout the Greek world, but most of all they flowed into Piraeus.

Metics in Fifth-Century Athens

Many rich residents of Athens, however, did not own land, since it was illegal for them to do so without special dispensation. These were the resident aliens known as metics, and they played a key role in the economy. Craftspeople and entrepreneurs who had come from all over the Greek world to conduct business in Athens, metics accounted for a significant proportion of the Athenian population. They could not vote or hold office; neither could their children or their children's children. They were forced to live in rented homes. But rented homes can be quite lovely, and metic families mingled comfortably with citizen families and suffered no social disabilities. A number of the central characters in Plato's works were metics, and the most famous Platonic dialogue, *The Republic*, was set at the home of the rich metic Cephalus, whom Pericles had invited to Athens from Syracuse. Citizens, metics, and slaves often worked side by side, sometimes for the same pay; a list of workers at one construction site included eighty-six laborers whose status can be determined—twenty-four citizens, forty-two metics, and twenty slaves. In a crisis, metics could be drafted into the armed forces.

Many of Athens' most distinguished intellectuals were metics, such as the philosopher Aristotle. Pericles' common-law wife Aspasia belonged to the metic class, and it was for this reason that he required a decree of the assembly to grant citizenship to their children. The inability of metic women to produce children who could enjoy Athenian citizenship played a large role in shaping the contours of Athenian society, creating two classes of women available as long-term partners to citizen men—metic mistresses and citizen wives. (In addition, a variety of prostitutes, both slave and free, were available for briefer encounters, and owners enjoyed the privilege of sexual access to their slaves.) Most metic women, of course, were housewives married to metic men. Slaves who were granted their freedom became metics rather than citizens. There were metics in some other poleis, but almost nothing is known of metics outside Athens.

The cultural achievements of sixth- and early fifth-century Greece were substantial, but the difficulties the city-states experienced in getting along with one another (and their aversion to uniting into a single political unit) would have a profound impact on the direction Greek civilization would take. The Thirty Years' Peace held a great deal of promise, but it was problematic in many ways. Dividing the Greek world openly into two spheres of influence—a Spartan land empire in mainland Greece and an Athenian naval one in the Aegean—was a dubious enterprise. From one standpoint, by drawing lines clearly the agreement seemed to hold out the hope of peace; but it also fostered a potentially dangerous bipolarity. The notion of submitting disputes to arbitration was all very civilized in the abstract, but with every state of any reputation allied with one side or the other, just who was going to act as mediator? No treaty, moreover, could change the fact that Megara still sat uneasily on the Attic border, or could diminish the commercial rivalry between Athens and Corinth. In 445 it was impossible to predict whether the peace would last.

TRANSLATIONS

Pomeroy, Sarah B. 1994. *Xenophon Oeconomicus, a Social and Historical Commentary.* Oxford: Clarendon Press.

Scott-Kilvert, Ian. 1960. *The Rise and Fall of Athens: Nine Greek Lives by Plutarch.* Harmondsworth, UK: Penguin.

SUGGESTED READINGS

Cohen, David. 1991. *Law, Sexuality, and Society: The Enforcement of Morals in Classical Athens.* Cambridge, UK: Cambridge University Press. What the framing and application of law reveal about sexual values and practices.

Ehrenberg, Victor. 1973. *From Solon to Socrates.* 2nd ed. London: Methuen. This remains a sensitive and thoughtful study of the evolution of Greek culture during the sixth and fifth centuries.

Fantham, Elaine, Helene Foley, Natalie Kampen, Sarah B. Pomeroy, and H. A. Shapiro. 1994. *Women in the Classical World: Image and Text.* New York and Oxford: Oxford University Press. An examination of the written and visual evidence for the lives of ancient women, placed within their historical and cultural context.

Hanson, Victor. 1989. *The Western Way of War: Infantry Battle in Classical Greece.* New York: Alfred A. Knopf. A gripping account of the experience of hoplite battle.

Just, Roger. 1989. *Women in Athenian Law and Life*. London and New York: Routledge. A study of how Athenian men sought to define and locate women.

Meiggs, Russell. 1972. *The Athenian Empire*. Oxford: Oxford University Press. A richly detailed examination of Athenian imperialism and the world that came under its sway.

Pollitt, Jerome J. 1972. *Art and Experience in Classical Greece*. Cambridge, UK: Cambridge University Press. A sensitive survey of Greek art that grounds it firmly in its historical context.

Pomeroy, Sarah B. 1998. *Families in Classical and Hellenistic Greece: Representations and Realities*. Oxford: Clarendon Press. An account of the Greek family as a productive, reproductive, and social unit.

7

GREECE ON THE EVE OF THE PELOPONNESIAN WAR

Avoiding war was particularly important when the Greeks had such precious achievements to protect in so many areas. From Sicily to Anatolia, remarkable temples to the gods proclaimed the grandeur of Hellenic civilization under the open sky. Greek ships plied the seas in all directions, enabling men and women hundreds of miles away to exchange their wares and profit from a wide variety of resources and skills. Novel experiments in government were in progress. The same diversity that fostered the dynamic creativity of the Greeks, however, also fragmented their world. The world of the *polis*, moreover, was in many ways a narrow one. Despite the growth of what the Greeks called democracy, ultimately each polis was grounded in the rule of an elite of free men over everyone else; and the inability of the *poleis* to get along boded ill for the future of Greece. Inevitably, prospects for the future were clouded by intermittent suspicions that the peace between the Athenian and Spartan camps might not endure.

GREECE AFTER THE
THIRTY YEARS' PEACE

After the signing of the peace in 445 BC, many Greeks were optimistic. The fact that their optimism was misplaced makes it easy to view the years before the outbreak of the Peloponnesian War in 431 as only a prelude to hostilities. Though it is important to try to understand events in their historical context instead of in terms of their consequences, hindsight also has some value. Viewed from the perspective of the war that followed, certain events of the 440s and 430s take on particular significance.

During this period the Athenians showed a marked interest in the west and in the northeast. Athens had multiple motives for accepting Megara into its alliance in 460, but access to the port of Pegae on the Corinthian Gulf had certainly been one factor, and the settlement of the Messenians at Naupactus several years

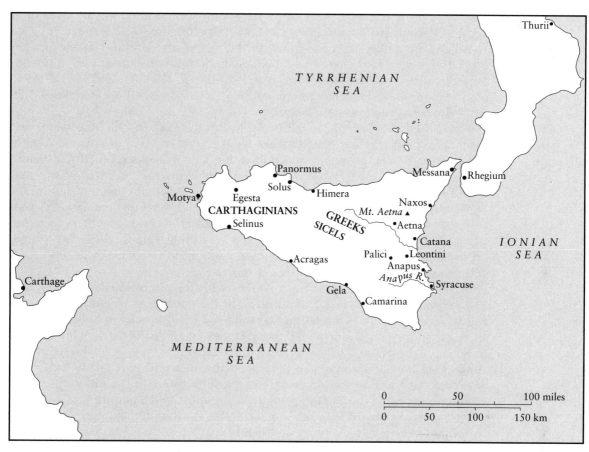

Figure 7.1. Sicily and southern Italy.

later provided a convenient stopping place for ships heading west. Probably also in the 450s Athens had contracted alliances with several Sicilian cities including Leontini, a city with a history of tense relations with Syracuse, a colony and ally of Athens' trade rival Corinth. Commerce with the western Greeks played a key role in the Athenian economy, and gradually the Greek cities of Sicily adopted Athenian currency.

Athens' growing interest in the rich lands to the west is confirmed by Pericles' decision to found a colony in the instep of Italy in 443. Thurii, however, was not an ordinary foundation, for the Athenians invited the other Greek states to share in founding a Panhellenic colony. Although the constitution of Thurii was democratic and the local coins were stamped with the head of Athena, the city adopted the laws of the Locrian lawgiver Zaleucus, and when a disagreement later led the colonists to ask the Pythia to whom they belonged, the Delphic oracle claimed them for Apollo, not Athens. Whatever Pericles' intentions for Thurii may have been, the Attic element in the population declined greatly over time, and the Corinthians do not appear to have taken offense.

Athens' immediate interest, however, lay in the area around Thrace and the Black Sea region. From here the Athenians imported hides, dyes, and, more importantly, grain and the timber they needed for their fleet. Around 445 the Athenians founded the Thracian colony of Brea, and a decade later Pericles led an Athenian squadron into the Black Sea.

Meanwhile, an alarming revolt broke out in the east. In 440, first Samos and then Byzantium rebelled, raising fears for the very survival of Athens' Aegean empire. Years later, according to Thucydides, some Greeks claimed that Samos "had almost managed to wrest from the Athenians their control of the sea" (8.76.4). When Samos' oligarchic government quarreled with the new democratic regime in neighboring Miletus, the Milesians together with some Samian exiles complained to Athens. One of three privileged allies (along with Lesbos and Chios) who contributed ships instead of paying tribute, Samos rebelled at Athens' order to submit the matter to arbitration, leading the Athenians to send forty ships to replace the oligarchy with a democracy.

Samos thereupon revolted from Athens with the aid of the satrap of Sardis. The subsequent revolt of Byzantium raised the specter of an empire-wide upheaval. The determined campaign that followed involved all ten of the Athenian strategoi and over 200 ships—160 from Athens and 55 from the remaining allies in the navy, Lesbos and Chios. When Samos fell after a long siege, the Athenians confiscated the Samian navy and established a democracy. A heavy indemnity was imposed and hostages taken. About the subjugation of Byzantium we know nothing except that the Byzantines agreed to return to the empire.

At the same time, Athens kept a hand in the northeast, planting the colony of Amphipolis on a strategic point on the Strymon River by the border of Macedonia and Thrace in 437. In addition to protecting Athens' access to grain, timber, and minerals, Amphipolis helped the Athenians monitor activities in the recently organized kingdom of the Thracian Odrysians to the north and east as well as in Macedonia to the west. But the fact that the town drew much of its population from neighboring towns undermined its loyalty to Athens, and in 424 it surrendered to Sparta.

Virtually nothing is known about how Spartans viewed the world between the Thirty Years' Peace in 445 BC and their declaration of war on Athens in 432. A hint is provided, however, by Thucydides' remark that the Corinthians claimed that they dissuaded the Spartans from attacking Athens at the time of the Samian rebellion: "We did not cast the deciding vote against you," they reported, "when Samos revolted from you, and when the Peloponnesians were evenly divided over whether to help them. We openly opposed it, saying that any city could punish its own allies" (1.40). If the story is true, then some members of the Peloponnesian League, including possibly Sparta, saw merit in attacking Athens in 440. Still, a war between Athens and Sparta was far from certain. At the same time that the fate of peace hung in the balance, moreover, Greece experienced a remarkable burst of cultural creativity.

THE PHYSICAL SPACE OF THE POLIS: ATHENS IN THE FIFTH CENTURY

The Greek world was both one and many: Though common features tied the city-states together, each polis was unique in culture. As so often in attempts to recover the world of Classical Greece, however, the bulk of our knowledge about the development of the polis during the later decades of the fifth century comes from Athens. Even during the war, Athenian dramatists continued to produce astonishing masterpieces. Some of our best evidence about fifth-century Athens is physical in nature, for the revenues of empire helped to adorn the imperial city with splendid buildings, many of which still impress and intrigue visitors today.

The Acropolis

A hill was a distinct advantage to a city-state. Though most people today associate the word "acropolis" with the Acropolis of Athens, in fact it was a feature common to many poleis, which relied for protection on a fortified citadel from which one could see far into the distance. In Athens, the Acropolis was the spiritual focus of the polis. Because of its height and steeply sloped sides, this naturally fortified area had been the residence of early rulers and had always been home to the chief gods of the Athenians. The sixth-century tyrant Peisistratus, like Pericles later, initiated an ambitious building project on the Acropolis, for he understood not only that such work would provide steady employment to the restless urban poor, but also that a beautiful city would create still more jobs, foster patriotism among all citizens, and attract wealthy, talented metics. It would be, as Pericles would later say in the pages of Thucydides, "the school of Greece." The Persian invasion of 480 BC destroyed the monuments and statues of Peisistratus's time. This rubble, in turn, was used as the foundation of the buildings constructed in Pericles' day on the Acropolis, largely financed by funds from the Delian League.

In the Classical period, the two principal architectural styles or orders were the Doric and Ionic. (The ornate Corinthian capital, invented in classical times, did not become popular until the Hellenistic period.) Though both orders were used for the same building purposes, they differed in details such as the shape of the columns and of their bases and capitals and in the features of the entablature, or structure that supported the roof. Architects strove to design buildings according to the principles of each order, rather than to invent new or highly individualized styles. The pleasure they took in their work was not the sort of delight one might take today in striking out in original and startling directions. Rather, Greek architects took from their work that special kind of satisfaction that comes from exercising creativity within the limits posed by an elaborate code of restraints. In this they resembled the tragedians.

The temple of Athena Parthenos ("the virgin") known as the Parthenon was a blend of Doric and Ionic elements. The rectangular structure with a ratio of eight

Figure 7.2. This model of the classical Acropolis shows the Panathenaic procession through the western gates (Propylaea), which are flanked on the right (south) by the temple of Athena Nike (Victory). The largest building is the Parthenon. The Erectheion is on the left (north) of the Parthenon.

columns on the front and back ends to seventeen on the sides was both aesthetically pleasing and appropriate to its commanding site on the acropolis. Greek architects knew that from a distance the eye would perceive straight vertical elements as thin in the middle and appearing to fall outward, and a horizontal foundation (stylobate) would appear to droop toward the center. As the Roman architect Vitruvius, who worked in the second half of the first century BC, explains, architects countered these illusions by subtle swelling (entasis) of the midportion of the columns, by tilting the columns and interior walls toward the interior lest they seem to be falling outward, and by increasing the height of the floor and steps toward the center. These refinements increase the impressions of solidity and height and some add strength to the building. Although, with the exception of the roof, the Parthenon was built of marble, like other Doric temples it preserves elements of earlier wooden construction, especially in the frieze where the triglyphs imitate the ends of three planks standing on their sides and follow the rule that all the corners of the frieze must end with a triglyph (see Figure 7.3).

Sculpture was an important feature of Greek architecture. The sculpture of the Parthenon depicted myths and history of Athena and Athens. The east pediment showed the birth of Athena while the west pediment illustrated the contest between Athena and Poseidon over primacy in Athens. A sculpted frieze running

Figure 7.3. The Doric and Ionic orders. The Doric order (left) may be a direct translation into stone of building elements that were originally made of wood. The more complex capital of the Ionic order is in a spiraled form known as a volute.

around the top of the exterior wall of the cella or "inner shrine" showed human figures, horses, sacrificial animals, and the twelve Olympian gods. Probably the array of human figures and animals depicts the procession at the Greater Panathenaic festival that was held every four years and the presentation of a new dress for the goddess by young girls who had helped to weave it.

The temple was not a place where worshipers congregated, but rather the private home of a divinity whose image was placed inside and a storehouse for the cult's belongings. Thus, within the cella of the Parthenon was a tall figure of Athena constructed by fitting sheets of ivory and gold over a wooden scaffold. Locked in a back room were the goddess' possessions, among which were the treasury of the city of Athens and, after the middle of the fifth century, that of

Figure 7.4. Plan of Parthenon showing exterior colonnade and cella (main room) within. The cult statue of Athena was kept in the cella and the state treasury was stored in the back room.

Figure 7.5. The Parthenon, built 447–438 BC, photographed in the twentieth century, seen from the east.

the Delian League as well. In front of the Parthenon on the west stood a huge bronze statue of Athena Promachos ("Athena the Warrior who fights in the front"). The goddess was portrayed standing, with her left hand holding her shield and her right arm holding her spear. The statue was nearly 30 feet tall: sailors rounding Cape Sounion could see the welcome glint of sunlight off the tip of the spear. Like the statue inside the temple, it was the work of the sculptor Phidias. Viewed by his contemporaries as the greatest sculptor of gods, Phidias also created a huge gold and ivory statue of Zeus at Olympia that was considered to be one of the seven wonders of the ancient world.

In contrast to the Doric, which was massive, solid, and plain, the Ionic order gave a slender, graceful, ornate impression. The Erechtheion, sacred to Poseidon Erechtheus, was the chief purely Ionic monument on the Acropolis. The building consisted of three Ionic porches. To support the roof, the south porch that faced the Parthenon employed six figures of maidens, called Caryatids (instead of columns). The building was begun in 421 BC, and because of the Peloponnesian

Figure 7.6. Parthenon east frieze, slab V, probably showing the presentation of the dress known as the peplos for the statue of Athena Polias at the Panathenaea. A section of the continuous frieze running along the top of the exterior cella wall. Other portions show a cavalcade of horsemen, religious officials, sacrificial animals, and the Olympian gods.

Figure 7.7. Plan of Erectheion (421–406 BC). This graceful temple was sacred to Athena, Poseidon, and the legendary Athenian king Erechtheus. The complicated shape was the result of needing to skirt Athena's sacred olive tree to enclose Poseidon's trident mark and perhaps the tomb of Erechtheus.

Figure 7.8. The Erechtheion, built 421–406 BC, photographed in the twentieth century, showing the Porch of the Maidens (Caryatids) that faces the Parthenon. Since this photograph was taken, the statues have been moved indoors to protect them from pollution and replaced with copies.

War the decorations may never have been completed. Many other buildings, temples, statues, and votive offerings adorned the Acropolis. Though little remains of these monuments nowadays except the bare marble framework of the major ones, in antiquity they were much more colorful: Some of the architectural and sculptural features were painted red and blue and were covered with gold leaf. Below the Acropolis, dramas were staged in honor of the god Dionysus. Spectators sat in the open air in a semicircle on the bare hillside watching the performances that took place below in the orchestra ("dancing place").

The structures that comprised Pericles' building program confirmed most Athenians in their support for the empire, for without the tribute pouring in from subject states such lavish public monuments would have been difficult to finance. They also enhanced Pericles' popularity, providing jobs as well as beautifying the city. At the same time, they provided an opening for Pericles' enemies—personal rivals or those who disliked the march of democracy—to undermine him by calling into question the propriety of diverting League funds to the aesthetic improvement of the hegemonic city.

The Agora

The part of a Greek city known as the *agora* was principally a center for secular human activity, though the gods, who were never excluded from human activities, also had their place. The agora served as a market, as a meeting place for the exchange of goods and of news, and as a focus of social, political, and judicial activities. Daily life for women was ideally indoors and for men outdoors. Men who stayed indoors were suspected of being effeminate and antisocial, and women who ventured outdoors were likely to have their chastity questioned. In the *Laws* Plato noted that the greatest good in the polis is that the citizens be known to each other, as the men (certainly not the women) would be if they saw one another every day in the agora. Aristotle distinguished human beings from other living creatures by their use of speech (though, again, women were placed in a different category and are characterized as ideally silent). Speaking was essential for the activities that took place in the agora.

The Athenian agora was a large level space at the foot of the Acropolis on the road from the main city gate. The area was cluttered with public buildings of which the most easily identified is the round structure called the Tholos, which housed the *boulē* and where official weights and measures were stored. The agora was also the site of law courts, altars, shrines, statues, inscriptions, fountains, drains, and trophies of war. On the western border stood a Doric temple that was dedicated either to Hephaestus, the god of crafts, or to Theseus, a legendary hero and king of Athens. It has withstood the ravages of time far better than the Parthenon and is still in remarkably good condition. Roofed, multipurpose colonnades called stoas flanked the agora. Sandwiched between the permanent structures and within the stoas as well were shops, bankers' tables, booksellers, wholesale merchants, schools, and people buying and selling the necessities of life.

One important place in Athenian life was not a building: The hillside of the Pnyx where the assembly met towered above the city. Throughout the fifth century, citizens sat either on cushions or directly on the rocky ground that sloped from south to north, filling an area of 15,000 square feet. Around 400 BC the meeting place was evened out and enlarged, and benches seem to have been added. The adult male citizens of Attica gathered in all kinds of weather to listen to speeches and debates, to make motions, and to hold high officials to account. In voting (which was by show of hands) they not only took into consideration what they had heard on the Pnyx but also made use of all the information they had garnered in the agora.

Rural Life in Attica

The growth of the urban center was not at the expense of rural areas. Public buildings were also located away from the city center. Gymnasiums and stadiums that required plenty of level space were often found in the suburbs, which were cooler and shadier and closer to plentiful supplies of water than could be found in central Athens. Cult centers and rural agoras, as well as fortresses and other structures for defense, were scattered throughout Attica. It was an easy walk, moreover, from city to country.

In the fifth century probably three-quarters of the citizens owned some rural property. Farming could be a part-time occupation that produced enough food to provide sustenance for a family. Many people still lived in villages, were loyal to their rural demes, and depended upon their family farms. Except for the spaces set aside for public activities, Athens was neither a beautiful city nor a comfortable one, and many propertied citizens were happy to leave it to artisans, to the urban poor, and to metics, who were not permitted to own land in Attica. The city had merely grown up in the Archaic and Classical periods without conforming to a town plan. Streets were irregular and narrow; housing in the city center was flimsy and sanitation poor. These problems were exacerbated when the entire population withdrew inside the city walls during the Peloponnesian War.

INTELLECTUAL LIFE IN FIFTH-CENTURY GREECE

Looking at the vibrant civilization of Greece in the middle of the fifth century, it would have been hard for anyone alive at the time to believe the horrors that lay ahead. Magnificent temples to the gods dotted the landscape, decked out with friezes that celebrated human and divine accomplishment. And throughout the Greek cities people had begun to explore new ideas about the universe and humanity's place in it.

Speculating About the Natural World

Greeks of Hesiod's day had viewed the earliest state of the universe as a formless void they called *chaos*. Out of chaos, they believed, the order of their own world had emerged—*kosmos*, a Greek word meaning both "order" and "beauty," hence the English word "cosmetics" for makeup, or "cosmetic surgery" to improve appearance. Mythology served the important function of grounding the growth of cosmos from chaos in various actions taken by the gods. The great contribution of the sixth-century Greek thinkers of Ionia had lain in their determination to abandon this mythological and religious framework and attempt instead to explain the world by material processes alone.

As we have seen in Chapter Three, the Ionian rationalists had focused on the natural world rather than on the values of the human community. Their speculations, however, raised inevitable questions about relations between gods and mortals, for they sought to enthrone human reason as the tool for understanding the universe and to replace divine plan (or caprice) with material forces. Anaxagoras from Clazomenae in Asia Minor (c. 500–428 BC) was one of many intellectuals who was drawn to the glittering city of Athens. Anaxagoras viewed material objects as composed of infinitely divisible particles and conceived of their organization as the work of a force he called *Nous* ("intellect"); from this came his nickname Nous ("the Brain"). The sun, he claimed, was not a deity but rather a white-hot stone a little larger than the Peloponnesus.

The workings of the universe also intrigued other fifth-century thinkers throughout the Greek world. Empedocles (c. 493–c. 433 BC), who lived in Acragas in Sicily, propounded a cosmogony based on the idea of four primary elements—earth, air, fire, and water. Physical substances, he argued, were produced when the twin forces of attraction and repulsion that he called "love" and "strife" acted upon these elements, combining them in various proportions. Maintaining that these combinations were randomly produced, Empedocles conjectured that monstrous forms had probably been created early in history but had perished through their failure to adapt.

An alternative view of how the world is made was put forward by Leucippus and Democritus. Like Anaxagoras, Leucippus, who seems to have been active around the middle of the fifth century, believed that matter was created of tiny particles, and his ideas were further developed by his pupil Democritus from Abdera in Thrace (c. 460–370 BC). In their view, moreover, the tiny particles were *atoma* ("uncuttable"). Ironically, then, the word for "atom," which was split in the twentieth century with such devastating consequences, originally meant "that which cannot be divided." In addition to atoms, so the theory had it, there was "void"; falling through void, atoms collided in a variety of ways to form visible matter. The theory did not encompass the influence of a divine being. What determined the manner of these collisions was a little uncertain—Leucippus insisted it was necessity and not chance, though other atomists disagreed—but the atomic theorists agreed on one thing: whatever was active in shaping the form of matter was a natural force and no divine being.

Though they certainly looked around them for models and paradigms, thinkers like Anaxagoras, Empedocles, Leucippus, and Democritus were essentially philosophers, not scientists. A mix of observation and systematic thinking, however, formed the basis of Greek medicine. Though prayer probably remained the most common Greek response to illness in antiquity, during the sixth century BC Greeks in Asia Minor began learning about anatomy from the observations Mesopotamians had made on animal entrails used in divination. By 500 BC, medical centers had been established on the island of Cos off the coast of Asia Minor and on the nearby peninsula of Cnidos. Some instruction also took place within the family; often the medical profession was passed down from father to son. Women were prohibited from practicing as doctors, but they frequently functioned as midwives.

Case studies formed the basis of the doctrines of Hippocrates of Cos (c. 460–c. 377 BC). The writings associated with Hippocrates' school included over a hundred works composed over a long period, and there is no way to know which of these might have been written by Hippocrates himself. Greeks did not develop many cures for diseases. The principal contribution of the Hippocratics lay not in any specific discoveries about medicine but rather in their commitment to seeking rational explanations of natural phenomena. Epilepsy, for example, had been labeled "the sacred disease" by the Greeks; in their treatise *On the Sacred Disease*, the Hippocratics took a different view, claiming that this notion was put forward by charlatans who, "having no idea what to do and having nothing to offer the sick . . . labelled the disease sacred in order to conceal their ignorance." (*On the Sacred Disease* 2) Another treatise, *Airs, Waters, Places*, examined the impact of climate on health, laying the foundations for epidemiology.

The largest corpus of Hippocratic texts deals with gynecology. Along with the general devaluation of women in Greek culture, women's reticence about speaking to male physicians sometimes cut doctors off from information vital to understanding female reproductive processes. In the absence of real data concerning symptoms and sexual practices, where women were concerned, speculation often substituted for the careful observation on which the Hippocratics prided themselves:

> If suffocation occurs suddenly, it will happen especially to women who do not have intercourse and to older women rather than to young ones, for their wombs are lighter. It usually occurs because of the following: when a woman is empty and works harder than in her previous experience, her womb, becoming heated from the hard work, turns because it is empty and light. There is, in fact, empty space for it to turn in because the belly is empty. Now when the womb turns, it hits the liver and they go together and strike against the abdomen—for the womb rushes and goes upwards towards the moisture, because it has been dried out by hard work, and the liver is, after all, moist. When the womb hits the liver, it produces sudden suffocation as it occupies the breathing passages around the belly.
>
> (*Diseases of Women* 1.7; Hanson 1975)

HISTORICAL AND DRAMATIC LITERATURE OF THE FIFTH CENTURY

In the verbal realm, the principal achievements of the Athenians during this period lay in history and in tragedy. Dozens of tragedians were active in fifth-century Athens, though only the works of Aeschylus, Sophocles, and Euripides have survived, and of these only a fraction of their output—seven each of Aeschylus and Sophocles, and nineteen of Euripides. History was the less common genre, but the two works that survived in their entirety—Herodotus' history of the Persian wars and Thucydides' history of the Peloponnesian War—enshrined in historical writing the model of the war monograph that has remained popular to this day.

Herodotus

Born in Halicarnassus in Ionia, Herodotus was heir to the traditions of Ionian rationalism and had a passionate curiosity about causes and origins. Why the Persians and the Greeks fought, what accounted for the Greek victory, how Darius came to rule Persia, where the Nile began, how the priestesses at Dodona came to be thought of as birds with human voices, where the Greeks got their gods—Herodotus used the Greek word *historia* ("inquiry") to describe his quest for understanding, and this word has given English and numerous romance languages their word for the investigation and analysis of the past: "history." He has set forth the results of his inquiry, he reports in the opening sentence of his work, "so that the actions of people shall not fade with time" and "so that the great and admirable monuments produced by both Greeks and barbarians shall not go unrenowned" (*The Histories* 1.1; Blanco, 1992).

Born probably shortly before Xerxes' invasion of Greece in 480, Herodotus was not old enough to remember the Persian wars, but he was able to interrogate his parents' generation. His interests were not confined to a particular series of historical events; like his somewhat younger contemporary Thucydides, he was fascinated by what history revealed about human nature and the way the world works. What he learned from his study of history was that power goes to people's heads, and that the mighty rarely meditate on their condition with sufficient judiciousness and reflection—that rulers hear what they want to hear, and rush headlong to their own destruction.

This paradigm appears early in his history in his imaginative reconstruction of a conversation between Solon, the Athenian lawgiver, and Croesus, the fabulously wealthy king of Lydia. During his travels, Herodotus maintains, Solon came to Croesus' palace, where the king made a point of having attendants give Solon a tour that would highlight Croesus' prosperity. Afterward, Croesus asked Solon if there was anyone in the world who struck him as particularly fortunate. Feigning innocence of Croesus' purpose in asking this question, Solon named a little-known Greek man who had died fighting for his city, leaving children behind him, and who was buried with honors. When Croesus was dissatisfied with this response, Solon offered an alternative example. Two young Argives, he related, when their mother needed to attend a feast of Hera and the oxen had not yet returned from the field, yoked themselves to the family wagon and pulled it several miles to the temple. Amid the great words of praise lavished upon the young men and on her for having such fine sons, their mother prayed to the goddess to bestow on her children whatever was best for humankind. Lying down to sleep in the temple, the youths never awoke, and the Argives dedicated statues to them at Delphi in commemoration of their excellence.

Resentful at not being named the most fortunate of men, Croesus spoke harshly to Solon, voicing his indignation at the notion that the Athenian should consider ordinary citizens more fortunate than a wealthy king like him. Solon in turn counseled him to think harder about what it means to be truly fortunate, cautioning him not to make facile judgments without waiting to see how things turn out in the end. "To me," he tells Croesus,

> it is obvious that you have great wealth and that you rule over many people, but it will be impossible for me to answer your question until I learn that you have happily ended your allotted life. After all, the rich man is not really happier than the man who lives from day to day unless good fortune stays with him and he dies painlessly, and in possession of all the good things life has to offer. . . . You have to consider how everything ends—how it turns out. For god gives many a glimpse of happiness and then withers them at their very roots.
>
> (*The Histories* 1.32; Blanco)

Croesus, however, does not listen. By carelessly misinterpreting a series of oracles, he loses his empire and comes to recognize Solon's wisdom.

It is not likely that Solon and Croesus really met. Solon's travels evidently preceded Croesus' accession to the throne around 560 BC. Herodotus has crafted this vignette to demonstrate the superiority of Greek over Persian ways of thinking—of the western dependence on the solid citizen over the eastern reverence for the powerful autocrat. Similar points are scored in Herodotus' characterization of the overconfident Xerxes. The implications of this are plain enough: For all their virtues, the Persians, like other eastern peoples, were dragged down by their habit of according immense power to a single individual, the king. Encouraging him in his childish self-confidence, they became slaves to someone who exaggerated his own importance not only vis-à-vis other mortals but, more dangerously still, in relation to the gods. In comparison, Greek civilization held all the promise that inhered in free institutions, in the rule of law, in respect for gods and the acceptance of human limitations.

In all this, Herodotus was a typical Greek, but in other respects he sought to undermine assumptions he saw in the world around him—assumptions about the inferiority of non-Greek cultures and the low intellect of women. Greek men, in Herodotus' view, needed to think harder and longer about their place in the world. To assist them in this project, he included in his history many stories about the intelligence of clever queens (such as Queen Artemisia of his native Halicarnassus) and a detailed account of the accomplishments of the Egyptians, stressing the greater antiquity of Egyptian culture in relation to Greek and suggesting Egyptian origins for the Greek gods.

Thucydides

Many intellectual currents of the fifth century flowed through Athens as Thucydides was coming to maturity and during the years when he composed his history of the long war in which he served. Clever speaking, careful observation, rational deduction, and a tragic view of the world can all be discerned in his work; unlike that of Herodotus, and the dramatic poets, however, his writing shows no interest in women. Whereas Herodotus, born a generation earlier, had conceived history as an interaction of divine and human forces, both vitally important, Thucydides saw the actions of people as pretty much exclusively responsible for how things turn out. A similar progression can be seen in the extant tragedians: Sophocles was somewhat more concerned with the human factor than Aeschylus, who was more drawn to the role and nature of the gods, and Euripides in turn—despite considerable interest in religion—gave human nature center stage.

Since Thucydides served as a general in 424, he must have been at least thirty in that year, and historians conjecture he was born around 460. He came from an aristocratic family with kinship ties to some of Pericles' rivals, but had enormous admiration for Pericles. His opportunities for research took an unexpected turn when he was exiled after failing to keep the Spartans from taking Amphipolis. From then on, he was able to gather a great deal of information from non-Athenian sources but could no longer attend meetings of the Athenian assembly. All we can be certain of concerning his life in exile is that he lived long enough to see Athens lose the war, which we know because he refers to Athens' defeat in his work.

Thucydides himself discusses his methodology at the outset of his history, stressing the lengths to which he went in his quest to determine the truth—and expressing impatience with those less committed to the search for knowledge. Most people, he complains, "expend very little effort on the search for truth, and prefer to turn to ready-made answers." His own approach will be different.

Document 7.1. Thucydides explains his methodology in his history of the Peloponnesian War, contrasting himself with less reliable reporters—including, it seems, Herodotus as well as rhetoricians given to virtuoso public displays.

One will not go wrong if he accepts the inferences I have drawn from the facts as I have related them, and not as they are sung by the poets—who embellish and exaggerate them—or as they are strung together by popular historians with a view to making them not more truthful, but more attractive to their audiences; and considering that we are dealing with ancient history, whose unverified events have, over the course of time, made their way into the incredible realms of mythology, one will find that my conclusions, derived as they are from the best available evidence, are accurate enough.

Even though people always think that the war they are fighting is the greatest there ever was, and then return to marveling at ancient wars once theirs has ended, it will be clear, after we examine the events themselves, that this war between Athens and Sparta actually was the greatest war there has ever been.

As to the speeches of the participants, either when they were about to enter the war or after they were already in it, it has been difficult for me and for those who reported to me to remember exactly what was said. I have, therefore, written what I thought the speakers must have said given the situation they were in, while keeping as close as possible to the gist of what was actually said. As to the events of the war, I have not written them down as I heard them from just anybody, nor as I thought they must have occurred, but have consistently described what I myself saw or have been able to learn from others after going over each event in as much detail as possible. I have found this task to be extremely arduous, since those who were present at these actions gave varying reports on the same event, depending on their sympathies and their memories.

My narrative, perhaps, will seem less pleasing to some listeners because it lacks an element of fiction. Those, however, who want to see things clearly as they were and, given human nature, as they will one day be again, more or less, may find this book a useful basis for judgment. My work was composed not as a prizewinning exercise in elocution, to be heard and then forgotten, but as a work of permanent value.

The Peloponnesian War 1.21–22; translated by
Walter Blanco, in Walter Blanco and Jennifer Roberts, eds.,
Thucydides: The Peloponnesian War. New York: W.W. Norton, 1998.

Thucydides has often been described as the world's first scientific historian, and his work has been cited for its objectivity. This characterization rests on a misunderstanding of what the writing of history really involves. History is not a science, and it cannot be objective, because it entails humans writing about other humans. Every omission, every connection, requires judgment. There is no limit to the number of decisions that confront historians. Herodotus was more disposed to put everything in and let his readers sort it out, but one consequence of this decision is that he has been criticized for being less analytical than Thucydides.

The Birth of Tragedy

Tragedy performed a central role in the spiritual and intellectual life of the polis. Wealthy citizens vied for honor and acclaim by undertaking the expense of training choruses, and during the festival of Dionysus in March actors and audience alike needed enormous stamina. Groups of actors performed four dramas in a day, and spectators had not only to follow the intricate poetry of the choruses but to turn up the next day and the day after that to compare the work of each playwright, to help determine who should receive the prize. A significant proportion of men—and perhaps women as well, though this is uncertain—attended the plays and no doubt continued among themselves a lively dialogue about the painful issues the dramas had raised. Even in eras of comparatively high literacy, ancient cultures remained oral to a considerable degree, and absorbing the complex imagery of Greek tragic choruses was not so difficult for people trained to listen and remember as it would be for most people today. Nonetheless, the popularity of performances that demanded serious intellectual work on the part of the audience tells us something about the richness of Greek culture. Over thirty tragedies have survived; what is missing, however, is any record (beyond the jokes in Aristophanes) of the discussions the performances must have inspired among friends and neighbors who had enjoyed this shared treasure of the community.

All parts in tragedy were played by men; masks facilitated the deception. They were shaped at the mouth rather like megaphones and so made for good acoustics. To be sure, they discouraged the nuanced portrayal of personality. This was not, however, considered a great loss, for Greek tragedy was never intended to be naturalistic. Characters in Greek tragedy were not like characters in modern films or novels, whom one might expect to recognize walking down the street, or whose subtler traits might appear in one's friends or neighbors. They represented humankind in all its aspiration—and frailty. They are not easy to like or dislike, for they were not intended to be lifelike, flesh-and-blood individuals.

Nor was the material of tragedy anything one could call a slice of life. Tragedy was meant to be heroic and grand, far removed from the trivial and the mundane. Plots were generally taken from the rich myths of the heroic age, but exceptions could be made for major events such as the Persian wars. (Even here, though, Aeschylus achieved a certain remoteness by setting the action of his *Persians* in faraway Asia, where people dressed exotically.) Formalities of several kinds limited the dramatist in his choice of material. No violence was permitted on stage, and all action had to take place within a twenty-four-hour period. Finally, the author had to contend with the challenge posed by the intricate meters of tragic verse.

Aeschylus

Aeschylus (525–456 BC) was the first of the famous tragedians of fifth-century Athens. He died in Sicily after a long life, during which he wrote perhaps seventy plays. Unfortunately only a handful of these survive. After his death the Athenians paid homage to the greatness of his work by decreeing that the archon should grant a chorus to anyone who wanted to produce one of his plays. Already in the time of Peisistratus, Thespis had expanded the range of the choruses honoring Dionysus by adding an actor who could carry on a dialogue with the chorus; now Aeschylus added a second actor. This innovation made possible real conflict and moved tragedy beyond tableau into the realm of drama. At the same time, drama remained firmly grounded in poetry, and verse remained the vehicle for both tragedy and comedy throughout antiquity.

Aeschylus' greatest surviving achievement is the trilogy known as the *Oresteia*, which treats the supreme difficulty of understanding and obtaining a just social and religious order. Apparently the sets of four dramas that playwrights entered in the competition generally involved three tragedies followed by a lighter work known as a satyr play, but the three tragedies did not need to treat the same theme, and frequently they didn't. In the case of the *Oresteia*, however, the three plays comprise one grand and complex drama, and this work is the only Attic trilogy that escaped destruction to be enjoyed today.

The Oresteia

The point of departure for the *Oresteia* was evidently Ephialtes' curtailment of the powers of the Areopagite Council, for the trilogy culminates in precisely the sort of trial that remained within the Council's purview—a murder trial. It seems likely that Aeschylus supported the reforms and chose this august drama as a vehicle by which to reassure conservative Athenians that the trying of homicide cases, the privilege with which Ephialtes had conspicuously not tampered, was in fact the ancient mission of this venerable body. In this way he could draw attention away from the significant limitations that had been placed on its jurisdiction. The material with which Aeschylus chose to convey his message was the familiar tale of the cursed house of the ancient hero Pelops and his descendant Agamemnon, commander-in-chief of the legendary expedition against Troy.

The first play, *Agamemnon*, portrays the Greek general's murder upon his victorious return from the Trojan War in a plot hatched by his faithless wife Clytemnestra and his cousin Aegisthus, who has become Clytemnestra's lover. Agamemnon's murder poses an agonizing dilemma for his children Orestes and Electra, for they are faced with a choice between killing their mother and allowing their father's death to go unavenged. Their pain and Orestes' eventual murder of Clytemnestra and Aegisthus form the subject matter of the second play, *The Libation Bearers*. As the play closes, Orestes finds himself pursued by the avenging earth goddesses known as the Furies. His suffering ends in the final play, *The Eumenides*. This play is set in Athens, where Orestes has taken refuge, hoping that a responsible government will afford him a fair trial. Athena's charge to the jury proclaims the glories of the Areopagus, the importance of justice, and the centrality of law.

Athena breaks the deadlocked jury's tie, and her grounds are revealing. Following Apollo's proclamation that it is the male and not the female who is the true parent, and bearing in mind her own birth (fully developed from the head of her father Zeus), she decides that the claims of the father trump those of the mother, justifying Clytemnestra's death. Now tamed, the Furies are given a new name, the Eumenides (Kindly Ones). Plainly Aeschylus conceives the creation of responsible government in Athens as the antithesis not only of tyranny but also of a disordered chaotic universe in which emotional and female forces of vengeance were paramount. The new world will be governed by orderly, rational institutions planned and staffed by men, with vengeance replaced by justice.

The choruses celebrated the awesome power of the gods while also exploring the nature of the human condition. "Sing sorrow, sorrow," the chorus chants toward the opening of his play *Agamemnon*, "but good win out in the end":

> Zeus: whatever he may be, if this name
> pleases him in invocation,
> thus I call upon him.
> I have pondered everything
> yet I cannot find a way,

only Zeus, to cast this dead weight of ignorance
finally from out my brain.

. . .

Zeus, who guided men to think,
who has laid it down that wisdom
comes alone through suffering.
Still there drips in sleep against the heart
grief of memory; against
our pleasure we are temperate.
From the gods who sit in grandeur
grace comes somehow violent.
                    (*Agamemnon* 160–166, 176–183; Lattimore 1959)

The genre established by Aeschylus would become one of the defining art forms of Greek civilization. Tragic drama, as it evolved throughout Aeschylus' career and in the hands of his successors Sophocles and Euripides, was in many ways the hallmark of Athenian greatness. Through Shakespeare and other great tragedians of Europe, this remarkable testament to the heroic struggle against human limitations forms an important part of a legacy that has endured to our own time.

Sophocles

Herodotus' warnings about the vicissitudes of fortune and the impossibility of judging a man's life until it is over are echoed in *Oedipus Tyrannus*, the most famous play of antiquity. Here the poet Sophocles (c. 496–406 BC) presents the seeming good fortune of Oedipus, the highly intelligent and respected ruler of Thebes in the Heroic Age—only to show us his life disintegrating as the drama unfolds. Sophocles wrote over a hundred plays. Like Aeschylus and other tragic poets, Sophocles reworked the familiar plots of Greek mythology, with their emphasis on agonizing family discord, to express his view of the world. Just after Herodotus' departure for Thurii Sophocles produced the first of three surviving dramas about the unfortunate house of Oedipus, the legendary ruler of Thebes who was fated to kill his father and marry his mother.

In the earliest of Sophocles' Theban plays, *Antigone*, the playwright asks us to contemplate the painful tensions that arise in Oedipus' family after his death. One of his sons, Polynices, has died fighting to take the throne of Thebes from his brother; naturally Polynices' sister Antigone wishes to fulfill her religious obligation and bury his body. But their uncle Creon, now king of Thebes, forbids anyone to take up this project on the grounds that Polynices was a traitor. Like many characters in Greek tragedy, Antigone now finds herself confronted with a painful choice. She must decide whether to honor her obligation to her brother and to the gods, which means facing death herself, or to obey the laws of the state and keep herself safe. She is headstrong and defiant; Creon is rigid and insensitive.

Though Sophocles is a conventional Athenian in his respect for the gods and their power to guide human life, in other regards he challenged conventional mores. Antigone's situation paralleled that of the Athenian girl known as an *epiklēros*, a girl with no surviving brothers, and it is hard to doubt that Sophocles' sympathies lie with the fatherless, brotherless girl who experiences all the helplessness that fell upon Athenian women who lacked male protectors. Sophocles, as his other plays confirm, sympathized with the plight of Greek women. Creon, however, makes a good case for the importance of a law that makes no exceptions for family members, and as an Athenian democrat Sophocles certainly saw the need to uphold the rule of law. But is the decree of an autocrat really law, especially when the populace is on Antigone's side? Sophocles fully recognizes the complexity of the tortuous choices Antigone and Creon must make, and he sees in their confrontation proof of the wondrous complexity of humankind and the communities humans have struggled to develop.

Document 7.2. The soaring poetry of the chorus celebrates the achievements of the human race in a memorable passage.

> Many the wonders but nothing walks stranger than man.
> This thing crosses the sea in the winter's storm,
> making his path through the roaring waves.
> And she, the greatest of gods, the earth—
> ageless she is, and unwearied—he wears her away
> as the plows go up and down from year to year
> and his mules turn up the soil.
> Gay nations of birds he snares and leads,
> wild beast tribes and the salty brood of the sea,
> with the twisted mesh of his nets, this clever man.
> He controls with craft the beasts of the open air,
> walkers on hills. The horse with his shaggy mane
> he holds and harnesses, yoked about the neck,
> and the strong bull of the mountain.
> Language, and thought like the wind
> and the feelings that make the town,
> he has taught himself, and shelter against the cold,
> refuge from rain. He can always help himself.
> He faces no future helpless. There's only death
> that he cannot find an escape from. He has contrived
> refuge from illnesses once beyond all cure.
> Clever beyond all dreams
> the inventive craft that he has
> which may drive him one time or another to well or ill.

Sophocles' *Antigone*. Antigone 11.332–368, Wyckoff, 1960.

Like Herodotus, Sophocles combined profound reverence for the gods with a compelling interest in the human dimension of life. In his plays, dialogue—the talking back and forth of humans—was expanded at the expense of the chorus; he also added a third actor where Aeschylus had used only two (not counting silent actors, who appeared on the stage but did not speak).

Euripides

In the spring of 431 Athenians and foreign visitors gathered in the theater of Dionysus to see Euripides' *Medea*. Plays by Euripides (c. 485–c. 406 BC) had been produced before, so the playwright was already known to the audience, but the subject matter for this drama was singularly shocking. Although the plots of Greek tragedy derived from familiar myths, Euripides enjoyed innovation, and there is some reason to believe that the ending of the play came as a surprise to the spellbound onlookers.

In *Medea* Euripides used the tale of Jason, the celebrated leader of the Argonauts in their quest for the Golden Fleece, to undermine conventional views of what makes a hero. In his adventures Jason had acquired a wife—Medea, a sorceress from Colchis, at the far end of the Black Sea. He has such confidence in the excellence of the Greek way of life that even when he has decided to abandon Medea to marry a Corinthian princess, he boasts of the benefits he has conferred on her by rescuing her from a barbarian land and transplanting her to Greece. Predictably, these arguments do not sit well with a highly intelligent witch who has the advantage of a non-Greek perspective. The bitter laments of Medea enable the audience to see things differently as she details the constraints on her life as a woman in a Greek city:

> We women are the most unfortunate creatures.
> First, with an excess of wealth it is required
> For us to buy a husband, and take for our bodies
> A master; for not to take one is even worse.
> And now the question is serious whether we take
> A good or bad one; for there is no easy escape
> For a woman, nor can she say no to her marriage.
> (*Medea* 231–238; Warner 1959)

Jason's shameful excuses for his actions, moreover, raise serious questions about a society that makes heroes of the kind of man who would rationalize his course of action on the grounds that his new marriage will give these children royal step-siblings. *Medea* was only one of the plays in which Euripides explored the dynamics of the conflict between reason and passion—reason, which could justify Jason in deserting the wife who had risked her life for him in her youth, and passion, which could move a mother to kill her offspring. Inevitably the agonizing conflict that marked plays like *Antigone* struck a particularly resonant chord with the audience in *Medea*, which was produced just as war was breaking out between two very different states with opposing views of the world.

CURRENTS IN GREEK THOUGHT AND EDUCATION

The convoluted arguments that help politicians who appear in Thucydides' narrative cloak ambition in fair-sounding words and the verses in which Euripides' Jason defends his action as calculated to improve his children's lives show the influence of the itinerant intellectuals who gravitated to Athens during the second half of the fifth century, the men who came to be known as the sophists, from the Greek word *sophistēs*, which means something like "practitioner of wisdom." Unlike the philosophers who sought to understand the world, the sophists contented themselves with teaching eager, paying pupils how to get by in it. Though their works do not survive except in fragments, it seems clear that they rejected facile assumptions concerning such topics as the connections between noble birth and true merit, the obligations owed to the gods, and the nature of law. Because of this, and because they enabled ambitious young men to speak effectively for or against any issue, they aroused suspicion in Athens.

Formal and Informal Education

The origins of the sophistic movement lie in the informal nature of Greek education, in its literary and aristocratic bias, and in its superficial nature. Since Homer's day, Greek children had learned primarily by watching the world around them and imitating respected elders. Few people in antiquity knew how to read, and most formal education involved listening and reciting from memory. Girls were rarely sent to school. Neither were most boys. The problem was not simply that poverty usually compelled children to stay home and work on the farm; the fact is that, with the exception of Sparta, Greek states did not provide public schooling. Parents of the upper classes, however, paid for their sons to be instructed in what was called *mousikē*, a subject that included the memorization of poetry. Since ancient poems were sung, mousike also involved learning to play the lyre. Beginning in the sixth century, more and more children also learned to read and write. Parents sometimes had daughters instructed in basic reading and writing skills in case they needed this knowledge to supervise household accounts or to manage temple properties if they became priestesses. Some instruction in math was also offered to children by private tutors and in schools, though not much was offered in the way of natural science or what we would call social studies. By the time boys progressed to the age at which adolescents today would enter college, moreover, they had ceased to be students and had become soldiers and citizens.

Most education went on in less formal settings, however, and this sort of education would continue throughout life. In childhood, girls would absorb the norms of appropriate social behavior from their mothers and aunts, boys from their fathers and uncles. As in many societies, the upbringing of the two sexes was designed to cultivate very different skill sets for males and females. These differences were most pronounced in the upper classes, for poor children of both sexes were likely to learn farming and craft skills from parents. Among the elite, however, a sharp differentiation occurred in adolescence, for at this juncture girls married and reproduced. Their education in home management continued at the hands of older relatives, and probably older slaves as well, who had considerable experience of child rearing. In addition, husbands sometimes took it upon themselves to give their wives vocational training in household management. In the *Oeconomicus*, written in the fourth century in the form of a Socratic dialogue, Xenophon describes how a husband, Ischomachus, trained his young wife to be a successful estate manager:

> [Socrates] said, "I would very much like you to tell me, Ischomachus, whether you yourself trained your wife to become the sort of woman that she ought to be, or whether she already knew how to carry out her duties when you took her as your wife from her father and mother."

> "What could she have known when I took her as my wife, Socrates? She was not yet fifteen when she came to me, and had spent her previous years under careful supervision so that she might see and hear and speak as little as possible. Don't you think it was adequate if she came to me knowing only how to take wool and produce a cloak, and had seen how spinning tasks are allocated to the slaves? And besides, she had been very well trained to control her appetites, Socrates," he said, "and I think that sort of training is most important for man and woman alike."
>
> (*Oeconomicus* 7.4–5; Pomeroy 1994)

While teenage girls might receive such instruction from their husbands, adolescent males were exposed to important influences of another kind. Books were expensive, and though literacy increased throughout the sixth and particularly the fifth century, learning still went on primarily in the interaction between two or more human beings, not in the interaction of a person with a written text. Relationships with somewhat older mentors formed a key element in the education of teenage boys. Just as younger teachers today often serve as role models for adolescents, so young men in Greece offered examples of manhood to those who were just developing into men. The one-on-one nature of these friendships, however—untrammeled by any need for a teacher to be evenhanded with an entire class of students—combined with different attitudes to sexuality to produce a significantly different dynamic. As we have seen in Chapter Four, the bond between a Greek male teenager and his adult mentor was often profoundly erotic. What we know about these relationships is somewhat compromised by a reticence about sex in the written sources and by the need many Greeks felt to stress the intellectual and spiritual bond at the expense of the sexual one. In his dialogue on love, the *Symposium*, Plato praises this bond for its value in the moral improvement of both the individual and society as a whole. "I would maintain," he writes,

> that there can be no greater benefit for a boy than to have a worthy lover from his earlier youth, nor for a lover than to have a worthy object for his affection. The principle which ought to guide the whole life of those who intend to live nobly cannot be implanted either by family or by position or by wealth or by anything else so effectively as by love. What principle? you ask. I mean the principle which inspires shame at what is disgraceful and ambition for what is noble; without these feelings neither a state nor an individual can accomplish anything great or fine.
>
> (*Symposium* 178b; Hamilton 1951)

The bond between the older lover (the *erastēs*) and the younger beloved (the *erōmenos*) shored up the stability of society by encouraging each generation (or half generation) to imitate the one that had gone before.

Erotic bonds, of course, that had begun in school might also be strong between men of a similar age. Xenophon portrays Socrates describing the passion of Critobulus for Cleinias:

> This hot flame of his was kindled in the days when they used to go to school together. It was the discovery of this that caused his father to put him into my hands, in the hope that I might do him some good. And without question he is already much improved. For a while ago he was like those who look at the Gorgons—he would gaze at Cleinias with a fixed and stony stare and would never leave his presence. . . . It does look to me as if he had also kissed Cleinias; and there is nothing more terribly potent than this at kindling the fires of passion. For it is insatiable and holds out seductive hopes. For this reason I maintain that one who intends to possess the power of self-control must refrain from kissing those in the bloom of beauty.
>
> (Xenophon, *Symposium* 4.23–24; Todd p. 577)

Finally, participation in the life of the city as a whole afforded an ongoing education to growing men, and to some extent to women as well, particularly those who served as priestesses. The poet Simonides put it well: *Polis andra didaskei* ("the polis teaches a man"). Only in mature life, however—by attendance, for example, at tragic dramas and the thoughtful discussions that no doubt followed in private gatherings—did this education entail any real questioning of conventional wisdom. In general, the purpose of Greek education was a blend of indoctrination and socialization calculated to foster the perpetuation of traditional values.

Figure 7.9. This vase depicts a mature bearded man courting a very young, barely adolescent boy.

All this changed when the sophists burst on the scene during the second half of the fifth century, sparking powerful tensions between the generations. Athens acted as a magnet for the philosophers and teachers of rhetoric who had sprung up throughout the Greek world as speculation about both the natural universe and the human community became increasingly popular among intellectuals. Democracy was grounded in skill in speaking and reasoning—in the ability to dissect and demolish the arguments of political opponents. The sophists offered to teach these skills. Sophists filled other needs as well, for they delighted in exploring tricky questions about the workings of the world. No common belief system marked the thinking of the various sophists, but they shared an enthusiasm for the kind of exercises in argumentation that are central to a great deal of higher education today.

The Sophists

Like much of the education that had gone before, the instruction offered by sophists benefited only a fairly small class of affluent students who could afford to pay. What the sophists had to offer, however, differed sharply from earlier education, for the sophists questioned conventional beliefs. One object of their explorations was the notion of *nomos*.

Herodotus had shown in his history the centrality of nomos to society. The Greek word meant both "law" and "custom"; there were state-sanctioned *nomoi* forbidding burglary, but there were also social nomoi regarding what to wear at your wedding and religious nomoi about how to worship Apollo. In a society that had existed for centuries without written law, only a blurry line divided a legal nomos and a conventional nomos based on tradition. The two, however, began to diverge the harder people thought about the problem. Herodotus' *Histories* demonstrated two different sides of nomos. On the one hand, the Greeks had fought the Persians in order to live by nomos rather than at the whim of a despot. On the other hand, the multiplicity of nomoi in different cultures reveals a diversity that suggests that local customs are the product of tradition rather than of abstract, unchanging principles of right and wrong. To demonstrate the force of nomos, Herodotus tells the following tale:

> During his reign, Darius called together the Greeks who were at his court and asked them how much money it would take to get them to eat the dead bodies of their fathers. They said they would not do it for any sum. Then he summoned a group of Indians known as the Callatiae, who eat the corpses of their parents. In the presence of the Greeks, and through a translator, he asked them how much money it would take for them to permit the burning of their parents on a funeral pyre. They gave a horrified gasp and demanded that he be silent.
>
> (*The Histories* 3.38; Blanco)

Each society, he concludes, considers its own customs to be best.

When this idea was assimilated to the speculations of the natural philosophers, an opposition evolved in many minds between the concept of *physis* ("nature"), and *nomos* ("convention"). The relationship between physis and nomos became central to Greek thought around Herodotus' time, for it carried powerful implications for the legitimacy of authority. If nomos was not the natural outgrowth of physis but actually existed in opposition to it, then the laws of the community were not necessarily to be obeyed, for they might have grown up randomly, endorsed by generations of unthinking traditionalists who had given no thought to their grounding in physis.

This concept of law varied conspicuously from the usual view that law ultimately came from the gods, and in fact the new ways of looking at the world had serious implications for relations between gods and mortals. One of the most renowned of the sophists who came to teach in Athens was Protagoras (c. 490–420 BC) of Abdera in northern Greece, who moved to Athens around 450 and spent most of the rest of his life there. He is best known for two sayings with religious implications. "Each individual person is the measure of all things—of things that are, that they are, and of things that are not, that they are not." Nobody, in other words, can tell you what is real or true—no state official, no parent, and no god. Another contention was still more provocative: it is impossible to know, Protagoras is said to have observed, "whether the gods exist, or how they might look if they do. Numerous obstacles stand in the way, such as the shortness of life and the difficulty of the subject matter."

There was an answer, however, to the question, "Just what do these people teach, anyway?" and that answer was rhetoric. Many Greeks believed there was no limit to what sophists would use rhetoric to defend. The anonymous treatise known as *Dissoi Logoi* (Double Arguments) reveals the moral relativism that many associated with sophists. Can sickness ever be good? Certainly, if you are a doctor. But what about death? Death is good for undertakers and gravediggers. The author goes on to enumerate the many examples of cultural difference found in Herodotus in order to demonstrate that no act is intrinsically good or bad. A mental universe in which nothing was purely good or patently evil was not one in which all Greeks wished to dwell.

For these reasons, the sophists drew to themselves a considerable amount of odium. They found themselves under attack not only in conversation but on the stage. In 423 Aristophanes produced the *Clouds*, in which the intellectuals of Athens—the "eggheads"—are derided as teaching a corrosive rhetoric that made a mockery of decent, sensible values. The man Aristophanes identifies as running the "think shop" was not, however, a sophist. Like some of Aristophanes' other characters, he was a real person, but not one who taught rhetoric or accepted fees. He was Socrates, and the disposition to identify him with the sophists contributed in no small measure to his execution just after the end of the war which broke out between Athens and Sparta in 431.

THE BREAKDOWN OF THE PEACE

The terms of the Thirty Years' Peace contained within them the seeds of war. Arbitration was meaningless when all the major states were lined up on one side or another; rules made in one sphere of influence might well have an impact on the other; and some states enjoyed an ambiguous status, with one foot in each camp. The full extent of the vulnerability of the peace was revealed by events that began in western Greece in 435.

A Provocative Alliance: Athens and Corcyra

In that year a civil war between the democrats and the oligarchs in the Corcyraean colony of Epidamnus moved the democrats to seek assistance from Corcyra. When their mother city turned them down for reasons we do not know, they were encouraged by Delphi to hand themselves over to their "grandmother" Corinth instead. Despite their own oligarchic leanings, the Corinthians welcomed the opportunity to make life hard for the Corcyraeans, with whom they had a long-standing feud, and agreed to assist the democrats. The Corinthians and Corcyraeans were soon fighting at sea.

This conflict set into motion a chain of events that had dramatic consequences for the Greek world. Needing an ally but unable to approach Sparta because of Corinth's membership in the Peloponnesian League, the Corcyraeans went to Athens instead. An alliance between Corcyra and Athens would not violate the terms of the Thirty Years' Peace, since the treaty permitted neutrals to join either side. The Athenians were nervous about offending Corinth by such an alliance, but they were even more apprehensive about the prospect of Corinth's defeating Corcyra in battle and obtaining for themselves Corcyra's substantial fleet. To gain those ships for Athens, therefore, they voted to make an alliance. They made a point of terming it a "defensive alliance" only, but this technicality fooled nobody; it was fairly clear that the Corinthians would indeed attack the Corcyraeans, and when they did, Athens would find itself at war with Corinth, one of the most powerful members of the Peloponnesian League.

This is precisely what happened. In the late summer of 433 a Peloponnesian fleet of 150 ships, 90 of them Corinthian, attacked the Corcyraeans off the island chain known as Sybota. With Athenian help, the Corcyraeans were ultimately victorious, and the Corinthians were furious. Prospects for peace between Athens and Sparta were receding.

The Problem of Potidaea

With chances of war now greatly increased, Athens issued problematic decrees against two members of the Peloponnesian League. The city of Potidaea on the Chalcidic peninsula was both a Corinthian colony and a member of the Athenian alliance. In the tense political climate, Potidaea's anomalous situation inevitably attracted Athens' attention, especially in view of the exceptionally close relations between Corinth and Potidaea, which even took its annual magistrates from Corinth. (Corinth's markedly contrasting relationships with its two colonies Corcyra and Potidaea are an important reminder of the many different possibilities for metropolis/colony ties.) During the winter of 433–432, the Athenians ordered the Potidaeans to dismiss their Corinthian magistrates, reject any future officials from Corinth, tear down their seaward defenses, and give hostages. When Potidaea refused these demands, Athens found itself involved in an expensive two-year-long siege in which Potidaea was aided by Corinth and the Macedonian king Perdiccas, whom the Athenians had alienated by supporting two rival claimants to his throne.

Athenian Decrees Against Megara

Around the same time, the Athenians took action against Megara. Because Thucydides considered the Megarian decrees only a pretext and not a major cause of the war, much is unclear about this third crisis. The Athenians apparently accused the Megarians of harboring escaped slaves and of cultivating some sacred and undefined land that lay between Eleusis in Attica and Megara and passed a decree against Megara, probably in 432, excluding Megarian merchants from all ports of the Athenian empire. This decree enabled the Athenians to inflict considerable harm on a member of the Peloponnesian League without technically infringing the terms of the Thirty Years' Peace, since there were few significant Greek ports outside the Athenian empire.

Even more than the other actions taken by the Athenian assembly during the 430s, the sanctions against Megara and the refusal to revoke them are associated with the name of Pericles. The plays of Aristophanes and Plutarch's biography of Pericles make it plain that some people considered the friction with Megara pivotal in bringing on the war and blamed Pericles for the outbreak of hostilities. Scattered references in Thucydides confirm this. In the autumn of 432 BC the Corinthians denounced the Athenians before the Spartan assembly. Although the Spartan king Archidamus urged caution, the Spartans voted that the Athenians had violated the Thirty Years' Peace. They then summoned delegates from the Peloponnesian League who duly voted to go to war with Athens.

Last-Ditch Attempts to Avert War

Hostilities did not immediately follow, but rather several months of diplomacy in which each side tried to portray the other as responsible for the impending war. Thus, the Spartans insisted that peace could be preserved if Athens would only "free the Greeks" (in other words, abandon their empire), expel any "cursed" Alcmaeonids in the city (Pericles was an Alcmaeonid on his mother's side), and rescind the Megarian decree; the Athenians demanded that the Spartans purify "the curse of the goddess of the Brass House," a reference to the impieties involved in the death by starvation decades earlier of Pausanias, who had taken refuge in the goddess' temple. In the end, after several months of fruitless negotiations, the impatient Thebans forced ambivalent Sparta's hand by attacking Athens' ally Plataea. Because Plataea enjoyed a special position in Greece as the site of a great victory against Persia in 479, this assault was considered particularly heinous. Afterward nobody could question that the Peloponnesians and the Athenians were at war.

Figure 7.10. Alliances at the outset of the Peloponnesian War.

ODRYSIAN KINGDOM

THRACE

Abdera
Neapolis
Maronea
Thasos
Thasos
Aenus

Samothrace

Cardia

Imbros

Sestos
Abydus

Sigeum • Troy

Lemnos

Tenedos

Antandrus

Methymna

Lesbos
Mytilene

Scyros

AEGEAN
SEA

Cyme
Phocaea

Chios

Erythrae • Clazomenae
Teos • Colophon
Notium
Ephesus

Carystus

Andros

Tenos

Samos

Myconos

Priene
Miletus

Delos

Iasus

Paros
Siphnos

Naxos

Halicarnassus

Cos

Cos

Caunus

Cnidus

Melos

Thera

Ialysus • Rhodes

Camirus

Rhodes
Lindus

Selymbria
Perinthus

Byzantium
Chalcedon

PROPONTIS

Cyzicus

Dascylium

Lampsacus

PHRYGIA

MYSIA

Adramyttium

LYDIA

Sardis

CARIA

RESOURCES FOR WAR

Thus ended the period of a half century between the Persian and Peloponnesian wars to which Thucydides gave the name the Pentakontaetia ("the Fifty Years") (actually forty-seven years). In the jockeying for position that went on during the months leading up to the Theban attack on Plataea, the Spartans seem to have come out ahead. Though it was they who had declared war, the Greek world was inclined to see imperialist Athens as the aggressor. When war broke out, Thucydides writes,

> Popular opinion shaped up in favor of the Spartans by far, especially since they had proclaimed that they were going to liberate Greece. Everywhere, city and citizen alike were eager, if at all possible, to join with them in word and deed, and everyone felt that any plan would come to a standstill if he himself could not take part in it. That is how angry most people were at Athens—some because they wanted to rid themselves of Athenian rule, and others because they were frightened lest they fall under that rule.
>
> (*The Peloponnesian War* 2.8; Blanco 1998)

The belligerents differed not only in temperament but also in the nature of their military strengths. The Athenians had far greater financial resources than the Peloponnesians, and an incomparably superior navy that included over four hundred Athenian and allied ships. Accordingly, Athens hoped to conduct as much of the war as possible at sea, while the Spartans would focus on the land. The Athenians were fighting essentially a defensive war, whose goal was to preserve the empire the Spartans sought to destroy. For Athens a stalemate would amount to victory. Sparta needed something more.

TRANSLATIONS

Blanco, Walter. 1992. *The Histories*, from *Herodotus: The Histories*, Walter Blanco and Jennifer Roberts, eds. New York: W. W. Norton.

Blanco, Walter. 1998. *The Peloponnesian War*, from *Thucydides: The Peloponnesian War*, Walter Blanco and Jennifer Roberts, eds. New York: W.W. Norton.

Hamilton, Walter. 1951. *Plato: The Symposium*. Harmondsworth, UK: Penguin.

Hanson, Ann. 1975. *Hippocrates: Diseases of Women*, in *Signs* 1.

Marchant, E. C. and O. J. Todd. 1968. *Xenophon in Seven Volumes*. IV. New York and London: Loeb Classical Library.

Pomeroy, Sarah B. 1994. *Xenophon: Oeconomicus, A Social and Historical Commentary*. Oxford: Clarendon Press.

Warner, Rex. 1959. *Medea*, from *The Complete Greek Tragedies, Euripides I: Four Tragedies*, David Grene and Richmond Lattimore, eds. Chicago: University of Chicago Press.

Wyckoff, Elizabeth. 1960. *Antigone*, from *The Complete Greek Tragedies*, David Grene and Richmond Lattimore, eds. Chicago: University of Chicago Press.

SUGGESTED READINGS

Beard, Mary. 2003. *The Parthenon*. Cambridge, MA: Harvard University Press. The history of the building from temple to medieval Cathedral to mosque and armory, the transfer of the Elgin Marbles to Britain in the nineteenth century, and the twentieth-century restoration.

Camp, John M. 2001. *The Archaeology of Athens*. New Haven, CT: Yale University Press. A thorough discussion of this important subject by a scholar who has spent many years in Athens.

Guthrie, W. K. C. 1971. *The Sophists*. Cambridge, UK: Cambridge University Press. A brilliant study of the issues regarding the sophistic movement, excerpted from the author's six-volume *History of Greek Philosophy*.

Harris, William V. 1989. *Ancient Literacy*. Cambridge, MA: Harvard University Press. A survey of the evidence for literacy and the lack of it in ancient Greece and Rome.

Hill, Ida Thallon. 1953. *The Ancient City of Athens: Its Topography and Monuments*. London: Methuen. A clearly written description with illustrations and plans of the architectural and sculpted antiquities at Athens, before the restorations that are now in progress began masking many of the major monuments.

Hurwit, Jeffrey M. 1999. *The Athenian Acropolis: History, Mythology, and Archaeology from the Neolithic Era to the Present*. New York: Cambridge University Press. An eminently readable history of the most famous hill in the Greek world.

Kagan, Donald. 1969. *The Outbreak of the Peloponnesian War*. Ithaca, NY: Cornell University Press. The first installment in Kagan's monumental four-volume history of the war.

Osborne, Robin. 1987. *Classical Landscape with Figures: The Ancient Greek City and Its Countryside*. London: G. Philip. An illustrated discussion of life in rural Greece, natural flora and agriculture, written by an author who plainly loves his subject.

Ste. Croix, G. E. M. de. 1972. *The Origins of the Peloponnesian War*. Ithaca, NY: Cornell University Press. An analysis of the available sources and an intensive study of the data concerning the Megarian decrees.

Vlastos, Gregory. 1991. *Socrates: Ironist and Moral Philosopher*. Ithaca, NY: Cornell University Press. An attempt to capture the essence of the philosopher, by one of the foremost students of the Platonic dialogues.

8

THE PELOPONNESIAN WAR

When war broke out between Athens and Sparta, few Greeks foresaw that it would be different from any war they had ever experienced or even imagined. The twenty-seven-year conflict cost thousands upon thousands of lives and proved a stern teacher. It enhanced many of the worst features of Greek society—competitiveness, jingoism, lack of compassion, and gross disregard for human life. At the same time, a number of extraordinary thinkers sought to focus attention on the problems people face in their attempts to live together: The writings of Thucydides, Sophocles, and Euripides showed vigor and spirit throughout the war years, and the comic dramatist Aristophanes continued to produce plays of irrepressible wit through three decades of fighting and for a generation afterward. The Peloponnesian War would alter the world the Greeks knew in many respects. Comfortable assumptions about the citizen-fighter and women's role in the polis would break down, and conventional morality and piety would face many challenges. Much, however, would stay the same—the polis as a political unit, the primacy of agriculture, the rivalries of the city-states, and the worship of the Olympian gods. The trauma occasioned by the war and its aftermath was also strikingly fertile, for the war supplied the impetus for many of the social, political, and intellectual changes we identify with the fourth century and the period after the death of Alexander in 323 BC that we call the Hellenistic Age.

THE ARCHIDAMIAN WAR (431–421 BC)

To many Greeks alive at the time, the decade of fighting that stretched from 431 to 421 seemed like a discrete entity in itself, and in fact this war has been given its own name—the Archidamian War, after the Spartan king and commander Archidamus. We owe the concept of a single Peloponnesian War extending from 431 to 404 to Thucydides. Another historian might have seen a continuous war extending from 460 to 404, or three wars—one from 460 to 446, one from 431 to 421, and another beginning somewhere between 418 and 415 and continuing to 404. Students of historiography (the writing of history) use the expression

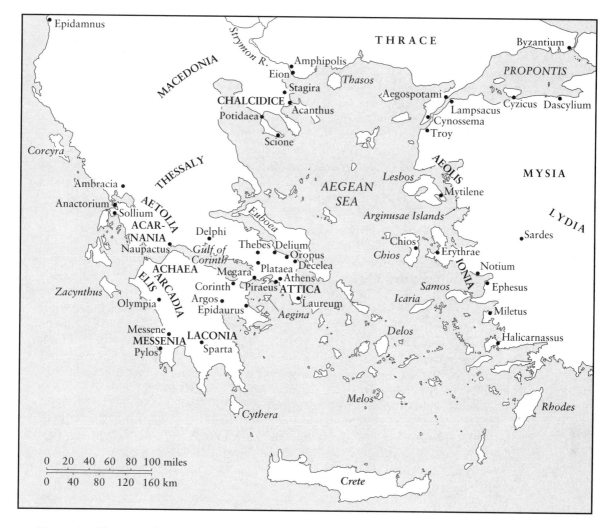

Figure 8.1. Theaters of operation during the Peloponnesian War.

"colligation," that is, "tying together," to describe the way historians "create" an event or a process by linking together separate events in such a way that they form a coherent whole. Joining what others might construe differently, Thucydides, the earliest and most important source for this period, has by colligation successfully enshrined in history the concept of what is today commonly known as "the" Peloponnesian War, the war of 431–404.

The Periclean Strategy and the Plague

Pericles devised an ingenious strategy for winning a war he conceived as essentially defensive, and it is a measure of his influence and eloquence that he was able to persuade his fellow Athenians to do something so conspicuously at odds with human nature. Harassing Peloponnesian territory with their navy, the Athenians declined to participate in hoplite battle with the Spartans. At Pericles' instigation, the Athenian farmers abandoned their land, taking with them what few household goods could be loaded on wagons, and huddled with the city-dwellers inside the Long Walls that linked Athens to Piraeus. These walls, Pericles rightly perceived, made Athens in essence an island. Food and other necessary goods would continue to be imported by ship from throughout the empire. The enemy, Pericles calculated, would tire of ravaging the land when nobody came out to fight. Seeing that the superior training and numbers of their infantry would do them no good, they would soon sue for peace. The Spartans, meanwhile, conjectured that the Athenians would grow restive cooped up in the overcrowded city throughout the campaigning season and, seeing their land being ravaged, would be unable to tolerate the frustration. They foresaw one of two consequences: either the Athenians would seek peace or they would overrule Pericles and come out to fight. In foreseeing that the enemy would give up after a couple of years, both sides miscalculated badly, but there was nothing intrinsically foolish in their thinking.

It was with reluctance and apprehension that the Athenians abandoned their homes and the familiar temples nearby, and when the farmers arrived in Athens only a few were able to find shelter with friends or relatives. Most had to seek out empty space in the city or bunk down in temples and shrines. Some wound up spending the summer campaigning season in the towers along the walls. Fortunately, the Athenians thought, the war would not last too long; but of course the Spartans knew this was just what they were thinking.

Though the first year of the war saw few casualties, by tradition the Athenians held a public funeral for those who had been killed. This much we know: Pericles was chosen to offer the eulogy. How closely the stirring paean to Athens that appears in Thucydides' history approximates what Pericles actually said is another question. We have no other versions of this speech. It could represent Thucydides' accurate recollection of what was said, or a faulty recollection, or a composition of his own; and even if Pericles said these things, his speech could have been written by someone else. In any event, the speech we have focuses not on the dead themselves but on the city of Athens and the way of life it represents—a way of life that is defined as the antithesis of everything Spartan.

It would be a mistake, Pericles suggested, to think that an easygoing polis such as Athens, with its love of words, of ideas, and of beauty, could not compete successfully in war with a highly regulated, militarized society like Sparta, where words are despised as a hindrance to action, people have little choice about how they live their lives, and anxious secrecy is the order of the day. "We love nobility without ostentation," Pericles says,

> and we have a virile love of knowledge. Furthermore, wealth is for us something to use, not something to brag about. And as to poverty, there is no shame in admitting to it—the real shame is in not taking action to escape from it. Finally,

while there are those who manage both the city and their own private affairs, there are others who, though wrapped up in their work, nevertheless have a thorough knowledge of public affairs. For we are the only people who regard a man who takes no interest in politics to be leading not a quiet life but a useless one. We are also the only ones who either make governmental decisions or at least frame the issues correctly, because we do not think that action is hampered by public discourse, but by not learning enough in advance, through discourse, about what action we need to take.

* * *

To sum up, I tell you that this city, taken all in all, is the school of Greece, and as far as I am concerned, any man among us will exhibit a more fully developed personality than men elsewhere and will be able to take care of himself more gracefully and with the quickest of wit.

(*The Peloponnesian War* 2.40–41; Blanco 1998)

Pericles' concluding charge to the women of Athens sat oddly on the lips of a man who lived with a companion far more visible and renowned than many of his fellow politicians:

And since I must also make some mention of womanly virtue to those who will now be widows, I will define it in this brief admonition: your greatest fame consists in being no worse than your natures, and in having the least possible reputation among males for good or ill.

(2.45; Blanco 1998)

This is certainly striking advice in a society as loquacious as the one Thucydides depicts in Athens. It is posited on a notion of woman as in every way the opposite of political man, in whose mind reputation counted for practically everything.

The next year brought a horrific surprise: a ghastly plague that attacked the population of Athens. Its origin is unknown, as is its precise nature—typhus, probably, or perhaps smallpox or measles—but it spread rapidly in the crowded, unsanitary environment of a city packed to capacity and beyond. Probably about a third of the populace died. Thucydides, who himself fell ill but recovered, took pains to record everything he could about the course and symptoms of the illness so that it would be possible for readers to recognize the disorder should it ever reappear: he reports the oral bleeding, the bad breath, the painful vomiting, the burning skin, the insomnia, the memory loss, the often fatal diarrhea and goes on to describe the way in which people reacted to the disease. A nihilistic lawlessness began to characterize life in the city:

Fear of the gods? The laws of man? No one held back, concluding that as to the gods, it made no difference whether people worshiped or not since they saw that all alike were dying; and as to breaking the law, no one expected to live long enough to go to court and pay his penalty. The far more terrible verdict that had already been delivered against them was hanging over their heads—so it was only natural to enjoy life a little before it came down.

(*The Peloponnesian War* 2.53; Blanco 1998)

Figure 8.2. This image of Pericles survives in a Roman copy of the head of a lost Greek bronze. Pericles was rumored to have worn a helmet in order to conceal the deformed shape of his head, which made him resemble the tyrant Peisistratus.

Demoralized by the plague and frustrated by being forbidden to march out and offer battle, some Athenians tried to open negotiations for peace with the Spartans, ignoring Pericles' cautions against this and in fact voting to depose him from the strategia (bringing forward some charge against him, as was common in Athens when politicians had ceased to please their constituency). Nothing much happened when Pericles was out of office except the long-awaited surrender of Potidaea. Finding that other leaders conducted the war no better, the Athenians returned Pericles to office at the next elections. Then he caught the plague and died.

Cleon and Diodotus: The Revolt of Mytilene (428–427 BC)

No one man replaced Pericles as the unquestioned leader of the Athenian people, but one of the most popular of the new politicians was Cleon (d. 422 BC), a brash and outspoken tannery owner who cultivated a flamboyantly anti-aristocratic persona.

Hated by Thucydides and pilloried by Aristophanes, Cleon has come before the tribunal of history at a desperate disadvantage. The 420s saw a change in the character of Athenian government. Though no formal distinctions divided rich from poor or separated social classes, still until the war Athenians had felt most comfortable with political power in the hands of men from old, wealthy families—men like Cimon and Pericles. Now this ceased to be true. Richer men still had the advantage in politics, but increasingly men whose fathers and grandfathers had recently made money in business began to compete successfully with those whose families had been living off their land holdings for generations. New words, moreover, crept into discussions of Athenian politics: *dēmagōgos* and its relative *dēmagōgia*, which first appears in the surviving literature in Aristophanes' *Knights*, produced in 424 BC. Literally a "leader of the people"—surely there is nothing wrong in that—in the hands of class-conscious critics the word demagogos came to signal a calculating politician who manipulated the voters for his own ends rather than letting himself be guided by patriotism and principle. In reality, however, there is no way to be sure of people's motives, and sometimes the word just betrays the class prejudice of the writer using it. Thucydides described Pericles as leading the Athenian people rather than being led by them. Did this mean Pericles was a demagogue too?

Cleon first appears in the pages of Thucydides in a dramatic debate that took place in 427. The year before, several cities on the island of Lesbos had revolted from the Athenian empire under the leadership of the Mytileneans, whose city was the largest. Though the Spartans had promised aid to the rebels, it never materialized, and in 427 the Mytileneans surrendered to Athens. The Athenians initially voted to put all the men in Mytilene to death and to sell the women and children into slavery, and they dispatched a boat to bring the news to the general in command on the island. The next day, however, some people at least had second thoughts, and a debate ensued. Cleon shows a cocky self-assurance in the dismissive way he addresses his audience: "I, for my part," he begins, "have often noticed before that democracies cannot rule over others, but I see it especially now in these regrets of yours about Mytilene . . ." (3.37; Blanco 1998). Deriding the Athenians for their openness and flexibility, he advocates a policy of harsh consistency. Bad laws that stay the same, he insists, are better than good ones that change. His studied anti-intellectualism contrasts pointedly with the praise of deliberation and debate in Pericles' funeral oration delivered three years earlier: Ordinary people, Cleon says, "run their cities far better than intelligent ones, for these want to seem wiser than the laws and to outdo whatever nonsense is said in public assemblies. . . . They are the downfall of cities because of this sort of thing" (3.37). In other respects, however, Cleon for all his crassness is plainly Pericles' heir. "You don't understand," he says, "that you hold your empire as a tyranny and that your subjects are schemers who are governed unwillingly" (3.37). Compare Pericles in his last speech: "You hold your empire like a tyranny by now. Taking it is thought to have been criminal; letting it go would be extremely dangerous" (2.63; Blanco 1998).

Diodotus, who is otherwise unknown, spoke against proceeding with the original plan, making a marvelous argument grounded in human psychology. Deterrence, he contended, was not as effective as commonly believed, because people who undertake risky ventures do so in the expectation that they will succeed, not fail. Furthermore, he argued, there was no merit in killing people even when they had surrendered, for to do so removed any incentive for surrender in future rebellions. He then made a key observation about the dynamics of the empire. "So far," he maintained,

> the populace in all of the cities is well-inclined toward you. Either they do not join in rebellion with the oligarchs, or, if they are forced to do so, they quickly turn against them. Thus, when you go to war you have the populace of the city you are attacking on your side.
>
> (*The Peloponnesian War* 3.47; Blanco 1998)

Though some might debate the accuracy of Diodotus' contention, it certainly makes us think twice about Thucydides' claim that the Athenian empire was universally detested in the subject cities.

Diodotus won the day, and a second boat was sent out to overtake the first. Envoys from Mytilene provided extra rations for the rowers and promised a large reward if they arrived in time. As it happened, the rowers on the original boat had been in no hurry to announce impending doom, and the second boat managed to arrive just as the death sentence was being announced. Instead of putting all the men to death and enslaving all the women and children, the Athenians executed the ringleaders of the revolt—who apparently amounted to over a thousand men.

The War Continues

The tendency to keep land in the family constricted social mobility in Greece, limiting opportunities for improving one's lot in life. As Thucydides points out, the war raging throughout Greece intensified the long-standing tensions between the aristocrats, who considered a lavish lifestyle to be their birthright, and the ordinary citizens struggling to make a living, for the former could expect help from Sparta and the latter from Athens. The result was *stasis* ("civil strife") more frequent and ferocious than ever before. Thucydides describes the agony that ensued when the democratic party in Corcyra gained the upper hand and, as allies of the demos, the Athenians under their admiral Eurymedon made no move to curtail the butchery. To avoid death at the hands of the democrats, some oligarchic partisans

> hanged themselves from trees. Others killed themselves in any way they could. Eurymedon remained at Corcyra for seven days with his sixty ships, during which the Corcyraeans ceaselessly slaughtered those among them whom they thought to be enemies. . . . One saw every imaginable kind of death, and everything that is likely to take place in situations like this did, in fact, take place—and even more. For example, fathers killed their sons; people were dragged from the temples and slaughtered in front of them; some were even walled up in the temple of Dionysus and left to die.
>
> (*The Peloponnesian War* 3.81; Blanco 1998)

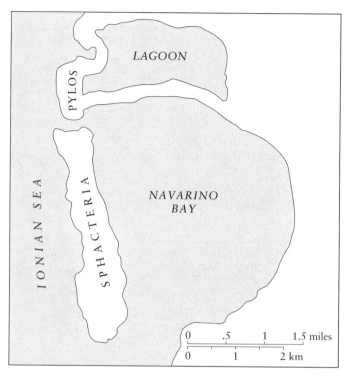

Figure 8.3. The Athenians achieved a great coup in marooning hundreds of Spartan soldiers on the island of Sphacteria shown here off the west coast of the Peloponnesus.

While operating in the west, the Athenians initiated a project which, while it would not determine the final outcome of the war, nonetheless had dramatic short-term effects. Held there by bad weather, the Athenian strategos Demosthenes (not to be confused with the famous fourth-century orator by the same name) decided to build a fort at Pylos, the legendary home of Nestor. This promontory combined with the narrow island of Sphacteria to enclose a body of water known today as the Bay of Navarino.

Fearing that Sphacteria might fall into Athenian hands, the Spartans recalled the army that was ravaging Attica and positioned 420 hoplites on the island. When the Athenians defeated the Spartans in naval combat, effectively marooning the hoplites on Sphacteria, the Spartan government panicked and sent envoys to Athens to plead for an armistice. So limited was the number of Spartans that their government was willing to do anything to get those hoplites back—even make a peace that took no account of their allies' interests. On the advice of Cleon, the Athenians refused, whether out of overconfidence or because they feared the fallout from a hasty peace that ultimately excluded key players like Corinth and Thebes.

The Spartans, then, remained on Sphacteria, and when Cleon made disparaging remarks about the failure of Athens' generals to capture them, he took for his particular target the respected strategos Nicias. A wealthy and religious man, Nicias had impressed many Athenians by the vast sums he spent on religious festivals, and his base of support lay with Athens' richer and more conservative voters—the sort of men who despised Cleon. Pointing his finger at Nicias, Thucydides reports, Cleon "said scornfully that if the generals were real men they could easily set out with an armada and capture the troops on the island. If he were in command, he continued, that was what he would do" (4.27; Blanco 1998). Nicias promptly suggested that Cleon himself be given a special commission to go to Pylos and get hold of the stranded hoplites. Against the expectation of upperclass Athenians, the inexperienced Cleon worked well with Demosthenes, and to the astonishment of all Greeks of all social classes, the Spartan soldiers surrendered rather than fight to the death. As 128 of the Peloponnesians had been killed in the fighting, the Athenians now had 292 bargaining chips with which to negotiate an end to the war. Seeing their position strengthened by the possession of hostages, the Athenians resolved to keep fighting rather than to make peace. This was probably a mistake, for any peace that Sparta made in order to regain its men was likely to alienate its allies and foster the disintegration of the Peloponnesian League.

The presence of Spartan hostages at Athens put an end to the annual invasions of Attica, but the war did not end, for in 424 the Spartans discovered what they had previously lacked, at least since the loss of Archidamus around 427: a charismatic general. As talented an orator as he was a strategist, Brasidas, by his campaigns up north in Chalcidice, very nearly won the war for Sparta, just as Demosthenes and Cleon had nearly won it for Athens at Pylos.

Figure 8.4. This bronze shield found in the Athenian *agora* was inscribed as booty taken from Pylos.

Brasidas and Chalcidice (424–422 BC)

Athens' hold on Chalcidice had always been fragile, and when some Chalcidic towns requested Spartan aid and were joined in their appeal by Athens' on-again, off-again ally Perdiccas of Macedonia, the Spartans promptly dispatched the dynamic Brasidas. Once in Chalcidice, Brasidas persuaded the towns of Acanthus, Stagirus, and Argilus to revolt from Athens. (His eloquence was great, but Thucydides stresses that fear of the Spartan presence was also a factor in these revolts.)

Though Brasidas had accomplished much for Sparta, the greatest prize lay ahead. Gaining possession of Amphipolis would require a little more effort, but this cherished Athenian stronghold was Brasidas' principal target, and in fact he brought it over to the Spartan side in less than twenty-four hours. Horrified by this loss, the Athenians banished one of their generals who had been offshore at Thasos when the catastrophe occurred: the historian Thucydides. The events of that snowy December night in the north played a large role in determining just what form Thucydides' history of the war, already begun earlier, would take. Just as they cut off the opportunity for hearing speeches delivered in the assembly and for picking up the latest scuttlebutt in the agora, they also ensured that Thucydides, freed from civic responsibilities and perhaps more trusted by foreigners now that he was on the outs with the home government, would have more reliable non-Athenian sources. Thucydides seems to know a great deal about Brasidas' thinking, for example; perhaps the two men got to know each other.

The following spring (423) the Athenians and the Spartans signed a year's armistice, but when the armistice expired in 422, Cleon, now a regularly elected general, met Brasidas in battle at Amphipolis. Greek generals fought in the front lines, and in the fighting both Cleon and Brasidas were killed.

The Peace of Nicias and the *Peace* of Aristophanes (421 BC)

The door to peace was opened by the deaths of the men Aristophanes called the pestles who were grinding down the mortar of war. Athens and Sparta had both had enough. Agriculture in Attica had been horribly disrupted and with it the trade between city and countryside that was the foundation of polis life, and the Athenians were unsettled by the patent unrest throughout their sphere of influence in the north. Sparta was nervous about continuing its war with Athens when the Spartan-Argive truce of thirty years was on the verge of expiring. A number of Spartan soldiers had died in captivity in Athens, and the Spartans were extremely eager to recover the survivors. Both sides were disturbed by the degree to which they had been compelled to hire mercenaries to keep the war going; it seemed like a bad precedent, and it was also costly. The other key players on the diplomatic scene, however—Corinth, Megara, and Boeotia—had somewhat less to gain from peace in general (although they had also experienced devastation during the war), and nothing to gain from the particular peace on which the Athenians and Spartans agreed. In fact, they refused to sign it. The highly problematic agreement known as the Peace of Nicias (named for the principal Athenian negotiator, Cleon's old rival) was essentially a victory for Athens.

Countless men and women throughout the Greek world had no doubt longed increasingly for peace during the ten years of the Archidamian War, but, as is often the case, we know most about the situation in Athens, from which the bulk of our written sources originate. Comic dramas, for example, were produced twice a year in Athens, both times at festivals of the god Dionysus. As at tragic competitions, several dramatists presented plays, but though we know the names of other comedians and fragments of their work remain, no whole plays by any hand other than Aristophanes' have survived from the fifth century. Obscene and boisterous, Aristophanes' plays also manifest a tender love of the countryside, a nostalgia for a simpler time, and a sober commitment to peace. Though Aristophanes' comic genius was unique, his values must have been congenial to the community; the decision whether to grant a chorus for training lay with the city magistrates, and of course prizes were awarded by citizen judges.

In 421, with an end to the war in sight, Aristophanes wrote his *Peace*; by the time it was presented, the treaty was close to becoming a reality. Here, parodying a lost play by Euripides, Aristophanes shows his protagonist Trygaeus riding on a huge dung beetle to the house of Zeus (accomplished on stage by a crane) to inquire why Zeus is destroying Greece by war. There he learns from Hermes that the gods have been alienated by the two sides' childish squabbling. The audience cannot have been entirely comfortable with Hermes' evenhanded allotment of blame. The gods, he says,

> were frequently for peace.
> But you guys wanted war. Laconians,
> when once they got a little piece of luck,
> would say, "By God, those Atticans will pay!"
> Or if it seemed that luck was on your side,
> and then the Spartans came about a peace,
> at once you'd cry: "We're being taken in!
> Athena! Zeus! we can't agree to this!
> If we hang on to Pylos, they'll come back. . . ."
>   (*Peace* 211–219)

He then explains that War has imprisoned Peace in a cave and, having obtained a huge mortar in which to grind down all the Greek cities, has sent his slave Tumult in search of pestles. Tumult, however, has learned that Athens and Sparta have recently lost their pestles—Cleon and Brasidas. Perhaps, then, there is some hope of setting Peace free.

Trygaeus finally persuades Hermes to help him organize the rescue of Peace. This is no mean task, since it is difficult to get all the Greeks to pull together on the necessary ropes even with divine assistance, but in time their efforts are successful. The blessings Peace will bring are celebrated in terms that reflect the concerns of the Athenian farmers in the audience:

Trygaeus: Fellow farmers! Stop and listen! Can you hear these
wondrous words?
No more spears, men, no more javelins, no more fighting with our swords!
We've got peace with all its gifts now, we can trade in
all that arming
For a happy, happy song as we march home to do
some farming.

Chorus: What a day, not just for farmers but for anyone worthwhile:
What a yearned-for, hoped-for vision! See how joyously
I smile
As I think about how soon I'll see the vines upon my land;
And the fig-trees that I planted as a youth with my
own hand!

(Peace 551–558)

The terms of the real-life peace were to be observed for fifty years. Athens was
to keep the empire with which it had entered the war; the treaty contained the
expression "the Athenians and their allies." Sparta was to return Amphipolis,
while Athens would abandon Pylos and the island of Cythera and release all prisoners of war. Though at tremendous cost in money and human lives, the Athenian
war goal had been met: The Spartans had failed to destroy the empire. Without even
trying, the Athenians had done much to weaken the Peloponnesian League. After a grueling war of ten years Sparta had suffered loss of life and loss of prestige.
Now she was about to lose her allies as well, and disaffection among them placed
the new peace in serious jeopardy.

Angry that no substantial damage had been done to the Athenian empire and
that two cities on the west coast, Sollium and Anactorium, remained in Athenian
hands, Corinth refused to sign the peace. Megara would not sign an agreement
that allowed the Athenians to retain its port Nisaea—as the Spartans should have
foreseen. The Boeotians, furious at the order to relinquish the border fortress of
Panactum to the Athenians, not only declined to sign the treaty but demolished
Panactum sooner than give it back. The Amphipolitans refused to return to the
Athenian empire and even began revering Brasidas rather than the Athenian
Hagnon as their founder; in retaliation, the Athenians held on to Pylos. The
chance for a productive alliance between the two most powerful states in Greece
was lost, and Thucydides viewed the Peace of Nicias as a false peace, a troubled
interlude before the resumption of hostilities.

BETWEEN PEACE AND WAR

Events were to prove that the thousands who had died in the Archidamian War
had given their lives for nothing. Though the Athenians and Spartans who desired

peace wanted it very badly indeed, they had to contend with formidable countervailing forces.

As a rule, it is dangerous to accord too large a role to high-profile individuals in shaping the course of history. At times, however, a particular person does seem to bear an extraordinary share of the responsibility for the way things turn out. Such was the case with the flashy Athenian aristocrat Alcibiades. Strategos for the first time in 420, Alcibiades had little prospect of making a name for himself in a tranquil world. His future glory was contingent on the disintegration of the fragile peace. To Alcibiades, even more than to the average Greek aristocrat, a life without glory was barely worth the name.

Alcibiades, Renegade Aristocrat

Alcibiades had been three when his father died, and he was raised in the home of his relative Pericles. Handsome, witty, athletic, charming, and sensuous, he was eagerly courted by lovers of both sexes. His rakish personality and flamboyant lifestyle were conducive to anecdote, and Plutarch tells several stories illustrating the opposition between the civic-mindedness of Pericles and the irresponsibility of his irreverent ward. One day, it seems, when Alcibiades had grown up and wished to speak to Pericles, he "went to his house, but was told Pericles could not receive him, as he was considering how to present his accounts to the people. 'Would it not be better,' asked Alcibiades as he came away, 'if he considered how to avoid presenting accounts to the people at all?'" (Plut. *Alcibiades* 7; Scott-Kilvert 1960).

Alcibiades never did like rules. His passions included his teacher Socrates, the breeding and racing of horses, and indeed competition in all its forms, on and off the track. His wealthy family had connections abroad, and despite his relationship to Pericles, his grandfather had been the Spartan *proxenos* at Athens—the man charged with representing Spartan interests in his home state. To the family connections that were his by birth, he added a marriage connection; his wife Hipparete belonged to one of the most wealthy and prominent families in Athens.

At first it appeared that Alcibiades' interest in reactivating the war would come to nothing. Although Elis and Mantinea joined the alliance Athens had formed with Argos, Sparta managed to defeat the new grouping in battle, scoring a decisive victory in Mantinea in 418 BC, and also succeeded in mending fences with its disaffected allies Boeotia and Corinth, thus in effect restoring the Peloponnesian League. Meanwhile tensions ran high among the various would-be leaders in Athens. An ostracism might have decided the rivalry of Alcibiades and Nicias, the hawk and the dove, but the two men seem to have panicked and mobilized their supporters to turn on a third man, Hyperbolus, instead.

The fact that ostracism was in reality something of an honor is underlined by Plutarch's claim that it was Hyperbolus' unworthiness that sparked this decision; a contemporary comic poet apparently quipped, "The man, indeed, deserved the fate, but not the fate the man." At this distance, it is impossible to determine whether the Athenians' distress at the outcome of the ostracism resulted from Hyperbolus' political insignificance or his social origins; those who had been ostracized earlier in the century came from aristocratic families. In any event, the Athenians now abandoned ostracism and turned to a different strategy for ensuring democratic control on government, making use of the *graphē paranomōn* ("indictment for illegal proposals") to punish politicians who brought forward proposals in conflict with existing laws. Like ostracism, however, this procedure was often used politically—a development that is not surprising, since, without a written constitution or bill of rights, only a highly subjective judgment could determine what new laws were and were not in harmony with the old.

The Destruction of Melos (416 BC)

The years that followed were marked by conflict in Athens and chaos in the Peloponnesus. A disturbing Athenian naval expedition stands out from these troubled years, memorialized in some of the most frequently read pages in Thucydides. In 416, probably at the instigation of Alcibiades, the Athenians dispatched ships to the little island of Melos, which was allied with neither Athens nor Sparta, and ordered it to join the Delian League. Hope of Spartan assistance moved the Melians to turn Athens down. Spartan aid did not materialize, and as punishment for their recalcitrance, the Athenians decided to kill all the Melian men and sell all the women and children into slavery—all of them. The ambivalence that had led them to limit their punishment of the Mytilenaeans to "ringleaders" in 427 was now a thing of the past. The episode plainly made a deep impression on Thucydides, who chose to include in his history a chilling rendition of the conversation between the Melians and the Athenians—the only sustained dialogue in his work. Melos was a tiny island in a remote locale. How did Thucydides know what was said there in such detail? He didn't. The set piece known as the "Melian Dialogue" shows us Thucydides experimenting with an art form closer to drama than to history.

Thucydides was not the only Athenian alive at the time who used his verbal talents to showcase the horrors of war and to explore its corrosive effect on morality. The following spring (415 BC) Euripides confronted the Athenians with his anguished *Trojan Women*. No one could seriously doubt that this exquisitely painful drama, ostensibly set in Troy in the aftermath of the city's fall, was designed to illustrate the dreadfulness of war in general and the current war in particular. The specter of the enslavement of the wives and sisters and daughters of the Trojan heroes and the execution of the young Astyanax, Hector's son, thrown to his death from the city walls, was all too evocative of recent developments: Many of those sitting in the audience had themselves done the killing at Melos. It also proved prophetic of events yet to come.

THE INVASION OF SICILY (415–413 BC)

While a small number of men met daily to practice singing the unsettling choruses in Euripides' sobering drama, many more busied themselves preparing for the largest military expedition in Athens' history. Pericles had warned the Athenians that attempts to expand their empire would undermine their chances of winning the war, but Pericles was long dead and his strategy had died with him. In the winter of 416–415 temptation had appeared to the Athenian assembly in the form of ambassadors from the Sicilian city of Egesta, an old ally. Their request for assistance against their neighbor Selinus provided a springboard for warmongers like Alcibiades. In a war with Egesta, Selinus could count on the backing of Syracuse, the most powerful city in Sicily—and a Corinthian colony. When Alcibiades advocated full support for Egesta and Nicias argued with equal passion against involvement in Sicily, the Athenians resolved on a peculiar compromise. Alcibiades would indeed be sent west with a large force, but he would be accompanied by two other strategoi—Lamachus, an experienced general, and Nicias himself, whose presence they hoped would serve as a check on Alcibiades' rashness.

The idea that Nicias' prudence would counter Alcibiades' impulsive nature was singularly wrongheaded. Shortly before the expedition was to sail, moreover, a bizarre nocturnal escapade in Athens sparked a scandal of extraordinary proportions that spilled over from religion to politics. Outside Athenian homes and temples stood religious images known as herms—stone pillars bearing images of the face and erect phallus of the god Hermes. They were meant to bring good luck and protection from danger. One morning not long before the expedition was to set sail, the Athenians awoke to find that nearly all these herms had been defaced—or rather dephallused.

Cultural differences make it hard for us fully to understand why Athenians reacted to this sacrilegious prank with utter terror and became convinced that a plot was afoot to overthrow the government, but this is exactly what happened. Though many were punished, responsibility for the project has never been determined. It may have been the work of one or more of the organizations known as *hetaireiai*. Drinking clubs composed of upper-class young men, often with oligarchic leanings, hetaireiai involved themselves in a variety of social and political activities. To democrats, they seemed sinister and potentially treasonous.

Not surprisingly, fingers were pointed at Alcibiades, precisely the sort of irreverent individual who would set his drinking companions on such an enterprise whether they belonged to a *hetaireia*, or not. Fuel was added to the flames by accusations that Alcibiades had staged a burlesque mocking the mystery rites celebrated at Eleusis, violating their secrecy by parodying them in front of the uninitiated. Since he had solid support among the adventurous sailors bound for Sicily, Alcibiades wisely demanded that he be tried at once, before the fleet left. Instead, his opponents waited to bring charges until the expedition had sailed.

The fleet the Athenians dispatched for Sicily was entirely out of proportion to the size or importance of its intended objective. It consisted of 134 triremes with 130 supply boats, a total of over 25,000 men. Dozens of merchant vessels decided to accompany the navy, hoping for profits. Both citizens and foreigners crowded the shore gazing with astonishment at the armada, which Thucydides says was the most expensive any Greek city had launched until that day. Of the many who sailed for Sicily, however, few returned. The Athenians received less support from the cities of Sicily and southern Italy than they had expected, and even the eager Egestans turned out not to have the resources they had claimed. Envoys dispatched to Egesta, it proved, had been duped into believing the city was rich when in fact it was poor. Thucydides tells how the various Egestans received the crews of the Athenian ships in their homes, rounding up as many gold and silver cups as they could find in town and in the neighboring cities and presenting them at parties as if they belonged to the host:

> They all used the same goblets, for the most part, and they showed so much of it everywhere that it absolutely awed the Athenian crewmen, who, when they returned to Athens, spread the news about the great wealth they had seen. Those who had been deceived in turn misled others, and they were all held responsible by the troops when word got out that Egesta did not have any money.
> (*The Peloponnesian War* 6.46; Blanco 1998)

Just about everything that could have gone wrong with the Sicilian enterprise did. Lamachus died fighting. Alcibiades was recalled to stand trial, and on the journey managed to jump ship and defect to Sparta. When in the winter of 415–414 envoys from Syracuse and Corinth came to seek Spartan aid for the Sicilian campaign, Alcibiades warned the Spartans that the Athenians were planning to conquer Sicily and Italy, attack Carthage, and then go after the Peloponnesus. The dispatch of a Spartan general to Sicily, he suggested, might be necessary if the Spartans wanted to prevent an Athenian takeover of the entire Greek world.

Nicias and Lamachus had occupied the plateau known as Epipolae west of Syracuse and had begun building a north-south wall with the idea in mind of blockading the city. Now in sole command, Nicias successfully moved the Athenian fleet into Syracuse's harbor, creating a real possibility of blockading the city, but the Spartans were determined to prevent the Athenians from conquering Sicily and had sent a talented commander, Gylippus, to see what he could do. The arrival of Gylippus with reinforcements changed the situation dramatically. Gylippus scaled the Epipolae heights via a pass that the Athenians had carelessly left unguarded— the same pass they themselves had used a few months before. The Syracusans, moreover, built a counter-wall that destroyed Athenian chances for a blockade.

Nicias was now suffering acutely from kidney disease and asked the Athenians to recall him. They refused. Convinced the situation was hopeless, he tried to dissuade them from continuing their efforts in Sicily by a long letter to the assembly maintaining that only a force as large as the original expedition could have any chance of success. To his horror, the Athenians sent Demosthenes out at the head of the proposed reinforcements. When he arrived with the second fleet and promptly suffered a serious reverse on the Epipolae heights, Demosthenes advocated withdrawal. Once more, however, religious anxiety intruded into the secular sphere. When everything was ready for the Athenians' departure, Thucydides related,

> and just as they were about to sail, there was an eclipse of the moon, which happened to be full. The event made most of the Athenians feel uneasy, and they urged their generals to stay; and Nicias, who was too inclined to believe in the

interpretation of omens and that sort of thing, refused even to discuss a move until after they had stayed for "three times nine days," as their seers decreed. This was the reason the Athenians stayed on after all their delays!

(*The Peloponnesian War* 7.50; Blanco 1998)

On learning that the Athenians had been planning to leave, the Syracusans attacked the Athenian fleet and blocked the exit from the harbor. A fierce battle ensued, with some two hundred ships rammed together in a tight space. The din made it impossible to hear the calls of the coxswains.

Unable to make their escape by sea, the Athenians resolved to depart over land, abandoning their sick and wounded. About 40,000 men set out on the dismal trek, the Syracusans hot on their heels. Nicias and Demosthenes became separated; the Syracusans caught up first with Demosthenes, who surrendered in the hope of saving his soldiers' lives. The Syracusans then overtook Nicias' army.

Document 8.1. Thucydides is at his narrative best in portraying the final collapse of the Athenian effort in Sicily.

The Athenians pushed on to the Assinarus River, all the while being devastated by the spears, arrows and stones coming from everywhere and by the hordes of cavalry and other troops. They thought that if they could just get across the river, things would be a little easier for them. They were desperate to stop the pain, to drink some water. When they got to the river, they broke ranks and ran into it, every man struggling to make the brutal crossing first as the enemy bore down. Driven to cross all together, they fell onto one another and trampled each other down. Some were killed immediately by their own spears; others got tangled up in their equipment and with each other and sank into the river. Syracusans positioned on the other bank, which was steep, hurled down spears at the Athenians, most of whom were jumbled together ravenously drinking from the nearly dry riverbed. The Peloponnesians went down into the river after them and did most of the killing there; and though it quickly became fouled, the Athenians nonetheless fought among themselves to gulp the muddy water clotted with blood.

Finally, with dead bodies heaped atop each other in the riverbed, and the army decimated, some in the river and others—such as got across—by the cavalry, Nicias surrendered himself to Gylippus, trusting him more than the Syracusans. He told Gylippus and the Spartans to do with him what they wanted, but to stop slaughtering his men. After this, Gylippus ordered his troops to take prisoners, whereupon the surviving men were brought in alive, except for the large number who had been hidden by individual Syracusan soldiers. They also sent a search party out after the three hundred who had broken through the sentries by night and captured them. . . . A large number, of course, were killed, for there was a great slaughter at the river, greater than any which occurred in the whole war.

The Peloponnesian War 7.84–85; translated by Walter Blanco, in Walter Blanco and Jennifer Roberts, eds., *Thucydides: The Peloponnesian War*. New York: W.W. Norton, 1998.

The Athenians had lost tens of thousands of men and accomplished nothing. For them, the outcome of the campaign was so horrific that they at first refused to believe the appalling news. Plutarch claims that word of the disaster first reached Athens by way of a hapless man who had reported it matter of factly to a barber in Piraeus as if it were common knowledge: The agitated barber promptly ran the 5 miles to Athens, where he repeated the tale. He was in the very process of being tortured as a troublemaker when messengers arrived to confirm the astonishing story. As Thucydides was later to write, "All was lost. Ships. Men. Everything" (7.87).

THE WAR IN THE AEGEAN AND THE OLIGARCHIC COUP AT ATHENS (413–411 BC)

The Greek world was as stunned by the Athenians' defeat at Syracuse as it had been by their victory at Marathon. The myth of naval superiority that had held the Delian League together was shattered. Athens' fighting force was vastly smaller than it had been in 431. Money was in short supply; previously one trierarch had been appointed for each ship, but soon after the disaster in Sicily the Athenians introduced the syntrierarchy, allowing two men to share the expense. For Athenian subjects, suddenly revolt became not merely an option but a powerful temptation. Alcibiades cruised the seas on Sparta's behalf, fomenting rebellion wherever he could. Meanwhile in Attica some twenty thousand slaves deserted to the Spartan king Agis, who at Alcibiades' instigation had established himself in a fort at Decelea in northeast Attica. The disappearance of the slaves from the mines prevented the continued tapping of the silver veins, and the strength of the encampment at Decelea interfered gravely with Athenian agriculture. Now the Spartans could ravage Attica all year, killing farm animals as they went and keeping Athens in a perpetual state of siege. Seeing success well within their grasp, the invigorated Spartans set about building a new naval force of a hundred triremes and began negotiating for Persian support.

Incredibly, it took Sparta eight years to bring Athens to its knees—eight years during which the Athenians, crippled by devastating losses in Sicily, survived the loss of the huge island of Euboea off the Attic coast and an oligarchic coup in the city. The history of these eight years is crowded with shifting alliances, plots and counterplots, murders and lies. Within Athens, lines between democrats and oligarchs appear blurred as key players in the political arena move back and forth between the parties, and a new creature appears, the "moderate"—a politician whose motives for keeping one foot in each camp are often impossible to determine: Sincere patriotism becomes increasingly difficult to distinguish from unprincipled time-serving. Spartans are divided as to how seemly it might be to barter the Ionians' freedom in exchange for Persian gold. Persians cannot decide which side, if any, to support. Alcibiades remains a wild card, cagily shifting position to suit the rapidly altering international situation—and to keep himself safe from the wrath of Agis, whose wife he appears to have seduced. The fortunes of battle swing wildly back and forth. In 413 Athens seemed to be finished; by 410 the Spartans sue for peace. Athens wins a stunning victory in 406 only to lose the war by 404.

Civil Strife in Athens

The burst of Peloponnesian energy that erupted in the wake of Athens' defeat in Sicily was short-lived. The Spartans soon reverted to their natural sluggishness. Their lukewarm efforts would have come to little had it not been for the dynamic energy of Alcibiades and for the tensions that erupted in Athens, setting the hoplites and the aristocratic elite against the thetes who manned the fleet.

For nearly a century after the clash between Cleisthenes and Isagoras, Athens had been free from the danger of civil war. Unrest erupted, however, when men of oligarchic inclinations played on the Athenians' anxieties about the failure of their democratic leaders to prosecute the war more successfully, particularly in Sicily. The machinations of Alcibiades provided a catalyst for a more substantial change in the government. Having worn out his welcome in Sparta—whether because of his alleged affair with the wife of King Agis or for some other reason—he had begun to plot a return to Athens. The entry of Persia into the equation provided the springboard he needed. In the years that followed the Athenian defeat in Sicily, Persian policy toward Greece was determined not primarily by the king, Darius II, but by the coastal satraps—Pharnabazus (the satrap of Dascylium) in the north, and Tissaphernes (the satrap of Sardis) in the south.

Tissaphernes in particular had a lively interest in Greek affairs, and indeed in Greek culture as a whole. At first he leaned toward Sparta, and in fact negotiated a series of treaties with Sparta in which the Spartans, uncomfortably but unmistakably, agreed to sell out the freedom of the Greek cities of Ionia in exchange for Persian gold. (Thus died the Spartans' claim to be the liberators of Greece.) Not long afterward, however, Alcibiades persuaded Tissaphernes that it might be better for Persia to let Athens and Sparta wear each other down. When Tissaphernes' support for the Spartan cause began to waver, Alcibiades sent word to Athens that he had it in his power to bring the Persians into the war on the Athenian side—but that their support would be contingent on replacing the democracy with an oligarchy. His support, of course, would be contingent on his recall.

That Alcibiades really believed he could persuade Tissaphernes to pour money into the Athenian treasury is unlikely, though not impossible. In the event, he couldn't, but by the time it became clear that the Persian support he had promised was illusory, the wheels had been set in motion for a change in government and Alcibiades' return. It is an index of how deeply the long war had shaken the Athenians that in 411 the assembly, some members intimidated and others just

Figure 8.5. This Greek-style coin struck by the Persian Tissaphernes reveals his desire to be identified with Greek culture.

demoralized, voted itself out of existence and placed the safety of the state in the hands of a new, provisional Council of four hundred, which, it was understood, would soon give way to a larger body of five thousand. Despite the way the war had undermined confidence in the democratic government, this vote was made possible only by the absence of the fleet, based now at Samos, for sailors, who were generally poor men, could be counted on to oppose any reforms that had the effect of limiting the franchise to property owners.

Experiments in Oligarchy

Neither of the reformers' notions was entirely new. Solon was believed by many people to have created a Council of four hundred—certainly such a body dated from approximately his time—and the five thousand were thought to correspond to the hoplite class. Sailors were right to be alarmed by such projects. What was really at issue here was the disenfranchisement of the lowest class in the Solonic census, the thetes. The notion of "hoplite democracy" had been Cimon's ideal, and he was not alone. From this moment many Athenians of antidemocratic tendencies began to make use of a new watchword, "the ancestral constitution," that is, a democracy limited to landowners, which they insisted was more traditionally Athenian than the upstart democracy that included the poor men who served as rowers in the fleet. This issue, which had seemed to be settled in 508 with Cleisthenes' victory over Isagoras, was now once again on the floor.

Carrying arms and flanked by an additional 120 men, the Four Hundred also entered the Bouleuterion where the council met, paid the councilors the balance of what was owing to them, and dismissed them. Their own despotic rule was also made easier by the ominous suspension of the *graphē paranomon*, the indictment for illegal proposals. There were now two Athenian governments—the oligarchy of the Four Hundred in the city and the democratic fleet stationed at Samos, which functioned as the assembly.

The belief that Athens' foreign affairs would do better under oligarchic guidance suffered serious setbacks when the peace with Sparta failed to materialize—and

Euboea successfully revolted from the Athenian empire. The hoplites whom the Four Hundred had set to fortifying the promontory of Eetionia at Piraeus mutinied, and the Five Thousand were promptly installed. They then recalled Athens' exiles, including Alcibiades, and governed Athens for eight months, from September 411 to June 410. Not a great deal is known about their government, though they seem to have limited the franchise to the hoplite class (cutting out the thetes who manned the triremes). Thucydides, who was frequently impatient with democracy, praised the government of the Five Thousand as a laudable blending of democratic and oligarchic elements.

The vigor the Athenians showed in rebuilding their fleet and carrying on the war despite acute domestic conflict was remarkable. After a victory at Cynossema, the Athenians, led by Alcibiades, scored a still more striking one at Cyzicus, where the Spartans lost their admiral-in-chief, Mindarus. The battle is memorable for the "laconic" dispatch the Athenians intercepted on its way to Sparta afterward: "Ships lost; Mindarus dead; men starving; can't figure out what to do." (It is also memorable as the first major encounter of the war not described by Thucydides: Thucydides' account breaks off shortly after Cynossema. From this point on the principal sources are Xenophon and Diodorus.) The victories in the east had been won by the cooperation of the Five Thousand in Athens and the fleet at Samos, and in June the democracy was formally restored at Athens. A number of the leaders of the Five Thousand remained powerful under the democracy. Among these was Hagnon's son Theramenes, who seemed to find a place for himself in any group. Animosity and suspicion were not entirely gone, however, and as one of its first official acts the restored democracy administered a loyalty oath, requiring each citizen to swear: "I will do my best to kill by word and by deed, by my vote and by my hand, anyone who overthrows the Athenian democracy, holds office under an undemocratic regime, or seeks to establish a tyranny either for himself or for someone else. If anyone else kills such a person, I will consider him clean in the eyes of gods and spirits" (Andocides, *On the Mysteries*, 97). The Spartans sought peace from the restored democracy, but only on the basis of the status quo. That the Athenians had regained their confidence is indexed by their refusal.

THE LAST YEARS OF WAR (407–404 BC)

In 407, however, the union of two powerful men dramatically altered the situation in the Aegean. Alcibiades was not the only Greek with charm. An enthusiastic friendship sprang up between Cyrus, son of the Persian king, and Lysander, the ambitious chief admiral of the Spartan navy. Ultimately, their alliance spelled doom for Athens.

That same year, Alcibiades, having raised a hundred talents for Athens by looting the coast of Caria, decided it might finally be safe to return home. It was an extraordinary circumstance—a man with so many friends that he was repeatedly elected to the board of generals but with so many enemies that he feared to set foot on Attic soil. Once more, however, his ascendancy in his native polis was remarkably brief. Within a matter of months, the Athenians lost twenty-two ships to Lysander at a naval engagement off Notium, where Alcibiades had left his personal pilot Antiochus in charge with orders under no circumstances to engage the Spartans. Antiochus, a friend of Alcibiades, probably had no business in a position of such authority, since he was not a trierarch, and Alcibiades had acted unwisely in putting him there; but the strength of the Athenian reaction attests to the continuing agitation of his enemies. Alcibiades' career at Athens was finished. It is certain that he was not reelected to the strategia, and it is likely that he was actually deposed before his term was out. Rumors circulated that he had fortified a castle in the Gallipoli peninsula as a refuge in case of emergency. Now that the emergency had materialized, he promptly withdrew to this very fortress. He never saw Athens again.

That spring the Athenians offered freedom to slaves who would join the navy that was about to set out for the area of Lesbos. There they scored an impressive victory in a huge naval battle off the Arginusae islands, sinking fully seventy-five Peloponnesian ships. Some twenty thousand Greeks lost their lives. The aftermath of the battle witnessed a bizarre frenzy of self-destruction. Though the Athenian navy was heartened by the victory at Arginusae, they knew that their admiral Conon and his fleet were blockaded at Mytilene. While the Athenian strategoi were debating whether to set about retrieving the sailors in the water or sail to Mytilene to rescue Conon's force, a sudden storm came up that made rescue impossible. When news of the casualties reached Athens, people began anxiously to cast blame on one another. The generals blamed the trierarchs Theramenes and Thrasybulus, and the trierarchs blamed the generals. Whether the men in the water were dead or alive is uncertain, but for Greeks the recovery even of bodies was important, since the souls of those left unburied would wander eternally in Hades, unable to find a resting place. The eight generals in command were summoned home for trial, and six chose to return. In violation of customary procedure—and over the protests of the philosopher Socrates, whose turn it happened to be to chair the assembly meeting that day—the generals were tried on a single slate, condemned, and executed. Ironically, after the death of his legitimate sons, Pericles had implored the Athenians to confer citizenship on his sons by Aspasia, and Pericles the Younger was among the generals put to death.

The Final Battle

Again, the Spartans offered peace on the basis of the status quo (though they were willing to evacuate Decelea); again the Athenians declined. Time, however, was running out, as was the pool of talented commanders—and of money. The next major battle would be Athens' last stand. Late in the summer of 405 BC Lysander, making good use of the subsidies he had obtained from his friend Cyrus, established a base in the city of Lampsacus in the Hellespont. In August the Athenian generals Conon and Philocles stationed their fleet 2 miles across the channel at Aegospotami. Alcibiades, seeing that the Athenians' position was highly vulnerable, descended from his fortress and advised them to move, but they disregarded his cautions. Attacking one morning when the Athenians had gone ashore for provisions, the Spartans captured 171 ships, and their infantry overwhelmed the Athenian camp. Understandably, the Athenians' carelessness gave rise to rumors of treachery. Only a handful of Athenian vessels escaped, one of them the official state trireme the Paralus, another commanded by Conon. Remembering the fate of the victors of Arginusae, Conon took refuge in Cyprus and did not return to Athens until he had engineered a victory over the Spartans at Cnidus in 394, ten years after the end of the war.

Lysander then called a meeting of the allies to solicit their thoughts about the proper treatment of the prisoners. The speeches made about the Athenians, Xenophon reports, were many and bitter,

> both with regard to all the crimes they had committed in the past and about the decree which they had passed to the effect that, if they won the naval action, they could cut off the right hand of every man taken alive; there was also the fact that, after capturing two triremes, one from Corinth and one from Andros, they had thrown every man in the crews overboard. It was Philocles, the Athenian general, who had all these men killed. Many other such stories were told, and in the end it was decided that all the prisoners who were Athenian should be put to death with the one exception of Adimantus. He had been the only man in the Assembly who opposed the decree for cutting off the hands of prisoners. He was also, it should be said, accused by some people of having betrayed the fleet. As for Philocles, who had thrown the Andrians and Corinthians overboard, Lysander first asked him this question: "What do you deserve for having been the first to act like a criminal toward your fellow-Greeks?" He then had his throat cut.
>
> (*Hellenica* 2.1.31–32; Warner 1979)

The Spartan victory at Aegospotami had cut off Athens from its principal source of grain; to make sure there would be no slip-ups, Lysander also decreed death as the penalty for anyone caught bringing grain to Athens. Lysander knew that the war was now over, and the Athenians would know it soon enough, for the Paralus was en route to Piraeus with the dismal tidings. The ship arrived at night, and as the news was reported, Xenophon relates, "one man passed it on to another, and a sound of wailing arose and extended first from Piraeus, then along the Long Walls until it reached the city. That night no one slept. They mourned for the lost, but more still for their own fate" (2.2.1; Warner). Late in the fall Lysander sailed victorious for Piraeus. Along the way he accepted the surrender of Athens' former allies and replaced their democracies with oligarchic governments beholden to Sparta. He also ensured still further stress on the Athenians' dwindling food supply by encouraging Athenian garrisons to return home. Samos persisted in its loyalty to Athens, in recognition of which the Athenians uncharacteristically granted the Samians citizenship. Agis, whose occupation of Decelea had played its desired part in the starvation of the city, moved down to the walls of Athens, where he was joined by Pausanias, his co-king. Miserable and terrified, the Athenians were at a loss for what to do. "They could see no future for themselves," Xenophon wrote, "except to suffer what they had made others suffer, people of small states whom they had injured not in retaliation for anything they had done but out of the arrogance of power and for no reason except that they were in the Spartan alliance" (2.2.10).

The mutability of fortune had been a commonplace in Greek literature, and the Athenians gathered in the theater in 415 had been given the opportunity to contemplate the cruelty of war's chances in Euripides' *Trojan Women*. Of those who prosper, the Trojan queen Hecuba had suggested, "consider no-one blest until he's dead" (509–510). This notion so reminiscent of Solon's warning to Croesus in Herodotus' cautionary tale was developed later in the play, as Hecuba underlines the foolishness of those who believe prosperity is secure:

> like someone who's gone mad, in changing moods
> fortune leaps wildly, now this way, now that:
> nobody ever prospers all the time.
>
> (*Trojan Women* 1204–1206)

In the end, Athens was spared. The Thebans, Corinthians, and other Spartan allies advocated doing to Athens precisely what had been done to Melos—killing all the adult men and selling all the women and children into slavery. The Spartans declined, pleading Athens' noble service to Greece during the Persian wars. The brutality of Lysander's temperament makes it more likely that the real motive was fear of the power vacuum into which Corinth or—more likely—Thebes could be counted on to rush.

Early in the spring the Athenians agreed to a treaty negotiated by Theramenes on the Spartans' terms: Athens would not only become Sparta's ally but would agree to the destruction of the Long Walls and the fortifications of Piraeus and would surrender all but a dozen ships. Exiles would also be recalled; these were largely men of oligarchic sympathies. The walls were pulled down, Xenophon says, to the merry accompaniment of flutes, for "it was thought that this day was the beginning of freedom for Greece" (2.2.23; Warner). The Spartans' actions, however, presaged ill for freedom. The willingness to sell out the Ionians to Persia and the establishment of pro-Spartan oligarchies in cities formerly in the Athenian empire were bad signs, and worse was to come.

TRANSLATIONS

Blanco, Walter. 1998. *The Peloponnesian War*, from *Thucydides: The Peloponnesian War*, Walter Blanco and Jennifer Roberts, eds. New York: W.W. Norton.

Scott-Kilvert, Ian. 1960. *The Rise and Fall of Athens: Nine Greek Lives by Plutarch.* Harmondsworth, UK: Penguin.

Warner, Rex. 1979. *Xenophon: A History of My Times [The Hellenica].* Harmondsworth, UK: Penguin.

SUGGESTED READINGS

Connor, W. Robert. 1992. *The New Politicians of Fifth Century Athens*. Indianapolis: Hackett. A nuanced but highly readable examination of the changing dynamics of Athenian political life in the fifth century.

De Romilly, Jacqueline. 1988. *Thucydides and Athenian Imperialism*. Trans. P. Thody. Reprinted Salem, NH: Ayer Co. Publishers. A classic study of Thucydides and the empire.

Ehrenberg, Victor. 1974. *The People of Aristophanes*. Reprinted New York: Barnes & Noble. A study of the sociology and economics of the Athenian state based on a close examination of data in Aristophanes' comedies.

Green, Peter. 1970. *Armada from Athens*. London: Hodder and Stoughton. A spirited account of the Athenian invasion of Sicily by a distinguished ancient historian.

Hornblower, Simon. 1986. *Thucydides*. Baltimore: Johns Hopkins University Press. A penetrating study of the "historian's historian."

Kagan, Donald. 2003. *The Peloponnesian War*. New York: Viking Press. A detailed but highly readable analysis of the war's military and diplomatic history.

Loraux, Nicole. 1986. *The Invention of Athens: The Funeral Oration in the Classical City*. Trans. Alan Sheridan. Cambridge, MA and London: Harvard University Press. An examination of the key role of the Athenian funeral oration in shaping ideals of civic life and defining what Athens was all about.

Meiggs, Russell. 1972. *The Athenian Empire*. Oxford: Oxford University Press. A history of Athens' relationship with its allies from the inception of the Delian League to the end of the Peloponnesian War, with chapters on the judgments made on the empire in both the fifth and fourth centuries and a chart recording tribute payments for the years 453 to 420.

Strauss, Barry. 1993. *Fathers and Sons in Athens: Ideology and Society in the Era of the Peloponnesian War*. Princeton, NJ: Princeton University Press. A sensitive analysis of Athenian society during the last decades of the fifth century that grounds conflict in intergenerational tension.

9

THE CRISIS OF THE POLIS AND THE AGE OF SHIFTING HEGEMONIES

There was nothing inevitable about the Spartans' ultimate victory in the war. Darius died in 404. Had the Athenians not been so careless at Aegospotami—or had they not been betrayed—the withdrawal of Persian support that would probably have attended on the king's death would gravely have compromised the Spartans' chances of winning the war. On the other hand, the long war taught Sparta a vital lesson about the centrality of naval power. When Sparta became a naval power, the Athenians lost an important advantage, lost the war, and lost their empire.

The economic consequences of the war were grave. Commerce by land and sea was disrupted; cities like Corinth suffered immensely. Agriculture suffered in most of Greece (although not, presumably, in Sparta, where helots continued to till the land); the redoubled labor of women and slaves was not sufficient to compensate for the death of farmers or their long campaigns away from home. A good deal of territory was ravaged, and livestock and farming implements destroyed as well as growing vines and olive trees. Some erstwhile farmers were driven to take service as mercenary soldiers, an increasingly popular profession. As usually happens in wartime, many women were forced to work outside the home, and the loss of thousands upon thousands of soldiers and sailors left many women without husbands. New patterns of labor within the *oikos* developed as well, as free women were more likely to work at home producing goods not only for in-house consumption but for sale as well.

In Athens, as many as fifty thousand people had probably died of the plague, many of them doing so before they could reproduce. War casualties seem to have included at least five thousand hoplite soldiers and twelve thousand sailors (including some three thousand executed by Lysander after Aegospotami). Probably the number of adult male citizens in 403 was half what it had been in 431. Some cities, like Melos and Scione, had been virtually annihilated. In Sparta, absolute numbers dropped less sharply, but the various classes began to redefine themselves, as the ranks of commanders as well as soldiers were swelled not only by distinguished *mothakes* ("children of Spartiate fathers and helot mothers") but also by helot fighters rewarded with freedom, known as *neodamodeis* ("new citizens").

The use of mercenaries and the periodic emergency enfranchisement of helots and slaves—there were one thousand neodamodeis in Sparta by 421 and probably at least fifteen hundred by the end of the war—blurred the lines that had traditionally divided citizens from noncitizens and eroded the concept of the citizen-soldier and the citizen-sailor, and the frequency of bloody civil strife eroded the concept of the *polis* itself. At the same time, however, the shattering of faith fostered a questioning spirit that opened the door to the reflections of Socrates, Xenophon, and Plato. The Peloponnesian War transformed the Greek world, but it did not destroy it.

OLIGARCHY AT ATHENS: THE THIRTY TYRANTS

Sparta's behavior throughout the Aegean soon put to rest any lingering notions that its decision to spare Athens arose from a policy of generosity. In states formerly allied to Athens Lysander set up "decarchies," that is, boards of ten pro-Spartan officials designed to ensure oligarchic government and loyalty to Sparta. For Athens itself plainly ten men would not suffice; there he forced the assembly to ratify a board of thirty. Athenian citizens, these thirty were sympathetic to Sparta and willing to sacrifice democratic principles, but they were not all committed oligarchs; they included, for example, the moderate Theramenes. The most prominent of those who came to be known as the Thirty Tyrants, however, left no doubt as to his political convictions. The oligarch Critias was a chilling figure—a pupil of Socrates, a relative of Plato, a brilliant intellectual, an avowed atheist, a passionate antidemocrat, a longtime admirer of the Spartan constitution, and, as events were to show, a man who would order murders by the hundreds without a qualm. Banished after the fall of the Four Hundred, to which he had belonged, Critias was now back with a vengeance. The Thirty, according to the author of the *Athenaion Politeia* sometimes attributed to Aristotle, "kept their hands off none of the citizens, but put to death those of outstanding wealth or birth or reputation, intending to put that source of danger out of the way, and also desiring to plunder their estates; and by the end of a brief interval of time they had made away with not less than fifteen hundred" (Ath. Pol. 35.4, Rackham 1961). They also fortified their position with seven hundred Spartan soldiers and a Spartan garrison commander similar to those Sparta had established in states throughout the Aegean that it had "liberated" from Athenian hegemony.

Not all the victims of the Thirty were citizens who could possibly have been conceived as political enemies; many were wealthy metics whose property the Thirty coveted. Inevitably the Thirty were apprehensive about the possibility of a resistance movement, and they suspected, with some justice, that such a movement might be spearheaded by Theramenes, who had made clear his alarm at the bloodbath. Summoned to the boule for a "trial" at which young oligarchs with concealed weapons had been stationed by prearrangement, Theramenes defended moderate government so convincingly that many listeners were persuaded. The reward for his eloquence was death. Critias promptly announced that Theramenes was not entitled to a trial after all and had him dragged to prison from the altar at which he had taken refuge. Forced to drink hemlock, the poison used soon afterwards to execute Socrates, Theramenes went out in style and not without irony, toasting Critias' health with his last drops.

Ultimately the Thirty were undone by their own abandon. Though Sparta had forbidden neighboring states to receive Athenian refugees, the murderous conduct of the Thirty had alienated many Greeks from Sparta, and neither Thebes nor Megara was disposed to turn the refugees away. It was in Thebes that Athenians under their leader Thrasybulus mounted an attempt to retake the city back for the democrats. In the fighting Critias was killed.

Because they expected Spartan aid, the oligarchs at Athens rejected Thrasybulus' call for peace and union between the two camps. As it happened, however, the murderous arrogance of Lysander and his associates was making many powerful men at Sparta nervous, including the kings Agis and Pausanias. Marching into Attica, Pausanias took the lead and masterminded not only the reconciliation of the various Athenian parties but also the eclipse (albeit temporary) of Lysander. Under his aegis, the Athenians agreed on the first recorded amnesty in history. The amnesty declared that only the Thirty and their chief officers could be brought to justice for crimes committed before 403; all others were compelled to renounce the many bitter grievances that had accumulated. In September, Thrasybulus led his men unopposed to the Acropolis, where they sacrificed to Athena for the salvation of the city and their own safe return. The work of reestablishing democratic Athens then began.

THE TRIAL OF SOCRATES (399 BC)

The Athenians came remarkably close to respecting the terms of the amnesty on which they had agreed. Nonetheless, decades of war followed by months of terror under the Thirty had taken a heavy toll, and there was no lack of people eager to assign blame for Athens' problems. The colorful Socrates had annoyed jealous parents whose young sons had lionized him, and though the Athenians were averse to breaking the amnesty law, some were open to bending it. Three Athenians—Anytus, Meletus, and Lycon—zeroed in on this eccentric old philosopher who haunted the public spaces of Athens confuting the careless in argument. Socrates (470–399 BC) had been quick to identify the drawbacks of democracy, and he had also been the teacher of (at least) two men who in different ways had harmed Athens: Alcibiades and Critias. The amnesty prevented his accusers from charging Socrates with inciting his pupils to treason, so instead they brought a rather odd three-pronged accusation: Socrates, they claimed, did not believe in

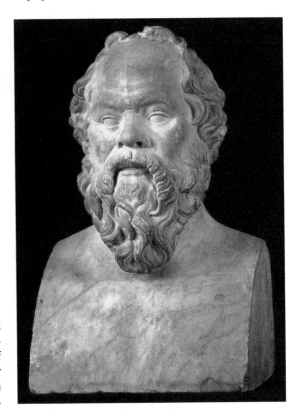

Figure 9.1. This bust of Socrates is commonly attributed to the fourth-century BC Greek sculptor Lysippus of Sicyon, considered to be the founder of the art of portraiture. A replica stands in the Louvre Museum in Paris.

the gods of the state; he taught new gods; and he corrupted the young. This sort of charge was unusual at Athens, but Greek states had no constitutional principles separating church and state or safeguards for protecting freedom of expression.

Since Socrates never wrote anything, we are dependent for our conception of him on the dialogues of his admirers Plato and Xenophon. Plato's pupil Aristotle observed about Socrates that the two things one could be certain of attributing to him were inductive reasoning and universal definition. We can be sure of a few other things. Socrates, an Athenian citizen, performed conventional civic services in Athens, fighting as a hoplite at Potidaea, Delium, and Amphipolis in the Peloponnesian War and serving as president of the assembly on the day of the Arginusae trial in 406. His avocation was discussing interesting philosophical questions with young men, questions that focused on the best way for humans to think and live; at least in his mature years, he was not particularly excited by natural science. He believed that the best way to develop ideas was in the give and take of conversation, and that the best way to educate people was to ask them a series of questions leading in a particular direction (now named for him "the Socratic method"). However painful it might be to find oneself the object of injustice, he was firmly convinced that doing wrong oneself was the only real misfortune that could befall a person. He had a keen wit and an engaging personality, and pupils flocked to him eagerly, though he had nothing that could be called a school. He was not a sophist; he became poor through his refusal to charge fees, and his goal was to inculcate moral excellence, which he viewed as the particular excellence of a human being. Like the sophists, however, he used clever arguments and subjected conventional notions to rational analysis, and like them he disrupted the customary bond that placed education in the context of the family, wounding Athenian parents whose sons preferred his company to theirs— and who gave his ideas greater credence. Whom, Socrates asks Meletus in Xenophon's rendition of his defense speech, do I corrupt? "By God," Meletus replies, "I know some—those you've persuaded to obey you rather than their parents" (Xenophon, *Apology of Socrates* 20). It is not surprising, therefore, that he was mistaken for a sophist, or that the sophists' shady reputation should have rubbed off on him. He was parodied in Aristophanes' *Clouds*, which showed him carried across the sky in a crane in a flaky educational establishment known as a "think shop."

He also spoke sharply about democracy. Whether it is fair to say that he opposed it and would have liked to see a different regime instituted at Athens is another question. Socrates enjoyed puncturing illusions, and it may be that had he lived under a monarchy or an oligarchy, those would have been the governments he spent his time undermining. But if anything can safely be gathered from Plato's dialogues, then Socrates was troubled by the notion of amateur government, in which anyone's opinion counted for as much as the next man's and in which a volatile assembly was swayed this way and that by rhetorical displays. Most people, he pointed out, aren't terribly thoughtful or analytical, so why should "most people," that is, the majority, make the life and death decisions that affect the polis?

This is a question any advocate of democracy must ask, and Socrates' insistence on asking it need not be taken as implying that he wanted decisions made by a minority. Combined with his association with Alcibiades and Critias, however, his pointed remarks about the foibles of democracy seemed downright unpatriotic, and he could easily enough be cast as a purveyor of dangerous ideas.

By Athenian custom, Socrates' trial took only one day. It is intolerably painful for most readers of Plato's *Apology of Socrates* to believe that the words written down by Plato were not actually spoken at Socrates' trial. Perhaps they were, and perhaps they weren't; Xenophon's account of Socrates' speech, also called the *Apology*, is less inspiring and much shorter. (The Greek word *apologia* does not connote "apologizing" in the modern sense but rather means a refutation.) Plato's rendition contains the famous dictum that "the unexamined life is not worth living" and constitutes an extraordinarily moving paean to intellectual freedom and the life of the mind. Shunning the strategy that he identifies as standard procedure in an Athenian courtroom—weeping, pleading, parading his children in front of the jury—Socrates, according to Plato, took the position that the best defense was a strong offense. Using the question-and-answer method for which he was famous and which had apparently gotten him into trouble, he demolished his accusers by demonstrating the inconsistencies in their allegations and then went on to explain in poignant detail the great service provided to the state by his relentless probing. His service to the state, he argues, is precious and irreplaceable. It is, literally, a godsend:

Know that if you kill me, I being such a man as I say I am, you will not injure me so much as yourselves; for neither Meletus nor Anytus could injure me; that would be impossible, for I believe it is not the gods' will that a better man be injured by a worse. . . . For if you put me to death, you will not easily find another, who, to use a rather absurd figure, attaches himself to the city as a gadfly to a horse, which, though large and well bred, is sluggish on account of his size and needs to be aroused by stinging. I think the god fastened me upon the city in some such capacity, and I go about arousing, and urging and reproaching each one of you, constantly alighting upon you everywhere the whole day long. Such another is not likely to come to you, gentlemen; but if you take my advice, you will spare me. But you, perhaps, might be angry, like people awakened from a nap, and might slap me, as Anytus advises, and easily kill me; then you would pass the rest of your lives in slumber, unless the god, in his care for you, should send someone else to sting you.

(*Apology* 30C–31A; Fowler 1914, adapted)

Socrates persuaded nearly half the jury of 501 Athenian citizens; he seems to have lost his case by about thirty votes. Meletus, the principal accuser, had proposed the penalty of death. Athenian procedure called for convicted defendants to recommend an alternative penalty, and it seems clear that Socrates' accusers expected him to propose exile—and would have been quite content to see him leave town. He did no such thing, suggesting first a reward for his benefactions or, alternatively, a small (but not trivial) fine. Xenophon ascribed this strategy to Socrates' wish to end a satisfying life before the sad realities of old age overtook him; it is also possible that Socrates was testing the jury to see if they understood who he really was and what he really provided to Athens. A number of those who had wanted him acquitted had a change of heart and voted for the death penalty. Socrates was then executed by one of the customary Athenian methods, being ordered to down a poisonous draft of hemlock.

At his trial, if we are to believe Plato, Socrates prophesied that the Athenians would bring great odium on themselves for killing him. He was right. Throughout subsequent history, the execution of Socrates is the most serious charge that has been brought by the critics of Athenian democracy. Socrates' death also made a deep impression on his brightest disciples, young aristocrats like Xenophon and Plato. Xenophon's works were very popular in ancient Rome and during the Renaissance. The dialogues Plato began soon after his teacher's death, in which Socrates served as a mouthpiece for his own thinking, became the foundation of Western philosophy. In this way the strains occasioned by the Peloponnesian War played a dramatic role in the history of ideas, as an enormous explosion of creativity burst forth in the very city that had gone down to defeat.

THE FOURTH CENTURY: CHANGING IDEAS, CONTINUING WARFARE

Already in the fifth century BC Greek thinkers had begun to ask the key questions about the human community that would be explored in new ways in the fourth.

What was the purpose of civic life? Were the laws of the polis in accord with nature or in conflict with it? Why were some people free and others not? Were the souls of men and women the same or different? Should Greeks war with other Greeks and enslave them when victorious? To these questions others came to be added. Did the autonomous city-state provide the best way of life? Was warfare worth the sacrifices it entailed? A smaller group debated larger questions—the nature of justice, of piety, of courage, of love. New genres took the place of the old as the search for meaning in life moved forward on different paths: Whereas the painful issues of human existence had been explored during the fifth century in tragedy and history, fourth-century thinkers developed the philosophical dialogue and prose treatise.

While some Greeks were subjecting their traditional values to scrutiny, others perpetuated the squabbles of the fifth century. In many poleis the economic problems arising from the war exacerbated class tensions and sparked bloody civil conflict. The eager involvement of Persia heightened an already chaotic situation. When an extraordinary individual arose to the north in the form of Philip of Macedon, the inability of the Greeks to work together productively had dramatic consequences, and the autonomous polis ceased to be the defining political institution of the Greek world.

The long years of fighting at the end of the fifth century had harmed the economy of many Greek states sufficiently to create a desire for both booty and revenge. The postwar poleis, moreover, showed remarkable resilience, and within less than ten years, the economy had rebounded sufficiently for people to contemplate new undertakings. The hostility of the Greek states soon found a focus, and that focus was Sparta. In 395 Sparta's old allies Corinth and Thebes were so bitter that they actually combined with Athens to attack their old hegemon; neither polis had gotten anything out of the war, and Sparta's proclivity for interfering with domestic governments caused considerable alarm. The war that ensued was known as the Corinthian War, since much of the fighting took place in the area of the isthmus. The first consequence of this futile war was the death of Lysander. Soon afterwards the Persian navy, commanded by the satrap Pharnabazus and the Athenian admiral Conon, defeated the Spartans decisively at Cnidus (394 BC) in southwest Asia Minor. When Conon returned victorious to Athens he joined his fellow citizens in rebuilding the Long Walls, assisted by a large infusion of Persian funds.

In fighting this pointless war, the Greeks deployed not only hoplites and sailors but also a wide variety of lightly armed troops including archers, slingers, and javelin throwers. A particularly useful brand of javelin thrower was the man known as the peltast, named for the small, round wicker shield he carried, the Thracian *peltē*. Enjoying a mobility impossible for the more heavily armed hoplites, these troops could be used to forage for supplies, to seize and defend passes, to ambush enemy soldiers, and to ravage hostile territory. They also played key roles in what were basically hoplite confrontations, for harassment at a distance by javelin-throwing peltasts made it difficult for the heavily armed enemy hoplites to retreat. A hardy band of peltasts backing up a hoplite force could easily turn the tide of battle.

The war ended on terms that all Greeks outside Sparta found intensely humiliating. The text of the dictated terms appears in Xenophon's *Hellenica*:

> I, King Artaxerxes, regard the following arrangements as just: 1. The cities in Asia and, among the islands, Clazomenae and Cyprus should belong to me. 2. The other Greek cities, big and small, should be left (autonomous) to govern themselves, except for Lemnos, Imbros and Scyros, which should belong to Athens, as in the past. And if either of the two parties refuses to accept peace on these terms, I, together with those who will accept this peace, will make war on that party both by land and by sea, with ships and with money.
>
> (*Hellenica* 5.1.31; Warner 1966)

It was most ironic that the guarantor of the peace was to be Persia's ally Sparta, since Sparta was getting a well-deserved reputation for meddling in the internal affairs of other states. In the guise of enforcing autonomy, Sparta promptly set about using force to dismantle a variety of existing arrangements. Mantinea, composed of five villages, was compelled to tear down its fortifications and dissolve itself into the five original communities. The Boeotian League was dissolved, and in 382 the Spartans occupied the Theban acropolis and installed a pro-Spartan government. The Spartan government then executed the head of the pro-Athenian faction at Thebes, Ismenias, on the grounds of conspiring with Persia. Sparta's record of collaboration with Persia made this turn of events particularly scandalous throughout Greece.

In 379, seven of the partisans of Ismenias who had taken refuge in Athens arranged to be brought to the pro-Spartan magistrates of Thebes, disguised as women who had been supplied for their delectation. Drawing their weapons, they easily overpowered and killed the oligarchs. The next day two Athenian generals and their regiments appeared, quite possibly as volunteers, and helped the Theban patriots expel the Spartan garrison. Nervous about Spartan reprisals, the Athenians condemned both generals to death and in fact executed the one who made the mistake of turning up for his trial. The Athenians' decision was quite reprehensible since their generals were clearly carrying out a policy that had the people's support.

Sparta, Athens, and Thebes

Not long afterwards, the Athenians allied with the Thebans for mutual protection against Sparta. They also moved forward with their plans to establish a new naval confederacy known as the Second Athenian League. The establishment of the League was commemorated in a decree which proclaimed that all allies "will remain independent and autonomous, enjoying the form of government they wish, admitting no garrisons or magistrates and paying no tribute. League policy was to be controlled by two bodies of equal weight, the Athenian assembly (*ekklēsia*) and the assembly of the allies (*synedrion*). Although no tribute was specified, a system of *syntaxeis* ("contributions") was set up to finance League operations. Periodic defaults make clear the ambivalence of some league members, but

Figure 9.2. The Decree of Aristoteles, 377 BC. The names of the cities that joined the alliance were inscribed on the same stone as the decree. As new states joined, their names were added.

the fact that about half the league's seventy-odd members were former members of the Delian League certainly needs to be thrown in with the other evidence concerning the popularity of Athens' earlier experiment in league leadership.

From this point on, the history of Greece involves a dizzying sequence of shifting alliances marked by two notable military victories and by outside interventions by eastern potentates such as Mausolus of Caria, technically a Persian satrap but de facto an independent ruler who operated from Halicarnassus (the home town of Herodotus), where he engaged Greek sculptors to construct the huge tomb for him that has given us our English word mausoleum. Mausolus saw the Athenian League as a serious obstacle to his ambitions, and he was quick to encourage any unrest he could detect; it was after receiving promises of Carian backing that Rhodes, Cos, and Chios revolted from Athens.

In mainland Greece, the Spartans and the Thebans met twice on the battlefield with dramatic results on both occasions. In the 370s Thebes was stronger than ever, led by two intimate friends, Epaminondas and Pelopidas. Both had been involved in the liberation of Thebes from the Spartans in 379. Pelopidas excelled primarily in generalship, Epaminondas in charismatic political leadership. On the plain of Leuctra, Epaminondas packed his left wing (normally the weaker side of a Greek formation) fully fifty shields deep. He also advanced in an oblique line so as to hold back the center and right wing while overpowering the enemy with the left at the point where he could expect the Spartan king Cleombrotus to be. The cutting edge of the Theban line was provided by the elite corps known as the Sacred Band, 150 pairs of select hoplites. Plato was probably thinking of the Sacred Band when he wrote that "if one could contrive that a state or an army should entirely consist of lovers and loved, it would be impossible for it to have a better organization than that which it would then enjoy through their avoidance of all dishonor and their mutual emulation; moreover, a handful of such men, fighting side-by-side, would defeat practically the whole world" (*Symposium* 178-179; Hamilton). The Sacred Band and the novel tactics of Epaminondas carried the day, killing nearly half the Spartans present including their king Cleombrotus. The remainder of the Spartan army withdrew, the legend of Spartan supremacy in hoplite warfare forever shattered.

When the Spartans' weakness became apparent to their allies, the Peloponnesus began seething with sedition. Democratic revolutions broke out in many cities, and a league was formed consisting of Mantinea, Tegea, and the communities of southern and central Arcadia. Arriving in the Peloponnesus to give support to the league, Epaminondas' army was unable to take the city of Sparta, but it ravaged Laconia—and succeeded in the liberation of Messenia. Helots were now to be citizens, and the new capital of Messene was founded on Mount Ithome. Epaminondas also founded a new capital for the Arcadian League, Megalopolis. This new foundation became the meeting place for the Council of Fifty that represented the communities of the league in proportion to their population, and of the Assembly of the Ten Thousand, open to all citizens. This development indexed a growing interest in experimenting with thoroughly amicable federations, a new phenomenon in Greece.

Within a few years and with comparatively little loss of life, Thebes under Epaminondas and Pelopidas managed to accomplish what generations of Athenians could not. Sparta was finished as an international power. This did not mean, however, that the Thebans achieved their goals. Pelopidas was killed fighting in Thessaly. Epaminondas' support in the Peloponnesus began to wane, and a number of Arcadian communities allied with Sparta—and Athens—against Thebes. Epaminondas met the alliance on the plain of Mantinea in 362 BC. Deploying the same strategy as at Leuctra and outnumbering the enemy by some ten thousand men, the Thebans were victorious. But Epaminondas himself was killed and with his dying breath counseled his countrymen to make peace.

For all his personal magnetism, Epaminondas seemed to have had no plan for Greece beyond replacing Athenian and Spartan imperialism with Theban imperialism. Ultimately Thebes gained nothing for itself, or for Greece, by its decade of military ascendancy. Though the liberation of Messenia offers great satisfaction to the enemies of slavery in all times and places, by knocking out Sparta as a military power Epaminondas performed a great service to Philip of Macedon, the future conqueror of Greece, something for which not all Greeks would ultimately be grateful. Philip was also the beneficiary of the agitation of Mausolus, who did so much to foment disaffection in the Second Athenian League. Late in 355 or early in 354, Athens was forced to recognize the independence of Byzantium, Chios, Rhodes, and Cos. Soon Lesbos and several other states also broke away from the confederation. The sanitized Delian League had not endured more than a generation.

LAW AND DEMOCRACY IN ATHENS

Whatever its successes or failures abroad, Athens had retained its domestic stability and continued to practice democracy at home interrupted by only two very brief experiments in oligarchy in the later fifth century, each occasioned by the strains of the long war and one of them imposed directly by a foreign power. A key building block of the democracy was the people's courts known as dicasteries (*dikastēria*). Athenian society was notoriously litigious, and in the hands of unscrupulous politicians court cases often became tools of factional strife. Trials of impeached officials—strategoi in particular—were frequently of a political nature, for impeachment at Athens was often used as a forum for a debate on foreign policy. Since decrees proposed in the assembly could be challenged by the graphe paranomon ("indictment for illegal proposals"), it can be argued that in fourth-century Athens the dicasteries rather than the ekklesia were the ultimate arbiters of policy. In the absence of a supreme court or a body of jurisconsults, dicasteries were also the arbiters of law. Courts were also used, of course, in the adjudication of private lawsuits and criminal cases with no political ramifications.

The Functioning of Dicasteries

All male citizens over the age of thirty were eligible to serve on dicasteries, and dicasts (jurors) were chosen each year by lot from those who volunteered. As we saw in Chapter Six, to ensure that the composition of the courts would reflect the voters of Athens, Pericles had instituted pay for jury service. The three obols a day, or half the average wage of a laborer, doubtless attracted the poor, who could not earn three obols another way, as well as comfortably retired older men who enjoyed the opportunity to sit with their fellow citizens in situations that often offered spellbinding entertainment. The number of dicasts allocated to a given case varied usually from 201 to 501 (odd numbers prevented a tie), although a larger body might be used for high-profile trials of a political nature, and some important political trials were held in the assembly itself. Large juries were designed in part to involve large numbers of citizens in decision-making, in part to discourage bribery. Further obstacles to bribery included an elaborate mechanism to select juries by lot and the custom of choosing them at the last possible moment before the trial. Small plaques, each inscribed with a dicast's name, were inserted into a *klērotērion*, an allotment device that distributed the names haphazardly among the daily juries. Voting was by secret ballot. Each dicast was given two pebbles or bronze discs, one of which had a hole punched through it; a herald would proclaim that "the pebble with the hole is a vote for the prosecutor, and the whole pebble a vote for the defendant." To cast his vote the dicast would throw the one he wanted to be counted into a copper receptacle and discard the other pebble into the wooden one.

As the case of Socrates reveals, the dicasts also determined the penalty. Precedents were not binding, so each jury was sovereign and its decision final. There could be no appeal to a higher court, for an Athenian dicastery was both the highest court and the people. Consequently dicasts functioned as judges as well as jurors.

Murder and the Courts

The earliest known laws in Athens and those that remained unchanged for the longest time concerned homicide. Since the Greeks believed that murder offended the gods, there were religious sanctions against homicide, and anyone who killed another person outside of wartime was considered polluted. At the same time a pressing religious and social obligation lay upon the male next of kin to avenge a death by killing the perpetrator, even if an act of homicide had been involuntary, say, as the result of a hunting accident. In accordance with basic principles of vendettas that operate across many societies, therefore, one homicide could evolve into an unending series of retaliations. The Athenians claimed to have founded the first law court in the world when Agamemnon's son Orestes came to Athens from Argos seeking absolution for the murder of his mother, whom he had killed in order to avenge his slain father. The Bronze Age myth that Aeschylus had fleshed out in his *Oresteia* had offered the playwright an opportunity to explain how law had come to replace family feud in just such a case. The court of the Areopagus in Athens adjudicated the case, marking the historic transfer of jurisdiction from the family to the state.

A personal element, however, remained, for accusations of homicide had to be brought by family members. Thus, while the murder of a slave by his or her master might be illegal, prosecution was unlikely in the absence of a citizen relative who could bring charges. Throughout Athenian history, self-help remained a central principle in law. (It also extended to helping friends and relations in a wide variety of instances. Citizens were expected to show both friendship and civic-mindedness by bringing cases on behalf of others who were wronged, such as orphans or girls of marriageable age without dowries.)

Besides the Areopagus there were four additional venues for murder trials. The court of the Palladion was used for unpremeditated killings, the Delphinion for justifiable ones (i.e., homicides committed in self-defense, or by a man who discovered someone in the very act of having intercourse with his wife, mother, sister, or daughter). The Prytaneion handled cases of unidentified murderers and cases in which an animal or an object such as a falling roof tile had caused a death. Finally, those who were already sentenced to exile for homicide and were on trial for an additional murder had to plead their cases on a boat off the coast of Phreatto to avoid polluting the land of Attica.

Conduct of Cases

The seriousness of the charges dictated the amount of time allocated to a trial, and the minutes were measured out by a water clock. The conduct of cases differed from those in modern Western courts in that the Greeks relied heavily on the testimony of witnesses not only as to the facts but also as to the character of the defendant. It was customary for witnesses to testify to the virtues of the accused and the public services he had performed—or to the calamities his family would experience if he was convicted. Though rules of time were stringently observed, rules of evidence were few, and defendants themselves were not discouraged from speechifying about their past services to the polis or from parading their vulnerable children before the jury. Even after the advent of writing, Greeks remained somewhat suspicious of texts, and jurors usually trusted the testimony given by witnesses under oath more than written evidence; they understood that a document such as a will could be forged. Slaves were often the optimal witnesses, for they were ubiquitous and often obliged to assist their owners in illicit activities. Theoretically, the testimony of slaves was admissible only if it had been given under torture, but we are uncertain how often such torture was actually inflicted. Following a guilty verdict, prosecutor and defendant proposed alternate penalties, as in the case of Socrates, and the jury decided between the two. The principle of self-help also meant that in private, or civil, cases the prosecutor had to execute the judgment himself. When the orator Demosthenes succeeded in convincing a jury that his guardians had dissipated the fortune his father had left, it was his own responsibility to try to collect the missing funds and property.

The Athenian Democracy in the Fourth Century

The survival of so many speeches and inscriptions from the fourth century enables us to see Athenian democracy in action more vividly in this period than was possible for the fifth century. In some ways the democracy changed after the restoration of 403, particularly in the constitution of various ad hoc boards of *nomothetai* ("creators of laws") to approve and review legislation. The fundamental principles, however, remained the same. All free adult males had a theoretically equal right to participate in government regardless of differential prestige and economic standing. Women and slaves were excluded, and it was difficult for resident aliens or their children to become citizens. Only men with two citizen parents could vote. Wealth and illustrious ancestry were distinct advantages in seeking public office. Boasting of your benefactions to the state was a good strategy if you needed to defend yourself in court, which was often the case in this litigious society. Although Solon's four classes were never formally abolished, it is clear that at least by the middle of the fourth century public offices were open to men of all groups. Many *thētes* and *zeugitai* were selected for offices chosen by lot, such as service on the *boulē*. Thus participation in government was widely diffused throughout the community of citizen males.

Jokes in Aristophanes' plays reveal a change in the dynamics of assembly attendance. The *Acharnians* (425 BC) alludes to the habit of roping citizens in with a cord covered with red paint that would smear the clothes of the recalcitrant, but when women dress as men and pack the assembly in the *Ecclesiazusae* (392 BC) until a quorum is reached, the real men of Athens complain that they arrived too late to get their pay. The carrot replaced the stick shortly before 400, when a small salary was instituted for attendance at the assembly. By Aristotle's time, it had gone from one obol to a drachma (six obols) for an ordinary assembly and a drachma and a half for the *kyria ekklēsia*, that is, the principal assembly of a prytany. At the level of assembly attendance, then, the government of the fourth century was somewhat more democratic than the fifth, for a higher number could afford to take time away from work, though it remained the case that attending meetings was easier for those who lived close by and those who worked for themselves. The large number of political issues ultimately decided in the courts was another democratic element.

As in the courts, where even criminal cases depended on volunteer prosecutors to set them in motion, the voluntary principle played a key role in the assembly. In the absence of organized political parties, concerned citizens took it upon themselves to initiate legislation. No well-defined group of officeholders saw itself—or was seen by others—as clearly marked off from the rest of the populace. By "politicians," people simply meant those who most enjoyed making proposals in the assembly and giving speeches in their support. The importance of oratory and debate to the functioning of the democratic system is attested in the Greek word that comes closest to our word "politician": *rhētōr*. Since *rhētores* shared common interests and habits, no doubt people were comfortable identifying a particular citizen they might see walking down the street as "one of the rhetores," but it is important to remember that there was no official "board of rhetores" to which such men belonged. Today it would be peculiar to identify someone who did not hold public office as a politician, but the Athenians saw nothing strange about it. It was precisely because of the power private citizens could gain through skillful oratory that the Athenians made sure to have the graphe paranomon on the books to ensure the accountability even of those who took part in public affairs without holding office. Those convicted of proposing something illegal were generally fined; three convictions deprived a citizen of the right to make further proposals.

THE FOURTH-CENTURY POLIS

Although the bulk of our evidence comes from Athens, most Greeks, of course, lived in other city-states. In the fourth century as in the fifth, some Greek poleis were governed by democracies, others by oligarchies that varied in their narrowness. As had always been the case in Greece, uneven distribution of wealth fostered ever-present tensions that threatened constantly to erupt and disturb the tenuous concord that united citizens, and changes of constitution were frequent.

Although warfare remained a fact of life, many people had come to question its efficacy in improving their situations. While some poorer citizens continued to welcome war for the pay it offered to rowers in the fleet, those who had land or commerce to protect were hesitant. The ideal of the citizen-soldier was wearing thin, and an increasing share of the fighting was conducted by mercenaries from outside. Agriculture remained the basis of the economy, but the devastation of the land during the Peloponnesian War had fostered a drift to the cities. By throwing people together, this development heightened the awareness of economic inequality and sharpened class bitterness. Plato and his pupil Aristotle both took it for granted that a polis consisted in reality of two cities, one of the many poor and one of the few rich. The division of citizens into haves and have-nots that had always marked Greek states was exacerbated in the fourth century by the increased poverty of the have-nots, bringing latent tensions to the surface.

Stasis

Bloodshed was common, and religious pieties were often ignored. In 392, Corinthian democrats violated the sanctity of temples by murdering oligarchs who had taken refuge there. Diodorus reports revolutions in Corinth, Sicyon, and Phlius and Xenophon recorded serious tensions in Tegea, Phlius, Sicyon, Pellene, and Elis. Diodorus, who shared the antidemocratic orientation of most ancient writers, took a certain satisfaction in relating the torture and murder of the elite by Argive democrats in 371, when class tensions erupted with violence exceptional even by Greek standards. After the execution of twelve hundred influential men, Diodorus contends,

> the populace did not spare the demagogues themselves. Because of the magnitude of the calamity the demagogues were afraid that some unforeseen turn of fortune might overtake them and therefore desisted from their accusation, whereas the mob, now thinking that they had been left in the lurch by them, were angry at this and put to death all the demagogues. So these men received the punishment which fitted their crimes as if some divinity were visiting its just resentment upon them, and the people, eased of their mad rage, were restored to their senses.
>
> (*Library of History* 15.58.4; Sherman 1952, adapted)

Beginning late in the fifth century, Greek intellectuals had begun calling for *homonoia* ("concord") among citizens, but the frequency with which the appeal was made reveals the discordant reality: In fact the slogan caught on during the contentious days of the Peloponnesian War. In praising the rule of law, Socrates had insisted in the pages of Xenophon's *Memorabilia* that throughout Greece homonoia was advocated by the "best men" (the *aristoi*). Aristotle, however, took a darker and more realistic view. In some states of his own day, he wrote in the *Politics*, the oligarchs in charge take an oath to be hostile to the demos and "plot whatever evil possible against the people" (1310a).

Not all poleis were constantly torn apart by stasis and debilitated by interpolis wars. Since the principal cause of internal weakness and vulnerability to outside attack was the frustrations of the poor, prosperity might act as a powerful deterrent. Megara with its brisk woolen trade flourished throughout the fourth century, and civil strife was rare. The progress of the economy was facilitated by peace with other poleis: The alliance between Corinth and Athens during the Corinthan War eliminated Megara's pivotal position in interpolis diplomacy, and the Megarians seem to have preserved their neutrality throughout that war. Megarian woolens found eager markets throughout Greece. Sheep grazed in abundance, and large numbers of slaves, probably mostly female, turned out well-made and inexpensive garments. The private homes of Megara were known for their elegance, and a variety of monuments decorated the city. The Athenian sculptor Praxiteles (370–329 BC) produced numerous statues of the gods for the sanctuaries of Artemis and Apollo and the temple of Aphrodite. Scopas, who contributed to the Mausoleum in Caria, also worked in Megara. Exactly what kind of government fourth-century Megara enjoyed is uncertain—Plato praised it but did not describe it—but it seems at least to have been fairly stable. Megara was not, however, entirely immune to the endemic stasis of the fourth century, for Diodorus reports an abortive uprising in the 370s.

Marginalized Workers in the Economy

The economy of each polis was different, but throughout Greece prestige attached to some kinds of work more than to others. Because social prejudices favored self-sufficiency through farming, or making money by selling the produce of one's land, free citizens tended to avoid involvement in commerce and banking, turning over these activities to metics and slaves. Such workers became important in the fourth century and often made considerable fortunes, for one phenomenon that distinguished the polis of the fourth century from that of the fifth was the rise of banking.

Bank owners trusted slaves to manage the daily operations of banks independently and even to travel with large sums of cash. Such slaves were highly skilled, usually literate, and very valuable. A slave who managed a bank could be completely responsible for his master's property. Therefore, a master might write a will freeing his bank manager on condition that he marry his widow and manage his bank in behalf of his minor children. Manumitted slaves became metics. Some of these metics, including a certain Pasio and Phormio, were among the wealthiest Athenians of the fourth century. In gratitude for their generous benefactions to the state, Athens rewarded them and their descendants with citizenship. Thus slaves in banking might experience rapid social mobility.

The stigma that attached to working for someone else was greater for women than for men; few women chose to work outside the home unless compelled to do so by poverty. In the fourth century as in the fifth, however, some women did work at service jobs outside their homes. Slave women were sometimes rented out by their owners, and former slaves, metics, and even citizen women in straitened financial circumstances worked at a variety of jobs. Some hired themselves out as nurses for other women's children; some sold goods in the marketplace; and older women often served as hired mourners at funerals. Although unacceptable for citizen women, prostitution was probably the work done most frequently by women outside the home. Some were put to work when they were still children. In Corinth, Nicarete, a former slave, purchased young girls from slaveholders and trained them for their work:

> Nicarete, who was the freedwoman of Charisius of Elis and the wife of his cook Hippias, bought seven girls when they were small children. She was an astute judge of natural beauty in little girls and furthermore she understood how to bring them up and train them skillfully, for she made this her profession and got her livelihood from the girls. She used to address them as daughters, implying that they were free women, so that she might extract the largest fees from those who wished to get close to them. When she had reaped the profit of the youthful prime of each, she sold all seven of them: Anteia, Stratola, Aristocleia, Metaneira, Phila, Isthmias, and this Neaera here . . .
>
> Neaera . . . was working with her body, although she was still very young, for she had not yet reached puberty.
>
> (Pseudo-Demosthenes, 59.18–20; Murray 1936)

Neaera's further adventures are also detailed in this speech, which is included in the corpus of Demosthenes although it was almost certainly written by someone else. Two of Neaera's clients purchased her from Nicarete to be their slave. But when these men were about to marry, they offered Neaera the opportunity to buy her freedom. Neaera borrowed her purchase price from former clients, and repaid them from her earnings as a free prostitute. Her attempt at social mobility was quashed, however, when she moved to Athens, married a certain Stephanus, and pretended to be an Athenian citizen. Apollodorus, an enemy of Stephanus (who had brought against him one indictment for an illegal proposal and another for murder), brought her to trial for false assumption of citizen rights. He also charged Stephanus with living with a non-Athenian woman as though she were his wife, and with giving Neaera's daughter in marriage to an Athenian citizen as being his own daughter born from a citizen woman.

PHILOSOPHY AND THE POLIS

The changing political situation in the Greek world helped shape Greek thought in each new generation, and the problems of the fourth-century polis were no exception. Philosophy evolved with the polis and survived it when Philip of Macedon brought the freedom of the independent city-states to an end in 338 BC. The Greek word *philosophos* means "a lover of wisdom," and for many years before Plato and Aristotle founded their famous schools in Athens, Greek thinkers had taken delight in searching for the underlying principles that shaped the cosmos and determined the life humans made in it. Democritus contended that he would "rather find the explanation for a single phenomenon than gain the kingdom of Persia." The truly prosperous man, Empedocles said, is one who enjoys the riches of a divine intelligence. Philosophers came in many shapes. Thinkers like Thales and Anaximander focused on the natural world. Others like Herodotus and Thucydides used the writing of history as a vehicle for their ideas about the human condition, while still others expressed them through dramas as did Aeschylus, Sophocles, and Euripides. In time, Xenophon and Plato would write dialogues and Aristotle treatises. These innovative thinkers explored the areas that still make up philosophy today—ethics, logic, epistemology (the philosophy of knowledge), metaphysics (the science of being), aesthetics, theology, philosophy of science, and social and political theory.

It was in the realm of social and political theory that philosophy was most closely tied to the polis. Because most surviving texts of political theory were composed in democratic Athens, one might imagine that they praised democracy. In fact, the opposite is true: The principal texts of Greek political theory were the work of intellectuals who were intensely critical of democratic government. Indeed, modern political scientists have observed that political theory—literally, "looking at the city-state"—was invented to show why democracy could not possibly work. It is the workings of democracy itself that reveal the ideology behind it.

Democracy and Political Theory

The anonymous satirist we call Old Oligarch had portrayed Athenian democracy with biting irony as a beautifully efficient way of guaranteeing the suppression of one class by another, but no surviving text treats the dynamics of democracy in a positive way. Reconstructing the theory behind democracy from written texts requires assembling patches from a variety of sources that engage the issue only obliquely. Thucydides' version of Pericles' funeral oration gives us a sense of what the Athenians at any rate prized in their government. At Athens, Pericles says, worth is assessed in terms of ability, not wealth or class. Athenians consider remaining aloof from politics a vice, not a virtue. They view debate as an aid to constructive action, not a hindrance.

Just as Thucydides, who was not particularly sympathetic to democracy, included Pericles' speech in his history, so Plato, one of democracy's sharpest critics, included a statement of democratic ideology in his dialogue *Protagoras*. There the famous sophist tells a quaint myth in support of his thesis that all people possess the rudiments of civic-mindedness. In earliest times, Protagoras says, people were unable to live together constructively in cities because of their lack of *politikē technē*, the skill of forming and managing a polis. Seeing this and fearing the destruction of the species, Zeus sent Hermes to bring *aidōs* ("shame") and *dikē* ("justice") to mortals. When Hermes asked Zeus whether these should be distributed to a select few, as was the case with the arts of medicine and other techniques, or to everyone, Zeus ordered him to give some to everybody, since "cities cannot be formed if only a few share in these skills as they do in the other arts" (322D). It is for this reason, Protagoras says, that when the Athenians come together to make decisions that require the sense of justice that goes into political wisdom "they take advice from everybody, since it is held that for states to exist everyone must partake of this excellence" (322E–323E).

Further clues are provided in the dozens of orations surviving from the fourth century, which praise freedom of speech, liberty, equality before the law, and the rule of law. Our best clue to the theory of democracy, however, is its practice. The Athenian democracy itself reveals what most men in Athens believed about government: They believed in a democracy of male citizens that required active participation on the part of these citizens, guaranteed by frequent rotation in office, and they believed that the average free man was qualified to make political decisions, as evidenced by the use of the lot and the taking of important decisions in the assembly by majority vote. They believed in trial by jury, and they feared the corruption that inhered in small groups more than the mob psychology that threatened large ones. They believed that the people had the right to call its officials to account with regularity and on the slightest pretext. They believed that the stability of the state was so crucial that it was reasonable to exile a man for ten years under the system known as ostracism even if he had done nothing to break the law. They believed in slavery and patriarchy. They believed that the control of women's sexuality was essential to the smooth functioning of the community and that the sequestration of women and girls was a good step in this direction. We know all this not because they wrote it down but because of how they chose to run their government and live their lives.

We know also that Greeks who did not live under democratic governments believed in the rule of law, which appears as a persistent leitmotiv in the literature of the fifth and fourth centuries. Its prominence begins with the efforts of Herodotus and Aeschylus to define and celebrate what it means to be Greek; for them living under law played a key role in shaping that identity and Herodotus stressed the Spartans' reverence for law. Euripides, however, connected law with democracy in his *Suppliants*, where he defined Athens even under Theseus as a place where

> Our city is not subject to one man.
> No, it is free, for here the people rule.
>
> (404–406)

Under a tyranny, one man governs, keeping the law in his private hands, and there is no equality:

> But when the laws are written down, the weak
> Enjoy the same protection as the rich.
>
> (434–435)

Although many Athenians identified their democratic constitution with the rule of law, Greek intellectuals sometimes saw things differently. Plato frequently identified democracy with tyranny, and his pupil Aristotle complained that the decrees of a democratic assembly were no different from the edicts of the tyrant.

Figure 9.3. This bust of Plato is a Roman copy of a fourth-century BC original.

Plato

It is certainly a tribute to Athenian democracy that it produced its own most astute critics. An aristocrat from one of Athens' most distinguished families and a relative of the oligarch Critias, Plato became a disciple of Socrates and was profoundly shaken by his death. The loss of his mentor, however, only heightened his creative powers. Over his lifetime, Plato composed numerous dialogues, in most of which the principal part is played by a character he identifies as Socrates. What is beauty? What is piety? What is justice? What is love? These questions were explored in Plato's Socratic dialogues. As Plato's thinking evolved with the passing of time, this "Socrates" had less and less in common with the historical Socrates and came to serve as a vehicle for Plato's own ideas.

Chief among these was the theory of Forms. Plato's belief in Forms was connected to his passion for definitions, for both depend on a conviction that seemingly disparate acts and items can nonetheless be classified in categories—that beautiful objects and acts and ideas, for example, all have something in common. In Plato's view, they all partake of the ideal Form of beauty. While a beautiful sunset might seem different from a beautiful mathematical proof or a beautiful young athlete, in fact what ties them together is more enduring than what sets them apart.

The relationship of appearance to reality in Plato's world view can perhaps be best grasped in the context of mathematics. A ring or a princely diadem or the

Figure 9.4. This bust of Aristotle dates from the Hellenistic Age.

perimeter of a hoplite shield might seem to the casual observer to be circles, but they are not circles in the same sense that the locus of all points in a given plane equidistant from a given point is a circle. They only look like circles; if you were to put them under a magnifying glass you would see that they were not circles at all, merely objects vaguely circular in appearance precisely because they bring to mind the Form of the circle. Only the circle depicted in the mathematical definition is a circle. Some people might say that these concrete objects are real circles whereas the geometrical concept is imaginary, but Plato was not one of these people. For Plato, only the concept is real. The tangible objects are debased copies, feeble imitations of the ideal Form. Plato, in other words, was an idealist and a dualist. He believed in an opposition between the physical world of appearances, which are deceptive, and the intellectual universe of ideas, which represent reality. The first is tawdry and serves only to distract people from ultimate truth; the second is noble, and to contemplate it ennobling.

In many ways Plato was a revolutionary. The close connection between appearance and reality was fundamental to Greek civilization. If you are rich and handsome, most of his contemporaries believed, then probably you are also good; if you are poor and ugly, probably you are bad as well. If everyone admires you, then all is right with the world; if you are despised, then you have no reason to go on. For most Greek men, reputation, power, and material success were central to happiness. Like Socrates before him, who preferred being right to being alive, Plato identified values that were more important than being well liked or envied.

In his dialogue on government and education, *The Republic*, he raised a key question about justice. Let us say, he proposed, that you had a magic ring that would make you invisible. Would you practice justice, or would you take the opportunity to grab as much power and wealth as you could, practicing injustice in the happy expectation of getting away with it?

As usual, Plato does not appear in this dialogue. His brothers Glaucon and Adeimantus, however, do, and they are quick to point out the customary Greek view that only convention, *nomos*, holds people back from committing injustice. The behavior that the man-made *nomoi* of punishment and disgrace discourage, however, is encouraged by *physis*, the natural instinct that urges people to take whatever they can get away with taking. This was the drive that Thucydides' Athenians at Melos had identified as the customary engine of human conduct: People, they had argued, "are always forced by the law of nature to dominate everyone they can" (5.105; Blanco). This sort of thing, Glaucon and Adeimantus say, is what the average person believes. It is up to Socrates to show that justice is in fact good for people.

This is a large task, and Socrates decides to shift gears and explore justice in the state in order to discover justice in the individual writ large. In the course of this exploration, he spins out threads that are even more revolutionary. The subject of the dialogue becomes an ideal state of Plato's imagining. It is a state divided into three classes, corresponding to Plato's conception of the tripartite nature of the soul. At the top are the guardians, who represent reason. Their supreme rationality, inculcated by years of education, qualifies them to govern. After them come the auxiliaries, who are characterized by a spirited temperament which suits them for the duties of soldiers. Last come the majority, who correspond to desire in the soul: They are not especially bright or brave and live only to satisfy their own material yearnings, and to perform the menial tasks the state requires for subsistence.

The education and lives of the guardians soon become the focus of Plato's attention. They will study for many years, approaching the understanding of the Forms by applying themselves to mathematics. Surprisingly, the guardians will be of both genders, and Plato advocates a unisex education for them.

Document 9.1. Though on the whole, Socrates argues, women are inferior to men in all skills besides weaving and cooking, nonetheless there will always be individual women who are more skilled than individual men. When Glaucon agrees, Socrates launches into his plan for having guardians of both sexes (though he always speaks of guardians and their wives, never guardians and their husbands).

SOC.　To conclude, then, there is no occupation concerned with the management of social affairs which belongs either to woman or to man, as such. Natural gifts are to be found here and there in both creatures alike; and every occupation is open to both, so far as their natures are concerned, though woman is for all purposes the weaker.

GLAU.   Certainly.

SOC.   Is that a reason for making over all occupations to men only?

GLAU.   Of course not.

SOC.   No, because one woman may have a natural gift for medicine or for music, another may not.

GLAU.   Surely.

SOC.   Is it not also true that a woman may, or may not, be warlike or athletic?

GLAU.   I think so.

SOC.   And again, one may love knowledge, another hate it; one may be high-spirited, another spiritless?

GLAU.   True again.

SOC.   It follows that one woman will be fitted by nature to be a Guardian, another will not; because these were the qualities for which we selected our men Guardians. So for the purpose of keeping watch over the commonwealth, woman has the same nature as man, save in so far as she is weaker.

GLAU.   So it appears.

SOC.   It follows that women of this type must be selected to share the life and duties of Guardians with men of the same type, since they are competent and of a like nature, and the same natures must be allowed the same pursuits.

GLAU.   Yes.

SOC.   We come round, then, to our former position, that there is nothing contrary to nature in giving our Guardians' wives the same training for mind and body. The practice we proposed to establish was not impossible or visionary, since it was in accordance with nature. Rather, the contrary practice which now prevails turns out to be unnatural.

GLAU.   So it appears.

SOC.   Well, we set out to inquire whether the plan we proposed was feasible and also the best. That it is feasible is now agreed; we must next settle whether it is the best.

GLAU.   Obviously.

SOC.   Now, for the purpose of producing a woman fit to be a Guardian, we shall not have one education for men and another for women, precisely because the nature to be taken in hand is the same.

GLAU.   True.

The Republic 455; translated by F. M. Cornford, *The Republic of Plato.* London and New York: Oxford University Press, 1945.

The guardians' lives will be unusual in many respects. The acquisitive principle that guides most people's activities will be alien to them, for Plato envisions a communistic regime within the guardian class; private property, though it exists for the other two classes, will be abolished for the top group. Nor will they have spouses in the conventional sense of the word. In short, they will have no oikoi—something that makes them eminently un-Athenian. Though they will not live in households, however, the guardians must reproduce in order to perpetuate the system. An elaborate mathematical scheme will dictate temporary couplings. (Plato was deeply influenced by the Pythagoreans, and he found in mathematics not only the embodiment of perfect abstraction but elements of mysticism as well.) Once born of these short-term "marriages," however, children will be mixed in with all the other children conceived around the same time and raised in common nurseries. Thus, no parent will know his or her own child and vice versa.

Like other utopias, Plato's is designed to demonstrate the shortcomings of real states. Whether he ever planned or even wished to see his Republic established is uncertain. What is clear is his dislike of the existing governments in Greece, and particularly of democracy. Tyranny and oligarchy are easiest to dismiss; nobody should have to live by the whims of a power-hungry autocrat, and money is no measure of merit. Democracy is harder to dispose of, but living under a government he did not like galvanized Plato into a vehement attack on a system he categorized as "an agreeable form of anarchy" marked by "an equality of a peculiar kind for equals and unequals alike" (558C; Cornford 1945). The debunking of the so-called equality of democracy was common to the thinking of fourth-century intellectuals. Aristotle and Isocrates shared Plato's preference for what they labeled "proportional" or "geometric" equality. It was the ratio between merit and privilege, they argued, that ought to remain constant. Such a system was far more equitable, they believed, than the "arithmetic" equality of democracy that accorded equal privilege to people of unequal merit. For Plato, giving equal political power to all alike was no different from giving all students the same grade regardless of their performance on papers and exams.

Good government, Plato concluded, will never come into being until philosophers and rulers are one and the same. Hoping to realize this goal in an immediate and concrete manner, he accepted an invitation to travel to Sicily, where he sought to educate the tyrant Dionysius II in philosophy, but Dionysius was already a mature adult, and the experiment was a complete failure. Closer to home, Plato founded a school in Athens that he called the Academy because of its location by the groves of the ancient Greek hero Academus. There men and a few women studied for years to achieve an enlightenment which, in Plato's view, would qualify them to participate in government—but which he acknowledged would in fact drive a wedge between them and their unenlightened fellow citizens. Former students at the Academy included many famous philosophers, astronomers, mathematicians, and even scientists. The presence of scientists at the Academy is a testimony to its breadth, for Plato himself was not drawn to science. How could he be, when he believed that only the eternal mattered—that the forms were the ultimate and only reality? Science deals with change and with motion. Like Parmenides, Plato conceived reality as unchanging and unchangeable. Without a mechanism for explaining change, Plato's idealist philosophy was antithetical to science.

Aristotle

It was Plato's star pupil Aristotle who founded the great institution of scientific learning at Athens, the Lyceum. His father had been a court physician in Macedon, and he had been trained in scientific observation from his youth. He was never happier than in the meticulous observation and classification of species. Scholars in all disciplines, but especially perhaps biologists, will recognize the delight he took in connecting the particular to the general, and in observing nature at work in all its perfection: Even in the animals that are not attractive to the senses, he wrote, "the craftsmanship of nature provides extraordinary pleasures to those who are able to recognize the causes in things and who have a natural inclination to philosophy" (*On the Parts of Animals* 645a 7ff). Certainly Aristotle thrived in the constantly changing world of nature, while Plato was happiest contemplating the eternal truths of mathematics. For Aristotle, the dynamic power of change accounted for a great deal of the excitement of mental life. And not only this: It was movement toward a particular end—teleology, from the Greek *telos* meaning "end" or "goal"—that he saw as the guiding force behind life. A prime mover, he argued, shaped the universe in accord with his ends. Only the prime mover was not itself moved. Loosely speaking, the prime mover was what most people would call God. Aristotle's philosophy was very popular in Europe during the Middle Ages, when Thomas Aquinas (1225–1274 AD) adapted it to Christian theology.

Aristotle was a less eccentric person than Plato. Though he came from the Ionian city of Stagira in northern Greece and hence did not belong in Athens the same way the blue-blooded Plato did, he was more firmly grounded in the customary relations of Greek society than Plato, who apparently never married or had children. He lived with two successive women, his wife Pythias and then, after Pythias' death, his concubine Herpyllis; he had a daughter and a son. After Plato's death in 347, when Aristotle had studied at the Academy for nearly twenty years, he left Athens and took up residence in Assos in Asia Minor. Several years later he returned to Macedon, where Philip had summoned him to serve as tutor to the young prince Alexander. It was upon his return to Athens in 335 that he established the Lyceum. He and his students conversed there while strolling through the colonnaded walks (*peripatoi*, which gave his followers the name "peripatetics" by which they are still known today). When he was accused of impiety in the burst of anti-Macedonian feeling that erupted after news of Alexander's death arrived in Athens, Aristotle left Attica. Looking back somberly at the trial of Socrates, he observed that he did not want the Athenians to sin a second time against philosophy. He died the following year, in 322.

That Aristotle loved science while Plato loved mathematics reveals a profound difference between the two men and their ways of engaging with the world of ideas. Live things excited Aristotle and inspired in him the desire to categorize them. The same urge would lead him to classify all the political arrangements familiar in his day in his famous work of political theory, the *Politics*. Where Plato had used reason as virtually his only tool in the quest for understanding, Aristotle placed tremendous importance on observation. His stay in northwest Asia Minor and the adjacent islands was particularly rewarding to him because of the opportunity it afforded him to study the lagoon of Pyrrha on Lesbos, which teemed with life. Though reason was not his only tool, he was the founder of the discipline of logic. To Aristotle we owe the articulation of the fundamental principle of the syllogism—the principle that tells us that if A yields B and B yields C, then A by itself must yield C. If Sneaky is a cat and all cats are mammals, then Sneaky must be a mammal. Since the Parthenon is in Athens and Athens is in Attica, then the Parthenon must be in Attica.

Whereas Plato had developed a framework for discussing politics so theoretical that scholars are often puzzled as to what real states he might have had in mind, Aristotle approached the question of the human community by amassing and analyzing a tremendous amount of data. In this project he was assisted by his students at the Lyceum, where 158 essays on constitutions of various poleis were drawn up. That all these have disappeared except for *The Athenian Constitution* is an incalculable loss to the study of Greek history. Aristotle was fascinated by issues surrounding government. His principal work of political theory is his *Politics*, which remained a cherished handbook throughout the medieval, Renaissance, and early modern periods.

In his conception of the universe at large, Aristotle differed with Plato on a key point—the existence of Forms. To Aristotle, as to the average person, Forms were not real. Only the combination of form and matter created something real. Plato, Aristotle thought, had failed, like Parmenides, to account for change. Aristotle also rejected the broad level of generalization at which Plato operated. In their views of the human community, however, the two men were quite similar. Both saw the polis as more than a practical arrangement for the exchange of goods and mutual protection; for them human existence and the existence of the polis were coterminous. (The lack of a state structure would make a fully human existence impossible, but a structure larger than the polis seemed unimaginable. Aristotle identified the largest possible size for the state at ten thousand citizens, the number who could be addressed by a speaker at one time.) Aristotle is famous for having said "man is a political animal." What he actually said is that people are animals whose nature it is to live in a polis. Only in a polis could individuals realize their social natures and grow through the sharing of ideas. This growth, however, was limited to a few people of intellectual gifts who belonged to a social class that guaranteed them leisure for contemplation. Powerful obstacles prevented the poor from participating in politics—especially the nonfarming poor, who did "banausic" labor, arduous jobs that compromised the mind along with the body. The best state, he concludes, will not make common laborers citizens, for citizens must have adequate property to ensure sufficient leisure for goodness and political activity. So much for democracy.

Both the blue-blooded Athenian aristocrat and Athens' most famous metic, then, were intensely class-conscious. Aristotle's political philosophy, however, differed from Plato's in two key respects. First, Aristotle believed in collective wisdom: A mass of people who are individually unwise, he argues, may surpass the wisdom of the few best men, just as potluck dinners may prove to be tastier than those hosted by a single individual. The masses, he claims, can be perfectly good judges of music and poetry, since "some appreciate one thing, some another, and taken together they appreciate everything" (*Politics* 1281b). For this reason, he is open to a compromise similar to that of Solon: Poor people in his ideal state would be allowed to choose officials and hold them to account, but not to hold office. Second, Aristotle had such a powerful belief in natural hierarchies—free over slave, Greek over non-Greek, adult over child, male over female—that he recurred with some frequency to this theme of the inferiority of women to men.

Whereas Plato's utopia entailed a unisex education aimed at producing guardian men and women who would govern together, Aristotle was a staunch supporter of patriarchy, which he believed had a solid basis in women's biological inadequacy. Women, he maintained, had colder bodies than men. For this reason, though they were able to provide matter for embryos, only men could provide the soul. In the womb, embryos that stopped short of full development for lack of heat became female. Thus women were literally half-baked. From this came the inferior strength he identified in a variety of species. The female, he contended, "is, so to speak, a deformed male" (*Generation of Animals* 737a). At times, as was the case with the Hippocratics, Aristotle's powers of observation deserted him when women were their subject. The twentieth-century philosopher Bertrand Russell quipped that Aristotle would not have claimed that women had fewer teeth than men if he had allowed his wife to open her mouth.

For all their differences, Plato and Aristotle shared a passionate conviction that the goal of philosophy was to enable selected people to pursue enlightenment in a republic of virtuous citizens. The state for them meant the polis, and it was central to the good life. Their thinking contrasts strikingly with that of most moderns, who are more likely to see the state as designed to grant individuals the freedom to pursue their private goals, particularly their economic ones. Though Plato and Aristotle were both intensely critical of democracy, they shared with the Athenian democrats an eminently Greek belief in the active nature of the polis. So far from an artificial institution whose chief goal was to redistribute goods and prevent crime, the polis was conceived by its residents as a force for the moral and spiritual improvement of its citizens. For this force to operate properly, citizens had to engage eagerly in political life; participation was a duty, not a right. The problems of the fourth century, however, raised serious questions about whether the polis as traditionally conceived was adequate to serve people's needs.

The fourth century BC witnessed an explosion of creative energy in many areas: Philosophy, biology, political theory, mathematics, and military science all made significant advances. Where all this fertility was leading is unclear. Solid foundations were established for intellectual traditions that lived and grew for centuries; many of them still flourish in altered—or unaltered—forms. The knowledge generated did not, however, offer salvation to Greece. The increasing specialization of the fourth century led to a division between generals and politicians that resulted in more professional military skills. Consequently, generals in the fourth century were better than those of the fifth. Their weapons and machinery were more versatile and sophisticated. New ways of thinking also led to specialized monographs like Xenophon's treatises on the art of horsemanship and the skills necessary for a successful cavalry commander, and the *Siegecraft* of the author known as Aeneas Tacticus. No good, however, came of these improvements. Greeks simply expanded the repertoire of available methods for killing.

The great texts of Greek political theory continue to be read today. The insight they afforded, however, seems to have had little real-life application in their own day. Plato's students never did take over Athenian government, and Aristotle's influence on his pupil Alexander was limited. Identifying those who are likely to govern best is always a challenge, and it contributes little to point out the imprudence of according sovereign power to a power-hungry tyrant, a clique of rich men, or an angry mob. It is precisely because wealth and birth have historically been the criteria for inclusion in the elite that democracy has become a popular alternative to oligarchy. It is one thing to advocate an aristocracy of intellect and another to design practical machinery for establishing one. It was a central tenet of Greek intellectuals that most people lacked capacity for growth. Plato and Aristotle worked on the assumption that the secret to reforming government was in nurturing the tiny minority that had this capacity. Their goal was basically to design a constitution that minimized the power prudence must accord to the mindless masses who might otherwise rise up and slaughter their betters.

To say that the polis ultimately failed because it lacked a truly democratic ideology would nonetheless be ridiculous on several counts. First, mighty empires have flourished for long periods without any democratic ideology whatsoever. Second, we know from the vigor and stability of fourth-century Athens that democracy was alive and well, albeit not in the minds of Greece's intellectuals. Third, the polis did not entirely fail. The collapse of polis ideology before the Macedonian onslaught was certainly noticeable in states like Athens and Sparta that had once enjoyed the privilege of framing their own foreign policies. Smaller poleis, however, had long been accustomed to eking out what dignity they could in the shadow of greater powers. The bustling city in fact remained the core of Greek civilization for centuries to come.

TRANSLATIONS

Cornford, F. M. 1945. *The Republic of Plato*. London and New York: Oxford University Press.

Fowler, H. N. 1914. *Plato: Euthyphro, Apology, Crito, Phaedo, Phaedrus*. Loeb Classical Library. Cambridge, MA, and London: Harvard University Press.

Hamilton, Walter. 1951. *Plato: The Symposium*. Harmondsworth, UK: Penguin.

Murray, A. T. 1936. Pseudo-Demosthenes, *Against Neaera*, from *Demosthenes*. Vol. VI. Loeb Classical Library. Cambridge, MA, and London: Harvard University Press.

Warner, Rex. 1979. *Xenophon: A History of My Times* [*The Hellenica*]. Harmondsworth, UK: Penguin.

SUGGESTED READINGS

Bryant, Joseph. 1996. *Moral Codes and Social Structure in Ancient Greece*. Albany: State University of New York Press. The connection between values and social organization from the Archaic period through the Hellenistic Age.

Cartledge, Paul. 1987. *Agesilaos and the Crisis of Sparta*. Baltimore: Johns Hopkins University Press. A close study of fourth-century Sparta.

Hansen, Mogens H. 1991. *The Athenian Democracy in the Age of Demosthenes*. Oxford and Cambridge, MA: Basil Blackwell. An engaging analytical study of Athenian democracy that is crammed with useful facts.

Hansen, Mogens H. 1991. *The Trial of Socrates from the Athenian Point of View*. Copenhagen: The Royal Danish Academy of Sciences and Letters. Discussion of the sources, a reconstruction of the trial, and an investigation of the political background of the prosecution.

Ober, Josiah. 1989. *Mass and Elite in Democratic Athens: Rhetoric, Ideology, and the Power of the People*. Princeton, NJ: Princeton University Press. A sociopolitical study of fourth-century Athens that uses the findings of modern social scientists to shed light on the ideology of the democracy as revealed in the work of the orators.

Sage, Michael, ed. 1996. *Warfare in Ancient Greece: A Sourcebook*. London and New York: Routledge. A collection of passages relating to Greek warfare, tied together by thoughtful and detailed commentary that includes critical readings of the sources themselves.

Sinclair, T. A. 1968. *A History of Greek Political Thought*. 2nd ed. Cleveland and New York: Meridian. A thought-provoking analysis of Greek political thinking from Homer through the Roman conquest.

Todd, S. C. 1993. *The Shape of Athenian Law*. Oxford: Oxford University Press. A detailed and analytical study of Athenian law dealing with both procedure and substance.

Tritle, Lawrence, ed. 1997. *The Greek World in the Fourth Century: From the Fall of the Athenian Empire to the Successors of Alexander*. London and New York: Routledge. A collection of essays on the problems of the fourth century, including chapters on Thebes, the Greeks of Asia Minor, and the states of western Greece.

Wood, Ellen Meiksins. 1988. *Peasant-Citizen and Slave: The Foundations of Athenian Democracy*. London and New York: Verso. The relationship between agrarian labor and democracy in Classical Athens.

10

PHILIP II AND THE RISE OF MACEDON

It is one of the paradoxes of ancient history that the Greek *poleis* maintained their independence as long as they did. Their tiny size and fractiousness made their escape from Persian conquest appear miraculous even in antiquity. The return of the threat of foreign conquest in the fourth century was not surprising, but the source of the threat was not the mighty Persian Empire but the hitherto insignificant kingdom known as Macedon or Macedonia.

The success of Macedon in conquering the Greek states was due partly to the political divisions and economic strains that inhibited the evolution of a consistent policy in Athens, partly to the mutual mistrust that prevented the formation of an effective united front by the leading poleis—Athens, Sparta, and Thebes. Credit, however, must also be given to the unique military and diplomatic gifts of Philip II, who became king of Macedon in 359 BC.

EARLY MACEDON

Herodotus claimed that Perdiccas, the first king of Macedon, was promised the land illuminated by the sun as his kingdom. The reality was different. For most of early Macedonian history, the kings of Macedon ruled a chronically unstable kingdom that was a state only in name. Sandwiched between Thessaly on the south, Thrace and the Chalcidian League on the east, Paeonia on the north, and Illyria and Epirus on the west, Macedonian kings struggled constantly to maintain their independence while simultaneously striving to assert their preeminence over the local dynasts, who ruled the various regions that made up the kingdom of Macedon.

Macedonia's geography made their struggle more difficult. Macedonia consisted of two distinct geographical regions: Lower Macedonia, the great alluvial plain created by the Haliacmon and Axius rivers during their course to the Gulf of Therma, and Upper Macedonia, the horseshoe of rugged uplands and mountains that stretched northwestward toward Illyria and Epirus. Lower Macedonia formed the heart of the kingdom of Macedon and supported a large agricultural population. Its mountainous hinterlands not only held extensive forests and rich mineral deposits but also sheltered various tribes who jealously guarded their freedom from the control of the lowland Macedonian kings. Uniting these two regions was the essential precondition for the growth and expansion of Macedonian power.

MACEDONIAN SOCIETY AND KINGSHIP

Were the Macedonians Greek? This question is the most contentious issue in Macedonian historiography. Conflicting claims to the territory of ancient Macedonia have made the question of the "Greekness" of the ancient Macedonians a burning issue. Modern nationalists may be confident of their answers, but contemporary ideology has little relevance to antiquity. Thus, while recent epigraphic discoveries suggest that "Macedonian" was a dialect of northwest Greek, it is clear that in antiquity neither Macedonians nor Greeks considered the Macedonians to be Greek. Except for the ruling Argead house, which was believed to be of Argive origin, Greeks viewed the Macedonians as barbarians like their Thracian and Illyrian neighbors.

More important, although Macedonian kings encouraged the Hellenization of the Macedonian nobility, Macedonian and Greek culture had little in common. Cities were the core of what was most distinctive in Greek civilization, but prior to Philip's reign, city life in Macedonia was limited to a few Greek colonies on the coast of the Gulf of Therma and dynastic centers such as Aegae and Pella. Most Macedonians were farmers or seminomadic pastoralists living in scattered villages and owing allegiance to Macedonian aristocrats. Other differences divided the two cultures as well, such as the polygamy of the Macedonian kings and the Macedonians' love of unmixed wine and their preference for tumulus burial instead of simple cremation or interment. Indeed, the lifestyle of the Macedonian nobility had more in common with that of Homeric heroes than with that of Classical Greeks. War and hunting were central to the life of a Macedonian noble. Before being recognized as an adult, a young man had to spear a boar without the aid of a net and kill an enemy. Feuds resulting from heavy drinking, competition for preference at the royal court, and rivalries over the favors of young men and women were common.

The monarchy was the central institution of Macedonian society. Like Louis XIV of France, a Macedonian *basileus* ("king") was an autocrat who could well say "I am the state." Theories that royal power was limited by an army assembly have been shown to be groundless. The army might acclaim a new king and witness trials of nobles, but the king made all appointments and grants of land and privilege, and only he responded to petitions. Treaties and alliances were made with him personally, and foreign allies pledged their support to him and his family. The king could even choose which of his sons would be his successor.

Macedonian kings were autocrats but they were not all-powerful. Greek political theorists equated monarchy and tyranny because of the supreme importance of the ruler's personality in the public and private spheres. This was especially true of Macedon, where the kings spent their lives in the midst of their *hetairoi* ("companions")—Macedonian nobles who formed their personal entourage. These nobles provided the kings with their advisers and the members of their bodyguard, and served in an elite cavalry unit commanded by the king. Not surprisingly, Macedonian kings sat on insecure thrones. Only two predecessors of Philip II died natural deaths; the rest died in battle or fell victim to conspiracies.

The Predecessors of Philip II

Philip II was the beneficiary of almost two centuries of patient state-building by his Argead predecessors. The process began in the late sixth century BC with an alliance between Amyntas I and Persia. The Macedonians were loyal allies, even supporting the Persian invasion of Greece in 480 BC. Not surprisingly, Amyntas' successor, Alexander I, encouraged the spread of stories after the Persian defeat testifying to his covert support of the Greek cause during the invasion.

Persian rule brought Macedon great advantages by shielding the kingdom from attack by its neighbors. After the Greek victory, Amyntas' fifth century BC successors—Alexander I, Perdiccas II, and Archelaus—extended their territory northwestward into Upper Macedon and eastward to the rich silver mine beyond the Axius River, making the kingdom the strongest power in the region. Macedon's growing power and resources attracted the attention of Athens and other Greek cities. Macedonian grain fed many of Athens' allies and subjects, and Macedonian timber was critical to Athens' fleet. For their part, the Macedonian kings used their wealth to win recognition as Greeks and Hellenize the royal court. Alexander I may have competed in the Olympic games, while Archelaus supported Greek artists and writers, such as the Athenian tragedian Euripides, who wrote two tragedies at Archelaus' court: the lost *Archelaus*, celebrating his host's alleged Argive ancestry, and the *Bacchae*, offering a terrifying evocation of the power of Dionysus. By the reign of Philip II, the Macedonian court was the principal cultural center in Macedon and the focus of the social life of the Macedonian aristocracy. Growing Macedonian power, however, threatened Athenian interests in the north Aegean, prompting Athens to support Macedon's Thracian neighbors and various pretenders to the Macedonian throne.

When Philip II came to power in 360, Macedon was faced by the most severe crisis in its history. Chronic instability had left the kingdom vulnerable to threats from both Greek and non-Greek enemies. Philip's own brother, Perdiccas III, had been killed in battle in 360 BC by the Illyrians together with four thousand Macedonian troops and much of the Macedonian aristocracy. Surrounded by enemies and beset by dynastic rivalries, the kingdom seemed on the verge of collapse.

Figure 10.1. Macedonia and its neighbors.

THE REIGN OF PHILIP II

Philip II was born about 382 BC, the last son of Amyntas III and his Illyrian wife Eurydice. Plutarch says that Eurydice learned to read in order to educate her children, but Philip's education ended abruptly with the defeat of his brother Alexander II and his own exile as a hostage in Thebes from 369 to 367 BC. His exile was not all loss. Philip's stay in Thebes soon after its victory at Leuctra gave him an invaluable insight into contemporary Greek politics and military tactics.

Philip returned to Macedon in 367 as the kingdom descended into chaos. Three kings ruled Macedon during the next seven years. Political instability also provided Philip with an unexpected opportunity, since the crisis following Perdiccas' death demanded a ruler capable of taking decisive action. That ruler could

Figure 10.2a. Silver tetradrachm of Philip II (359–336 BC). Obverse: Head of Zeus. Reverse: Mounted Macedonian king—probably Philip II—wearing Macedonian hat and cape.

Figure 10.2b. Silver tetradrachm of Philip II (359–336 BC). Obverse: Head of Zeus. Reverse: Jockey commemorating the victory of Philip's horse at Olympia in 356 BC.

only be Philip, since he was the sole surviving adult Argead. Not surprisingly, Philip quickly supplanted his infant nephew Amyntas as king of Macedon.

When Philip took power in 360, Macedon was threatened by foreign enemies and rival claimants to the throne supported by the Thracian king Seuthes II and the Athenians, still hoping to regain Amphipolis. In the next two years the situation changed dramatically. After neutralizing the Thracians and Athenians through astute diplomacy, Philip quickly defeated both the Paeonians and Illyrians and regained control of western and northwestern Macedonia. Philip's brilliant diplomacy paved the way for his decisive military victories over the Paeonians and Illyrians in 358 and set the pattern for the rest of his reign.

Success followed success during the remainder of the decade. Alliance with the Molossians in Epirus secured Macedon's western frontier and freed Philip to turn eastward and seize the Greek cities on the coasts of Macedon and the gold mines of Mount Pangaeus that financed his plans for the rest of his reign. In less than a decade, Philip had freed Macedon from the enemies that had threatened its survival since the sixth century. At the same time far-reaching reforms gave the kingdom unprecedented military strength and political cohesion.

The Reforms of Philip II

Philip II's reign coincided with a revolution in military tactics and weaponry that ended the Greek hoplite's dominance of the battlefield. By introducing these innovations to Macedon, Philip transformed it into the preeminent military power in southeastern Europe. His most important military reform was the reorganization of the Macedonian infantry. Philip created a new phalanx to replace the old undisciplined militia that had served Macedonian kings so poorly in the past. The six companies of the new phalanx were recruited from each of Macedon's traditional territorial divisions, but they were equipped with new weapons and assigned a new role in battle. Each member of the phalanx wore a metal helmet and carried a small shield and a short sword. His principal weapon, however, was an enormous pike that could be as much as 18 feet long, allowing the soldier to

Figure 10.3. The Macedonian phalanx.

strike a blow before his enemies could close and use their shorter weapons. The presence of the phalanx in a battle forced Philip's enemies to modify their tactics to cope with it and allow the companion cavalry to deal a decisive blow to an enemy force already confused by the phalanx and the elite guard units protecting its flanks.

Philip also strengthened the bonds between the army and the king by sharing its hardships and dangers, as his loss of an eye and other wounds attested. He conferred a new title on the common soldiers, *pezhetairoi* ("foot companions"), suggesting that they too, like the nobles, were the king's personal companions. The rage of Alexander's soldiers at the thought of sharing this status with Persians revealed the strength of the bond Philip had forged with them. The bond between the king and the Macedonian nobility also changed. Perdiccas III's disastrous defeat had devastated the Macedonian nobility and enabled Philip to replenish the royal companions with Greeks and non-Greeks who flocked to Macedon in search of opportunity and wealth. Members of the old nobility also benefited, receiving commands in Philip's new model army. Their sons became royal pages, personally serving the king and providing Philip with future officers, while also serving as hostages for the loyalty of their families.

Theopompus, the historian of Philip's reign, sarcastically characterized his new companions as men more suited to be "courtesans" than "courtiers." Still, they were loyal to Philip, and he rewarded them with land and treasure gained by his victories. Projects such as the draining of marshland in Lower Macedonia and the foundation of colonies such as Philippi further strengthened royal power and resources. As a result, Philip possessed what no previous Macedonian king had ever had before: a loyal base of support for his policies.

Philip Becomes a Force in Greece

Philip's predecessors had tried to avert the danger posed by a united Thessaly by supporting Larisa against Pherae and its Theban allies. Not surprisingly, Philip also intervened in Thessaly following the conclusion of an alliance between Phocis and Macedon's old enemy Pherae.

Phocis had emerged in the mid-350s as a major power in central and northern Greece, and the alliance of Pherae and Phocis alarmed both Larisa and Thebes, forcing them to seek Philip's aid. Philip initially underestimated the threat posed by the alliance of Pherae and Phocis. Although Philip suffered two severe defeats at the hands of Phocis in 353—the most serious of his entire reign—he crushed them a year later at the Battle of the Crocus Field. This battle transformed Philip's position in Greece. After occupying Pherae and exiling its tyrant, Philip was appointed by the Thessalian League *archōn* ("commander-in-chief") of Thessaly, uniting Thessaly and Macedon and virtually doubling the military forces at his disposal. It also allowed Philip to expand his influence deep into central Greece.

While Philip was busy in Thessaly, central Greece was convulsed by the Third Sacred War. The war originated in Thebes' attempt to humiliate Phocis by having the Delphic Amphictyony severely fine the Phocians in 357 for cultivating sacred land. Phocis' response was unexpected. Long Thebes' main rival in central Greece, Phocis had grudgingly recognized Theban suzerainty at the Battle of Leuctra. In 357, the Phocians made a desperate effort to regain their independence. Instead of submitting to Theban blackmail, they seized Delphi and used Apollo's treasures to recruit mercenaries. Athenian and Spartan hostility frustrated Thebes' attempt to avenge the sacrilege, allowing Phocis to subdue much of central Greece.

Conflicts with Thrace and Olynthus delayed Philip's intervention until 347. Although Macedonian power tipped the scales against Phocis, Philip sought to prevent Thebes from profiting from his victory by secretly negotiating surrender terms with Phocis. Facing the traditional penalty for such sacrilege—execution of all adult males—the Phocians accepted the relatively mild terms offered by Philip and surrendered in the summer of 346. Phocis' cities were broken up into their constituent villages, and the Phocians agreed to repay Delphi at a rate of sixty talents per year. Finally, Philip gained Phocis' votes in the Delphic Amphictyony, thus giving him a voting majority on the Amphictyonic Council. All Greece learned the full extent of Philip's new influence in Delphic affairs a year later, when he presided over the Pythian games. Philip's triumph in the Sacred War also temporarily calmed relations between Macedon and Athens.

Philip, Athens, and the Peace of Philocrates

Tense relations between Athens and Philip dated to the beginning of his reign when he bought Athenian neutrality by promising to restore Amphipolis and then not only seized it but also captured Pydna, Methone, and Potidaea, thereby eliminating Athens' principal allies in the north Aegean. Athens delayed responding to Philip's actions for almost a decade. This was largely the result of the economic devastation caused by the Peloponnesian War, which limited Athens' ability to pursue a wide-ranging foreign policy in the early fourth century. Athenian power was further constrained in the 350s by the defection of several key allies from the Second Athenian League and by an important political innovation: the establishment of the Theoric Fund.

Eubulus (c. 405–c. 335 BC), Athens' leading politician, persuaded the Athenians to pass a law assigning all fiscal surpluses to the Theoric Fund, which funded public benefits such as repairing roads and fortifications and religious participation including distributions to Athenian citizens at religious festivals; it was named after the "theatrical" performances that were part of these celebrations. The orator Demades rightly called the Theoric Fund "the glue of the democracy," since it reduced tension between the rich and the poor. It also, however, encouraged a pacifist foreign policy in two ways: by lessening the poor's need for the pay they received for rowing in the fleet and by increasing their concern that surplus funds would be redirected to military expenditures and their benefits reduced should war break out.

Eubulus' cautious financial policies had dramatic results. Athenian revenues rose from 130 talents to 400, enabling Athens to construct new triremes and to

Figure 10.4. Polyeuctus' posthumous portrait of Demosthenes was erected in the Athenian *agora* in 280 BC and survives in this Roman copy. It shows the orator as gaunt, worried, and thoughtful. (Note: The position of the hands is reproduced incorrectly in this copy.)

improve the docks and fortifications. The Laurium silver mines were reopened and foreigners encouraged to settle in Attica and become metics. Only the threat of Macedonian military intervention in central Greece in the late 350s prompted the prosperous Athenians to finally take strong action.

With a Macedonian invasion of Attica seemingly imminent, the Athenians dispatched an expeditionary force in 352 to occupy Thermopylae, to block the Macedonian advance. The motion was made by a close associate of Eubulus. In a crisis, Athens' security overrode any scruples Eubulus and his supporters may have had about dipping into the Theoric Fund. Otherwise, however, Athens failed utterly to hinder the Macedonian king's growing influence in northern and central Greece. Athens' actions in the early 340s were similarly ineffective. When Olynthus tried to shift alliances from Macedon to Athens, Philip turned on his former ally. Athens' ineffective response to Olynthus' appeals for help in 348 allowed Philip to capture the city, raze it, enslave its citizens, and to dismantle the Chalcidic League, Macedon's only potential Greek rival in the north Aegean.

Although Athens' restraint as Philip's power grew was prudent, its inability to regain Amphipolis or aid its allies was humiliating. Not surpisingly, some Athenian politicians demanded a more aggressive Athenian policy toward Macedon. The most prominent of these politicians was the orator Demosthenes. Demosthenes' fame was such that the Roman statesman Cicero called his speeches against Mark Antony "Philippics" after Demosthenes' speeches against Philip. Originally a supporter of Eubulus, by 351 Demosthenes had become disenchanted with Eubulus' policies and begun to forge a new political identity. In the *First Philippic*, Demosthenes revealed his new views, attacking Philip and urging the Athenians to prepare for war by building a strong navy. Although Demosthenes continued to advocate resistance to Philip, even he recognized that the fall of Olynthus, Philip's triumph in the Sacred War, and the defection of Euboea made peace imperative if Athens was to avoid total disaster.

The Athenian politician Philocrates negotiated peace with Philip in the summer of 346. Negotiating the treaty and securing its approval by the Athenian assembly was a contentious process. Because the Peace of Philocrates quickly collapsed amidst bitter recriminations, the details of its negotiation remain unclear, but not its significance. Faced with the alternatives of fighting Macedon or accepting Philip's terms, Athens chose the latter. Athens abandoned its claim to Amphipolis, accepted the exclusion of its Phocian and Thracian allies from the treaty, and agreed that the city and the Second Athenian League would become allies of Philip and his descendants. Athens' inability to prevent the growth of Macedonian power and influence in Greece was clear to all.

The Aftermath of the Peace of Philocrates

The Peace of Philocrates ratified Philip's supremacy in northern and central Greece. His diplomatic triumph was, however, short-lived. As the likelihood of war with Macedon receded, support for the treaty dissipated. Philip's treatment of Phocis also cast doubt on the credibility of the treaty's negotiators, who had promised that the Phocians would suffer no harm. When Philip also gained Phocis' two votes on the Amphictyonic Council, the Athenians and Spartans angrily refused to send deputations to the Pythian games.

While Philip's critics in Athens steadily undermined the Peace of Philocrates and its supporters, Philip's proposals to strengthen the peace were rebuffed. Athens again demanded that he return Amphipolis. Philocrates, the architect of the peace, was indicted for bribery and fled into exile, while Demosthenes, who had helped negotiate the treaty, unsuccessfully impeached his fellow envoy Aeschines in order to protect himself. Only Philip's need for peace in Greece during his Thracian campaign in 342 prevented him from taking strong action against Athens. He finally declared war in 340, when Athens joined Persia to frustrate his siege of the Hellespontine city of Perinthus. Athens responded with its own declaration of war.

The actual outbreak of hostilities was delayed for another year. First, Philip unsuccessfully besieged Byzantium; then he campaigned against the Scythians, who ruled the hinterlands of modern Romania's Black Sea coast and threatened Macedonian control of Thrace. Nevertheless, he still gave Athens a sharp reminder of the potential consequences of war with Macedon by capturing the entire Black Sea grain fleet in 340 BC, thereby threatening Athens with starvation.

Philip's long-awaited opportunity to strike directly at Athens came in 339, when he accepted the Delphic Amphictyony's invitation to lead a sacred war against the city of Amphissa, near Delphi. By the end of the year the Macedonian army was in Phocis, within easy striking distance of Athens. Almost a decade later Demosthenes proudly reminded the Athenians that only he had dared address the assembly, when they learned of Philip's presence in Phocis.

> At dawn the next day the Prytaneis called the Council to the Chamber, and citizens moved into the Assembly. . . . The Council appeared, announced the news they had received, and brought forward their informant to repeat it. The herald then voiced the question "Who desires to speak?" No one moved. The question was repeated several times without a man standing up, though all the strategoi were there, all the orators, and the voice of Athens called for a word to save her. . . . I came forward and addressed the Assembly.
>
> (*On the Crown*, pp. 169–172; Saunders 1975)

The Athenians' despair was understandable. Few Peloponnesian cities had heeded Demosthenes' appeal to join in resisting Philip, so when battle was finally joined in late summer 338 at Chaeronea in Boeotia, Philip faced only the levies of Athens, Thebes and the Boeotian League and a handful of Peloponnesian units. A monumental stone lion still gazes over the plain of Chaeronea, marking the site of this pivotal battle in world history. Little is known about the battle itself beyond two facts: Greek casualties were heavy, and the decisive blow was struck by the companion cavalry led by Philip's eighteen-year-old son and heir, Alexander. A thousand Athenians were killed and another two thousand captured; the Thebans' cherished Sacred Band was annihilated. Philip's triumph was complete. After Chaeronea, resistance to Philip's authority in Greece would have been futile. All that remained to be determined was the form Macedonian domination of Greece would take.

Figure 10.5. This lion burial monument marks the graves of 254 Thebans buried at the site of the Battle of Chaeronea.

PHILIP'S PLANS FOR GREECE

Philip's immediate concern after his victory at Chaeronea was how to deal with his two principal enemies. The Thebans were treated with exemplary harshness. As Thebes had a long record of collaboration with Persia and was Macedon's chief rival for power in Greece, Philip set out to break the city's power. Theban and other Boeotian prisoners were released only after payment of a heavy ransom. Thebes' political leaders were either executed or exiled. A Macedonian garrison was installed on the Cadmea, the city's acropolis. Finally, Thebes was stripped of its traditional position of leadership in the Boeotian League.

Philip's treatment of Athens was dramatically different. Capturing the city would require a difficult siege, and its fleet could threaten his projected Persian campaign. Consequently, Athens escaped significant punishment despite its leading role in the war. Athenian prisoners were returned without ransom, and the Athenian dead were escorted back to the city by an honor guard led by Alexander and Antipater, Philip's most trusted general. Nor did Philip object when Demosthenes, his most implacable opponent, delivered the funeral oration over the dead of Chaeronea.

Philip's actions were well received. Many Greeks welcomed the humiliation of Thebes, whose arbitrary behavior since the Battle of Leuctra had bred widespread resentment. Athens, for its part, showered the city's former enemies with honors, making Antipater and Alexander Athenian citizens and establishing a cult in Philip's honor in one of the city's gymnasia. Athenian suspicion of Philip, of course, did not disappear: A law passed in 337 promised severe penalties for conspirators against the democracy. Officially, however, relations were friendly. Antipater and Alexander were not the only Macedonian subjects to benefit from the thaw in relations between Philip and Athens. As was mentioned in the previous chapter, one person who took advantage of the new political climate was the philosopher Aristotle, a close friend of Antipater and the former tutor of Alexander. Aristotle returned to Athens in 335 and stayed until 322, when anti-Macedonian sentiment forced him to flee to Euboea, where he died. Philip's conciliatory policy toward Athens, however, had more practical goals, winning Athens' acquiescence in his plans for Greece, and it succeeded. Not only did Athens offer no further resistance to Macedonian preeminence in Greece, the Athenians also agreed to send representatives to the general meeting of Greek states at Corinth that Philip called in the summer of 337 BC.

The Corinthian League

Representatives of all the major Greek states except Sparta met at Corinth to learn Philip's plans. The centerpiece of the new order was an alliance, referred to by historians as the Corinthian League, but which Philip called simply "the Greeks." Its stated goals were two: to maintain a common peace in Greece and to avenge the Persian aggression against the Greeks. The alliance council (*synedrion*) was empowered to pass decrees binding on member states, to arbitrate disputes between them, and to try individuals accused of treason. Member states also received pledges of mutual nonaggression and support against attack or internal subversion. Not surprisingly, the delegates approved Philip's proposals and appointed him *hēgēmon*, ("leader") of the alliance and commander of the war against Persia.

Document 10.1. Oath of Members of the League of Corinth

(338–337 BC). Fragment of an Athenian inscription recording the oath sworn by the Athenians when they ratified the treaty establishing the League of Corinth.

Oath. I swear by Zeus, Earth, Sun, Poseidon, Athena, Ares, and all the gods and goddesses. I will abide by the peace, and I will not break the agreements with Philip the Macedonian, nor will I take up arms with hostile intent against any one of those who abide by the oaths either by land or by sea. I will not seize in war by any device or stratagem any city or fort or harbor belonging to those who share the peace. Nor will I suppress the kingdom of Philip or of his descendants or the constitutions in force among any of those [who share the peace], when they swore the oaths concerning the peace. I will not commit any act that contravenes the agreements nor will I permit any other to do so. If any one breaks the agreements, I will assist those who have been wronged in accordance with their requests. I will fight against those who break the common peace just as the common council and the leader (*hēgemōn*) decide. . . .

Inscriptiones Graecae 2.236.

Although the primary purpose of the League of Corinth was to legitimize Philip's domination of Greece, it also reflected important trends in contemporary Greek thought. Ever since the end of the Peloponnesian War, Greek politicians and thinkers had tried to end the chronic political and social unrest that plagued Greece. The philosopher Plato, as was described in the previous chapter, offered in the *Republic* and the *Laws* utopian visions of ideal cities free of *stasis*. More pragmatic thinkers denounced wars between Greeks as civil wars, while insisting that wars against barbarians were inherently just or even desirable as a way of reducing internal tensions in Greece. These ideas were embodied in the so-called "common peaces," such as the King's Peace and its successors, that are so characteristic of fourth-century Greek diplomacy.

The most prominent just-war theorist was the Athenian educator Isocrates. Isocrates was almost one hundred years old when the Battle of Chaeronea was waged. Throughout his long career as a speech writer and teacher of rhetoric, he had argued that the solution to Greece's problems was conquering a portion of the Persian Empire to which economically deprived and potentially dangerous segments of Greek society then could emigrate. Isocrates had appealed unsuccessfully to various Greek rulers to lead a united Greece in a crusade against Persia, so Philip must have seemed his last chance to see his dream realized. Unfortunately, we do not know how Philip reacted to Isocrates' letter urging him to lead such a crusade after his victory at Chaeronea, but by uniting in the League of Corinth the ideas of a "common peace" and a crusade against Persia, Philip was exploiting ideas that had been circulating widely in Greece.

The Death of Philip II

Philip's planned invasion of the Persian Empire was well timed. The 330s were a time of severe crisis for Persia. The power of the able but ruthless king Artaxerxes III (358–338 BC) rivaled that of the founders of the empire. He had ended the satrapal rebellions that had disrupted the reign of his father Artaxerxes II (405–359 BC), reestablished Persian authority in Phoenicia and Asia Minor, and even reconquered Egypt. Philip's enemies such as Demosthenes appealed to Persia for assistance against Macedon, but in vain, since Artaxerxes III had been assassinated in 338 BC, precipitating a dynastic crisis that lasted for almost two years.

Philip exploited the chaos within the Persian Empire by sending an expeditionary force commanded by his trusted general Parmenio across the Hellespont in early 336 BC. The Macedonian army's march south along the Anatolian coast incited revolts in various Greek cities against their pro-Persian tyrants. At Eresus on

Lesbos, the new government established a cult to Zeus Philippios, while the Ephesians placed a statue of Philip in the temple of Artemis. Parmenio's success augured well for the invasion Philip intended the next year. Fate, however, intervened.

Philip was assassinated at Aegae in summer 336 by Pausanias, a member of his own bodyguard. Philip's assassination climaxed a political crisis that had begun with his seventh marriage in 338. For most of his reign Philip's queen had been his fourth wife, the Epirote princess Olympias, the mother of his designated heir, Alexander. Philip's other marriages had served diplomatic ends without threatening Olympias' position at court. His seventh marriage, however, was different, since Philip married a young Macedonian woman named Cleopatra, thereby allying himself for the first time with a powerful Macedonian noble family.

Whatever Philip's reasons for his marriage to Cleopatra—ancient writers explained it as a disastrous infatuation with a younger woman—its consequences quickly became evident. In short order both Olympias and Alexander fell from favor and fled into exile, amidst talk that Philip intended to supplant his son with a "Macedonian" heir. The threat to Alexander's position, however, proved short-lived; Cleopatra bore Philip a daughter named Europa. The child's name bore witness to Philip's pride in his accomplishments, but a woman could not succeed to the Macedonian throne. Without a son to replace Alexander, Philip had to reconcile with him. A mutual friend, Demaratus of Corinth, effected the rapprochement. Although Olympias remained in exile in Epirus, Alexander returned to Pella and resumed his place at court. The crisis over the succession had ended, it seemed, without serious consequences.

Indirectly, however, Philip's ill-advised marriage to Cleopatra proved his undoing. Philip became embroiled in the enmities of her family, and one of them involved his assassin, Pausanias. According to Aristotle, Pausanias killed Philip because the king had ignored extreme abuse of him by Cleopatra's uncle Attalus. Pausanias had been raped by Attalus' servants to avenge the death of a young relative of Attalus, whom Pausanias had slandered because Philip had preferred the latter as his lover. Unwilling to offend Cleopatra's family, Philip tried to palliate Pausanias' grievance by promoting him to the coveted rank of royal bodyguard. The wedding of Philip's daughter Europa at Aegae gave Pausanias an opportunity for revenge. As Philip led a splendid procession into the theater, Pausanias rushed forward and stabbed the king to death before the startled eyes of the guests from all over the Macedonian empire. So ended the reign of the most controversial of all Macedonian kings.

Since antiquity, historians have had difficulty assessing Philip and his achievements. Polybius was bewildered by Theopompus' observation that "Europe had never produced a man like Philip," which seemed contradicted by his lurid catalogue of Philip's "crimes and follies," including his unbridled sexuality and drunkenness, his betrayal of his friends and allies, and his destruction of Greek cities. The problem, of course, was perspective. The second-century BC historian Polybius found it difficult to sympathize with Theopompus' Greek view of Philip as a foreign, malignant force in Greek affairs and not as the founder of Macedonian greatness.

Both points of view have merit. Philip's influence on Greek affairs undeniably was largely negative. The destruction of cities such as Amphipolis, Methone, Stagira, and Olynthus is well documented. Philip was, however, first and foremost king of Macedon, and his primary concern was the welfare of Macedon, not Greece. In that regard he succeeded. During the twenty-four years of his reign, Philip transformed Macedon from a kingdom on the verge of dissolution to a unified state, ruling an empire that extended from the Danube to southern Greece. Whether his plans to extend Macedonian power into Asia were as grandiose as those carried out later by Alexander cannot be known. Nevertheless, it is clear that without Philip's legacy of a united, powerful Macedon the achievements of Alexander and his successors would have been impossible.

TRANSLATION

Saunders, A. N. W. 1975. *Demosthenes and Aeschines.* Harmondsworth, UK: Penguin.

SUGGESTED READINGS

Adcock, F. E. 1957. *The Greek and Macedonian Art of War.* Berkeley and Los Angeles: University of California Press. Clearly written introduction to Greek and Macedonian ideas of war.

Andronicos, Manolis. 1984. *Vergina: The Royal Tombs.* Trans. Louise Turner. Athens: Ekdotike Athenon. Beautifully illustrated account of the discovery of the Macedonian royal cemetery at Vergina.

Borza, Eugene N. 1990. *In the Shadow of Olympus: The Emergence of Macedon.* Princeton, NJ: Princeton University Press. Insightful history of the kingdom of Macedon from its origin to the reign of Philip II.

Cawkwell, George. 1978. *Philip of Macedon.* London: Faber & Faber. Perceptive biography of Philip from a Greek viewpoint.

Ellis, J. R. 1976. *Philip II and Macedonian Imperialism.* London: Thames and Hudson. Lucid treatment of Philip's reign from a Macedonian viewpoint.

Sealey, Raphael. 1993. *Demosthenes and His Time: A Study in Defeat.* New York: Oxford University Press. Important revisionist biography of the Athenian statesman.

11

ALEXANDER THE GREAT

Alexander the Great changed the world the Greeks knew forever, and the effects of his conquests reverberate to this day. News of recent events in Afghanistan and Iran echoes the names of places he passed through, destroyed, built, and changed, and by which he, in turn, was changed. Alexander's death in 323 BC marked the end of the Classical period. Yet, rarely has an epoch-making reign begun in such uncertainty as that of Alexander.

Philip II had transformed Macedon into the leading military power in the region, controlling an empire that stretched from the Danube River to central

Figure 11.1. In this portrait of Alexander, leonine hair adds to his ferocity. Roman marble copy after the head of an original Greek statue of about 330 BC. Inscribed "Alexandros, son of Philip of Macedon."

Greece, but his assassination on the eve of his projected invasion of Asia threatened all of his achievements with ruin. Alexander III was only twenty years old at the time of his father's death in the summer of 336 BC. Omens were later said to have forecast his rule. His mother, Olympias, even claimed to have dreamed that lightning struck her womb. Although Philip had offspring from several of his wives, Alexander was treated as his father's heir throughout Philip's reign and carefully groomed for his future role. A series of Greek tutors including Aristotle provided him with an education in Greek literature and culture. From them Alexander gained his lifelong love of Homer and his determination to equal or excel the exploits of his legendary ancestors, Heracles and Achilles.

Alexander also had practical training in kingship, governing Macedon in Philip's absence, and suppressing a Thracian rebellion. He even commanded the companion (*hetairoi*) cavalry in the decisive Battle of Chaeronea in 338 BC. Nevertheless, Alexander's succession was not assured. Olympias and his closest friends and advisers were in exile, and there were rumors implicating Olympias and him in Philip's assassination. There was also talk of other possible successors including the former king (*basileus*), Amyntas IV. Antipater, Philip's most senior commander, saved the succession for Alexander, however, by quickly presenting Alexander to the Macedonian troops at Aegae for the traditional acclamation as king.

CONSOLIDATING POWER

Alexander's personal role was never more important than in the critical first year of his reign. Philip's senior commanders urged the young king to proceed cautiously, consolidating his base in Macedon and conciliating Macedon's northern subjects and allies, even at the risk of losing influence in Greece. Not for the last time Alexander rejected the advice of the Macedonian old guard in favor of decisive action.

Greece first claimed Alexander's attention. Immediately after Philip's funeral, Alexander made a sudden and dramatic appearance there, forcing anti-Macedonian politicians at Athens and Thebes to abandon plans to exploit the confusion after Philip's assassination to free Greece. Alexander was confirmed quickly in Philip's former positions as *archōn* of Thessaly and *hēgemōn* of the Corinthian League, and Greek support for the war against Persia was reaffirmed. After returning from Greece, Alexander campaigned in the spring of 335 against the Thracians and Illyrians, thereby making clear that Philip's death would bring no easing of the Macedonian yoke.

Alexander's campaign extended as far north as the Danube. Only sketchy accounts of the course of events survive, but it is clear that his main target was the Triballi, who had humiliated Philip in 339 after his victory over the Scythians. The Triballi's attempt to hold a key pass against Alexander failed, thanks to the discipline of his Macedonian troops, who cleared a path for the wagons their enemies sent careening down the mountain in the hope of breaking their line. Triballian resistance quickly collapsed, allowing Alexander to launch an amphibious assault on an island where the Triballi had placed their women and children for safety. The other Thracian tribes submitted after a dramatic raid across the Danube into the territory of the Getae. He also concluded a treaty of friendship with a group of Gauls, the vanguard of a migration that would greatly affect southeastern Europe and Anatolia in the early Hellenistic period. Alexander completed his first major campaign by inflicting a severe defeat on his father's old enemy, the Illyrian king Cleitus. Although he received the first of his many battle wounds during the campaign, the Illyrian threat to Macedon's western frontier that had loomed over so many of his predecessors was at an end.

Alexander's long absence in the north sparked rumors of his death in Greece. Hope was mother to the fact. Demosthenes even introduced a supposed eyewitness of Alexander's death to the Athenian assembly. The Thebans revolted, besieging the city's Macedonian garrison on the Cadmeia, the acropolis of Thebes, and inviting other Greek states to join them in the struggle for freedom. Forced marches by Alexander, however, brought the Macedonian army to Thebes before the rebellion could spread, persuading Athens and Sparta to withhold their support. When the Thebans nonetheless spurned his demand for surrender, the city was stormed and sacked. Alexander ordered that Thebes' Boeotian neighbors decide the city's fate; and they, ever resentful of Thebes' past efforts to subdue them, decided that the city should be destroyed and the remaining Thebans sold into slavery. Alexander carried out the decree, sparing from destruction only Thebes' temples and the descendants and house of its illustrious poet, Pindar.

Greeks long remembered the destruction of Thebes as one of the great atrocities of their history. Alexander himself was said later to have given special consideration to personal requests by individual Thebans. For the moment, however, his calculated use of terror achieved its purpose of discouraging resistance to Macedonian rule in Greece. For the second time in a little over a year, the Corinthian League acknowledged Alexander as its hegemon and affirmed its support for his policies. Alexander, for his part, moderated the severity of his demands on the Greeks, abandoning his call for the surrender of anti-Macedonian leaders at Athens and elsewhere in Greece.

Similar ruthlessness was employed in Macedon. While Alexander won popularity among his subjects with measures such as freeing Macedonians from all personal obligations except military service, he quickly eliminated all potential rivals. Olympias had Philip II's last wife Cleopatra and her daughter Europa brutally murdered and the male members of Cleopatra's family were executed. Amyntas IV, Alexander's sole legitimate rival for the throne, who had survived throughout the whole of Philip II's reign, also was sacrificed to the new king's need for security. Their supporters fled to their only possible refuge, Persia, leaving Alexander as the unchallenged ruler of Macedon.

Invasion of Asia

With Macedon secure, Alexander invaded Asia in the spring of 334 BC. His army was fully 37,000 strong: its core was the 12,000 Macedonian phalanx troops, supplemented by 3000 hypaspists ("royal guards") and 1800 companion cavalry. It also included special light-armed units from Illyria and Thrace and almost 9000 allied Greek infantry and cavalry. A fleet of almost 200 Greek ships supported his troops and maintained his communications with Europe.

Alexander's first actions in Asia were bold, even theatrical. He was the first Macedonian to land on Asian soil, leaping ashore and casting his spear into the land to claim all that he conquered as territory won by the spear. He then went to the traditional site of Troy, where he sacrificed to Athena, asked pardon of the legendary Trojan king Priam for invading Asia, and paid homage to his supposed ancestor Achilles.

The symbolism suited the leader of the Greek crusade, but serious problems lay behind all the bravado. Alexander had been compelled to leave almost half his Macedonian troops with Antipater to control Greece and Macedon. In Asia, everything won by Philip in 336 had been lost except for the bridgehead at Abydus. Worse yet, Alexander had sufficient funds for only a brief campaign; and his friends did not control the government and army. In Macedon, Antipater governed as his regent. Moreover, Alexander's second-in-command in Asia was Parmenio, a friend of Antipater and a former ally of Cleopatra's family, whose relatives held key commands in the army's critical cavalry units. Alexander needed a quick victory to achieve the goals of his campaign and to liberate him from the control of the Macedonian aristocrats who had made him king. Fortunately, the Persians proved to be "convenient enemies."

The Battle of Granicus (334 BC)

The vast extent of the Persian Empire slowed mobilization of its main forces to confront threats on its frontiers, forcing satraps to rely on their garrison troops to cope with invasions. Satraps normally employed a defensive strategy that would deny the enemy use of local resources until the Great King could mobilize and bring the empire's main forces to bear on the invader. The Anatolian satraps, who were unwilling to risk the losses in revenue and the destruction of royal lands that such a strategy would entail, chose a bolder course, deciding to confront Alexander directly in battle in the hope of killing him.

The strategy almost worked. The Persians met Alexander at the River Granicus, the modern Koçabas, in northwest Anatolia. The details of the battle itself are disputed, but it is clear that the Persians nearly succeeded in killing Alexander, who stood out clearly in the flamboyant "armor of Achilles" that he had taken from the temple of Athena at Troy. Only the daring action of Cleitus the Black, the brother of Alexander's nurse, saved the king from certain death: At a crucial moment Cleitus sliced off the arm of a Persian noble who was about to deal a fatal blow to an already dazed Alexander.

Because the Persians had staked everything on killing Alexander, the failure of their plan brought disaster. Their army was totally destroyed. The fate of the Greek mercenaries who formed the core of the Persian army was particularly harsh. Alexander ordered the slaughter of all but two thousand of them as traitors to the

Figure 11.2. Alexander's campaign.

Greek cause. The survivors were sent to Macedonia to work in chains. Alexander boldly announced his victory to the Greek world by sending to Athens three hundred suits of Persian armor as a dedication to Athena with the inscription: "From Alexander, the son of Philip, and the Greeks, except the Spartans."

Alexander's victory at the Granicus changed the character of the war, depriving the Persians of their ability to mount an effective defense in Anatolia while fomenting rebellion in Greece. Although the Phoenician fleet freely cruised the Aegean, the Greeks as a whole refused to commit themselves to the Persian cause. Alexander's forces, meanwhile, swept south along the west coast of Anatolia. In quick succession the satrapies of Lydia, Caria, and Lycia fell. By the spring of 333, Alexander had reached Gordium, the capital of the ancient kingdom of Phrygia, near modern Ancyra in central Anatolia. In less than a year, Isocrates' once seemingly impossible dream of severing Anatolia from the Persian Empire had been realized.

Alexander's rapid conquest of Anatolia exposed the contradiction in his position as hegemon of the League of Corinth and king of Macedon. As hegemon he was required to respect the commitments he and Philip had made to the League of Corinth. Consequently, he punished captured Greek mercenaries and turned deposed pro-Persian tyrants over to the league council for trial. As king of Macedon, however, he dealt with conquered territory as he saw fit, and increasingly his interests as king overrode his obligations to the League and his concern for Greek opinion.

Greek Reaction

Alexander made his supremacy clear immediately after his victory at the Granicus. Greek and non-Greek cities that surrendered were ordered to obey their new Macedonian satrap and to pay the same tribute they had paid to the Persians. When it became clear that his previous severity had only stiffened the resolve of Greek mercenaries in Persian service to fight, he eased the terms for their surrender. Similarly, he encouraged democratic factions in the Greek cities of Asia when they offered their support to the Macedonian forces. The newly "liberated" cities, however, found that freedom had limits. They no longer paid "tribute" to the Persians, but they now made financial "contributions" to the Macedonians and were severely punished if they objected. Inscriptions from Chios and other Asian cities also document Alexander's readiness to intervene in the internal affairs of cities.

Alexander's relationships with his new non-Greek subjects was similar. Although his first Asian satraps were Macedonians, he soon began to court local support. In Caria, he entrusted the civil administration of the area to Queen Ada, who ruled as a widow like her predecessor Artemisia, who had commanded her own ships at the Battle of Salamis. Ada showed her affection and gratitude by adopting Alexander as her son and heir. Control of military affairs, however, remained in the hands of a Macedonian garrison commander responsible to Alexander. Still, the policy was clear. Non-Greek leaders who recognized Alexander could expect royal favor and promotion.

Although Isocrates had dreamed of a new greater Greece in Anatolia, the true situation was more accurately reflected in the symbolism of Alexander's dramatic severing of the "Gordian knot." According to a famous legend, rule over Asia was promised to whoever loosed the complex knot that connected the drawpole to the wagon the first Midas had ridden when he became king of Phrygia. While he was at Gordium, Alexander fulfilled the prophecy by slashing through the knot with his sword, allowing no doubt that a new king had arisen in Asia.

A severe fever that brought Alexander to the brink of death delayed the departure of the Macedonian army from Anatolia until the summer of 333. His brush with death revealed to everyone his unique importance to the expedition. Without an heir, Alexander was indispensable. Only he held the army together and gave its actions force and direction. The army's dependence on Alexander would only increase as its march carried it farther and farther away from Macedon.

The Battle of Issus (333 BC)

After his illness, Alexander made a characteristically bold decision. Instead of seeking to confront the forces of Darius III directly in Mesopotamia, Alexander moved south along the Syro-Palestinian coast toward Egypt. Behind this decision lay a risky calculation. Having disbanded his own Greek fleet, Alexander hoped to end Persian naval operations in the Aegean by depriving the Persian fleet of its bases.

The strategy was daring and almost resulted in catastrophe. Alexander marched south along the coast during the late summer and fall of 333. At the same time, Darius III led the Persian Empire's main forces northwestward from Babylon, hoping to trap Alexander in Anatolia. On learning Alexander was advancing toward Syria, Darius followed in his rear, thereby severing Alexander's communications with Anatolia and his Macedonian base. Darius, however, failed to exploit his advantage by allowing Alexander to choose to confront the Persian army at Issus, a narrow coastal plain in Cilicia. Prevented from fully deploying his forces, Darius was unable to benefit from the Persians' numerical superiority.

Callisthenes, Aristotle's nephew and the campaign's official historian, treated the Battle of Issus as a Homeric contest between Alexander and Darius III in which victory resulted from a cavalry charge led by Alexander on the center of the Persian line. Darius was forced to abandon his army and flee. A famous painting of the late fourth century BC brilliantly depicted this moment; a mosaic copy

Figure 11.3. This late Hellenistic mosaic from Pompeii is believed to be a copy of a fourth-century BC painting depicting the Battle of Issus. It demonstrates that the legend of Alexander had reached places he himself had never visited.

of this painting was discovered at Pompeii and is now preserved in the Naples Museum. The flight of Darius turned the defeat of the Persian army into a fearful rout. Years later, Ptolemy I recounted in his history of Alexander how his units had crossed streams on the piled up bodies of dead Persian soldiers.

Alexander's victory at Issus was a fundamental turning point in his campaign. The main Persian forces had been destroyed and Darius III had fled in disgrace. The royal treasure stored at Damascus quickly fell into Alexander's hands and ended the financial problems that had threatened his plans since their inception. Alexander had even captured Darius' family, including his mother, wife, daughters, and son and heir to the Persian throne.

Alexander had not merely defeated the Great King: he had humiliated him. This humiliation continued, as Alexander summarily rejected Darius' written offer of friendship and alliance in exchange for his family's return. He also accorded the Persian royal family the protection and public deference to which their former station entitled them, but which they had lost when Darius deserted them. The symbolism was clear and unambiguous: Henceforth Alexander was the arbiter of the fate of the Achaemenids. The Greeks also understood the significance of Alexander's victory. After Issus all hope of Persian aid against Macedonian rule had to be abandoned. Not surprisingly, the rest of Greece remained passive when Antipater crushed a Spartan rebellion in 331 BC.

FROM ISSUS TO EGYPT: CONQUEST OF THE EASTERN MEDITERRANEAN (332–331 BC)

While Darius fled eastward, Alexander resumed his march toward Egypt. Most of the Syrian and Phoenician coastal cities surrendered, successfully concluding Alexander's plan to defeat the Persian fleet by depriving it of its bases. The situation is less clear with regard to the interior of Syria and Palestine, but the surrender of the Samaritans in northern Judaea suggests that the peoples of these areas also quickly came to terms with Alexander.

Only Tyre and Gaza resisted Alexander, and his response was characteristically vigorous. When the Tyrians rejected Alexander's request to enter the city and sacrifice to his ancestor Heracles in the guise of their chief god Melqart, he besieged the city for almost eight months. After its capture in August 332, Tyre also suffered the same brutal fate as Thebes: slaughter of most of the male population and sale of the surviving women and children. The decision by Gaza's Persian governor, a eunuch named Batis, to maintain his loyalty to Darius resulted in a similar fate for his city two months later. The fall of Gaza gave Alexander the greatest prize of the first phase of his Asian adventure: Egypt.

Alexander in Egypt

Alexander's stay in Egypt dramatically altered his view of himself and his public image, but the conquest of Egypt itself was anticlimactic, since Mazaces, the last Persian satrap of Egypt, surrendered his satrapy without a fight.

Unlike most of the other peoples of the ancient Near East, the Egyptians had never accepted Persian rule. Severe Persian repression had followed Egyptian rebellions during the fifth and fourth centuries BC. Not surprisingly, therefore, the Egyptians welcomed Alexander's army during its march to the ancient capital of Memphis, where he held Greek-style games and sacrificed to Zeus. At the same time, Alexander also carefully avoided the errors of his Persian predecessors, publicly honoring the Apis bull, the living incarnation of Ptah, chief god of Memphis, and other Egyptian deities. Alexander doubtless accomplished much during the six months he spent in Egypt, but the sources concentrate on only two episodes: his consultation of the oracle of Zeus-Ammon and the establishment of Alexandria, the first city he founded.

The oracle of Zeus-Ammon, about 300 miles west of the Nile in the oasis of Siwah, was one of the three principal oracles patronized by the Greeks. The report of Alexander's visit to Siwah was a tale of miracle and romance. Unseasonable rains provided water, and sacred animals, such as snakes or crows, served as guides. Unfortunately, Alexander revealed neither his motives for consulting the oracle nor its reply to him. Ancient and modern historians have proposed widely differing explanations for his visit, suggesting that he desired to duplicate his legendary ancestor Heracles' visit to the oracle or to surpass the Persian king Cambyses, who had failed to conquer the oasis; or to obtain divine approval for the new city of Alexandria.

All the ancient accounts agree, however, that the decisive moment of his visit was when the chief priest of the oracle greeted him as "Son of Ammon." Through the process historians call syncretism ("the unification of religious beliefs"), Greeks equated Ammon with Zeus. The Greeks, therefore, understood that the priest had recognized Alexander as a son of Zeus. Whether or not the priest was merely according Alexander the welcome traditionally granted a king of Egypt, Alexander clearly took it as a divine sign that Olympias rightly claimed that there had been something more than mortal about his birth.

Alexander had probably selected the site for his new city during his trip to Siwah, but the actual foundation of Alexandria occurred after his return from the oracle in April 331. Strong Homeric associations probably influenced his choice of the site: Just offshore was the island of Pharos made famous by the *Odyssey*. It was also ideal for a great commercial center, with Pharos creating a sheltered anchorage and Lake Canopus linking it to the Nile and the interior of Egypt. Understandably, the sources depict Alexandria as destined for greatness, telling how birds consumed the sacred flour with which Alexander was marking its boundaries, thereby indicating that the city would nourish people from all over the world.

Founding Alexandria was Alexander's last major act in Egypt. It is difficult to assess the full significance of Alexander's conduct in Egypt, but his actions in Egypt as a whole indicate significant continuity between his policies in Egypt and those he followed in the territories conquered earlier in the campaign. This is particularly clear with regard to Alexandria, which was founded as a Greek *polis* with citizenship limited to Greeks and Macedonians. Alexander's organization of Egypt itself likewise followed the model he had used in Anatolia. Thus, although

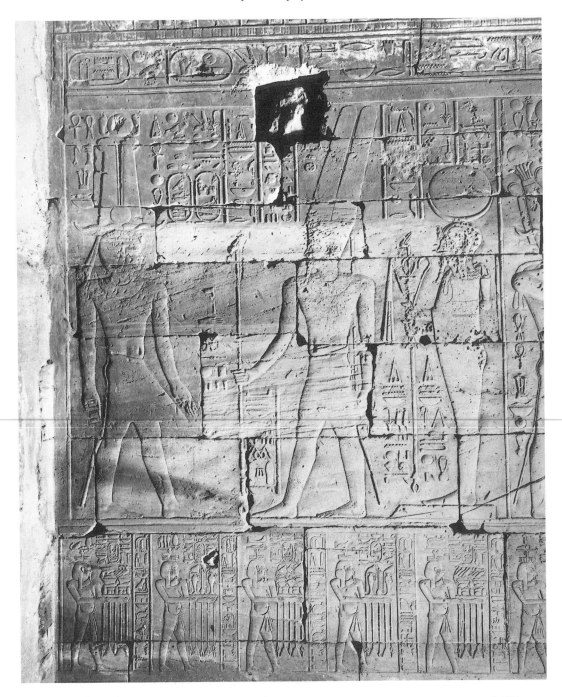

Figure 11.4. Representation of Alexander as Pharaoh before Ammon-Ra and Khonsu-Thoth in the Bark shrine at Luxor temple at Thebes. C. 330–325 BC.

he did not appoint a single satrap for all of Egypt, Alexander retained much of the Persian organization of Egypt, including the requirement that Egyptians pay tribute. Both Egyptians and Greeks exercised only civil authority. Military power remained in the hands of Macedonian officers.

Only in one area was there significant change, but that area was the most important of all: Alexander's self-image. The revelation of his divine parentage at Siwah struck a responsive chord in Alexander. It confirmed his sense of his own uniqueness and heightened his personal identification with his heroic ancestors Heracles and Achilles. Henceforth, his unshakable belief in his connection to his divine father Ammon would be the linchpin of his personality. His belief in his divine descent also opened a rift between him and the older Macedonians. They could not accept Alexander's view of his special tie to a "barbarian" god and the implied slight to Philip, the king they believed responsible for Macedonian greatness.

FROM ALEXANDRIA TO PERSEPOLIS: THE KING OF ASIA (331–330 BC)

Shortly after founding Alexandria, Alexander left Egypt to seek a final and decisive confrontation with Darius III. Darius, for his part, made one last desperate effort to avoid battle, offering Alexander marriage to his eldest daughter, cession of all territory west of the Euphrates River, and an enormous ransom for his family. Darius' offer was unprecedented. It involved division of the empire, surrender of several of its richest satrapies, and permanent exclusion of Persian power from the shores of the Mediterranean.

Parmenio probably spoke for many when he advised Alexander to accept Darius' proposal. Alexander, however, would have none of it, curtly observing that he would accept it too—if he were Parmenio! Faced with Alexander's refusal, Darius hastily gathered together another army to face the Macedonians. The two armies finally met on October 1, 331 BC, at Gaugamela in northeastern Iraq. Thanks to the capture of the Persian plans in Darius's headquarters after his defeat, the Battle of Gaugamela is the best documented battle in Greek history.

The Battle of Gaugamela (331 BC)

Learning from his defeat at Issus the previous year, Darius carefully chose a battlefield that suited the strengths and weaknesses of his army. Because his new army was particularly strong in cavalry, but weak in first-line infantry, Darius hoped that the broad plain of Gaugamela would allow the Persian cavalry to envelop Alexander's Macedonians, while terror weapons such as scythed chariots and elephants would confuse and disrupt the superior Macedonian infantry. Despite Darius' careful preparations, however, the battle of Gaugamela ended just like the battle of Issus with an attack by Alexander and the companion cavalry on the center of the Persian army. Darius fled the battlefield and sought refuge in eastern Iran. Although Alexander failed to capture Darius, the heartland of the

Persian Empire was now his for the taking. With justification, his troops saluted him as king of Asia.

Alexander captured Babylon, Susa, and Persepolis in rapid succession. His treatment of his three great prizes, however, differed. Alexander entered Babylon in triumph in mid-October, 331. As in Egypt, he sought to conciliate the influential Babylonian priesthood, offering sacrifice to Babylon's chief god Marduk and ordering the reconstruction of his temple that the Persians had destroyed a century and a half earlier as punishment for a Babylonian rebellion. He rewarded the satraps who had surrendered Babylonia and Susa by leaving them in their positions. Far different, however, was the fate of Persepolis and its citizens.

The Destruction of Persepolis

Persepolis was the spiritual center of the Persian Empire where major public rituals of Persian rule such as the new year's festival and the ceremonial presentation of their tribute to the Great King by his subjects took place. There also Greek ambassadors had abased themselves before Persian kings since the reign of Darius I. Persepolis was therefore identified with Persian rule in the eyes of Greeks

Figure 11.5. Palace of Persepolis.

and Persians alike, and its treatment would send a clear message to both peoples. The message Alexander chose to send was vengeance for the destruction wrought during the Persian wars of the early fifth century BC. Just before leaving Persepolis in April, 330 BC, the Macedonians torched the city's palaces.

A large entourage of noncombatants including slaves, women, children, and entrepreneurs of all types accompanied the army. It was said that during a drunken revel an Athenian, the courtesan Thaïs, suggested to Alexander and his friends that Persepolis be burned in revenge for the Persians' destruction of Athens in 480. Thaïs may have inspired the actual burning of Persepolis, but Alexander clearly had decided at the time of its capture that the city was to be destroyed. Despite its surrender, Persepolis suffered the same fate as Thebes and Tyre. In the twentieth century American archaeologists excavated Persepolis and the last Shah of Iran restored the site. The excavations have also revealed that its palaces were completely stripped of their treasures, the accumulated wealth of two centuries of Persian imperial rule, before they were set on fire. With the flames rising over the ruins of Persepolis, Alexander unmistakably signaled the triumphant end of the Greek crusade.

THE HIGH ROAD TO INDIA: ALEXANDER IN CENTRAL ASIA

As Alexander watched Persepolis burn, he could not know that the next four years would be the most difficult of the campaign. At first, his good fortune seemed to continue unabated. Darius had fled eastward from Media, leaving Ecbatana to fall into Alexander's hands with its treasures intact. Having secured Persia and Media, Alexander discharged his remaining Greek troops. All that remained was to capture Darius III himself and put an end to the long line of Achaemenid rulers.

The Death of Darius (330 BC)

Leaving Parmenio behind at Ecbatana to secure his communications with the west, Alexander raced after Darius. He hoped to intercept him before he could reach Bactria, modern Afghanistan, and continue resistance from there. Before Alexander could overtake the fleeing Great King, however, he learned that a cabal of eastern satraps headed by Bessus, the satrap of Bactria, had assassinated Darius III in July, 330 BC. Worse yet, Bessus had escaped to Bactria, where he had assumed the throne of Persia as Artaxerxes IV.

The assassination of Darius III changed the dynamics of the campaign. Alexander had hitherto acted in Persia as the avenger of past Persian misdeeds. It was a stance that was popular with Greeks but hardly calculated to attract Persian support. Darius' assassination allowed Alexander to escape from this dilemma by assuming the role of his successor and acting as defender of Achaemenid legitimacy against the regicides. To symbolize his new role Alexander adopted a style of dress that combined both Macedonian and Persian royal style. Darius' body was brought back to Persia and buried with full royal honors. A rumor even spread that Darius' last wish had been that Alexander avenge him.

Alexander's strategy was clever and effective. While Persian nobles and even some surviving members of the Achaemenid house joined Alexander, Bessus alienated potential supporters by failing to confront Alexander directly. As a result, resistance melted away as Alexander moved farther into eastern Iran. Finally, in the spring of 329, Bessus' fellow regicides, fearful for their own survival, betrayed Bessus to Alexander in exchange for a pardon and confirmation in their offices, just as they had betrayed Darius III before. Acting as the successor of the Achaemenids, Alexander turned Bessus over to his Persian supporters for trial and execution as a regicide.

The Struggle for Bactria and Sogdiana (330–327 BC)

As Alexander marched farther and farther east, the miraculous and romantic elements of his epic increased. It was even rumored that, like a mythical hero, he enjoyed a tryst with a mythical non-Greek woman: an Amazon queen. Unfortunately, Alexander's ignorance of conditions in eastern Iran almost cost him everything he had gained through his astute dynastic policy. Unaware of the close ties between the peoples of eastern Iran and the Scythians and the intricate network of tribal relations in the region, Alexander ignited rebellion throughout much of Sogdiana and Bactria by trying to establish a controlled border between Sogdiana and Scythia at the Jaxartes River. The revolt lasted almost three years. By the time it ended in 327, Alexander had suffered the worst military defeats of the entire campaign and developed a whole new approach to the control of conquered territory.

Alexander replaced Iranian satraps with Greek and Macedonian officials. He also settled Greek mercenaries and discharged veterans in military colonies at strategic sites in Sogdiana and Bactria. Most important, however, the crisis in central Asia starkly revealed the growing tensions in the army and even within Alexander's court itself.

Macedonian Unrest

No Greek or Macedonian army had campaigned for so long or so far away from home, and Alexander's soldiers became more reluctant to advance ever farther into Asia. Alexander had barely dissuaded his troops from going home as soon as they learned of Darius' death. The miseries of the subsequent struggles in Bactria and Sogdiana only increased their frustration and longing for home. More worrisome to his officers was Alexander's abandonment of the traditional Macedonian style of kingship and the growing prominence of Iranians and Iranian practices at court. The most dramatic example of the trend was Alexander's marriage in the spring of 327 to Roxane, the daughter of a powerful Sogdian noble.

The marriage was politically astute, since it brought Alexander the alliance of one of the principal tribal chieftains in Bactria and Sogdiana, and then, as now,

Figure 11.6. Fresco from Pompeii believed to be a Roman copy of a late fourth-century BC original depicting Alexander captivated by love of Roxane.

the support of such men was the key to controlling the area's fierce peoples. To his officers and soldiers, however, the fact remained that Alexander's queen and the potential mother of his successor was not a Macedonian or even a Greek but an Iranian! Of course, Alexander's own mother also was not Macedonian but from Epirus, and his rivals in Macedonia had tried to use his hybrid lineage as a reason to deny him the throne.

286   *A Brief History of Ancient Greece*

Alexander's unsuccessful demand for the ritual prostration known as *proskynēsis* on the part of all members of his court further increased tension at court. Ancient and modern writers have connected Alexander's desire for proskynesis and his claim to be son of Ammon, but they disagree as to his intentions. According to the historian Arrian, for example, Alexander desired that by performing ritual prostration people would recognize his divine descent from Ammon, while the biographer Plutarch, on the other hand, thought that Alexander hoped to use proskynesis as a device to dominate his eastern subjects.

Most modern scholars adopt a view similar to that of Plutarch, especially since Persians viewed proskynesis as an affirmation of the hierarchical order of society. Whatever Alexander's intentions, however, he underestimated the resistance to his plans. Greeks and Macedonians saw proskynesis as a recognition of divinity and an unwelcome reminder of past Persian arrogance. They tolerated its performance by Persians at Alexander's court, but not his effort to make them also perform it. It is not surprising, therefore, that for the first time there was open resistance to Alexander's policies and even conspiracies against his life.

The first sign of trouble appeared late in 330 and involved Parmenio's son, Philotas, the commander of the companion cavalry, who was executed for failing to inform Alexander of an alleged plot to kill him. Whether the charges against Philotas were true or not, Alexander henceforth took seriously the possibility of conspiracies against him and acted accordingly, ordering the assassination of Philotas' father Parmenio. Alexander of Lyncestis, a son-in-law of Antipater, who had been held under arrest since the beginning of the campaign, was also executed. Alexander even instituted censorship of his soldiers' and officers' correspondence.

These measures muted the rancor at court, but they did not eliminate discontent. The most dramatic incident was Alexander's drunken murder in autumn 328 of Cleitus the Black, who had saved his life at the Granicus. Cleitus' offense was criticizing Alexander's efforts to accommodate the Persians and his belittling the contribution of his officers and soldiers to his successes. More seriously, Alexander was nearly assassinated six months later by a group of his own pages, who claimed at their trial that they hoped to free the Macedonians from Alexander's growing tyranny. As with Philotas, Alexander was implacable in the face of disloyalty by members of his personal entourage. The pages were summarily tried and executed. Callisthenes, Alexander's historian and the pages' tutor, who had publicly opposed the introduction of proskynesis, was arrested and later died under mysterious circumstances.

By the summer of 327, Sogdiana and Bactria had been secured. That happy outcome, however, had required years of hard fighting and suffering and had resulted in major changes, especially in the army. Forced to cope with a mobile and resourceful enemy, Alexander reorganized his army to allow greater flexibility. In particular, he extensively recruited Iranian units to supplement his steadily dwindling supply of Macedonian and Greek troops.

Equally important changes occurred in Alexander's court. Men personally tied to Alexander, such as Perdiccas, Craterus, Lysimachus, and Ptolemy, had replaced the Macedonian "old guard." These men would play critical roles in the turbulent events that followed Alexander's death. Finally, the relationship between Alexander and his soldiers had altered in a subtle but significant way. Their loyalty remained unchallenged, but, as events in India were to demonstrate, Alexander would never again be able to count on their unquestioning obedience.

INDIA AND THE END OF THE DREAM

When Alexander entered India in the summer of 327 BC, he believed he was approaching the end of the inhabited world. For Greeks and Persians alike, India was the land of the Indus River, essentially modern Pakistan. Aristotle believed that beyond India there was only a great desert and then ocean. Although Darius I had incorporated India into the Persian Empire, Persian rule had long since ended when Alexander entered the region. He believed he would be campaigning in a land that Dionysus, Heracles, and the legendary Assyrian queen Semiramis had failed to conquer, a land where cannibals and monstrous men and animals lived, where cloth grew on trees, and ants mined gold. What Alexander actually found was almost as remarkable and at least as strange to him: a vast subcontinent occupied by a network of peoples and states, who viewed him as a new piece to be played in their complex political chess game.

As the Macedonian army descended through the Khyber Pass to the plain of the Indus River in the summer and fall of 327, it encountered some of the fiercest resistance in the campaign. Opposition ended only at Taxila, whose ruler, called

Figure 11.7. The Greek view of the inhabited world.

Taxiles, had already solicited Alexander's aid while he was still in central Asia. Taxila was one of the principal centers of Indian religious thought. There Alexander met with a group of "naked philosophers"—ascetic Indian holy men, one of whom, Calanus, even joined his expedition.

Taxiles had sought Alexander's aid against his eastern neighbors, Abisares, the ruler of Kashmir, and especially Porus, whose kingdom included all the territory between the Jhelum and Chenab rivers. When Abisares offered his submission, Alexander moved against Porus in early 326.

The Battle of the Hydaspes (326 BC)

The two armies met at the Hydaspes River, the modern Jhelum. There Alexander found that Porus had established a strong defensive position, using his infantry and his two hundred elephants to form a living wall along the east bank of the river. Solving this difficult military problem took all of Alexander's tactical skills and involved a daring secret crossing of the flooded river. In the end, the outcome was the same as that of his earlier battles: the total destruction of his enemy's forces. Much to the displeasure of Taxiles, however, Alexander spared Porus. Instead, impressed by the nobility of his defeated opponent, who asked only to be treated "like a king," Alexander restored his kingdom to Porus and even added new territories to it.

Although Alexander did not realize it at the time, the confrontation at the Hydaspes was to be his last pitched battle. As the army marched farther eastward through the Punjab, morale dropped steadily. The crisis came when Alexander reached the river Hyphasis, the modern Beas. Exhausted by the stresses of fighting and marching during the endless rains of the summer monsoon, terrified by

Figure 11.8. Silver five-shekel coin from Babylonia (c. 326–323 BC). Obverse: Alexander attacking Porus on his elephant. Reverse: Alexander holding scepter and thunderbolt, attributes of Zeus.

rumors of yet another great river valley occupied by great kingdoms possessing thousands of war elephants, and doubtful that they would ever return home, the army mutinied. This time not even Alexander could persuade his soldiers to go on. Ultimately, Alexander yielded, defeated by his own army, and agreed to return to the Indus, where he had already ordered the construction of a great fleet.

The End of the Campaign

As Alexander kept his plans to himself, ancient and modern historians have speculated about his ultimate goals. After he had defeated Darius and taken control of the Persian Empire, why did he continue to push ever eastward? Did he have a master plan for world conquest when he left Macedonia, or did his ambitions grow with each new success? Unfortunately, no definitive answer is possible. Whatever Alexander's ultimate intentions may have been, his army forced him to adopt a more modest goal: the conquest of the Indus River Valley to its mouth.

From early winter 326 to midsummer 325, Alexander's army moved steadily southward against heavy resistance. The tale of slaughter told in the ancient sources is unparalleled elsewhere in the campaign. Finally, in July 325, the army reached the mouth of the Indus. On an island near its mouth, Alexander made offerings to gods for whom his father Ammon had ordered sacrifices; then he sailed out onto the Indian Ocean to pray to Poseidon for a safe voyage to Babylonia. The preparations for the journey home had begun.

Results of the Indian Campaign

Alexander's invasion was the first major incursion into India from the west since the reign of Darius I almost two centuries earlier. Like that of Darius, Alexander's campaign produced a flood of new information about India and its peoples. Also like the Persians, the Macedonians were to remain only briefly in India. Little more than a decade after Alexander's death the Macedonian presence had disappeared from the Indian landscape and from Indian consciousness. While Greek and Indian artistic traditions mingled to produce Gandara art and to establish a stylistic vocabulary for expressing Buddhist traditions in human form, Indian culture forgot the historical Alexander and remembered only the romantic Alexander of medieval legend.

The ephemeral character of Alexander's achievements in India suggests to some historians that he lost interest in the area once his army's mutiny halted his advance to the Ganges Valley, but this is to confuse results with intentions. Alexander's political arrangements in India indicate that he intended to maintain control of his Indian conquests after his return to the west. Three Macedonian satraps supported by strong detachments of mercenary troops governed the Indus Valley. Loyal local rulers such as Taxiles retained their thrones under the supervision of one of the Macedonian satraps. Three new Greek cities were founded in the northern satrapy, and several foundations were also planned for the other satrapies. Finally, the expanded kingdom of Alexander's ally, King Porus, protected the

Figure 11.9. Indian statue of Buddha showing Greek influence.

Macedonian eastern flank. Alexander had planned carefully for his Indian do-main, but the resources available to his agents proved inadequate to maintain Macedonian rule in this remote part of his empire.

RETURN TO THE WEST

Alexander left India for Persia in late August 325. He intended to lead his army through Gedrosia, an arid region in southwestern Pakistan. His purpose was to establish supply depots for his fleet, which was to follow the time-honored route along the north coast of the Indian Ocean from the mouth of the Indus River to the Persian Gulf. Nearchus, the commander of Alexander's fleet and one of his closest friends, later claimed that Alexander, ever the competitor, was also deter-mined to surpass Semiramis and Cyrus the Great of Persia, who lost their armies in Gedrosia. For almost two months, Alexander's men struggled through the arid wastes of Gedrosia. Including the wives and children of his soldiers and camp fol-lowers, possibly as many as eighty thousand souls comprised what was virtually a moving city. Before the army finally reached Carmania and safety, thousands died, including most of the soldiers' families, who were swept away together with the bulk of their possessions in a flash flood. Only news of the safe arrival of the fleet at the head of the Persian Gulf in December 325 BC, after an adventure-filled voyage that included encounters with whales and exploration of a "haunted" island, lessened Alexander's sense of having barely escaped total disaster.

Reorganization of the Empire

Alexander's return from India sparked turmoil throughout his empire. Eight satraps and generals—both Macedonians and Iranians—were quickly deposed and executed. One of Alexander's oldest friends, the royal treasurer, Harpalus, fled to Athens with a huge fortune looted from the king's funds and a private army of six thousand mercenaries. The ancient sources argued that the upheaval was caused by the deterioration of Alexander's character. Modern admirers cite his outrage at the reports of corruption and oppression by his officials. The truth is more complex. Some victims of the king's wrath, such as the governors of the satrapies along his line of march through Gedrosia, clearly were scapegoats for a disaster that was largely of Alexander's own making. Others were victims of court politics and jealousies, but as the Roman historian Curtius Rufus (10.1.7) perceptively noted, most were guilty of the one unforgivable crime: They had assumed Alexander would not survive and had begun to exploit his empire for their own personal benefit.

Alexander's actions were not limited to punishing overly ambitious and corrupt subordinates. He also attempted to prevent similar problems in the future. All satraps were ordered to disband their mercenary forces. When roving bands of penniless cashiered soldiers threatened the security of his Asian realm, Alexander ordered the cities of Greece to permit their exiles to return home. Fully twenty thousand exiles are said to have heard Aristotle's son-in-law Nicanor read the royal decree at Olympia in the summer of 324 BC. Reintegrating them into their various cities was to cause turmoil in Greece for years to come, sparking a last desperate attempt by the Greek cities to free themselves from Macedonian rule after Alexander's death.

Uniting Greek and "Barbarian"

Almost as serious a threat to Alexander was the dismay of his veteran Macedonian troops at the changes in their relationship to their king. In the early spring of 324 Alexander celebrated the conquest of India in grand style. Decorations were distributed to officers of the army and fleet. The climax of the celebration was a grand marriage ceremony in which Alexander himself took as wives daughters of Artaxerxes III and Darius III, although he was already married to Roxane, following the precedent set by his father Philip II, who had married at least seven women from territories he had conquered. In the same ceremony ninety of Alexander's principal officers married noble Persian and Median wives. Gifts also were distributed to ten thousand of his soldiers who had followed Alexander's example and married Asian women, and the king paid their debts.

The good feelings quickly dissipated when Alexander introduced into the army thirty thousand young Iranian troops trained to fight in Macedonian style, whom he referred to as his "Successors." Their name suggested that they were eventually to replace his Macedonians. It is not surprising, therefore, that when Alexander announced at Opis in the summer of 324 that he intended to discharge and send home veterans who were too old or too ill to fight, the army mutinied. The soldiers demanded that the king discharge them all and sarcastically urged that he henceforth rely on his father Ammon. Only after Alexander reassured them that his Macedonians were his only true "companions" did the mutiny subside.

The victory of his veterans was only symbolic. Although Macedonians occupied seats of honor at a great banquet Alexander held at Opis to celebrate the end of the mutiny, he remained steadfast in carrying out his original plans. He discharged the veterans shortly thereafter and sent them back to Macedon, while retaining the children produced by their marriages to Asian women with him as the nucleus of a new generation of soldiers loyal only to himself. In the meantime, the integration of Iranian units into the army continued.

Death in Babylon

The final year of Alexander's reign was full of activity and unfulfilled plans. It began with a personal tragedy. In November 324, Hephaestion, Alexander's most intimate friend, drank himself to death. The grief-stricken king executed Hephaestion's doctor and ordered a monstrous ziggurat-like monument to Hephaestion to be built at Babylon. When he believed he had received approval from Ammon, he ordered the Greek cities to grant his dead friend heroic honors. It may also have been at this time that Alexander also demanded that the Greeks worship him as a god.

On his arrival at Babylon in the spring of 323, Alexander received delegations bearing congratulations and petitions from the Greeks and other peoples of the Mediterranean. He also began to formulate plans for his next major project, the conquest of the Arabians, who, he claimed, had not sent an embassy to honor him. But omens of his impending death were already being bruited about. In desperation, the Babylonian priests even revived the ancient substitute-king ritual: a criminal was seated on the king's throne dressed in the royal regalia, then executed in the hope of averting the doom threatening the king.

This frantic effort was to no avail. On May 29, Alexander fell ill at a party hosted by one of his officers. After suffering from fever and delirium for almost two weeks, he died on June 10, 323 BC. According to later legends, he was the victim of a plot concocted by Aristotle and Antipater, whom he had decided to replace as his regent in Europe. More likely, his body, exhausted by the strain of constant campaigning and numerous wounds, was unable to fight off a disease, possibly malaria, that he contracted while at Babylon. He was not yet thirty-three years old.

THE ACHIEVEMENTS OF ALEXANDER

Hero or villain, the world was not the same after Alexander had passed through it. From the Mediterranean to India, Eurasia had been linked together and would remain so until the end of antiquity. Alexander's plans for his empire are not known, partly because Alexander did not expect to die when he did. There is, however, a more fundamental reason. When the Roman emperor Augustus was told that at the time of his death Alexander was perplexed about what he should do next, he expressed his surprise that Alexander did not consider governing his empire a greater challenge than conquering it. Not surprisingly, his papers contained only schemes for grandiose monuments and future campaigns, not plans for the governance of his empire. He may have thought it sufficient to simply replace the top echelon of Persian administrators with Macedonians, Greeks, and native rulers loyal to him. It would be his successors who would shape the details of the new political order that would replace the Persian Empire and provide the framework for social and cultural relations in much of western Asia for the rest of antiquity.

SUGGESTED READINGS

Bosworth, A. B. 1988. *Conquest and Empire: The Reign of Alexander the Great.* Cambridge, UK: Cambridge University Press. Unsentimental and clearly written political and military history of Alexander's reign.

Engels, Donald W. 1978. *Alexander the Great and the Logistics of the Macedonian Army.* Berkeley and Los Angeles: University of California Press. A fascinating account of the practical problems of supplying Alexander's army during its long campaign.

Roisman, Joseph. 1995. *Alexander the Great: Ancient and Modern Perspectives.* Lexington, MA: D. C. Heath. Valuable collection of primary and secondary sources dealing with principal controversies concerning Alexander.

Stoneman, Richard. 1997. *Alexander the Great.* London: Routledge. Brief biography clearly describing Alexander's reign and its significance.

Wheeler, Mortimer. 1968. *Flames over Persepolis: Turning-Point in History.* New York: Reynal and Company. Illuminating survey of the archaeological evidence for Alexander's campaign.

12

THE NEW WORLD OF THE HELLENISTIC PERIOD

Alexander's conquests changed forever the world the Greeks knew. Formerly citizens of minuscule city-states on the fringes of the Persian Empire, the Greeks came to share the rule of a vast territory that stretched from the Mediterranean to India. This enormous "cosmopolis" (literally, "a city-state comprising the world") was unified only by the use of Greek as the common language of government and culture and by the creation of islands of Greek culture in settlements scattered in the region. The cosmopolis served as a huge arena for the military and political struggles of the Hellenistic period. Against this bloody backdrop, Greeks and non-Greeks tried to retain traditional values while living in a world vastly different from that of their grandparents. Although the modern world owes much to the classical *polis* and the culture it nurtured, in many respects its closest affiliation is with this new era that historians call Hellenistic.

The Hellenistic period spans the three centuries from the death of Alexander in 323 BC to the death of Cleopatra VII of Egypt in 30 BC. In many ways, the Hellenistic age anticipated the problems faced by modern imperial powers in ruling large multiethnic states. Most of the popular Hellenistic philosophies like Stoicism, Epicureanism, Cynicism, and Skepticism spoke to the needs of people who shared many of the same interests and anxieties as people today. In the arts also the repertoire of themes and styles expanded far beyond that typical of the Classical period. This was particularly true of sculpture, where the patronage of kings and rich individuals freed professional artists to break out of the Classical focus on the idealized young male to explore themes that challenged their technical skills, such as depicting with sympathy the emotions of defeated athletes, the ravages of old age, and the lives of children, women, and even non-Greeks.

THE STRUGGLE FOR THE SUCCESSION

When Alexander died suddenly in 323 BC, the Persian Empire had disappeared, but no regime had emerged to replace it. Only Alexander's charismatic personality had

Figure 12.1. This statue of an old woman is either a Hellenistic original of the third- or second-century BC or a Roman marble copy.

held his empire together. A new king had to be chosen quickly, but there was no heir. Although his wife Roxane was pregnant, only Alexander's mentally deficient half-brother Arrhidaeus survived of his family. A regency, therefore, was inevitable but who would lead it and in whose interest?

On his deathbed Alexander had given his signet ring to his chief minister, Perdiccas, and his bodyguards and the cavalry supported Perdiccas' proposal to wait for the birth of Roxane's child. The Macedonian infantry, however, mutinied and demanded that Arrhidaeus become king. Only a bizarre compromise averted civil war: If Roxane's child were male, he and Arrhidaeus would be joint kings! When Roxane gave birth to a son, he and Arrhidaeus were proclaimed kings as

Alexander IV and Philip III. Although the immediate crisis was over, events were to prove the truth of Alexander's prophecy that there would be great "funeral games" over his corpse.

For almost half a century Alexander's successors fought over his empire. Only when the last of them died in 280 BC did a new political system emerge dominated by three kingdoms, each ruled by a Macedonian dynasty: the Ptolemies in Egypt, the Seleucids in western Asia, and the Antigonids in Macedon and northern Greece. This arrangement formed the framework for political and social life in Egypt and western Asia for over two centuries and nurtured a vibrant culture that endured through later antiquity and the middle ages.

THE REGENCY OF PERDICCAS

More was at stake after Alexander's death than the selection of his successor. Decisions also had to be made concerning the goals of the new imperial government. Conquest and expansion characterized Alexander's reign, and on his deathbed Alexander was planning to invade Arabia. Perdiccas had no interest in such projects. The exhausted soldiers demanded that Alexander's final plans be abandoned. The fantastic career of conquest that had begun a decade earlier was over. The time for consolidation of Macedonian rule and enjoyment of the fruits of victory had arrived, or so the soldiers thought.

With the succession settled, Perdiccas quickly organized the regency, beginning by reallocating the satrapies of the empire. The sources anachronistically highlight the satrapies assigned to Alexander's successors: Cappadocia to Eumenes, Egypt to Ptolemy, Thrace to Lysimachus, and much of western Anatolia to Antigonus the One-Eyed. Cappadocia, however, had yet to be conquered, the corrupt usurper Cleomenes of Naucratis held Egypt, and much of Thrace had been lost in a Thracian rebellion. Perdiccas understandably needed to avoid alienating the powerful Macedonian satraps in Asia to survive, and such appointments met this need.

Perdiccas' other decisions were equally cautious. Three men were to govern the empire in the name of the kings: Antipater, Alexander's strategos in Europe; Craterus, Alexander's most prominent field commander; and, of course, Perdiccas himself. Macedonian unity was preserved, and Perdiccas' principal rivals shared the governance of the empire. Marriages of two of Antipater's daughters to Perdiccas and Craterus were to seal the alliance. Nevertheless, Perdiccas' position began to crumble almost immediately.

Revolts broke out at both the eastern and western ends of the empire. Alexander's Asian subjects had remained quiet during the crisis after his death; not so the Greeks. The Greek settlers in central Asia revolted first. Bactria was to become home to a remarkable Greek kingdom that would exert a significant influence on the cultures of central Asia and India, but that was in the future. In 323, twenty-three thousand Greek settlers mutinied and started to march home. Perdiccas responded promptly, forcing the survivors to return to Bactria. The European Greeks revolted at almost the same time.

The roots of the European uprising lay in the decree of 324 concerning the return of exiles, which threatened many Greek cities with social and political upheaval, but none more so than Athens and Aetolia. In desperation, Athens hired a mercenary army and launched the strongest naval force mobilized by the city since the Peloponnesian War. Victory initially seemed to be almost within the Greeks' grasp. Antipater was besieged in the Thessalian city of Lamia, from which the revolt gets its name, the Lamian War (323–322 BC). But then events turned against them. The Athenian fleet was decisively defeated at the Battle of Amorgos, while Macedonian reinforcements from Asia freed Antipater and helped him defeat the Greek army at Crannon in Thessaly in 322. Antipater intended that there should be no further revolts. The League of Corinth was dissolved and with it the last traces of the fiction that the Greeks were allies and not Macedonian subjects. Athens was severely punished, and the democracy was dismantled. Demosthenes committed suicide, and other democratic leaders were executed. Twelve thousand Athenians failed to qualify for citizenship and were disfranchised. Athens was again ruled by an oligarchy maintained in power by a foreign garrison.

The Death of Perdiccas

While Antipater was occupied with the Lamian War, Perdiccas was struggling to control the satraps in Asia, especially Antigonus the One-Eyed, the satrap of Phrygia, who had refused to help Eumenes take control of his satrapy of Cappadocia. To save himself, Antigonus fled to Macedon with the news that Perdiccas was planning to marry Cleopatra, Alexander's sister, despite his promise to wed one of Antipater's daughters. Antigonus' news outraged Antipater and split the regency, but Ptolemy ignited the wars of Alexander's successors by diverting Alexander's funeral cortege to Egypt. Perdiccas could not ignore so direct a challenge to his authority, but his invasion of Egypt in 321 failed when Ptolemy opened the Nile dikes, drowning thousands of Perdiccas' soldiers. Demoralized by defeat and seduced by Ptolemy's promises, Perdiccas' officers assassinated him.

The victors quickly met at Triparadeisus in Syria to reorganize the regency. Antipater replaced Perdiccas as regent for the kings, and the satrapies were reassigned yet again. Ptolemy and Lysimachus retained their satrapies, and Seleucus received Babylon as his satrapy. Eumenes was condemned to death, Antigonus the One-Eyed, appointed *strategos* in Asia, was ordered to hunt him down. Antipater himself returned to Macedon with the two kings. For the first time since Alexander had crossed into Asia over a decade earlier, a king would occupy the royal palace at Pella.

At first glance, little had changed. The empire was intact, and Philip III and Alexander IV were still joint kings. Nevertheless, appearances were deceptive. Perdiccas had failed to control the Asian satraps; and Antipater was unlikely even to try. Indeed, by taking the kings back to Macedon, he had made clear that Macedon was central in his view of the empire. The person best situated to exploit the new situation was Antigonus the One-Eyed, who controlled all royal forces and resources in Asia.

THE PRIMACY OF ANTIGONUS THE ONE-EYED

Antigonus' rise to preeminence in Asia was rapid. He quickly expelled Eumenes from Cappadocia and was on the verge of subduing him when Antipater's sudden death in 319 BC set off a new round of conflict. Antipater's son Cassander refused to accept his father's choice of Polyperchon as regent for the two kings and fled to Antigonus, precipitating the formation of a grand alliance of Antigonus, Cassander, Ptolemy, and Lysimachus against the new regent.

The struggle lasted for three years, ending with the collapse of the royal cause in both Europe and Asia and the destruction of the Argead house itself. Polyperchon enjoyed a brief period of success when Olympias joined the struggle on his side—but her passion for her grandson Alexander IV led to the murder of Philip III and his queen Eurydice and the alienation of much of the Macedonian aristocracy, which rallied to Cassander. Shortly after the death of Philip III, Olympias met a similar fate, leaving her grandson and Macedon in the hands of Cassander. Although Cassander claimed to be regent for Alexander IV, he was in reality the new ruler of Macedon. Alexander IV and Roxane were confined under house arrest in Amphipolis, never to be seen in public again.

A similar fate befell the royal cause in Asia. Although Eumenes managed to avoid defeat for three years, the end came in 316 when his own soldiers betrayed him to Antigonus, who ordered his immediate execution. As in Europe, so in Asia, a victory won in the name of the heirs of Alexander resulted instead in the usurpation of Argead rule. Antigonus quickly appointed his supporters to key satrapies. Not surprisingly, Seleucus quickly abandoned Babylon and fled to Ptolemy. Although officially only strategos in Asia for Alexander IV, Antigonus actually controlled the child-king's vast Asian territories as securely as Cassander did his European ones.

The "Freedom" of the Greeks

Antigonus' triumph was brief. In 315 his allies demanded that he share the territories that he had captured. Antigonus responded with an ultimatum of his own demanding that his rivals recognize all Greek states as free. Although these ultimatums were propaganda, Antigonus' invocation of Greek freedom was a shrewd attempt to build Greek support. Antigonus never freed the Greek cities he controlled, but he was right to believe that his proclamation would be well received in Greece. Already in 319, when Athens had rebelled, Polyperchon promised to restore democracy and freedom to the Greeks. Antigonus hoped that his proclamation would have a similar effect among Cassander's other embittered Greek subjects when he invaded Macedon. Antigonus' invasion of Macedon, however, never materialized. Ptolemy defeated Antigonus' son Demetrius at Gaza in 312 BC, and helped Seleucus return to Babylon, where he incited defections among the eastern satraps. In 311 with his southern and eastern fronts in ruins, Antigonus made peace with his former allies.

In the Peace of 311 Antigonus admitted that his attempt to gain control of all of Alexander's empire had failed. The treaty provided that Cassander would remain as strategos in Europe, Antigonus would continue as strategos over all Asia, Ptolemy and Lysimachus would retain their satrapies, and the Greek cities would be free. In return for an empty pledge to support the principle of Greek freedom, Antigonus had accepted the division of the empire as it had existed at the beginning of the war.

Antigonus' Last Gamble

The Peace of 311 was merely a truce that Antigonus and his rivals used to rebuild their strength. War resumed in 307 when Demetrius invaded Greece with a mandate "to free all the cities of Greece." Success was immediate. Demetrius liberated Athens from Cassander and restored the democracy. The next year he occupied Cyprus, seizing Salamis in the first of the epic sieges that would gain him the sobriquet Poliorcetes ("the Besieger"), and inflicted a crushing defeat on the fleet Ptolemy sent to relieve the city. Demetrius' victory transformed the political world. Alexander's successors had maintained they were only agents of the child-king Alexander IV even after his death in 310, but when the news of Demetrius' victory reached Antigonus' army in Syria, his soldiers acclaimed Demetrius and Antigonus as kings, thereby publicly admitting the end of the Argead dynasty.

Like Homer's heroes, Macedonian kings were military leaders, and it was the glory of Demetrius' victory at Salamis that justified the acclamation of his father and himself as king. Within a year Cassander, Lysimachus, Ptolemy, and Seleucus also assumed the title "King," thus affirming their independence. The struggle for control of Alexander's legacy that had been interrupted by the Peace of 311 had begun again. The end came in 301, when Lysimachus and Seleucus defeated Antigonus and Demetrius at Ipsus in central Phrygia. Antigonus was dead, trampled by Seleucus' elephants, and Demetrius was in headlong flight, their dreams of empire in ruins.

BIRTH PANGS OF THE NEW ORDER
(301–276 BC)

After his death, Antigonus' enemies divided his territories in Asia. Lysimachus received Anatolia north of the Taurus Mountains, while Seleucus added to Babylonia and Iran the coastal regions of southern Anatolia, Syria, and Mesopotamia. The division of western Asia into two huge kingdoms should have created tension along their mutual borders, and so it would have except for an unforeseen development. In 301, Ptolemy had occupied Judaea, Phoenicia, and southern Syria. To protect himself, he formed an alliance with Lysimachus that was sealed by the marriage of Lysimachus to Ptolemy's daughter Arsinoë (the future queen Arsinoë II of Egypt), and of Ptolemy's younger son, the future Ptolemy II, to Lysimachus' daughter. Seleucus responded by allying with Demetrius, the son of Antigonus the One-Eyed, who now ruled a "sea empire" comprising his father's fleet and a handful of ports in the Aegean. The renewal of war seemed imminent, but it was delayed for over a decade.

Figure 12.2. The Hellenistic world.

Tanais

ARAL SEA

Hypanis R.

COLCHIS

Phasis

CASPIAN SEA

CHORASMIA

Trapezuz

ARMENIA

Araxes R.

Lake Van

Lake Urmia

HYRCANIA

PARTHIA

amosata

Nisibis

MEDIA

Carrhae

Gaugamela

•Arbela

Tigris R.

MESOPOTAMIA

Ecbatana

Dryra Europos

Seleucids

Euphrates R.

Antiochea

Seleucia

Cunaxa

Susa

Babylon

Pasargadae

Persepolis

PERSIAN GULF

During the 290s, the kings concentrated their efforts on the development of their kingdoms. Lysimachus fought against the Getae, who lived across the Danube, while founding or reorganizing several cities in Anatolia including Ephesus. Ptolemy designed the administration of Egypt, but the most active king was Seleucus, who founded numerous cities and military settlements in Syria, including his great new capital of Antioch near the mouth of the Orontes River. As thousands of Greeks emigrated to Egypt and western Asia, the new cities grew and prospered, acquiring large populations and splendid public buildings and amenities unknown in Aegean Greece.

The Final Struggle

Demetrius Poliorcetes possessed a "kingdom" without a territorial base. In 294 he remedied that deficiency, seizing Macedon from the feuding sons of Cassander. His success, however, was brief. For Demetrius, Macedon was only a stepping-stone to Asia, but before his invasion was ready, his rivals struck. Lysimachus and Pyrrhus, the king of Epirus, invaded Macedon and forced Demetrius into prematurely launching his Asian campaign in 286. The result was inevitable. Outnumbered and ill, Demetrius surrendered to Seleucus and lived out the last few years of his life under house arrest near Antioch.

Demetrius' conquerors did not long survive him. Taking advantage of a bitter succession crisis in Thrace, Seleucus invaded Lysimachus' kingdom. The forces of the two aging monarchs—both were over eighty—met in early 281 at Corupedium (the "Field of Crows"), in Phrygia. At the end of the battle, Lysimachus lay dead on the field and Seleucus, it seemed, finally had achieved the dream that had haunted Perdiccas and Antigonus the One-Eyed and his son: the reunion of Alexander's empire. Seleucus did not long enjoy his triumph, being assassinated by an exiled son of Ptolemy, Ptolemy Ceraunus ("the Thunderbolt"). The Thunderbolt's moment of glory also passed quickly. In 279, he fell in battle, defending Macedon against Gauls, whose migration from Western Europe home had begun in the early fourth century.

The Gallic threat was brief, but it had significant consequences. The Gauls soon transferred their terror to Anatolia, but only after being defeated at Delphi and Lysimacheia by the Aetolian League (the organization of the city-states of Northwest Greece) and Antigonus Gonatas ("Knockknees"), the son of Demetrius Poliorcetes. Their victories over the Gauls transformed the position of both the Aetolians and Antigonus, legitimizing the emergence of the former as the preeminent power in central Greece and the protector of Delphi and the latter as king of Macedon. The final pieces of the new political system that had so gradually and painfully emerged from the wreckage of Alexander's empire had fallen into place.

THE POLIS IN THE HELLENISTIC WORLD

Despite the turmoil of the Hellenistic period, one aspect of Greek life remained unchanged: The polis remained the center of Greek life. Old poleis such as Athens and Ephesus prospered. War between poleis actually declined, and arbitration of disputes became routine. Even the particularism of the classical polis was partially overcome by the Aetolian and Achaean leagues, strong federations, which expanded their membership to include cities outside central Greece and the northern Peloponnesus.

Political trends that had appeared in the fourth century BC intensified in the Hellenistic period. Virtually all Greek cities now claimed to have democratic governments. The claim, however, was largely empty since democracy increasingly signified little more than that a city-state was not ruled by a tyrant. Meanwhile, the average citizen's role in government declined as aristocratic oligarchies increasingly managed affairs from behind the scenes. Wealthy men and women made generous gifts to their cities, including aqueducts, feasts, schools, and various types of charities. Numerous inscriptions documenting their generosity and public service attest to the patriotism of these new leaders as well as the poleis' need for such men and women to rescue them from recurrent financial, diplomatic, and social crises.

Athens and Sparta

Although the democracy was never fully restored, Athens flourished as the cultural center of mainland Greece. Hellenistic Athenian culture differed greatly from that of the classical city. The change is most obvious in drama, where the

Figure 12.3. This Roman bronze statuette reflects the lost statue of the *Tychē* (Fortune) of the city of Antioch by Eutychides. Here Fortune is personified as a goddess wearing a crown representing the city walls.

grand tragedies and biting political comedies of the Classical era were replaced by a lighter genre known as New Comedy. The plays of Menander (344–c. 292 BC), its most famous practitioner, reflect the new political order and the interests of its upper-class audience.

Menander had been a pupil of Theophrastus, Aristotle's successor as head of the Lyceum, and a friend of Demetrius of Phaleron, Cassander's governor of Athens. A Hellenistic critic wrote, "O Menander and O life, which one of you has imitated the other?" Menander's plays depict a Greece populated by swaggering mercenaries, impoverished citizens living next door to wealthy people, courtesans and pimps, spendthrift youths, and respectable young women whose destiny is marriage. Menander's characters are engrossed in their private worlds, as though weary of war and political upheaval.

Slaves are ubiquitous in New Comedy and in Hellenistic Athens. Constant warfare had reduced many people to slavery, while slave dealers took advantage of the practice of exposing unwanted newborns. Greeks had long used child exposure, especially of females, to limit family size. Infant exposure forms the theme of several of Menander's plots (with happier destinies for their children than those that awaited them in real life). Significantly, the chief divinity in New Comedy is Tyche ("Fortune"), a fitting emblem of this chaotic era.

The altered temper of the times manifested itself also in philosophy. Plato and Aristotle had directed their teachings to affluent men interested in the political life of the autonomous poleis. Hellenistic philosophies, however, aimed to help people cope with a vast world over which they had little control. Two of the most important schools of Hellenistic thought flowered in Athens: Stoicism and Epicureanism. Born in Cyprus, Zeno (335–263 BC), the founder of Stoicism, was a friend of Antigonus Gonatas and lived in Athens, teaching at the Stoa Poikile ("Painted Porch"). For this reason his followers received the name of Stoics (i.e., "Porchers").

Zeno's philosophy reflected the new political order. The earth stood at the center of the universe with Zeus its prime mover. Just as cosmic motions never changed and Zeus remained king of the gods, so monarchy was the divinely ordered system of government. Revolution, consequently, violated the natural organization of the world, whereas patriotism and public service harmonized with the cosmic order. Serenity could be achieved only by those confident that they had fulfilled their duties to others. Stoicism, thus, entailed a large dose of humanitarianism and public service.

Zeno urged his followers to seek an inner tranquillity that was proof not only against agonizing pain but also against excessive pleasure as well. He did not, however, advocate withdrawal from social and political life. Stoics were to uphold justice, but not to engage in any serious attempts at reform. Stoics consequently considered slaves spiritually as free as their owners, but they did not try to abolish slavery. In keeping with their belief in an orderly universe, Stoics thought life was rational and could be planned. Epicurus (341–270 BC) taught a very different philosophy in the school he established in his home in Athens called "The Garden," including women among his students. Adopting the atomic theory of Leucippus and Democritus, he rejected their determinism. Although he agreed that atoms fell in straight lines from the sky, Epicurus argued that the multiplicity of substances in the universe arose from periodic swerves in the atoms' paths, causing them to collide at a variety of angles. Like the kingdoms carved out by Alexander's successors, the universe was created by chance combinations, and would perish and regenerate by chance.

The gods had little role in this philosophy. Epicurus deduced that gods exist since people saw their images in dreams, but they had no interest in humans, living, instead, serene, untroubled lives, indifferent to prayers, offerings, and rituals. (The good news was that the horrific punishments associated with the underworld were fictions; the bad news was that the gods were not interested in listening to complaints, offering solace, or avenging injustices.) After death, the atoms that had comprised the soul and body of each person merely dissolved and recombined to form new entities.

Understandably, Epicurus viewed happiness on Earth as the purpose of life. He defined happiness as the attainment of *ataraxia*, an untroubled state free from excessive pleasure and pain, much like the serenity advocated by Zeno. Unlike Zeno, however, Epicurus advocated withdrawal from activities that might bring pain, both the quest for love or money (which Stoics also saw as problematic) and participation in politics (which Stoics praised). For Epicureans, anything that might threaten ataraxia was to be avoided. Though today "Epicurean" connotes indulgence in pleasure, particularly fine dining, Epicurus actually counseled moderation in food and drink in order to avoid indigestion and hangovers. Epicureans also approved of sex, provided love with all its pitfalls was avoided.

Despite their differences, Stoics and Epicureans shared a common goal: attaining tranquillity in a turbulent world. A similar aim characterized two other philosophical schools popular in the Hellenistic period: Cynicism and Skepticism. The principal theorist of the Cynic movement, Diogenes of Sinope (c. 400–325 BC), maintained that civilization was unnatural. Denying that humans had needs different from those of animals, Diogenes scandalized contemporaries and earned the name of the Cynic ("dog," "*kuōn*" in Greek) by brazenly maintaining that people should follow instincts just as animals do, even urinating and masturbating in public. The Skeptics also shared the Cynics' and Epicureans' disillusionment with Greek public life. Skepticism became popular around 200 BC. Stressing the impossibility of certain knowledge, Skeptics urged withdrawal from the world. The quest for truth and power, after all, was hopeless. Today, the words "skeptical" and "cynical" suggest people who are not easily persuaded. In this, Hellenistic philosophies contrast sharply with those of Plato and Aristotle, who believed that knowledge was possible and could be gained through education.

While Athens continued to attract intellectuals, the center of philosophical speculation in the Hellenistic era shifted not only away from Athens but also away from mainland Greece in general. Stoic thinkers came from places like Cyprus and Syria, while Tarsus, Alexandria, and Rhodes became the most famous Stoic university towns. Stoicism ultimately took root in the Roman Empire, fortifying the minds and souls of men and women seeking to cope with and participate in the government.

Almost as remarkable was the fate of Sparta. After a century-long decline in which the number of Spartiates dwindled to fewer than a thousand and tensions between rich and poor became acute, two reformer kings, Agis IV (262–241 BC) and Cleomenes III (235–222 BC), revived Sparta's "Lycurgan" institutions. Debts were canceled, land was redistributed, and the traditional Spartan educational system, the *agōgē*, was reestablished. Sparta briefly became the Stoic model state. The Stoic notion that individual suffering is part of some great natural scheme and should be endured attracted Spartans as did the idea that austerity was preferable to self-indulgence. For a few years, Spartan arms were invincible and the city seemed on the verge of dominating the Peloponnesus again. Greek intellectuals celebrated the Lycurgan system. Their dreams of Greek renewal were shattered when the joint forces of Macedon and the Achaean League crushed the Spartans at Sellasia in 222 BC. As the fate of Sparta revealed, not even the strongest polis could resist the power of the Macedonian kingdoms.

THE MACEDONIAN KINGDOMS

Greek literature contains little information about the organization of the new Macedonian kingdoms. Fortunately, archaeological evidence in the form of inscriptions and papyri has remedied this deficiency, revealing that the Hellenistic kingdoms were conquest states based on two fundamental principles: first, that the kingdom and its population belonged to the king; and second, that the king's business took precedence over all other considerations. These two principles were common to all the Macedonian kingdoms. Thanks to the rich papyrological evidence, however, their operation is clearest in the case of Ptolemaic Egypt.

Ptolemaic Egypt

Egypt's wealth lay primarily in its agricultural land, which, as heirs of the Pharaohs, the Ptolemies claimed to own. For practical purposes, however, the Ptolemaic

Figure 12.4. This gold octodrachm showing the deified Ptolemy II and Arsinoë II was minted by Ptolemy III (246–221 BC).

government divided Egyptian land into two categories: royal land for basic agricultural production and "released land," which was used to provide soldiers with land grants, reward government officials, and support Egypt's numerous temples. The rest of the economy was also tightly organized. Activities such as textile, papyrus, and oil production were state monopolies, intended to generate the maximum revenue for the king from fees and taxes. The system was managed by a bureaucracy headquartered in Alexandria but with agents—both Greek and Egyptian—in even the smallest village. To ensure that the king's work was done, every adult from peasant to immigrant soldier was registered according to place of residence and economic function. The king managed the whole system as an autocrat whose word was law, while the institution of a cult of the living ruler, his wife, and his ancestors legitimized royal rule while offering subjects a public means of demonstrating their loyalty and gratitude for the "benefits" provided them.

Egyptian and cuneiform texts indicate that there was continuity between Egyptian and Persian administrative practices and Hellenistic state organization. Ptolemaic Egypt and Seleucid Asia, for example, maintained many of their traditional administrative structures, together with many of their key institutions, and remained divided into their traditional subdivisions, such as nomes and satrapies. Not surprisingly, the Greek terminology of many of our sources often proves upon analysis to be a facade, hiding traditional preexisting institutions.

In Hellenistic Egypt and Asia, the temples still played major roles in the social and economic lives of their peoples. Egyptian priests used the names of the Greek gods, equated the Macedonian and Egyptian calendars, and translated royal titles into Greek in order to give a Hellenic cast to Egyptian religious traditions. This continuity is not surprising, since the Ptolemies and Seleucids were both Macedonian kings and also pharaohs and kings of Babylon, whose responsibilities had included support of traditional institutions.

Epigraphical and papyrological evidence has revealed "irrationalities" and inefficiencies in the kingdoms' operations. Ptolemaic Egypt and Seleucid Asia were personal autocracies. Official documents describe their governments as consisting of the "king, his friends" (the king's personal entourage), "and the army." Their power was restrained only by fear of losing the support of their armies and generals, who could unseat a king if provoked too far. Government officials were political appointees with often multiple and even conflicting responsibilities, who filled posts assigned them by the king irrespective of their experience and qualifications.

Instead of smoothly functioning bureaucratic machines Hellenistic governments were inefficient and often arbitrary instruments, primarily designed to extract the maximum revenue from their rulers' subjects. Documents such as the letters of Ptolemy II (282–246 BC) forbidding lawyers from assisting individuals in disputes concerning taxes bear witness to the kings' insatiable need for money to support their ambitious foreign policies and grandiose domestic projects. Similarly, the numerous royal orders forbidding government officials from exploiting the king's subjects for personal gain and amnesties for unfulfilled obligations to the government attest to the inherent inefficiency and corruption of these systems in actual practice.

HELLENISTIC SOCIETY

The new Macedonian monarchies not only posed a threat to the independence of the cities of Aegean Greece, they also created unprecedented opportunities for individual Greeks. Whatever Alexander's plans for the governance of his empire may have been, his successors clearly decided to rely on Greek immigrants to staff the upper levels of their governments.

New Opportunities in a Colonial World

The resulting opportunities were greatest for Greek men, who quickly formed a powerful class of expatriate civilian and military officials. Inscriptions and papyri document the wealth and influence of members of this new governing class, such as Apollonius, the chief financial officer of Ptolemy II, and Zenon, the Carian immigrant who managed his estate. Less glamorous, but equally real and far more numerous, were the multitude of minor, but potentially lucrative, administrative jobs required to govern the new kingdoms. The court poet Theocritus spoke the literal truth when he described Egypt as a land of opportunity for immigrants and characterized Ptolemy II as a "good paymaster."

Document 12.1. Letter of King Ptolemy II to Apollonius concerning the revenues of Egypt (259 BC).

King Ptolemy to Apollonius, greeting. Since some of the advocates listed below are intervening in fiscal cases to the detriment of the revenues, issue instructions that those advocates shall pay to the crown twice the additional tenth and that they shall no longer be allowed to serve as advocates in any matter. And if any of those who have harmed the revenues be discovered to have served as advocate in some matter, have him sent to us under guard and have his property assigned to the crown.

The Amherst Papyri (eds. B. P. Grenfell and A. S. Hunt,
Vol. 2, London, 1901, Nr. 33) translated by Stanley M. Burstein,
The Hellenistic Age from the Battle of Ipsos to the Death of Kleopatra VII.
Cambridge, UK: Cambridge University Press, 1985, pp. 121–122.

Opportunities expanded also for women, although not to the same extent. As in the case of men, they were greatest for women of wealth. Queens like Arsinoë II and Cleopatra VII of Egypt stand out in the ancient sources, but some Greek cities allowed women to hold minor public offices in return for their willingness to use their wealth for civic purposes. Some educated women even pursued careers, such as the Cynic philosopher Hipparchia and the professional musician

Polygnota of Thebes, who won honors at Delphi. More women, however, benefited from the modest changes in their rights that occurred in the colonial society of the Macedonian kingdoms, where marriage contracts and other legal documents reveal women capable of conducting their own business and seeking legal redress for their husbands' misconduct. Not surprisingly, the explosion of new opportunities and royal patronage made the Hellenistic period one of the great creative ages of Greek civilization.

Document 12.2. Marriage Contract of Heracleides and Demetria (311 BC). The improved legal position of married women in the Hellenistic period is clear in this marriage contract from Egypt. The diverse origin of Greek immigrants to Egypt is evident in the variety of ethnics among the witnesses to Heracleides' and Demetria's marriage contract.

Seventh year of the reign of Alexander, the son of Alexander, fourteenth year of the satrapy of Ptolemy, month of Dius. Marriage contract of Heracleides and Demetria. Heracleides, a free born man, takes as his lawful wife Demetria, a free born woman from Cos, from her father Leptines, from Cos, and from her mother Philotis. Demetria will bring with her clothing and ornaments worth 1,000 drachmas. Heracleides will furnish to Demetria everything that is appropriate for a free woman. We shall live together in whatever place seems best in the common opinion of Leptines and Heracleides.

If Demetria shall be detected devising something evil for the purpose of humiliating her husband Heracleides, she shall be deprived of everything she brought to the marriage. Heracleides shall declare whatever charge he may make against Demetria before three men whom both approve. Heracleides may not introduce another woman into their home to insult Demetria, nor have children from another woman, nor devise any evil toward Demetria for any reason. If Heracleides shall be detected doing any of these things and Demetria declares this before three men whom both approve, Heracleides shall return to Demetria the dowry of 1,000 drachmas which she brought, and he shall pay to her in addition 1,000 silver Alexandrian drachmas. Demetria, and those with Demetria, shall be able to exact payment, just as though there were a legal judgment from Heracleides himself, and from all of Heracleides' property on both land and sea.

This contract shall be wholly valid in every way wherever Heracleides produces it against Demetria, or Demetria and those with Demetria produce it against Heracleides, in order to exact payment. Heracleides and Demetria each have the right to preserve their contracts and to produce the contracts against each other. Witnesses: Cleon of Gela, Anticrates of Temnos, Lysis of Temnos, Dionysius of Temnos, Aristomachus of Cyrene, Aristodicus of Cos.

Elephantine Papyri (ed. O. Rubensohn, Berlin, 1907, No. 1, lines 1–18).

ALEXANDRIA AND HELLENISTIC CULTURE

Alexandria was the most famous and enduring of Alexander's foundations, and the site of his tomb. The first three Ptolemies transformed it into the foremost city of the Hellenistic world with a multiethnic population including Macedonians, Jews, Greeks, and Egyptians. The clearest symbol of Alexandria's dynamism and originality was its signature monument, the Pharos. Built by Ptolemy II, the Pharos was the first skyscraper, a 400-foot-high polygonal tower topped by a statue of Zeus Soter ("Savior") whose beacon fire guided ships to Alexandria. The Ptolemies also made Alexandria the cultural center of the Greek world. Like Alexander, Ptolemy I and his immediate successors encouraged prominent Greek scholars and scientists to come to Egypt. With the enormous wealth of Egypt at their disposal, they could afford to subsidize intellectuals, encouraging artistic and scientific work by establishing cultural institutions of a new type.

The Ptolemies' principal cultural foundation was the "Museum," so-named because of its dedication to the nine Muses, the patron goddesses of the arts. There distinguished scholars, supported by government stipends, could pursue their studies in congenial surroundings including dormitories, dining facilities, and pleasant gardens. To assist the Museum's scholars, Ptolemy I established (with the aid of Demetrius of Phalerum) a library intended to contain copies of every book written in Greek. The library's collection is said to have ultimately reached 700,000 papyrus rolls.

The Ptolemies' passion for their library was legendary. Ptolemy II supposedly sponsored the Greek translation of the Jewish Bible, the *Septuagint*, and Ptolemy III allegedly stole the official Athenian copy of the works of the three canonical tragedians. Even the books of visitors to Egypt were seized—the owner received a cheap copy—if the library lacked them. The library offered unprecedented resources for scholarly research in every field of intellectual endeavor (despite sneers at the occupants of Ptolemy's "bird coop" who were expected to earn their keep). Doctors and writers receiving government stipends served as physicians and tutors to the royal family, and celebrated its achievements. The scholar and

Figure 12.5. Tetradrachm of the Roman emperor Commodus (AD 180–192) struck at Alexandria, showing ship(s?) passing the Pharos.

poet Callimachus catalogued the library in 120 books, thereby laying the foundation for the history of Greek literature. In his poem *The Lock of Berenice* Callimachus also celebrated the transformation into a comet of a lock of hair dedicated by Berenice II in 246 BC to commemorate the beginning of the Third Syrian War. In a similar vein, Theocritus' seventeenth *Idyll* extravagantly praised the first decade of the reign of Ptolemy II, comparing the king and his sister-wife Arsinoë II to Zeus and Hera.

The work of Alexandrian intellectuals was not limited, however, to satisfying the whims of their royal patrons. Alexandrian writers made important innovations in Greek literature. In his *Idylls*, brief dialogues or monologues set in an idealized countryside, Theocritus introduced the pastoral mode into Western literature. Callimachus inaugurated the tradition of "learned" poetry in works such as his *Hymns* and *Aetia*, in which he retold in elegant verse obscure myths and the origins of strange customs and festivals collected from all over the Greek world. Callimachus' younger contemporary and rival Apollonius of Rhodes reinvigorated the old epic genre with his acute psychological portraits of Jason and Medea in his vivid retelling of the story of Jason and the Argonauts, the *Argonautica*. Euhemerus, an ambassador of Cassander to Ptolemy I, used the utopian travel romance to propound in his *Sacred Tale* the radical idea that the gods had once been great rulers worshiped after their deaths for their gifts to humanity like contemporary kings.

The Visual Arts

The visual arts reflect the combination of old and new that is a distinctive feature of the Hellenistic Age. Classical artists had perfected a limited number of artistic genres or types such as the idealized figure of an unemotional youthful nude male. This type of figure continued to be sculpted as a heroic representation of Hellenistic kings. Hellenistic art is, however, characterized by variety and experimentation, providing dramatic renderings of a cross section of humanity experiencing a variety of emotions under extreme stress as in the case of the Laocoön, where the doomed effort to escape a horrible death is captured in stone; or the Boxer, where the pathos of defeat is equally vividly depicted in bronze. Sculptors particularly delighted, however, in exploring every aspect of the female nude as illustrated by the various depictions of Aphrodite at her toilette. Sculpture thus provides strong evidence of the new focus on the individual as special and unique, rather than only a citizen of a polis.

The production of small terra-cotta figures began in the fourth century and flourished in the Hellenistic period. These mold-made figurines were relatively inexpensive and popular throughout the Greek world. They are our best evidence for the visual arts as a reflection of reality, portraying people of all ages, every social status, and a range of ethnicities, including chubby children; stooped, stout, and wrinkled elderly people; elegant and graceful society women; and members of the lower classes. Small bronze sculptures, though more expensive, also depict a broad variety of people.

a

Figure 12.6a. Laocoön (Rome). Dramatic representation of the Trojan priest Laocoön and his two sons being killed by sea serpents as punishment for advising the Trojans not to bring the Trojan horse into the city. **b.** (Facing page) Bronze Boxer (Rome). Brilliant study of an aging athlete. Cleaning has revealed that his body is covered with wounds represented by red copper inlays. **c.** (Page 314) Crouching Aphrodite (Rome). The goddess Aphrodite represented as a beautiful woman interrupted by an unseen viewer as she washes her shoulder and neck.

c

Portraiture on coins and in sculpture was also fostered by interest in the individual and in the personality. Hellenistic portraits sought not only to portray the actual features of the subject, but also to influence the viewer's perception of the character. The Ptolemies, for example, adeptly used visual imagery to gain support for their regime. Like Alexander, who encouraged belief in his own divinity and was worshiped as a god after his death, Hellenistic rulers manipulated religion to legitimize their use of absolute power. Members of the ruling dynasties were portrayed on coins and in sculpture with the attributes and epithets of gods and heroes. The political and propagandistic value of sculpture is obvious in the image of Alexander in the company of Egyptian divinities (Chapter Eleven, Figure 11.5) and in the sculpture of Arsinoë II portraying her as an Egyptian goddess. Viewers would immediately understand that Alexander and his successors were not mere mortals but incarnations of divinities, and the rightful rulers of Egypt and the Greek world.

Many monuments Hellenistic rulers commissioned are now known only through images on coins, Roman copies, and verbal descriptions. These convey a

a   b   c

Figure 12.7. Miniature Hellenistic sculptures. **a.** Terra-cotta figurine of old nurse and child. Late fourth century BC. **b.** Terra-cotta figurine of schoolgirl reading papyrus roll. **c.** Bronze statuette of black youth in craftsman's garb. Third to second century BC.

vivid impression of the wealth and power of the monarchs and proud cities who constructed them. Artists traveled wherever such patrons beckoned. Bravura characterizes many major Hellenistic sculptures such as the Victory (Nikē) of Samothrace dedicated by the Rhodians to commemorate their victories over Antiochus III of Syria (222–187 BC). Victory is portrayed alighting on the prow of a ship. Her wet and windblown dress reveals the contours of her body, while the cloth, flaring out behind the goddess, illustrates the drama and restlessness characteristic not only of the art but also of Hellenistic life. Her raised wings also suggest that her presence is not necessarily permanent. Like the goddess Tychē (Fortune), Victory can be fickle.

The visual arts also reveal nostalgia for a safer and more secure past. Portraits of philosophers, poets, and other historical figures decorated public areas and private enclosed spaces such as libraries (cf. Demosthenes, Chapter Ten, Figure 10.4). Some authors were even worshiped as divine. For example, portrait busts

Figure 12.8. Limestone statue of Arsinoë II in Egyptian style. A hieroglyphic inscription on the back pillar of Arsinoë's portrait indicates that the figure was dedicated not long after her death and deification in 270 BC. Her corn curls were painted black, and the face and parts of the body were originally gilded. The full, curved lips, highly arched brows, and large, wide-open eyes are depicted in the Egyptian style, but the queen carries a double cornucopia, an attribute of Greek goddesses referring to their powers of fertility.

Figure 12.9. (Facing page) Victory (Nike) of Samothrace. The colossal statue known as the Winged Victory dates from around 200 BC. Louvre Museum, Paris.

of Homer (about whose appearance nothing was known) were common, no doubt because the *Iliad* was the most widely read book in the Greek world and was used as a text in school. Nevertheless, despite the reverence for the past, the visual arts allowed Hellenistic Greeks no doubt that the world had changed drastically since the days of Achilles and the bards who first recited his exploits in regular lines of verse.

Figure 12.10. This sculpted relief of the Apotheosis of Homer by Archelaus of Priene, found in Bovillae, Italy, dates from around 221–205 BC. The deified poet, seated at the lower left, holding a scroll and scepter, is crowned by Calliope (the Muse of epic poetry). The other figures include Zeus and Mnemosyne (Memory), as well as their daughters, the Muses. The sculpture was probably made for a poet who was victorious in a competition at Alexandria.

Scholarship and Science

Hellenistic intellectuals also made fundamental contributions in the areas of literary scholarship and applied science. Callimachus and philologists such as Zenodotus and Aristarchus founded the critical study of Greek language and literature, preparing texts of Homer and other poets that are the ancestors of those we still use. The mathematician and geographer Eratosthenes established the principles of scientific cartography, and produced a strikingly accurate estimate of the circumference of the earth. The physicist Ctesibius pioneered the study of ballistics and the use of compressed air as a source of power, while other scientists experimented with the use of steam to operate simple machines. More mundanely, an unknown Ptolemaic technician invented the *saqqiyah*, an animal-powered water wheel still used today in Egypt and the Sudan.

The doctors Herophilus and Erasistratus made fundamental discoveries concerning the anatomy and functions of the human nervous, optical, reproductive, and digestive systems by dissecting corpses, and even vivisecting criminals provided by the government for the "advancement of science." The Hippocratic Oath also dates to the Hellenistic period and enjoins physicians to promise to respect their teachers and to hand on their knowledge only to their teachers' sons and apprentices. Doctors are to swear to abstain from harming any person and to refrain from practicing abortion and euthanasia and from divulging what patients tell them in confidence. Since there was no licensing of physicians in antiquity and many conflicting medical doctrines and views of the physician's ethical role, the oath was by no means universally adhered to by Greek physicians, as is obvious from medical texts that discuss abortion, and from the use of vivisection. Royal patronage did, however, have a drawback. Areas that did not receive royal largess tended to stagnate. Thus, apart from the *Elements* and *Optics* of the mathematician Euclid, the Alexandrian contribution to the theoretical sciences and philosophy, which were of limited interest to the Ptolemies, was undistinguished.

SOCIAL RELATIONS IN THE HELLENISTIC WORLD

Greek cultural preeminence tends to obscure the fact that Greeks were a minority in the Hellenistic world, even in cities like Alexandria and Antioch. Not surprisingly, therefore, historians differ in their interpretations of relations between immigrant Greeks and the native populations, some seeing the Hellenistic cities as "melting pots" in which Greek and non-Greek cultures and peoples blended into a new cosmopolitan civilization, and others as capitals of segregated societies in which social status and privilege were determined primarily by ethnicity and in which the ethnicities that counted were Macedonian and Greek. A considerable degree of social and cultural segregation was, of course, inherent in the demography of the Hellenistic kingdoms because of the predominantly urban character of Greek settlement. Studies of Egyptian villages have revealed an almost total absence of either Greek residents or Greek influence on daily life.

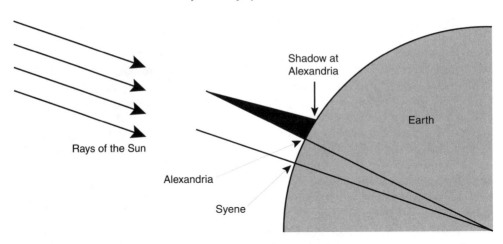

Figure 12.11. Eratosthenes' Calculation of the Circumference of the Earth. Eratosthenes measured at Alexandria the shadow cast by a pointer at noon of the summer solstice when the sun was directly overhead at Aswan. By applying two simple geometric theorems—the angles of similar triangles are equal and equal angles sweep out equal arcs—he concluded that the 5000 stade distance between Alexandria and Aswan represented 1/50 of a sphere with a circumference of approximately 250,000 stades, a little over 30,000 miles (assuming a stade equaled 8 1/3 miles).

Segregation was not limited, however, to the countryside. Non-Greeks were not citizens of the Hellenistic cities and lived in separate residential quarters. Greeks, Egyptians, and Jews even used separate legal systems in Egypt. Ethnic prejudices and tensions are also well documented by papyrological evidence. Theocritus characterizes petty street crime as "an Egyptian game," and an agricultural worker complains of being treated with contempt "because I am a barbarian." Prophecies of the end of Macedonian rule are common in both Hellenistic Egyptian and Jewish literature, and Hellenistic history is replete with rebellions intended to achieve that goal.

The Place of Non-Greeks

Nevertheless, the picture of the Hellenistic kingdoms as totally segregated societies distorts ancient reality. Greek translations of Egyptian literature prove that at least some Greeks were interested in contemporary Egyptian culture. More important, the native populations of the Hellenistic kingdoms were not united in their reaction to Macedonian rule.

As in the past, the security of the Hellenistic kingdoms depended on the support of the local gods and their priesthoods. Although the Ptolemies strictly supervised the temples of Egypt, they also generously subsidized them and their priests, as is illustrated by the extensive temple building they sponsored. Study of the Egyptian evidence for Hellenistic Egypt is only in its infancy, but papyri document the prosperity of priestly families, which acquired large estates and

Figure 12.12. The Rosetta Stone. 27 March 196 BC. Fragment of a black granite stele found at the Rosetta mouth of the Nile containing a trilingual (Greek, Hieroglyphic [Middle Egyptian], and Demotic [vernacular late Egyptian]) inscription recording a decree passed by a synod of the priests of Egypt commemorating the coronation of Ptolemy V (204–180 BC) as king of Egypt.

spent large sums on lavish tomb furnishings and dedications to the gods. Their prosperity also provided the basis for a vigorous revival of Egyptian culture, resulting in a variety of new literary and artistic works that are only now being studied and appreciated. It is not surprising, therefore, that Egyptian priests congratulated Ptolemy V for suppressing a native rebellion that threatened them as much as him.

Opportunity was not limited to the religious elite. Village officials also prospered by exploiting their role as intermediaries between the Greek-speaking central government and its Egyptian subjects. Not surprisingly, priests and local officials both were singled out for reprisal during native uprisings. Similar patterns of royal patronage of temples and priestly prosperity characterize Seleucid Asia, where the Seleucid monarchs subsidized Babylonian temples and the temple of Yahweh at Jerusalem and received the loyal support of their respective priesthoods.

Social and cultural factors also moderated ethnic segregation in the Hellenistic kingdoms, especially demography. Although the Ptolemies encouraged Greek immigration with generous rewards including grants of land, the actual extent of immigration was limited and mostly male in character since most immigrants were soldiers. The number of ethnic Greeks in the Hellenistic East was, therefore, probably small and intermarriage was not uncommon so that over time Greeks assimilated somewhat to the social and cultural mores of their non-Greek neighbors. This was particularly true in the area of religion, since Greeks, like other polytheists, were already predisposed to honor the gods of countries in which they lived.

Hellenistic Religion

Greek religion underwent a profound change in the Hellenistic kingdoms. Paganism and polytheism were flexible, nondogmatic religious systems, open to new divinities and to the reshaping of old ones with the result that the powers of the old Olympian gods were often redefined, since they could no longer be conceived as defending Greeks against non-Greeks. In Egypt, for example, Ptolemy I ordered the creation of a new god to serve as Alexandria's new patron deity. The new god, Sarapis, was a synthesis of Egyptian and Greek elements, combining aspects of Hades, Dionysus, Zeus, and Osiris. Outside Alexandria, Greeks worshiped traditional Egyptian gods such as Isis and Osiris, aided by the traditional Greek practice of identifying their own gods with those of other peoples (syncretism).

In the process Egyptian gods also changed. Practices alien to Greek religious traditions, such as animal worship or mummification, were purged from the new Hellenized cults, while the Egyptian gods assimilated to the Greek gods with whom they were identified. Isis, for example, was originally the wife of Osiris and mother of Horus in the charter myth of the Egyptian monarchy, but through her identification with Aphrodite, Demeter, and Athena, she assumed a character unprecedented in Egyptian tradition: queen of the universe, benefactress of all people, and creator of civilization. Thus accommodation between Greek and non-Greek culture occurred.

⌸⌸

Document 12.3. The Praises of Isis (first century BC or first century AD). The Hellenization of Egyptian religion is evident in this inscription from the city of Cyme in northwest Anatolia with its universalization of Isis' power and identifications of Greek and Egyptian gods (Hephaestus: Ptah, the creator god of Memphis; Hermes: Thoth, god of wisdom and inventor of writing; and Cronus: Geb, god of the earth and father of the royal gods of Egypt).

Demetrius, the son of Artemidorus, who is also called Thraseas, a Magnesian from Magnesia on the Maeander, an offering in fulfillment of a vow to Isis. He transcribed the following from the stele in Memphis which stands by the temple of Hephaestus.

I am Isis, the tyrant of every land; and I was educated by Hermes, and together with Hermes I invented letters, both the hieroglyphic and the demotic, in order that the same script should not be used to write everything. I imposed laws on people, and the laws which I laid down no one may change.

I am the eldest daughter of Cronus. I am the wife and sister of King Osiris. I am she who discovered the cultivation of grain for people. I am she who is called goddess by women. By me the city of Bubastis was built. I separated Earth from sky. I designated the paths of the stars. The sun and the moon's course I laid out. I invented navigation.

I caused the just to be strong. Woman and man I brought together. For woman I determined that in the tenth month she shall deliver a baby into the light. I ordained that parents be cherished by their children. For parents who are cruelly treated I imposed retribution. Together with my brother Osiris I stopped cannibalism.

I revealed initiations to people. I taught people to honor the images of the gods. I established precincts for the gods. The governments of tyrants I suppressed. I stopped murders. I compelled women to be loved by men. I caused the just to be stronger than gold and silver. I ordained that the true be considered beautiful. I invented marriage contracts. Languages I assigned to Greeks and barbarians. I caused the honorable and the shameful to be distinguished by Nature. I caused nothing to be more fearful than an oath. Anyone who unjustly plotted against others I gave into the hands of his victim. On those who commit unjust acts I imposed retribution. I ordained that suppliants be pitied. I honor those who justly defend themselves. With me the just prevails.

I am mistress of rivers and winds and the sea. No one becomes famous without my knowledge. I am the mistress of war. I am the mistress of the thunderbolt. I calm and stir up the sea. I am in the rays of the sun. I sit beside the course of the sun. Whatever I decide, this also is accomplished. For me everything is right. I free those who are in bonds. I am the mistress of sailing. The navigable I make unnavigable whenever I choose. I established the boundaries of cities.

I am she who is called Thesmophoros. The island from the depths I brought up into the light. I conquer Fate. Fate heeds me. Hail Egypt who reared me.

Inscriptiones Graecae 12.14; translated by Stanley M. Burstein,
The Hellenistic Age from the Battle of Ipsos to the Death of Kleopatra VII.
Cambridge: Cambridge University Press, 1985, p. 147.

Over time the lack of rigid barriers between Greek and local societies resulted in situations in which many individuals, who are referred to as "Greeks" in Hellenistic sources, were not so much persons of Greek birth as of Greek culture—people, that is, who had received a Greek education, adopted a Greek lifestyle (and frequently a Greek name), and worshiped their old gods under Greek names.

Likewise, many "Greek cities" in the Near East were simply renamed local settlements with citizen bodies composed of such acculturated non-Greeks. Some Jews sought to transform Jerusalem into such a Greek polis in the early second century BC, but other Jews led by the Maccabees vigorously opposed them. The conflict escalated when Antiochus IV forbade the Jews to carry on their traditional religious practices, and in 167 BC had the temple of Yahweh rededicated to Zeus. The festival of Chanukah commemorates the Maccabees' triumph over Antiochus and his supporters. The books of First and Second Maccabees in the *Apocrypha* illuminate the Hellenistic world from the viewpoint of a subject people and reveal that the mass of the population of the Hellenistic kingdoms rejected Hellenization.

Macedonian rule in Egypt and western Asia lasted for almost three centuries. Scholars evaluate its significance differently, some emphasizing the spread of Greek culture in the region and others viewing it as a transitory period of colonial rule in which Greek culture was little more than a veneer with limited influence. Not surprisingly, the truth is more complex. Hellenization did occur, but primarily in the major urban centers of the region. Likewise, native traditions endured and even flourished, but their vigor was short-lived, surviving often exclusively among women. Education, culture, and elite status had always been closely connected in the region. The privileged position enjoyed by Greek culture, however, severed that link, encouraging native aristocrats to abandon their traditional cultures and Hellenize. The establishment of the Macedonian kingdoms, therefore, marked the beginning of the end of the ancient civilizations of Egypt and the ancient Near East.

SUGGESTED READINGS

Lewis, Naphtali. 1986. *Greeks in Ptolemaic Egypt.* Oxford: Clarendon Press. Account of life in Ptolemaic Egypt as reflected in the careers of eight Greeks and Egyptians.

Momigliano, Arnaldo. 1975. *Alien Wisdom: The Limits of Hellenization*. Cambridge, UK: Cambridge University Press. Pioneering study of cultural interaction in the Hellenistic period.

Pollitt, J. J. 1986. *Art in the Hellenistic Age*. Cambridge, UK: Cambridge University Press. Standard treatment of Hellenistic Art.

Pomeroy, Sarah B. 1984, 1989. *Women in Hellenistic Egypt: From Alexander to Cleopatra*. New York: Schocken Books (1984); with a new foreword and addenda, Detroit: Wayne State University Press (1990). Wide-ranging survey of the social, economic, and legal status of women in Ptolemaic Egypt.

Shipley, Graham. 2000. *The Greek World after Alexander: 323–30 BC*. London: Routledge. Comprehensive account of all aspects of Hellenistic history with full discussion of sources and contemporary scholarship.

Walbank, F. W. 1992. *The Hellenistic World*, Rev. ed. Cambridge, MA: Harvard University Press. Lucid brief history of the Hellenistic kingdoms from their foundation until the Roman conquest.

EPILOGUE

In many ways the early third century BC was the climax of ancient Greek history. Macedonian power and Greek culture reigned supreme in western Asia. New Greek cities were founded throughout the region, and a person could travel almost to India speaking only Greek. The heyday of the Hellenistic kingdoms, however, was brief, as their survival itself was called into question shortly after their founding.

The Seleucids' kingdom proved the most vulnerable. From Antioch the Seleucids struggled to maintain control of the Asian territories of Alexander's empire. Seleucus I (311–281) gave up his claims to Alexander's conquests in India to Chandra Gupta (c. 324–300), the founder of the Maurya dynasty, who had already conquered northern India. Further territorial losses followed in the third century BC. While Seleucus' successors fought over the royal succession, enemies attacked their western and eastern frontiers. In the west, the Attalids of Pergamum seized control of much of Anatolia; in the east, the Parthians (Iranian-speaking nomads) and rebellious Greek settlers carved out kingdoms for themselves in eastern Iran and Bactria.

The Ptolemies' hold on Egypt was more secure. Not until 170 BC did an enemy succeed in breaching Egypt's defenses. Nevertheless, Ptolemaic authority in Egypt also weakened significantly in the third century BC. Native rule was reestablished in southern Egypt in the last decades of the century, while succession crises sapped the dynasty's strength. By 200 BC, the Ptolemies ruled only Lower and Middle Egypt. With the total collapse of the Hellenistic state system in sight, Antiochus III (223–187 BC) and Ptolemy V (204–180 BC) launched vigorous counteroffensives that seemingly restored their dynasties' authority. Before the Seleucids and Ptolemies could fully consolidate their power, however, disaster struck in the form of the Romans. Roman expansion into the eastern Mediterranean was so dramatic and unexpected that the historian Polybius could justifiably ask the deceptively simple question: How could anyone not be interested in knowing how the Romans overthrew the world created by Alexander in less than half a century?

Although Roman relations with Egypt dated to the 270s BC, Rome first intervened in the political life of the eastern Mediterranean in the 190s BC, defeating

Philip V of Macedon and Antiochus III. The Romans did not annex any territory after their victories, preferring instead to pose as the defender of Greek freedom. The Senate's refusal to brook potential rivals to Roman preeminence in the region, however, effectively undermined all the Hellenistic kingdoms. By the mid-second century, Macedon had been transformed into a Roman province. Meanwhile, the Seleucids, weakened by dynastic rivalry and subversion often abetted by Rome, were locked in a losing struggle with the Parthians. This struggle gradually reduced their kingdom to a few cities in Syria that Rome finally occupied in 63 BC. The Ptolemies survived their Seleucid rivals by a generation, but only because the Senate could not agree on which senator would take credit for the annexation of Egypt. That debate ended in 31 BC, when Octavian defeated Antony and Cleopatra VII at Actium in northwest Greece. With their suicides in 30 BC the long succession of Alexander's successors finally ended.

In the end, Rome and Parthia turned out to be the ultimate heirs of Alexander's legacy, having extinguished the kingdoms of his successors. The demise of the Hellenistic state system did not mark the end of Greek civilization, but it did change its character and role. In the eastern portions of Alexander's empire, Greek civilization gradually disappeared. Macedonian and Greek rulers were responsible for the flowering of Greek culture in the Hellenistic East, and their patronage ended with the disappearance of their kingdoms. Deprived of political support, Greek culture withered as the new Parthian rulers of the Middle East sought to rally support from the non-Greek elites of their territory by favoring local traditions. In the west, however, Greek culture flourished thanks to Roman support.

Although the Roman conquest of the eastern Mediterranean was marked by brutality that belied the promise of "freedom" the Romans had made to the Greeks in 196 BC after the defeat of Philip V, it was not the whole story. The Romans were no strangers to Greek culture. Greek influence on Roman culture dated from the beginnings of Roman history and continued long after Greece had become merely a minor province of the Roman Empire. Not surprisingly, Greek

Figure Epilogue 1. Coin portrait of Cleopatra VII, who ruled Egypt from 51 to 30 BC.

literature and art were familiar to many upper-class Romans. Some senators, like Fabius Pictor (c. 220 BC), the father of Roman history, even wrote books in Greek. By the first century BC Roman culture was saturated with Greek influence. Rome's gods and myths had been recast in terms of Greek mythology. Latin writers constantly echoed their Greek predecessors, so that a work like Virgil's *Aeneid*, Rome's national epic, has to be read against the background of the *Iliad* and the *Odyssey* to be fully appreciated. Virgil's contemporary, Horace, was only recognizing reality when he wrote that "Greece, though a captive, captured her fierce conqueror, and brought the arts to rustic Latium" (*Epistles* 2.1).

Because of the Hellenization of the Roman upper class, the Romans made the support of Greeks and Greek culture the linchpin of their rule of the eastern Mediterranean. Greeks enjoyed privileged status, and Greek cities provided the framework for Roman provincial administration.

The result was a remarkable renaissance in the cultural life of the Greek cities during the first two centuries AD. Evidence of this renaissance is visible in the ruins of the splendid public buildings that everywhere in the eastern Mediterranean dominate the remains of Greek cities and the honorary statues that nowadays crowd our museums. Greek writers, such as the historian Appian and the orator Aelius Aristides, celebrated the benefits of the *Pax Romana* ("Roman Peace"). Science and philosophy also flourished. Galen's medical works and Ptolemy's syntheses of astronomy and geography remained authoritative for more than a millennium. The Egyptian-born Neo-Platonist Plotinus created the last great philosophical system of antiquity, a philosophical mysticism—loosely based on the works of Plato— that was Christianity's most formidable intellectual rival. Only in one area of Greek life was there no renaissance: the civic and political culture of the Greek cities themselves. Instead, during these same two centuries, the last vestiges of the *polis* tradition of self-government disappeared. As the moralist and biographer Plutarch candidly observed, "Nowadays, when the affairs of the cities no longer include leadership in wars or the overthrowing of tyrannies or acts of alliances, what opening for a conspicuous and brilliant public career could a young man find?" Plutarch answered his own question by pointing out that "there remain the public lawsuits, and embassies to the Emperor" (*Precepts of Statecraft* 805a–b; Fowler). Not surprisingly, men such as Arrian, who was governor of Cappadocia under the emperor Hadrian (117–138 AD) and a historian of Alexander, abandoned their *poleis*, and found rewarding careers in the service of Rome.

While Greeks and Greek culture prospered under Roman rule, the same was not true of the non-Greek cultures of Egypt and the Near East. Roman patronage heightened the value of Greek culture and Roman citizenship. Non-Greek cultural traditions and institutions were not repressed, but they were devalued. In the second century AD the Syrian writer Lucian expressed the cultural priorities of the new regime in his autobiographical essay *The Dream*, stating that without a Greek education a man could only be an "artisan and commoner, always envying the prominent and fawning on the man who was able to speak," while the educated man was "honored and praised, in good repute among the best people, well regarded by those who are preeminent in wealth and breeding . . . and considered worthy of public office and precedence" (*The Dream* 9–11). Lucian's calculation was correct. His Greek education and literary skill brought him fame and a lucrative post on the staff of the Prefect of Egypt.

Some peoples, such as the Jews, resisted the assimilatory pressures of Roman imperial society, sometimes violently. Others found in the new Christian church opportunities for the satisfaction of the ambitions of their elites. Increasing numbers of non-Greeks, however, followed Lucian's example, especially after 212 AD when the emperor Caracalla erased the legal barriers between Greeks and non-Greeks by conferring Roman citizenship on virtually all inhabitants of the empire.

The process of assimilation was not always free of friction. Complaints of Greek prejudice and cultural chauvinism are frequent in the writings of Hellenized non-Greeks such as, for example, the Hellenized Syrian rhetorician Tatian, who urged Greeks not to despise non-Greeks and their ideas since most Greek practices "took their origin from barbarian ways" (*Address to the Greeks* 1.1). Nevertheless, by late antiquity a significant portion of the social and intellectual elite of the eastern provinces of the Roman Empire consisted of Hellenized non-Greeks. The local languages of the region survived in the vernacular speech of the urban lower classes and the countryside and even found new written expression in the literatures of Syriac and Coptic Christianity. But the traditional cultures of Egypt and the Near East died, as the native elites that had patronized them for millennia gradually deserted them. Meanwhile, the dominant strand in the intellectual life of the eastern Mediterranean basin became what scholars call Hellenism, essentially a cosmopolitan form of Greek culture loosely based on Classical Greek literature. In this form Greek culture continued to flourish in the lands conquered by Alexander the Great and influenced the medieval civilizations of Byzantium and Islam and through them the culture of western Europe and the Americas.

TRANSLATION

Fowler, Harold N. 1936. *Plutarch's Moralia*. Vol. X. Loeb Classical Library. Cambridge, MA and London: Harvard University Press.

GLOSSARY

acropolis—Literally, the "upper city," the citadel of a city or town. Many citadel hills had been the sites of Mycenaean palaces and remained as special places in *polis* life. The most famous is the Acropolis of Athens, the religious center of the city, which was magnificently adorned with temples in the fifth century.

agora—In Homer, the term for the "place of gathering," the assembly of the people. In the city-state period it denoted the public space of a city or town, being both the marketplace and civic center. Lingering in the agora was the best way to inform oneself about public affairs, make business contacts, and collect gossip.

Amphictyonic Council—The governing body of an ancient league of Delphi's neighbors, the Delphic Amphictyony, that administered the oracle. It also conducted the Pythian games and dealt with transgressions against the oracle and its territory. The members were *ethnē*, of which the most important were the Thessalians, Phocians, Boeotians, Dorians, and Ionians. Votes were unequally divided among the members, so that Philip II's acquisition of the twelve Thessalian and two Phocian votes gave him a majority of the council's twenty-two votes and control of the Amphictyony.

archon—A common title (meaning "leader") for the highest ranking magistrate in the early city-states. During the Classical period, even when the *strategoi* had become the most important officials in Athens, nine archons continued to be chosen (by lot) to serve judicial and administrative functions.

aristocracy—The term *aristokratia* ("power in the hands of the best men") was coined, probably in the fifth century, possibly to describe the rule of the elite in preference to the less noble-sounding *oligarchia*. Aristocratic power and exclusiveness were strongest in the early Archaic period and gradually weakened as strong democratic sentiments emerged in the city-states.

331

assembly—One of the two primary elements of Greek governance (see boule). From the Dark Age on it was made up of the adult males of the community. In the Dark Age, the assembly (called *agora* in Homer) had limited power vis-à-vis the chiefs, although its concurrence was crucial. By the Classical period it had become the deciding body of state policy. In Athens, the assembly or *ekklesia* met in the open air on the hill called the Pnyx about forty times a year.

barbaros—Term for all people who were not Greek in language and culture, so that the highly civilized and generally admired Egyptians and Persians were *barbaroi*. Increasingly from the fifth century on, however, barbaroi came to be stigmatized as the inferior "others," lacking the mental and moral capabilities that belonged naturally to Hellenes.

basileus—The term for the legitimate monarch, the "king." In Mycenaean society, the title *pasireu* denoted a village or district adminstator; in the Dark Age *basileis* were the warrior-chiefs who ruled the villages and districts. The hierarchy of basileis was replaced in the Archaic Age by oligarchies of landed aristocrats.

boule—Term for the "council," which was one of the two primary governing institutions of the Greeks (see "assembly"). Composed of the chiefs and other influential men in the Dark Age, it became the major organ of aristocratic power in the Archaic Age. In Classical Athens, the *boulē* consisted of five hundred men chosen by lot; it prepared business for the assembly and also tried certain court cases.

cella—The inner shrine of a temple. A gold and ivory statue of Athena, over 38 feet high and now lost, stood in the cella of the Parthenon.

city-state—See polis.

currency, Athenian—Units of Athenian currency included the obol, the drachma, the mina, and the talent. Six obols made a drachma; one hundred drachmas made a mina; and sixty minas added up to a talent. In fifth-century Athens, a silver drachma coin was considered good pay for a day's labor by an unskilled worker and was probably a living wage for a small family. A drachma was the standard daily pay for a rower in the fleet. Maintaining a trireme cost a talent a month.

demagogos—Literally, a "leader of the people." Term used by some Athenians to categorize democratic politicians, particularly after Pericles' death. Usually it had negative connotations and suggested that such a man was self-interested, unlike a true statesman, who cared for the welfare of the state.

democracy—A form of government in Classical Greece that permitted all free male citizens some degree of participation in politics, regardless of wealth or family background. Despite ideologies of equality, economic inequalities prevailed and generally brought political inequalities with them. Athens encouraged democratic governments in its allies.

demos—A territory and the people who live in it; thus, "the land" and "the people." It occurs in the Linear B tablets in the form *damo*, meaning, possibly, a village community and its free inhabitants. Although always retaining its official meaning of "the (whole) people," aristocrats increasingly used it as an exclusive term for the "commoners," or the "masses."

dicasteries (dikasteria)—Democratic courts at Athens. A dicasterion was composed of hundreds of adult male citizens chosen by lot from those belonging to the pool of jurors known as the heliaia (q.v.). Both the last-minute element of the choice and the large size of the juries discouraged bribery, especially since Athenian court cases had to be decided in a single day and there was no appeal from its decisions. Beginning around the middle of the fifth century, jurors received a small amount of pay for their services.

dokimasia—The scrutiny Athenian citizens had to undergo before assuming a position in the government. Political enemies often used this procedure as a means of keeping a man out of public office.

drachma—See currency, Athenian.

ekklesia—See assembly.

ephor (*ephoros*)—"Overseer," an office found in Sparta and in other Dorian states. In Sparta a board of five ephors was elected annually by the assembly; the senior ephor gave his name to the year. The ephors had great power in the Spartan state, including general control over the kings' conduct.

epikleros—A brotherless Athenian girl compelled to marry her nearest male relative to produce a son to inherit her father's property. Although often translated "heiress," the epikleros could not herself inherit but only transmit property.

ethnos—Term for a group of people who shared a common identity and territory, but were not politically united, preferring local self-government. From the sixth century BC on, Greek *ethnē* acted as unified states by forming federations of local and regional segments of the *ethnos*. By the fourth century, ethnic confederacies and leagues played a prominent role in the geopolitics of Greece.

genos—A category of families claiming descent from a single male ancestor. A *genos* was led by its most prominent family and played a prominent part as a political group in the Archaic Age. In the Classical period *genos* membership continued to confer social prestige on their constituent families.

gerousia—The "council of elders" (from *geron* "old man"). Term used at Sparta and in other *poleis* for the aristocratic council. The Spartan *gerousia* consisted of the two kings plus twenty-eight men over age sixty who served for life.

graphe paranomon—Athenian procedure used from the late fifth century BC to indict a man for making an illegal proposal in the assembly. Since there was no Athenian constitution and illegality was difficult to determine, the procedure was usually used as a form of political attack. Those convicted were generally fined; three convictions barred a citizen from making further proposals.

guest-friendship (*xenia*)—A form of ritual friendship, whereby a "stranger" (*xenos*) entered into a hereditary relationship of mutual friendship with a man from another *demos*, each obliged to offer hospitality and aid when they visited each other's community. A prominent feature of Homeric society, *xenia* continued throughout antiquity, eventually becoming the more formal diplomatic relationship of proxeny.

hegemon—A state or individual who headed an organization of states. Athens, for example, was the hegemon of the Delian League, Sparta of the Peloponnesian League. A hegemon was said to exercise hegemony, hence the period of Theban ascendancy in the 360s BC is known as the Theban hegemony.

hektemoroi—A term used in Solonian Athens meaning "sixth-parters," referring, presumably, to poor farmers who had fallen into debt to wealthy landowners and had to hand over to them a sixth of their produce under penalty of enslavement for their debt.

heliaia—The body of prospective jurors from which dikasteria (q.v.) were selected. Any adult male citizen might present himself for participation.

Hellenes—Greek name for themselves. They had a myth of an eponymous ancestor, Hellen, who was the son of Deucalion, the Greek Noah, and the father of the eponymous ancestors of the Dorians, Ionians, and Aeolians. The common name (and the supporting myth) probably arose relatively late, perhaps in the eighth century BC.

helots—Term for groups of conquered people in Greece forced by their conquerors to work as serfs on their former lands. It is most commonly associated with Sparta, where helots probably outnumbered citizens by a ratio of seven to one. The Spartan way of life both depended on and was formed by the state's ownership of thousands of helots in Laconia and Messenia. Fear of helot uprisings often discouraged Sparta from engaging in distant campaigns.

hetaira—Term meaning literally "female companion" and normally used for courtesans in Classical Athens. *Hetairai* usually came from the metic class. Often more cultivated than citizen women, they were trained to be entertaining and interesting rather than to be thrifty managers of households. Since Pericles' citizenship laws of 451–450 made it impossible for a man to marry a metic woman, many Athenian men formed long-term associations with hetairai simultaneously with their legal marriages to Athenian women. Although some hetairai functioned as entrenched mistresses or even common-law wives, others were essentially prostitutes.

hetaireiai—The military systems of some cities such as those in Crete grouped men in *hetaireiai* or "bands of companions," but the word is most commonly associated with hetaireiai or social clubs with political overtones, often of an anti-democratic nature in Athens. The mutilation of the herms in 415 was allegedly the work of such a hetaireia, and hetaireiai probably played a part in the oligarchic revolutions of 411 and 404.

hetairos—"Companion" or "comrade." In the Dark Age, follower-bands of *hetairoi* formed the military and political support of the chiefs who recruited and rewarded them. For associations of hetairoi for in the city-states, see *hetaireiai*. In Macedonia, the hetairoi were an elite band of warriors and advisors who formed the retinue and personal bodyguard of the kings.

hoplite—*Hoplitēs.* The heavily armored infantryman, named from his distinctive shield (*hoplon*). Hoplites were the dominant military arm from the seventh century on, gradually undergoing changes in weaponry and tactics. Because Greek governments did not issue arms to their soldiers, hoplites tended to come from the middle class, men able to afford armor and swords.

kleros—An allotment of farmland sufficient to support a citizen-family; it was passed on in perpetuity in the male line. In oligarchic states, full citizenship was frequently tied to the possession of a certain amount of land.

kore—"Maiden." Term for the life-size or larger marble Archaic statues of clothed females, made as cult offerings or grave markers. The term *kouros* ("youth") is used of the corresponding nude male statues.

liturgies—An indirect system of taxation at Athens whereby the rich were required to use their own money to finance public services such as the training of a chorus for dramatic performances or sending a delegation to a religious festival in another state. The trierarchy was the most expensive, requiring a man to maintain a trireme for a year and to equip and train its crew.

megaron—A large rectangular building that served as the focal point of Mycenaean palaces. Its function as the "great hall" of the ruler continued in the reign of the Dark Age chiefs. In the city-states the ancient *megaron* achieved immortality as the basic plan of the Greek temple.

metics—Resident aliens in a Greek state. We know most about metics in Athens. Although they lacked citizenship, metics mingled comfortably in Athenian society and were called on for help in wartime, but they were not permitted to own property or represent themselves in court.

metropolis—"Mother-city." Term for a *polis* that founded a colony. The relationship between the mother-city and the new *polis* was normally very close, combining economic, political, and spiritual ties.

mina—See currency, Athenian.

myth—All cultures possess myths, traditional tales that treat aspects of life that are important to the collective group (e.g., marriage, initiation, food, cultural institutions, human-divine relations, etc.). The Greeks knew many such orally transmitted stories going back to the second millennium BC and continually enriched by additions from the mythologies of the Near East. Greek historians depended on myths to reconstruct the preliterate past. Modern researchers attempt to glean from them historical or psychological realities.

nomos—Custom or law. Sometimes it corresponds to the English word "mores," connoting a way of doing things that is deeply embedded in a value system. It can also be used, however, in a legal context; thus, for example, the rules laid down by Solon were called his *nomoi*.

nomothetai—Athenian officials set up after the restoration of the democracy in 403 BC. The *nomothetai* reviewed and ratified the laws of Athens.

obol—See currency, Athenian.

oikist—The *oikistēs* (note the root of *oikos*) was the "founder" and the leader of a colony sent out by a mother-city (*mētropolis*). The *oikistēs* had great authority in the new settlement and was often deified after his death.

oikos—"Household." The fundamental social and economic unit in Greek society, comprehending the family group, its house, land, animals, and property, including slaves.

oligarchy—*Oligarchia* ("rule by a few men") replaced the system of ranked chieftains as the standard form of government in the early city-states. Opposition from below the narrow ruling circle caused most oligarchies to broaden inclusion in state affairs. Democratic *poleis* were subject to oligarchic revolutions, as in Athens in 411 and again in 404 BC. Throughout the fifth and fourth centuries, tension between oligarchs and democrats—which often added up to tension between rich and poor—was a constant factor in Greek political life and sometimes erupted in bloodshed.

paramount—An anthropological term referring to the highest ranking leader of a community or group. The major warrior-heroes of the Homeric epics, who rule over other leaders as a "first among equals," represent the paramount chiefs who ruled during the tenth to eighth century BC.

pediment—The elongated triangular spaces that sat on top of the columns on the front and back of Greek temples. They were frequently adorned with elaborate relief sculpture.

peltasts—Lightly armed Greek soldiers who carried light throwing spears and small, round shields. They were deployed as skirmishers either alone or in concert with hoplites. Although used during the Peloponnesian War, their importance increased dramatically in the fourth century.

pentakosiomedimnoi—The highest of the four property classes in the Solonic system. To qualify for membership, the *pentakosiomedimnoi* or "500-measure men" each needed an estate that produced at least 500 *medimnoi* (bushels) of produce in any combination of oil, wine, or grain.

perioikoi—"Those who dwell about," the term used for neighboring peoples subordinate to a dominating *polis*. The chief example is Sparta, which treated the people of the perioecic communities of Laconia and Messenia as half-citizens, who possessed local autonomy and were obligated to military service but had no say in the conduct of policy.

phalanx—The tactical formation of a hoplite army, consisting in the Archaic and Classical periods of ranks of heavy infantry, usually eight deep. The phalanx introduced by Philip II of Macedon consisted of six brigades of fifteen hundred men each. Each phalangite was armed with a short sword, a small round shield, and a long pike (*sarissa*) up to 18 feet long, and they fought in rectangular formations sixteen men deep.

phratry—A subdivision of the tribe (*phylē*) and, theoretically, a kin group. In Classical times phratries were well-defined social groups concerned with defining descent and, therefore, citizenship. Every citizen family in Athens belonged to a phratry.

phylai—"Tribes." The term for the large descent groups into which a *dēmos* was divided. Ionian communities had four such "tribes," Dorian communities three. The tribes functioned as organizational units in the city-states. In his reform of the Athenian government, Cleisthenes bypassed the four traditional tribes and divided Attica politically and militarily into ten new *phylai*.

polemarch—The office of *polemarchos* ("war leader") was common to many early city-states. As army commander for a specified term, usually a year, and subject to the policy of the aristocratic council, the polemarch was limited in his power. Circa 500 BC, the military functions of the Athenian polemarch were transferred to the board of ten *strategoi* (see strategos). After 487 BC, when the polemarch became appointed by lot, his functions became mainly legal and ceremonial.

polis—"City," "town." From the eighth century on, *polis* designated a political community, composed of a principal city or town and its surrounding countryside, which together formed a self-governing entity, the "city-state." The small polis was the principal form of Greek community, numbering in the high hundreds by the fifth century BC.

probouleutic—The term for the council's (*boulē's*) function of preparing state business for consideration in the assembly.

probouloi—In Athens, a committee of ten older men that was set up to direct the government in 413 BC. The establishment of the *probouloi* resulted from the shock engendered by the disaster in Sicily.

proskynesis—Greek name for the Persian ritual greeting offered by social inferiors to their superiors and by all Persians to the Persian king. In its simplest form, *proskynēsis* involved merely blowing a kiss. Proskynesis to the Persian king, however, required full prostration before the ruler. Although Persians did not believe that their king was divine, Greeks and Macedonians considered proskynesis appropriate only to deities and resented attempts to make them perform it.

proxeny—The term used for a diplomatic arrangement whereby citizens in one state, called *proxenoi*, looked after the interests of other states in their communities. The *proxenos* was highly honored by the foreign state he represented. The system of proxeny (*proxenia*) developed from an earlier system of *xenia* or private "guest-friendship" (q.v.).

prytanis—One of the titles for the presiding magistrate (or a college of magistrates) in a city-state. In the reorganization of the Athenian *boulē* (508 BC), ten boards of fifty *prytaneis* each, chosen by lot from the ten new "tribes" (*phylai*), took turns as the officials in charge of the daily business of the *boulē* and *ekklēsia* for a tenth of the year. Each group of fifty men comprised a prytany.

redistributive system—The term for the kind of economic and political arrangements found in the Bronze Age kingdoms of the Near East and Greece, where most of the agricultural and manufactured production of a region was controlled from the center (the king and his palace), which redistributed the resources as it saw fit. In the Greek city-states, by contrast, the government exercised only limited control over production and distribution. See liturgies.

rhetores—The men who chose to involve themselves intensively in Athenian politics during the fourth century, proposing decrees and making speeches in the assembly. It is often translated "politicians."

Satrap—Title of the governors of the principal territorial subdivisions of the Persian Empire, then of Alexander III's empire, and later of the Seleucid kingdom.

satrapy—Originally a province of the Persian Empire. Alexander III retained the satrapal system of the Persian Empire as the administrative framework of his empire. After the division of Antigonus the One-Eyed's empire in 301 BC, the term was used to designate the largest territorial subdivisions of the Seleucid kingdom.

sophists—Itinerant intellectuals who taught and gave speeches during the latter part of the fifth century BC. Some were primarily teachers of oratory, while others engaged in thoughtful speculation about society that challenged entrenched conventions. Plato made the discrediting of the sophists an important part of his dialogues, accusing them of substituting showy rhetorical displays for real wisdom such as Socrates possessed.

stasis—The term first for a group of men who take the same "stand" in a political dispute—a faction—and then by extension the act itself of taking sides. In the city-states *stasis* (civil strife) occurred between oligarchical factions and between the rich and the poor. At its worst, stasis entailed bloodshed; thus containing it within nonviolent bounds was a principal objective of the city-states.

stele—A stone slab inscribed with a text, a decoration, or both. Stelae could be used to indicate graves, military victories, or property boundaries. Important texts such as legal decrees and treaties might also be inscribed on them.

strategos—The common term for a "military leader." In Athens, after 487, the ten strategoi were the only elected high officials; thus most influential fifth-century politicians were strategoi. In the early Hellenistic era, *stratēgos* (general) was the title of the highest-ranking Macedonian military commander in Europe and Asia. The four attested strategoi of this period were Antipater, Polyperchon, and Cassander in Europe and Antigonus the One-Eyed in Asia.

symposion—In Archaic and later periods the after-dinner "drinking party," made up of a small number (between fourteen and thirty) of men, was a frequent event in adult male social life, primarily among the elite. The *symposion* was an important bonding ritual among young aristocrats and (like the *hetaireiai*, q.v.) was often the occasion of factional plotting. Meaning "drinking together," it is the origin of the English word symposium.

synedrion—A representative council such as that of the Second Athenian Confederacy or the Corinthian League. The *synedrion* of the Second Athenian Confederacy was composed of a single representative from each member state and ruled the confederacy jointly with the Athenian assembly; policy decisions had to be ratified by both bodies. The synedrion of the Corinthian League consisted of representatives of the member cities and *ethnē* of the League. The latter synedrion was responsible for upholding the Common Peace that established the Corinthian League and was empowered to arbitrate disputes among its members and to try individuals accused of betraying its goals.

synoecism (*synoikismos*)—The term used for the process whereby several separate communities were formed into a single political union. Synoecism also referred to the actual movement of people from several communities into a new composite settlement.

talent—See currency, Athenian.

thes—The term for a free man who was forced by his poverty to hire out as a laborer for wages. In Athens, according to the economic divisions attributed to Solon (c. 600 BC), the *thētes* (plural) formed the lowest class of citizens.

tholos (plural tholoi)—A type of monumental above-ground stone tomb (shaped like a beehive) favored by the elites of the Late Bronze Age. In the Classical period, circular structures, also called *tholoi*, served as temples and public buildings.

trireme—Term for the standard form of Greek warship (*trieres*) in the Classical period. Propelled by three banks of oars, and attaining speeds of nine knots, the trireme used its bronze ram to disable enemy ships.

tyranny (*tyrannis*)—The illegal seizure and control of governmental power in a *polis* by a single strong man, the "tyrant" (*tyrannos*). Tyranny occurred as a phase in many city-states during the Archaic period, and is often seen as an intermediate stage between narrow oligarchy and more democratic forms of polity. In the late fifth and the fourth century, a new kind of tyrant, the military dictator, arose, especially in Sicily.

wanax—"Lord," "master." The title of the monarchical ruler of a Mycenaean kingdom. In the form *anax* it appears as the title of gods and high-ranking chiefs in Homer.

xenia—See guest-friendship.

ART AND ILLUSTRATION CREDITS

i   Papyrus roll containing speech of Hyperides. London, The British Library, Papyrus 115, cols. 27–34. Photo: Library. Reprinted by permission of The British Library.

ii   Cup depicting lessons in music and reading, Douris painter, Athens. From H.D. Amos & A.G.P. Lang, *These Were the Greeks* (Chester Springs: Dufour Editions, Inc., 1982), p. 162, Fig. 15.1. Reprinted by permission of the Staatliche Musseen Preussischer Kulturbesitz, Berlin.

1.1a   Plan of the Minoan palace at Knossos. From Raimond Higgins, *The Archaeology of Minoan Crete* (London: The Bodley Head, 1973), p. 41.

1.1b   Plan of the Mycenaean palace at Pylos. From Donald Preziosi and Louise A. Hitchcock, *Aegean Art and Architecture* (New York: Oxford University Press, 2000), p. 157, Fig. 97. Reprinted by permission of publisher.

1.1c   View of the ruins of the Minoan palace at Phaistos. Photo: The J. Allan Cash Photo Library, London.

1.2   Fresco of a fisherman from Thera. Athens, National Archaeological Museum. Photo: Bildarchiv Preussischer Kulturbesitz, Berlin.

1.3a   Inlaid dagger. Athens, National Archaeological Museum. Photo: Hirmer Fotoarchiv, Munich.

1.3b   Plan and cross section of the Kato Phournos *tholos* tomb, Mycenae. Photo: British School, Athens.

1.3c   Interior vault of a *tholos* tomb, Mycenae. Photo: Hirmer Fotoarchiv, Munich.

1.3d   Gold mask from shaft graves, Mycenae. Athens, National Archaeological Museum. Photo: Foto Marburg/Art Resource, New York.

1.4b   The *megaron* hall at Pylos. Photo: Alison Franz.

1.4c   "The Lion Gate." Photo: Bildarchiv Preussischer Kulturbesitz, Berlin.

1.5a   Linear B tablet from Pylos. From Donald Preziosi and Louise A. Hitchcock, *Aegean Art and Architecture* (New York: Oxford University Press, 2000), p. 158, Fig. 98. Reprinted by permission of publisher.

1.5b   Linear B tablet from the Mycenaean-ruled Knossos. From Donald Preziosi and Louise A. Hitchcock, *Aegean Art and Architecture* (New York: Oxford University Press, 2000), p. 158, Fig. 99. Reprinted by permission of publisher.

1.6a   Statue of goddess figure from Knossos. Herakleion, Crete, Archaeological Museum. Photo: Foto Marburg/Art Resource, New York.

1.6b Gold ring from Knossos. Herakleion, Crete, Archaeological Museum. Photo: Hirmer Fotoarchiv, Munich.

1.6c Scene on a gold ring from Late Bronze Age Mycenae. From Donald Preziosi and Louise A. Hitchcock, *Aegean Art and Architecture* (New York: Oxford University Press, 2000), p. 139, Fig. 87. Reprinted by permission of publisher.

1.7a Bronze plate armor and boar's tusk helmet. Nauplion Museum. Photo: German Archaeological Institute, Athens.

1.7b Vase showing line of soldiers on the march, Mycenae. Athens, The National Archaeological Museum. Photo: Archaeological Receipts Fund (TAP).

2.1a Submycenaean vase. Athens, Kerameikos Museum K2616. Photo: German Archaeological Institute, Athens.

2.1b Late Protogeometric vase. Athens, Kerameikos Museum K576. Photo: German Archaeological Institute, Athens.

2.2a Reconstruction of chief's house at Lefkandi. Hugh Sackett, The British School at Athens. Photo: The British School at Athens.

2.2b/c "Village chieftain's house" at Nichoria. From William A. McDonald et al., *Excavations at Nichoria in Southwest Greece: Vol. III, Dark Age and Byzantine Occupation* (Minneapolis: University of Minnesota Press, 1983), pp. 36–37, Figs. 2-22 and 2-23. Reprinted by permission of publisher.

2.2a "Ordinary" Dark Age house. From William A. McDonald, *Progress into the Past: The Rediscovery of Mycenaean Civilization*, rev. ed. (Bloomington: Indiana University Press, 1990), p. 368, fig. 103. Reprinted by permission of publisher.

2.3a Gold jewelry from the tomb of a rich Athenian Woman. Athens, Agora Museum. Photo: American School of Classical Studies at Athens.

2.3b Terra-cotta chest with five model granaries. From Anthony M. Snodgrass, *Archaic Greece: The Age of Experiment* (London: J.M. Dent and Sons, Ltd., 1980), Fig. 1. Reprinted by permission of the American School of Classical Studies at Athens.

2.4a Graffiti on eighth-century vases. Transcriptions: L. H. Jeffery, LSAG in J. N. Coldstream, *Geometric Greece* (Huntingdon, England: A&C Black Publishers Ltd., 1977), p. 298. Reprinted by permission of publisher.

2.4b Late Geometric vase from the Dipylon cemetery. Athens, National Archaeological Museum NM192. Photo: German Archaeological Institute, Athens.

2.5a Geometric krater from Athens. Paris, Louvre. Photo: Herve Lewandowski, Réunion des Musées Nationaux/ Art Resource, New York.

2.5b Large Late Geometric grave amphora from the Dipylon cemetery. Athens, National Archaeological Museum 804. Photo: German Archaeological Institute, Athens.

2.5c A detail of Figure 2.5b. Athens, National Museum. Photo: German Archaeological Institute, Athens.

2.6 Bronze statuette of man and centaur. New York, The Metropolitan Museum of Art 17.190.2072. Gift of J. Pierpont Morgan, 1917. Photo: Museum.

3.2 Corinthian vase with depiction of a hoplite battle. Rome, National Museum of the Villa Giulia. Photo: Hirmer Fotoarchiv, Munich.

3.3a Athenian amphora. Boston, The Museum of Fine Arts 01.8037. Henry Lillie Pierce Fund. Photo: Museum.

3.3b A *symposion* scene on an Athenian red-figure calyx krater. Munich, Staatliche Antikensammlungen und Glyptothek. Photo: Museum.

3.4 Statue of an Egyptian nobleman. Boston, The Museum of Fine Arts 07.494. James Fund Purchase and Contribution, August 8, 1907. Photo: Museum.

3.5   Marble *kouros*. New York, The Metropolitan Museum of Art 32.11.1. Fletcher Fund, 1932. Photo: Museum.

3.6   Marble *kouros*. Athens, National Archaeological Museum NM3938. Photo: Museum.

3.7   Kore of Euthydicos. Athens, Acropolis Museum. Photo: Bridgeman-Giraudon/Art Resource, New York.

3.8   Relief sculpture depicting the battle of the Gods and the Giants. Delphi, Archeological Museum. Photo: Nimatallah/Art Resource, New York.

3.9   The *agora* in the Archaic period, c. 500 BC. After J. Travlos 1974. Used with permission of the American School of Classical Studies at Athens, Agora Excavations.

4.2   Bronze statuette of a running girl. London, The British Museum. Photo: Museum, courtesy of trustees.

4.3   Hilaire Germain Edgar Degas' "Young Spartans." London, The National Gallery. Photo: Museum, courtesy of trustees.

5.1   Water jar from Athens depicting women at a fountain house (*Hydria*) by the Priam Painter. The Toledo Museum of Art 1961.23. Photo: Museum.

5.2   *Tetradrachm*, Athens. New York, American Numismatic Society 1957.172.1033. Photo: Society.

5.3   Detail of Attic red-figure *psykter*. New York, The Metropolitan Museum of Art 1989.281.69. Gift of Norbert Schimmel Trust, 1989. Photo: Museum.

5.4   Statues of the tyrannicides Harmodius and Aristogiton. Naples, National Museum. Photo: Hirmer Fotoarchiv, Munich.

5.6   Delegations bringing tribute to Persepolis. Photo: Barbara Grunewald © Bildarchiv Preussischer Kulturbesitz, Berlin.

5.8   Herm of Themistocles. Ostia, Archaeological Museum. Photo: Antike Porträts © Bildarchiv Preussischer Kulturbesitz, Berlin.

5.9   *Ostraka* discovered in the Athenian agora. Agora Excavations. Photo: American School of Classical Studies at Athens.

5.10 Reconstruction of the Athenian trireme of the Classical period. Photo: Paul Lipke/Trireme Trust, Montague, Mass.

6.1   Section of Athenian Tribute List incription. Athens, Epigraphic Museum. Photo: Museum.

6.3   Bronze charioteer. Delphi Museum. Photo: Foto Marburg/Art Resource, New York.

6.4   Roman copy of *diskobolos*. Rome, National Museum. Photo: Hirmer Fotoarchiv, Munich.

6.5a Reconstructions of the east pediment of the temple of Zeus at Olympia. From Bernard Ashmole, *Architect and Sculptor in Classical Greece* (London: Phaidon Press, 1972), p. 25.

6.5b Seer from east pediment. Olympia Museum. Photo: Museum.

6.6   Marble relief depicting girl with doves. New York, The Metropolitan Museum of Art 27.45. Fletcher Fund, 1927. Photo: Museum.

6.7   Attic vase c. 470 BC. Boston, The Museum of Fine Arts 63.1246 Ca. 470. William Francis Warden Fund. Photo: Museum.

6.8   Attic black-figure vase depicting crafts people at work. Boston, The Museum of Fine Arts, 01.8035. Henry Lillie Pierce Fund. Photo: Museum.

6.9   Detail of Attic red-figure wedding bowl by the Washing Painter. Munich, Staatliche Antikensammlungen und Glyptothek. Photo: Museum.

6.10 Black-figure vase, attributed to the Amasis Painter. New York, The Metropolitan Museum of Art 31.11.10. Fletcher Fund, 1931. Photo: Museum.

7.2 Model of Periclean Acropolis. Toronto, The Royal Ontario Museum 956.118. Photo: Museum.

7.3 The Doric and Ionic orders. From John Boardman, ed., *The Oxford History of Classical Art* (New York: Oxford University Press, 1997). Reprinted by permission of publisher.

7.4 Ground plan of the Parthenon. From John Boardman, ed., *The Oxford History of Classical Art* (New York: Oxford University Press, 1997). Reprinted by permission of publisher.

7.5 The Parthenon today. Photo: Werner Forman Archive/Art Resource, New York.

7.6 Parthenon east frieze, slab V. London, British Museum. Photo: Foto Marburg/Art Resource, New York.

7.7 Ground plan of Erechtheion. From J. Travlos, *Pictorial Dictionary of Ancient Athens* (New York: Praeger Publishers), 1971, pp. 216–217. Reprinted by permission of Greenwood Publishing Group, Inc.

7.8 Erechtheion, Athens Acropolis. Photo: The J. Allen Cash Photo Library, London.

7.9 Red-figure vase depicting man courting adolescent boy. Oxford, The Ashmolean Museum 1967.304. Photo: Museum.

8.2 Herm of Pericles by Cresilas. Photo: © Bildarchiv Preussischer Kulturbesitz, Berlin.

8.4 Bronze shield with graffiti. Agora Excavations. Photo: American School of Classical Studies at Athens.

8.5 Coin struck by Tissapherenes. New York, American Numismatic Society 1967.152.462. Photo: Society.

9.1 Bust of Socrates by Lysippus. Paris, Louvre. Photo: Bridgeman-Giraudon/Art Resource, New York.

9.2 Decree of Aristoteles. Athens, Epigraphic Museum. Photo: Museum.

9.3 Bust of Plato, Roman copy. Paris, Louvre. Photo: Erich Lessing/Art Resource, New York.

9.4 Hellenistic bust of Aristotle. Paris, Louvre. Photo: Herve Lewandowski, Réunion des Musées Nationaux/Art Resource, New York.

10.2a Silver tetradrachm of Philip II (Obverse: Zeus; Reverse: Mounted Macedonian king). Oxford, The Ashmolean Museum, Plate 28, No. 512. Photo: Museum, Heberden Coin Room.

10.2b Silver tetradrachm of Philip II (Obverse: Zeus; Reverse: jockey commemorating victory of Philip's horse at Olympia). Oxford, The Ashmolean Museum, Plate 28, No. 513. Photo: Museum, Heberden Coin Room.

10.3 The Macedonian Phalanx. From Arther Ferrill, *The Origins of War: From the Stone Age to Alexander the Great* (New York: Thames and Hudson, 1985), p. 177. Reprinted by permission of publisher.

10.4 Polyeuctus' portrait of Demosthenes. Copenhagen, Ny Carlsberg Glyptotek, cat. 436a, IN 2782. Photo: Glyptotek.

10.5 Burial monument at Chaeronea. Photo: SEF/Art Resource, New York.

11.1 Portrait of Alexander as hero-king. Paris, Louvre Museum. Photo: Giraudon/Art Resource, New York.

11.3 Mosaic from Pompeii. Naples, National Museum 10020. Photo: Alfredo D'Agli Orti, 1990 © Bildarchiv Preussischer Kulturbesitz, Berlin.

11.4 Alexander as Pharaoh. Chicago, The Oriental Institute of the University of Chicago P.38387/N.43812/CHFN 9246. Photo: Museum.

11.5 Palaces of Persepolis. Photo: " Lloyd Cluff/CORBIS.

11.6 Fresco depicting Alexander and Roxane, Pompeii. From Andrew Stewart, *Faces of Power: Alexander's Image and Hellenistic Politics* (Berkeley: University of California Press, 1993), Fig. 6. Pompeii, Soprintendenza archaeoligica di Pompeii, Villa dei Misteri.

11.7 The Greek view of the inhabited world. From N. G. L. Hammond, *A History of Greece to 322 BC*.

11.8 Silver five-shekel coin from Babylonia. London, The British Museum. Photo: Museum, courtesy of trustees.

11.9 Indian statue of Buddha showing Greek influence. Rome, Museo Nazionale d'Arte Orientale. Photo: Scala/Art Resource, New York.

12.1 Statue of old market woman. New York, The Metropolitan Museum of Art 09.39. Rogers Fund, 1909. Photo: Museum.

12.3 Roman bronze statuette copy of the Tyche of Antioch by Eutychides. New York, The Metropolitan Museum of Art 13.227.8. Rogers Fund, 1913. Photo: Museum.

12.4 Gold octodrachm showing Ptolemy II and Arsinoe II. New York, American Numismatic Society 1977.158.112. Photo: Society.

12.5 Tetradrachm of Commodus. London, The British Museum. Photo: Museum, courtesy of trustees.

12.6a Laocoon group, Rome. Vatican Museum. Photo: Nimatallah/Art Resource, New York.

12.6b Bronze boxer, Rome. Rome, Museo Nazionale Romano delle Terme. Photo: Scala/Art Resource, New York.

12.6c Crouching Aphrodite, Rome. From John Boardman, *The Oxford History of Classical Art* (New York: Oxford University Press, 1997), p. 192, Fig. 190. Rome, National Museum of the Terme.

12.7a Miniature sculpture of old nurse with child. New York, The Metropolitan Museum of Art 10.210.38. Rogers Fund, 1910. Photo: Museum.

12.7b Miniature sculpture of school girl reading a papyrus roll. Hamburg, Museum für Kunst und Gewerbe. Photo: Museum.

12.7c Bronze statuette of black youth. New York, The Metropolitan Museum of Art 18.145.10. Rogers Fund, 1918. Photo: Museum.

12.8 Limestone statue of Arsinoe. New York, The Metropolitan Museum of Art 20.2.21. Rogers Fund, 1920. Photo: Museum.

12.9 The "Winged Victory." Paris, Louvre Museum 2369. Photo: Alinari/Art Resource, New York.

12.10 Sculpted relief of the Apotheosis of Homer. London, The British Museum. Photo: Werner Forman Archives/Art Resource, New York.

12.12 The Rosetta Stone. London, The British Museum. Photo: © Bildarchiv Preussischer Kulturbesitz, Berlin.

Epi. 1 Coin portrait of Cleopatra VII. London, The British Museum. Photo: Museum, courtesy of trustees.

INDEX

Note: Page numbers in bold refer to illustrations.